Praise for *Claiming a Continent*

'... a lively and thorough overview of Australian history ... Day's themes of conquest and dispossession fit easily with the preoccupations of the 1990s about post-Mabo race relations and the desirable ethnic mix for Australia. He is a historian for our times.'

— *Australian Book Review*

'*Claiming a Continent* provides a massive revision of Australian history and is anything but conventional: its focus is unremittingly on white affairs in terms of the true owners of the claimed continent. It is an account of the long, fluctuating conflict between white Australians and Aborigines, from the unequal physical encounters of the 19th century through the apparent defeat and final subjugation of indigenous people in the first half of this century, to the revolutionary re-drawing of the lines in the Mabo judgement and its enshrining legislation.'

— *The Australian*'s Review of Books

'Encompassing a broad sweep from first white settlement through to the present, this substantial but highly accessible volume considers the themes of cultural contact and contested space; the results of racist policies rigorously pursued against Aborigines and non-European immigrants; the forging of a national identity through participation in far-flung colonial wars; and the problematic nature of belonging to a nation thus wrought. David Day's lively panorama conveys the facts succinctly, explains the various currents in historical thinking, makes good use of quotes and juxtapositions, and provides a coherent background for further study. Ideally suited as core text for upper-secondary and first-year tertiary courses, and deserving of a broad general readership.'

— *The Australian*

'In a bold reinterpretation of the major themes of European settlement in Australia, Day's provocative synthesis of historical writing is every bit as jolting to the status quo as was Germaine Greer's *The Female Eunuch* more than two decades ago.

It is a powerful, moving and extremely convincing study that every Australian at all interested in where we have come from, what we have done and where we are going, should read; it is also a must for school curriculums, a long-awaited antidote to a shamefully long and embarrassing silence.

It is just possible that David Day is our most important historian of the present era; he is certainly the most provocative.'

— *Canberra Times*

'Day has seized upon a thread which unifies the post-Cook story of this country: the ever-present insecurity of white usurpers of an already-occupied land in regard to the validity of their oft-claimed right to do so. In a vigorous, witty, shrewd and often irreverent retelling of this history, Day illuminates the origins and persistence of a virulent white-supremacist strand in our "national psyche", while offering reasons for cautious optimism as settler claims and those of the dispossessed begin to merge. An important, coherent, lively and timely book.'

— Judges' comments in awarding the Non-Fiction Prize to
Claiming a Continent at the 1998 South Australian Festival Awards for Literature

Praise for *John Curtin: A Life*

'Splendid and admirable ... this at times gripping and at times deeply affecting study is a fine biography of a complex, flawed, self-sacrificing but ultimately triumphant personality — one of the great figures of Australian history.'

— Greg Sheridan, *The Weekend Australian*

'The most important characteristic that this biography shares with its subject can be summarised in one word: unflinching ... [Day is] an excellent biographer and a first-rate historian ... he deserves every reader's commendation for staying the honest course.'

— Kim Beazley, *The Age*

'Among the book's real strengths is that it provides a great deal of history as well as biography ... Curtin survives these pages as one of the few inspiring figures in Australian political life.'

— Michael Sexton, NSW Solicitor-General, *The Sydney Morning Herald*

'David Day's magisterial biography ... ranks with Geoffrey Serle's *Monash* and David Marr's *Patrick White* as one of the greatest Australian biographies.'

— Barry Jones, *Labor Herald*

'Thought-provoking, even haunting ... the man who probably qualifies for nomination as Australia's most provocative historian has done it again.'

— David O'Reilly, *The Canberra Times*

'*John Curtin: A Life* is the product of solid historical research, but Day's real triumph is that he sustains interest for nearly 600 pages. His well-paced narrative guides the reader through more than six decades of Australian history and is never less than engrossing.'

— Ken Spillman, *The West Australian*

CLAIMING A CONTINENT

A NEW HISTORY OF AUSTRALIA

DAVID DAY

HarperCollins*Publishers*

To Michael, Emily and Kelly

HarperCollins*Publishers*

First published in Australia in 1996
This edition published in 2001
Reprinted in 2001
by HarperCollins*Publishers* Pty Limited
ABN 36 009 913 517
A member of the HarperCollins*Publishers* (Australia) Pty Limited Group
http://www.harpercollins.com.au

HarperCollins*Publishers*
25 Ryde Road, Pymble, Sydney NSW 2073, Australia
31 View Road, Glenfield, Auckland 10, New Zealand
77–85 Fulham Palace Road, London W6 8JB, United Kingdom
Hazelton Lanes, 55 Avenue Road, Suite 2900, Toronto, Ontario M5R 3L2
and 1995 Markham Road, Scarborough, Ontario M1B 5M8, Canada
10 East 53rd Street, New York NY 10022, USA

National Library of Australia Cataloguing-in-publication data:

Day, David, 1949– .
   Claiming a continent: a new history of Australia.
   New ed. Includes bibliography and index.
   ISBN 0 7322 6976 8
   1. Australia – History. I. Title.
994

Cover photograph by Philip Quirk/Wildlight
Design by Judi Rowe, HarperCollins Design Studio

Set in Garamond 10.5/12.5
Printed and bound in Australia by Griffin Press on 70gsm Bulky Book Ivory

9 8 7 6 5 4 3 2
05 04 03 02 01

ABOUT THE AUTHOR

David Day has written widely on Australian history and the history of the Second World War. Among his many books are *Menzies and Churchill at War* and a two-volume study of Anglo-Australian relations during the Second World War. His much-acclaimed history of Australia, *Claiming a Continent*, won the prestigious Non-Fiction Prize at the 1998 South Australian Festival Awards for Literature and has been revised and updated for this edition. An earlier book, *Smugglers and Sailors*, was shortlisted by the Fellowship of Australian Writers for their Book of the Year Award. His most recent work, *John Curtin: A Life*, won the 2000 Queensland Premier's Literary Awards' Prize for History and was shortlisted for the 2000 NSW Premier's Literary Awards' Douglas Stewart Prize for Non-Fiction.

Day graduated with first-class Honours in History and Political Science from the University of Melbourne and was awarded a PhD from the University of Cambridge. He has been a Junior Research Fellow at Cambridge, founding head of History and Political Science at Bond University, official historian of the Australian Customs Service, Keith Cameron Professor of Australian History at University College, Dublin, and Professor of Australian Studies at the University of Tokyo. He is currently an ARC Senior Research Fellow at LaTrobe University in Melbourne, and is working on a biography of Ben Chifley, to be released later this year by HarperCollins.

Other books by David Day:

Menzies and Churchill at War (1986)
The Great Betrayal: Britain, Australia and the Onset of the Pacific War, 1939–42 (1988)
Reluctant Nation: Australia and the Allied Defeat of Japan, 1942–45 (1992)
Smugglers and Sailors: The Customs History of Australia, 1788–1901 (1992)
Contraband and Controversy: The Customs History of Australia from 1901 (1996)
(ed.), *Brave New World: H. V. Evatt and Australian Foreign Policy 1941–1949* (1996)
(ed.), *Australian Identities* (1998)
John Curtin: A Life (1999)

CONTENTS

1

'EVERY TRIBE HAS ITS OWN DISTRICT'

On 26 January 1988, more than a million Australians crowded the rocky shores of Sydney Harbour to watch 11 sailing ships plough their way through a welcoming armada of small boats. The ships were celebrating the bicentenary of the European occupation of New South Wales by recreating the voyage of the First Fleet. They were also symbolically reasserting the original British claim of proprietorship over New South Wales, based upon 'discovery' by Captain James Cook in 1770 and the subsequent landing by Captain Arthur Phillip and his party of marines and convicts in 1788. Also on the rocky shoreline were thousands of Aborigines who had travelled from throughout Australia to contest the assumptions underlying the celebration and to reassert the primacy of their own pre-existing claim to the continent.

The picturesque panorama on Sydney Harbour was part of an ongoing and universal drama that occurs whenever different societies contest the occupation of the same territory. One of the most important forces in the shaping of human history has been the constant movement of peoples across the face of the world onto the lands of others and the subsequent, prolonged process of asserting claims of legal, effective and moral proprietorship over those supplanted lands. An examination of the ways in which this process has been played out across Australia over the last 200 years is fundamental to understanding the ways in which European society has gradually been shaped until it has come to comfortably occupy that island continent.

One of the most important Australian history books during the last few decades was Geoffrey Blainey's *The Tyranny of Distance* which explored the ways in which distance has shaped the development of Australia. Other historians have chosen different routes by which to explore Australian history, with the doyen of recent Australian historians, the late Manning Clark, interpreting it in his sagacious, six-volume *History of Australia* in terms of the establishment of European civilisation in a barbaric wilderness. Others have used class, race or, more recently, gender as ways of reinterpreting Australian history.

More than anything, though, the history of modern Australia has been the ongoing story of the struggle by European Australians to claim the continent of Australia as their own. Using methods that range from brutal massacres of the original Aboriginal inhabitants to the more subtle appropriating of Aboriginal Dreamtime stories, European Australians during more than 200 years have tried to supplant the claims that countless generations of Aborigines have established over their separate territories during a period of occupation that stretches back for tens of thousands of years.

There are three different layers to the claim of proprietorship that European Australians have tried to establish over the continent. The first is a legal claim that is asserted when, for instance, a flag is run up a pole by the discoverer of a new land and that land is claimed on the basis of first discovery. Or it might be made on the basis of conquest. The second is a claim of effective proprietorship that is made by the physical occupation of that land, the dispossession of its original inhabitants and its defence against possible counterclaims by rival supplanting societies. The third is a claim of moral proprietorship, which is rather harder to define but comes into existence, usually over an extended period of time, as the supplanting society gradually develops links to the landscape and realises that there is no other place it can call 'home'. It took many British Australians until the Second World War and after before they accepted that Australia, rather than Britain, was 'home'. More importantly, a claim of moral proprietorship requires the descendants of the original inhabitants, if there are any, as well as outsiders, to acknowledge that the supplanting society has established a legitimate claim to the land.

Although the British government of the time did not acknowledge it, there was a pre-existing society enjoying just such a sense of proprietorship when Captain Arthur Phillip nudged his 11 convict ships into what has become known as Sydney Harbour. The British invaders did not consciously come as invaders of what Cook had styled as New South Wales. Instead, they came flourishing a legal claim based upon Cook's supposed discovery. This was backed by an effective claim based upon their occupation of Sydney Cove and their exploitation of its immediate hinterland. And overlaying it all was a moral claim based upon the 'gifts of European civilisation' which they were about to bestow upon the Aborigines and their fulfilment of their God's injunction to make the earth fruitful.

For nearly two centuries, the claims of the British went largely unchallenged. In 1962, Manning Clark began his massive history with a sentence that he came to regret. 'Civilisation', he wrote, 'did not begin in Australia until the last quarter of the eighteenth century.' From that sentence flowed more than a million more words about the establishment of European civilisation in Australia. More crucially, though, the implications of that sentence served to justify the continued dispossession of the Aborigines who, Clark argued, had lived for millennia in a 'state of barbarism'.

Certainly, the officers of the first fleet of British invaders believed they were stepping ashore on a continent that had not felt the heel of civilised man. Strictly speaking, of course, the officers and Manning Clark were correct if civilisation is defined, as it commonly is, as being a literate society with cities marked by fine buildings of government, religion, commerce and learning. Traditionally, the concept of civilisation has had a Eurocentric orientation, with the archetypal civilisation being that of the Greeks. Civilisation was Europe's gift to the rest of the world. Or so Europeans used to believe. Many people now rightly question the assumptions of cultural superiority that the British officers brought amongst their mental baggage in the First Fleet.

The question of civilisation is not, and was not then, a value-free definition but was usually used to contrast with its opposite—savagery and barbarism. By defining the Aborigines as uncivilised, the British also implicitly justified their dispossession. However, the more that Europeans have learnt about the accomplishments of the Aborigines, the more they have come to acknowledge and even admire them. They have come to realise that Aboriginal society has a rich culture, a systematic set of laws governing their lives, an oral tradition preserving their history, and ways of living off the land fruitfully without placing their environments under intolerable stress.

Aboriginal society could not reflect the usual European trappings of civilisation that allowed for everything from universities to organised warfare, from worldwide trading companies to inquisitions. Such civilisations were built upon the surplus production of agriculture and pastoralism that allowed for specialised occupations in the towns and cities. Aborigines lacked important advantages enjoyed by Europeans and, to a lesser extent, Africans and Americans. The Australian continent is singularly lacking in significant river systems that in other continents provided the basis for a sedentary lifestyle. Moreover, there were no animals or fowl in Australia capable of domestication. There were no sheep, pigs, goats, cattle, horses, chickens or turkeys.

There were also few plants suitable for cultivation. Even the Incas had llamas and guinea pigs and plants such as corn that were suitable for cultivation and storing and upon which a settled civilisation could be constructed. Given their limited resources, it can be argued that the Aborigines maximised the potential of the continent. Aboriginal technology was certainly more primitive than 18th century European technology. However, its stone tools, fish traps, hunting weapons and relatively nomadic lifestyle were well adapted for the Australian environment. As an early European visitor to Australia remarked, the Aborigines' lack of a civilisation to which Europeans could easily relate was due mainly 'to the nature of the country they inhabit' rather than to any deficiency on the part of the Aborigines.

It could even be argued that Aborigines were more sophisticated than Europeans have proved to be in Australia. While the Aborigines lived for hundreds of centuries in Australia, changing their lifestyles in reaction to gradual changes in the environment and sometimes even shaping that environment to maximise their returns from it, just two centuries of European occupation have seen almost irreparable harm done to the environment through greed or ignorance. Europeans are now drawing on Aboriginal methods of land management to take care of their national parks and to live successfully in arid areas. So the question of whether Aboriginal society was 'civilised' or 'savage', with all the pejorative connotations that those terms imply, is best answered by suggesting that it was as 'civilised' as it was capable of being, given the resources of the Australian environment. It was certainly not a static, Stone Age society as it was for so long alleged to be by Europeans anxious to justify their act of dispossession.

Recent archaeological evidence has revealed the relative sophistication of the continent's early human occupants while also successively extending the length of human occupation of the continent. The oldest and most complex cave paintings in the world are found in Australia, with some depicting animals that have been extinct for more than 18 000 years. Although dating of them is difficult, it has been suggested that painting may have been carried on in Australia as early as 60 000 years ago. Ground stone axes, as much as 20 000 years old, that have been found in Australia are older than any yet found in Europe, Africa or the Middle East. The oldest ritual burials in the world appear to have taken place in Australia. On the shores of Lake Mungo, near Broken Hill in far western New South Wales, the skeleton of a man was unearthed lying on his side with hands clasped to his face. Over the body had been scattered red ochre as part of the burial ceremony. That man had died more than 30 000 years ago. But he was far from being the earliest human inhabitant of Australia.

When Manning Clark published the first volume of his monumental history in 1962, it was generally believed that Australia had been occupied for about 10 000 years. There were few archaeologists looking for evidence of a more extended occupation. The first chair of Australian prehistory had only been appointed in 1961. It did not take long for such people to push back the arrival of humans in Australia to 40000 years and, more recently, to 60000 years. Although evidence from a cave in Arnhem Land has confirmed the presence of humans in Australia 60000 years ago, dating techniques beyond this time become increasingly imprecise and open to argument. Nevertheless, there have been some claims that the human occupation of Australia could be doubled to 120000 years.

Studies from soil samples taken from Lake George near Canberra show a dramatic change in the vegetation of that area approximately 120000 years ago. The change was from trees that were susceptible to fire, to trees such as the eucalyptus that were resistant to fire. The foliage would burn during a bushfire, but the tree would survive to sprout with new growth. With no evidence to suggest a natural cause for any increase in fires through lightning strikes or other means, archaeologists have argued that the most likely cause for this change in vegetation is the coming of the first Australians with their methods of firestick farming, the systematic firing of the bush that Aborigines use to flush out game and burn off old grass and encourage new growth and thereby provide food for the animals they hunted.

Further circumstantial evidence points to an occupation of the continent of 100 000 years or more. The lowering of the seas during an ice age at that time shortened the sea crossing between the extended Australian continent and the nearest islands providing stepping stones from Asia to just 50 kilometres. This would have allowed island dwellers to see much more easily the smoke from lightning-induced bushfires on a land that was tantalisingly out of sight. The smoke may have created the impression that the land was inhabited. It may have been this mistaken belief that induced these early humans to embark on what must surely have been one of the first crossings of the open sea. It was a landmark voyage in the world's maritime history, the first and only seaborne occupation of an uninhabited continent.

These early voyagers would have encountered a continent that is very different from the one we know today. It was much larger, joined by land to Tasmania and New Guinea. It was also much less arid, with freshwater lakes and rivers providing subsistence across the interior where today there are only intermittent rivers, salt pans and desert. There were also mega-fauna, the giant kangaroos and other prehistoric mammals, lizards perhaps nine metres long and even a giant meat-eating marsupial, living in the ancient Australian landscape. Their disappearance from that landscape suggests that a new predator had appeared on the scene equipped with skills and weapons to hunt them to extinction, probably at the same time as they were coming under stress from climatic and vegetational changes that saw the Australian continent become more like the relatively arid place we know today.

Although humans may have appeared on the Australian continent somewhere between 60 000 and 120 000 years ago, it is likely that they came at two widely separated times. Archaeological evidence has revealed a heavy, almost neanderthal-looking human. Some of these ancient skeletons are more than 1.8 metres tall with massive bone structures, and it is likely that their ancestors were part of the first wave of arrivals perhaps 120 000 years ago. The other type was a smaller, more slender type with thinner bones. It is likely that these people arrived around 50 000 years ago. Despite the wide physical differences between the two types, it seems that the later arrivals did not exterminate or drive out the pre-existing inhabitants. Archaeological evidence suggests that they co-existed and interbred to produce the modern Aborigines who are, as a result, perhaps the most physically diverse population in the world.

While we can know with some precision the type of physical world these first Australians would have encountered when they stepped ashore in Australia, we will never know with any precision the mental universe they inhabited. We can only speculate from observations of modern hunter–gatherer societies and by extrapolating backwards from the mental world of modern-day Aborigines. Prominent in that mental world is the abiding sense of their spiritual links to the land from which they obtain their daily sustenance. Those links would have been gradually developed during the millennia of their occupation of the continent.

Aborigines have come to believe that their ancestors were created by spirits during the mythical Dreamtime period and that these spirits remain embodied in various land formations, in animals and in plants. Accordingly, each Aboriginal group has ties of ownership to a particular territory, or to a cluster of territories interspersed with a cluster belonging to another group. Some groups have a clearly defined boundary to their territory which is defended against outsiders who breach the customary access routes. Other groups have a more permeable boundary and identify their territory more by the natural features, such as rivers, mountains or caves, that are contained within it.

While taking a harsh view of Aboriginal intruders who are not members of the extended kinship group, it was accepted that subgroups within the extended cultural group could gather together on land for which one of the subgroups had primary responsibility in order to hunt game or otherwise exploit the seasonally available resources. The permeable nature of Aboriginal boundaries reduced the scope for conflict over the boundaries themselves, although not over the primary rights to the economic resources of particular territories.

The separate identities of the subgroups and their links to their separate territories were expressed in carvings and painting and preserved in ceremonies where singing and dancing were used to act out the relationship to the land. As Stephen Davis and Victor Prescott explain,

[T]he land was given form by ancestral beings who traversed the landscape, conferring territories and naming each locality. Each named locality within the total territory can be identified by senior custodians of the territory. Names are recited in a particular order. When asking a senior custodian the extent of his territory he will, most often, name all localities on the territory to which the ancestral being travelled and performed all the daily activities of life in the creative epoch. The names are recited in the order in which they were visited. This naming of localities matches the order in which names appear in the song cycle during the performance of rituals involving clans from the wider ritual group with which the clan identifies.

This clearly delineated, ritualistic relationship between Aborigines and their territories did not necessarily negate the possibility of the 'ownership' of particular territories, or parts of territories, being challenged and possibly transferred from one subgroup to another.

Over the long human prehistory of the Australian continent, there would have been much scope for challenging claims of proprietorship asserted by particular subgroups over certain territories. Climatic changes and consequent vegetational changes over extended periods of time would have seen the imperceptible movement of groups from their traditional areas. The rising sea levels that drowned much of the former coastline would have forced a gradual move to new areas, as would the increasing aridity of the interior, with the drying up of the many inland lakes and rivers that formerly provided a rich lifestyle for its human inhabitants.

In more recent times, anthropologists have observed changes in their attachment to particular sections of land by Aboriginal groups as they move into new areas or outsiders encroach on their land. Although their Dreamtime stories have an aura of unchanging immutability about them, it is unlikely that Aboriginal groups were any more static in their relationship to the land than were other ancient societies. Davis and Prescott cite an instance where a clan was dying out and its territory was contested by related clans. To make good their claim, one clan 'set up a permanent camp site' on the contested land while also 're-emphasising the relative importance of the major sites' on this disputed territory in their ritual cycle. Overall, though, there was a relatively enduring continuity between Aboriginal groups and the territory in which they lived.

As the Presbyterian clergyman the Reverend John Dunmore Lang observed in the 1830s:

[T]heir wanderings are circumscribed by certain well-defined limits, beyond which they seldom pass, except for purposes of war or festivity. In short, every tribe has its own district, the boundaries of which are well known to the natives generally...

Thus, when Captain Arthur Phillip raised the English flag in Sydney Cove on 26 January 1788, he was beginning the dispossession of a people who were not only in secure occupation of their separate territories but who collectively enjoyed a claim of legal, effective and moral proprietorship over the continent as a whole. Despite having secured such an abiding sense of proprietorship during countless millennia, they were destined to have their claims trampled by challengers from half a world away.

Recommended Reading

Geoffrey Blainey, 1982, *Triumph of the Nomads*, Macmillan, Melbourne.

C. M. H. Clark, 1962, *A History of Australia*, Vol. 1, Melbourne University Press, Melbourne.

S. L. Davis and J. V. R. Prescott, 1992, *Aboriginal Frontiers and Boundaries in Australia*, Melbourne University Press, Melbourne.

Josephine Flood, 1992, *The Archaeology of the Dreamtime*, Collins, Sydney.

R. L. Kirk, 1983, *Aboriginal Man Adapting*, Oxford University Press, Melbourne.

D. J. Mulvaney, 1975, *The Prehistory of Australia*, Penguin, Melbourne.

2

'A PURE STATE OF NATURE'

Once Europeans began to explore beyond the circumscribed boundaries of their medieval world, it did not take them long to discover the existence of an island continent at the very antipodes of their known earth. Within about 30 years of Columbus's voyage to America in 1492, it now seems clear, the Portuguese had reached as far as the formerly unknown east coast of Australia. Although the existence of this island continent was unknown to Europeans, it had been widely believed by speculative geographers that a substantial continent must exist in that part of the globe.

As soon as people came to accept that the world was round, they also postulated the existence of an undiscovered continent in the Southern Hemisphere that would balance the continents of the north and stop the world becoming wobbly and spinning off out of the solar system. In the wake of Columbus's discovery of the Americas, the vision of another such undiscovered continent caught the imagination of Europe, particularly when it was enhanced by the widespread belief that it was rich in mineral wealth. In 1540, England's King Henry VIII was assured by an adventurer eager for his patronage that a land to the south-east of China would be found to have 'all the golde, spices, aromatikes and pretiose stones' together with 'all other thinges that we have in estimation'. Although Henry was apparently not

9

attracted by the allure of this prospective land, there is mounting evidence that the Portuguese might have been.

The Portuguese had reached Ceylon and what is now Indonesia by the 1520s and embarked on a voyage of discovery in 1521 for the fabled islands of gold. Because of the fragmentary nature of the evidence that remains, what they found remains a matter of some dispute. Maps drawn between 1540 and 1570 by a school of cartographers in the important French port of Dieppe reveal an extensive continent named 'Java La Grande' to the south-east of Sumatra. It has been argued by some geographers that the Java La Grande on these so-called Dieppe maps is really Australia, although its coastline is not immediately recognisable as such. However, by redrawing it using Mercator's projection, which was not then in use, and by making adjustments based upon knowledge of 16th century navigational methods, geographers have produced a coastline with an uncanny resemblance to the Australian east coast. From it, they argue that the maps prove the east coast of Australia was visited by the Portuguese 250 years before Captain Cook's claim of first discovery. Others have argued that the coastline is a representation of Indochina or a composite of other South-East Asian coastlines.

Some geographers believe that the Dieppe maps were French copies of Portuguese originals which are assumed to have been destroyed in the devastating earthquake and fire that raged through Lisbon in 1755. They explain the absence of Java La Grande from surviving Portuguese maps of the period as being due to the necessity to conceal from the Spanish their presence on the east coast of Australia, pointing out that the Spanish had been apportioned that part of the world by the Pope. However, Helen Wallis, the former keeper of maps at the British Library in London, has proposed a simpler solution, suggesting that a French expedition to Sumatra in 1529 brought back intelligence to Dieppe of the recent Portuguese discovery of Java La Grande which was then incorporated into subsequent maps produced at that port. Because of the destruction of Portuguese records in Lisbon and the British shelling of Dieppe in 1694, the map evidence is necessarily fragmentary and inconclusive.

Further confirmation of a Portuguese discovery might have come from the remains of what is believed to have been a Portuguese sailing ship wrecked on a south-west Victorian beach. The wreckage was sighted last century but was subsequently buried beneath shifting sandhills. Recent rewards offered by the Victorian government have prompted serious efforts by a number of people using modern technology to locate and disinter the remains of this putative Portuguese vessel. But they have been unsuccessful. Furthermore, a set of keys that are believed to be Portuguese, and which were reported to have been found beneath several feet of sand during the early years of Melbourne's settlement, have also disappeared.

Whatever the truth or otherwise of the Portuguese 'pre-discovery' of Australia, it had no discernible effect on the subsequent efforts of the early voyagers. The Portuguese seem not to have followed up their charting of Australia's eastern coast, presumably because they found nothing of value to draw them back. While the French incorporated the Portuguese discovery on their maps, they made no early attempt to see the land for themselves. Moreover, the map-makers of Dieppe and elsewhere persisted with portraying a mysterious great south land, which they often dubbed Terra Australis Incognita, as stretching at several points from Antarctica up into the tropics. Much of it lay squat in the centre of the south Pacific, to the east of Australia.

The Spanish were the first Europeans to sail into the Pacific when Ferdinand Magellan, although of Portuguese origin, headed a Spanish expedition in 1519 which rounded the tip of South America and eventually reached the Philippines where Magellan was killed. Over the next half-century, the Spanish developed their maritime links across the Pacific between Mexico and the Philippines, occupying those islands in the 1560s as a base from which to trade their American silver for the sought-after riches of the East. Once established in the Philippines, and with a sea route secured to South America, the Spanish attempted to find and colonise the fabled great south land.

A Spanish expedition sent into the south-west Pacific in the 1560s only succeeded in finding the Solomon Islands, which they named in anticipation of the gold they expected to find there. Although no gold was found, the allure was sufficient to attract another expedition in the 1590s which failed even to find the Solomons. A further expedition, which set out in 1605 under the command of Fernandez de Quiros, searched for the famed Terra Australis, or great south land, to claim it for Spain and found instead an island to the north-east of Australia in what we now call the New Hebrides group. De Quiros proclaimed to his king that he had found a land as great in extent 'as all Europe and Asia Minor' and claimed accordingly 'all this region of the south as far as the Pole', naming it Austrialia del Espiritu Santo. When he tried to buttress his legal claim with an effective claim by establishing a settlement called New Jerusalem as a base from which to convert the indigenous inhabitants, the intruders were driven off. Still the stories persisted of a Terra Australis Incognita abounding in wealth of all description.

The Dutch helped to settle the matter when they extended their trading empire to the East Indies (present-day Indonesia), dislodging the Portuguese. Initially, the Dutch trading vessels used to cross the Indian Ocean from Madagascar to Java, a route that often left ships becalmed in the tropics. In 1611, a Dutch captain discovered that he could make faster time using a dog-leg route, using the prevailing winds in the southern Indian Ocean to head due east for around 3000 miles before turning north to Java. With no accurate method of determining longitude, considerable guesswork was involved in such voyages. A miscalculation would see a Dutch ship fetch up on the western coast of Australia, as an unsuspecting captain did just five years after the new route was proven. There, on an island off the coast, Dirk

Hartog hammered in a post on which he nailed an inscribed pewter plate proclaiming that his ship had arrived there on 25 October 1616.

Hartog's visit was fleeting and accidental, but the plate he left behind established Holland's claim to the as yet unnamed land he had discovered. The parts of the western coast sighted by successive Dutch captains were usually named after the ship in which they sailed. As these names accumulated on maps showing their discoveries, so Holland buttressed its claim of legal proprietorship over this western coastline of a continent that some described as Terra Australis Cognita, in contrast to the mythical Terra Australis Incognita. But the Dutch made no attempt to supplement their claim by settling the land and thereby establish a claim of effective proprietorship over it.

The Dutch exploration of the coastline could discover nothing worth having, despite repeated efforts to do so with a series of voyages being launched to chart the lands to the south and east of Batavia. As the Dutch captain Jan Carstensz reported in 1623 after skirting the south coast of New Guinea and charting the Gulf of Carpentaria without discovering the passage to the Pacific that lay between New Guinea and Cape York Peninsula,

> [W]e have not seen one fruit-bearing tree, nor anything that man could make use of: there are no mountains or even hills, so that it can be safely concluded that the land contains no metals, nor yields any precious woods ... In our judgement this is the most arid and barren region that can be found anywhere on the earth; the inhabitants, too, are the most wretched and poorest creatures that I have ever seen in my age or time ...

The disappointed discoverer headed home to Batavia after leaving behind a nailed-up board on a tree proclaiming his feat to any who might come after him. Another Dutch claim was made on the Australian continent.

The deliberate discoveries of Carstensz and others, and the accidental discoveries by Dutch ships heading for Batavia, gradually filled in further swathes of the southern oceans on seafarers' maps, making it increasingly difficult for them to sustain the idea of a huge continent stretching north from Antarctica into all the oceans of the world. It was increasingly believed that the mythical land must be mainly contained within the south Pacific to the east of Terra Australis Cognita. As a largely incidental consequence of the ongoing search for it, the blank parts of the north and west Australian coastline were gradually filled in. The bleak succession of reports that observers brought to Batavia about this southern continent failed to dent the Dutch desire to discover the great south land.

With the passage to the Pacific apparently blocked in the east, the Dutch East India Company's governor-general in Batavia, Anthonie Van Diemen, despatched Abel Tasman to the south in 1642 in search of the great south land

and of a passage to the Pacific that might allow the Dutch to attack Spanish settlements in Chile. Taking a route that would allow his two ships to catch the prevailing winds, Tasman went west to Mauritius from where he sailed to a southern latitude that would have taken him clear to New Zealand. When heavy seas forced him north, he chanced upon the west coast of Tasmania, which he named Van Diemen's Land without realising it was an island. On the south coast of Van Diemen's Land, without making contact with any of its Aboriginal inhabitants, Tasman erected a flag of the Dutch Prince Frederik Henry to signify his country's claim of legal proprietorship over it. Another accidental Dutch discovery had been made, and a legal claim secured, on what Tasman took to be part of the coastline of the barren southern continent.

After taking just ten days to chart part of its coast, Tasman continued in search of his real goals, a southern passage to the Pacific and the great south land. Crossing the Tasman Sea, he came upon the west coast of New Zealand, which he did not realise was two islands, and made a similar claim of legal proprietorship, naming it Staten's Land. He was satisfied that he had found part of the great south land and that it was joined to another land discovered in the South Atlantic of that name. Only when the latter land was discovered to be the small island of South Georgia was New Zealand renamed. His exploration of New Zealand's coast was cut short when four of his crew were suddenly set upon and killed by Maoris while seeking fresh water at a point Tasman named Murderers' Bay. Leaving New Zealand, Tasman was satisfied from the size of the prevailing easterly swell that nothing of consequence lay between New Zealand and Chile. He could therefore claim to have fulfilled the two parts of his mission: to discover the great south land, and to prove a viable sailing route from the East Indies to Chile. Accordingly, he returned to Batavia by way of Fiji, Tonga and the north coast of New Guinea. His cautious discoveries left open the question of the great south land's reputed riches and its true extent.

Although Van Diemen was disappointed in Tasman's failure to follow up his discoveries, he despatched him again in 1644, this time to continue the Dutch search for a passage to the Pacific between New Guinea and Cape York Peninsula and also to discover whether there was any way of reaching the new-found Van Diemen's Land by means of a north–south passage that was thought to begin on the southern coast of the Gulf of Carpentaria. There was still speculation that the southern continent was separated by sea from a land named on some maps as New Carpentaria, which stretched south from Cape York Peninsula. In other words, western and eastern Australia were divided in two. Tasman was unsuccessful on both counts and brought back further dismal accounts of the commercial prospects of the southern continent. Van Diemen reported to his directors in Holland that there was 'nothing profitable, only poor, naked people walking along the beaches; without rice or many fruits, very poor and bad-tempered people in many places'. Nevertheless, Tasman's voyages had filled in further stretches of the Australian coastline such that subsequent maps published by the Dutch affirmed their legal claim to the island continent by naming it New Holland.

Through his voyages, Tasman had proved that New Holland was not part of the fabled great south land and that it was clearly not attached to Antarctica. However, he left unresolved the question of whether New Zealand was part of the western coast of a great south land. What Tasman's voyage also did was to dismiss any idea of New Holland being a treasure trove of wealth to rival that of the great south land. The Dutch picture of a rather desolate New Holland was reinforced for British minds by the voyage of the buccaneering Englishman, William Dampier, who sailed south from the East Indies in 1688 and landed on the north-west coast of New Holland where he remained for six to ten weeks. He came away with a report that discouraged any further discoveries, describing it as an arid, largely lifeless place occupied by inhabitants who consequently were 'the miserablest People in the World'. His account was published in 1697 as *A New Voyage Round the World* and was widely read in Europe, helping to deter further investigation of New Holland.

The publication of Dampier's book was too late to prevent the Dutch from sending an expedition from Holland in 1696 under the command of Willem de Vlamingh to chart the west coast of New Holland, to look for any survivors of Dutch shipwrecks and to assess again its commercial prospects. Reaching Rottnest Island off the south-west coast of New Holland, the Dutch took samples of its fragrant sandalwood trees before exploring the Swan River, site of Perth, on the adjacent coastline. Although the country was of a more fertile and appealing nature than the coast further north, there was nothing of value to the Dutch to be found. Continuing north along the coast, de Vlamingh found the pewter plate Hartog had left 80 years earlier. He sent it to Holland as evidence of the Dutch discovery, along with a watercolour of the coastline on which the position of Hartog's claim was marked. He then replaced Hartog's plate with another so that the Dutch claim of first discovery might remain intact. It was the most noteworthy discovery on another disappointing Dutch expedition, with the explorers taking their leave of the western coastline at North West Cape by firing volleys 'in farewell of the wretched South Land'.

Undeterred by these dire discoveries along coastlines devoid of interest to European eyes, the map-makers and adventurers simply argued that there were two southern lands. New Holland was one, while the other one—the one with all the riches—lay to the east of New Zealand, as Tasman's discoveries indicated. Dampier seemed to believe this as well and returned in 1699 with the backing of the English navy, touching once again on New Holland's west coast at Shark Bay, where he confirmed his desolate view of its commercial potential, later shooting an Aborigine while searching for fresh water. Sailing off in search of Terra Australis Incognita, he got no further than New Britain before being forced to turn back. His ship was rotting under him and finally sank at Ascension Island *en route* to England.

European interest in the mythical great south land did not end with the disappointment of Dampier's second voyage. But the British seafarers preferred to concentrate their attention on robbing the Spanish of the silver that was sent by galleon from Mexico to the Philippines, a quest that kept them far from the southern Pacific latitudes in which the great south land was believed to be situated. And only desultory interest was maintained in the known barrenness of the Australian continent, despite Jonathan Swift positioning his imagined Lilliput off the west coast of New Holland. Gulliver's fictional travels were made credible by the relative lack of knowledge in Europe about the reality of the South Seas, with much of the south Pacific still unseen by European eyes. It took three voyages of the relentless explorer Captain James Cook finally to destroy the idea of the great south land and at the same time to reignite European interest in New Holland.

Cook was sent to the Pacific in 1770 by the Admiralty to observe the transit of Venus from Tahiti. These observations were crucial for improving the accuracy of navigation. Once that was done, Cook was to head south from Tahiti in search of the mythical south land. The British Admiralty had already made two earlier attempts to locate this land. Once in 1764, when they sought it in the south Atlantic, and once in 1766 when they looked in the south Pacific. Neither voyage was successful, although the mariners on the latter voyage had mistaken distant cloud banks in the south Pacific for land and returned with tantalising suggestions that such a continent might exist. They also brought back the first tales of the South Sea paradise of Tahiti. There were still large, unexplored areas of the southern oceans in which to look for the great south land.

Britain was motivated in this by interests of trade and empire, as well as by Enlightenment-inspired ideas of exploration and scientific inquiry for their own sake. Britain had been excluded or expelled from most of the Americas, while the west coast of Canada was being opened for fur trading. The furs provided a lucrative article of trade that could be exchanged in China for the tea that was so keenly sought in Europe. A scramble of imperial powers tried desperately to dominate this trade. Russia used its control of Siberia as a base from which to control it; Spain, Britain's traditional rival, controlled most of the western American coastline and had possession of the Philippines; American traders from the Atlantic coast were moving into the north Pacific; and the French were showing an interest in expanding there. If Britain could take possession of the great south land, and if its mythical riches were proved to exist, then Britain might pre-empt all its rivals and make a credible bid for supremacy in the Pacific.

Cook did as instructed. Taking his leave from Tahiti after three pleasant months living among its people, Cook explored the southern reaches of the Pacific but without success. Finally, he headed for New Zealand hoping to take up where Tasman had left off and discover definitely whether New

Zealand was part of the great south land. By circumnavigating both islands, Cook discovered that New Zealand was two islands rather than the west coast of the great south land. Before leaving, he claimed for Britain that part of New Zealand uncharted by Tasman. He was then faced with the question of returning home. He could retrace his route by heading east directly across the extreme south Pacific to confirm once and for all whether the great south land existed. Or he could track up the east coast of New Holland and seek supplies in the Dutch East Indies before proceeding home to England.

The south Pacific route was, according to Cook, 'what I most wished because by this route we should have been able to prove the existence or non existence of a Southern Continent which yet remains doubtfull'. But the condition of his ship made taking such a route with winter approaching unwise. The westerly route to the Cape of Good Hope was also dismissed, wrote Cook, 'as no discovery of any moment could be hoped for in that rout'. So the coast of New Holland it was. There is a suggestion that it was the pressure from his officers, perhaps based upon fear of mutiny from sailors anxious to reach a replenishment port, that dictated Cook's course.

Although he was aiming for Van Diemen's Land, Cook sighted Australia on 20 April 1770 at a more northerly point on the coastline, which he named Point Hicks after the young, tuberculosis-stricken officer who had first seen it. Although he was in a position to settle the question of whether Van Diemen's Land was a separate island, he did not sail south to do so. Instead he headed north according to his prearranged plan to sail along the east coast. His aim was to replenish his supplies of wood and water and make what discoveries he could along the way without diverting from his course to the Dutch East Indies. Clearly he saw that anything he might discover in New Holland would be of little account compared with the momentous discovery that had eluded him—the great south land.

Being the navigator that he was, Cook carefully charted the east coast as he tracked north but spent little time closely examining the countryside. However, even from his shipboard vantage point, he was already realising that the east coast was different from the desolation that Dampier had described on the west coast. Sailing past, Cook described it as 'green and woody', while the botanist Joseph Banks thought it had 'the appearance of the highest fertility'. This judgment would have been based upon the tall eucalypt trees that were visible from the ship and which their European experience suggested were indicative of fertile soils. Cook tried at one stage to send a boat ashore for a closer look, but it took in water and he was forced to retrieve it. It was only when he reached the sheltered waters of a large bay on 29 April that he finally anchored the *Endeavour* and spent time ashore exploring the possibilities of New Holland.

His first meeting with the Aborigines was not propitious. A couple of them brandished their spears when Cook's boat tried to land. Attempts by a

Tahitian interpreter to speak with them proved fruitless, as did the throwing ashore of nails and beads. Cook had sailed with good intentions. The Tahitian had been taken on board as an interpreter to establish friendly relations with the supposedly civilised inhabitants who were believed to inhabit the great south land and thereby avoid the bloodshed in which the Spanish empire had been soaked. But New Holland was not the great south land and these Aborigines were not civilised in ways that Cook and his company could comprehend. So, when their attempts at friendship were rebuffed, Cook ordered small shot to be fired to sting them into submission. Not surprisingly, subsequent attempts to establish friendly relations were met with suspicion. Nothing that the British left for them as tokens of friendship were touched by the naked Aborigines. The language and cultural barrier was much too wide to be bridged during a fleeting visit. 'All they seem'd to want was for us to be gone', wrote Cook, which he did after just eight days' investigating the shores of Botany Bay and collecting fresh water and wood for the onward voyage.

Exploration of the surrounding countryside produced conflicting impressions. Cook saw the relative lack of trees and undergrowth as a blessing, suggesting that 'the whole Country or at least great part of it might be cultivated without being oblig'd to cut down a single tree'. Banks the botanist just saw swamps and sandy soil on which trees were incapable of growing. In another place, Cook claimed to have found 'a deep black Soil which we thought was capable of produceing any kind of grain'. Cook also praised the capability of the harbour to shelter ships. It was Cook's account that was published and further embellished by its editor, John Hawkesworth. And it was given added emphasis by the gradual transformation in the name given to the bay—from Sting Ray Harbour, after the giant stingrays caught by the sailors in the bay's shallow waters, to Botanists Bay and finally to Botany Bay, thereby buttressing Cook's word picture of the area as a fertile meadow awaiting the white man's plough. Had the name Sting Ray Harbour been retained, as a repellent balance to Dampier's Shark's Bay in the west, the British might never have settled Australia when they did, if at all. The alluring appellation of Botany Bay would help to convince the British government of its potential for supporting European agriculture while also conflating in European minds the imagined world of the great south land with the newly described realities of New Holland's eastern coast.

Cook's brief visit to Botany Bay convinced him of various vital facts that would be instrumental in determining the subsequent relations with the Aborigines. He was convinced from his observations that they were nomadic, that they lived mainly on shellfish and did not cultivate the land or erect permanent habitations upon it. It was, Cook wrote, in 'a pure state of Nature', with the British visitors not having seen 'one Inch of Cultivated land in the Whole Country'. Moreover, Cook believed from his observations that the Aborigines were not numerous and, because of the apparent scarcity of animal life, that they lived solely on the coast. He also judged them to be 'a timorous and inoffensive race'.

All these observations seemed to justify a claim of legal proprietorship by Cook, without seeking approval from the Aborigines, over the coast he had 'discovered'. Accordingly, he 'caused the English colours to be display'd a shore every day and an inscription to be cut out upon one of the trees near the watering place seting forth the ships name &c'. The inscription was not to advise the Aborigines of their dispossession but was faced out to sea to advise subsequent European explorers that they had been preceded by Cook and therefore they had no right to claim it for themselves on the basis of first discovery.

At least Columbus had bothered to formally involve the native inhabitants when going through the rituals associated with claiming the islands he had 'discovered' off the Americas nearly three centuries before. Then again, the language difference made it unlikely that the 'Indians' would have realised the import of Columbus's action. And the end result in the Americas was the same as it was to become in Australia. Like Columbus, those simple acts by Cook had legally dispossessed the Aborigines in British eyes. Whether the claim would be followed with an invasion of their territory depended upon the official reaction to Cook's report.

As he continued north along the east coast, the accounts of the countryside by Cook and Banks varied, sometimes describing it as green and fertile and sometimes as dry and sandy. Cook sailed past Sydney Harbour without attempting to enter it and he missed Newcastle harbour altogether. In far-north Queensland, the *Endeavour* struck part of the Great Barrier Reef, tearing a great hole in the hull. For a day, the ship was stuck fast and in great danger of sinking before the hole was plugged. The ship then sailed to the coast where a river provided shelter for six weeks of repairs. It was here, at the site of the later Cooktown, that the ship's company had closer contact with the Aborigines. Initially their relations were relatively good. The Aboriginal men even ventured on board the ship, although the women always kept well clear. But tension returned when the Aborigines tried to take some large turtles lying on the *Endeavour*'s deck. When they were prevented from doing so, they set fire to dry grass nearby, sending the sailors scurrying to rescue their tents and animals. Shots were fired to make the Aborigines retreat before amicable relations were restored. Although little meaningful communication took place between the two alien groups, relations were sufficiently cordial for the visitors to discover what they took to be the Aboriginal name for the strange hopping marsupial they had sighted for the first time, the kangaroo.

Once the *Endeavour* was repaired, Cook continued along the east coast to the tip of Cape York Peninsula where he landed on an offshore island to take possession, in the name of King George III, of the whole east coast which he named New South Wales. As an additional move to ensure that his act of claiming would endure, at least on subsequent maps, Cook named the small island Possession Island. In his instructions from the Admiralty, he had been told to take possession only with the consent of the natives if that could be obtained. But the Lords of the Admiralty had been referring to Terra Australis Incognita in those instructions. And that was meant to be populated by a people sufficiently 'civilised' to make treaties with. As far as Cook was concerned, this land clearly was not.

His legal claiming of the east coast was buttressed by Cook's naming of all the prominent features that he could discern from his passing offshore vantage point. Their appearance on subsequent maps of the coast would leave no doubt about Cook being their discoverer. With the naming of Botany Bay and other features along the east coast, Cook was planting solid English names on what he regarded as the otherwise unnamed soil. He thereby disregarded the Aboriginal claim to be the first discoverers and rightful occupiers of the continent and namers of its geographical features. Had he spent more time on shore and managed to communicate more effectively with the Aborigines, Cook may well have done as subsequent explorers of its interior did and adopted some Aboriginal names for its mountains, bays and rivers.

Cook was more careful about acknowledging the rights of the Dutch, leaving the western portion of New Holland for the Dutch who had first 'discovered' it. So legal proprietorship of the continent's eastern coastline, together with all its bays and rivers, was claimed by Cook on the basis of discovery. From there, Cook sailed homeward a bitterly disappointed man. As he subsequently complained to a friend in Whitby, he had 'made no great discoveries, yet I have explored more of the South Sea than all that have gone before me'. Paramount in Cook's disappointed mind was his failure to prove conclusively the existence or otherwise of the great south land.

The publication of Cook's journals caused the European view of New Holland, based upon Dampier's account, to be modified. 'This Eastern side', wrote Cook, 'is not that barren and Miserable Country that Dampier and others have described the Western Side to be.' Instead, he claimed that 'most sorts of Grain, Fruits, Roots, &c of every kind would flourish here', while there was food for 'more Cattle at all seasons of the year than can be brought into this Country'. That said, both he and Banks reserved most of their praise for the more fertile landscape of New Zealand. European interest in New South Wales was mainly as a source of scientific inquiry rather than commercial profit. It was a place where the seasons were reversed, where four-legged animals hopped, where trees shed their bark rather than their leaves. The *Endeavour* had returned with its hold crammed with such curiosities.

The European view of the Aborigines also changed somewhat from Dampier's view of them as being the most miserable creatures on God's earth to a view more approximating the romantic, Rousseauistic view of the 'noble savage' living, as Cook phrased it, 'in Tranquility'. Physically, they were 'far from being disagreeable and their voices are soft and tunable'. Instead of being 'the most wretched people upon the earth', as he might have concluded of the Aborigines in comparison with the Tahitians and the Maoris, Cook considered that 'they are far more happier than we Europeans ... The Earth and sea of their own accord furnishes them with all things necessary for life; ...they live in a warm and fine Climate and enjoy a very wholsome Air'. Cook had been impressed with their refusal to accept the trinkets and other trade goods that had been so eagerly accepted, and even demanded, at other places they had called upon. However, his admiration for their lifestyle did not prevent this generally humane and discerning seafarer from showing a complete disregard for their land rights.

Although publication of Cook's journals moderated Dampier's view of New Holland, it did not arouse much English interest in the southern continent, which had nothing of value to trade with Europeans. Its east coast had relatively few harbours, and no large rivers had been seen which might allow easy access to the continent's interior; its inhabitants, though perhaps epitomising the currently popular view of the 'noble savage', were among the most primitive peoples in the world; and the continent's soil seemed fertile in parts and indifferent in others. Overall, the best that could be said for New Holland, or at least its eastern coast, was that it seemed capable of growing a range of European plants and therefore of supporting a European settlement. But why bother sending people halfway around the world to grow what could be grown at home, or imported from nearby, at a fraction of the expense?

Recommended Reading

J. C. Beaglehole (ed.), 1962, *The Endeavour Journal of Joseph Banks 1768–1771*, Vols 1 & 2, Angus&Robertson, Sydney.

J. C. Beaglehole, 1974, *The Life of Captain James Cook*, A & C Black, London.

J. C. Beaglehole (ed.), 1955–74, *The Journals of Captain James Cook on his Voyages of Discovery*, Hakluvt Society, Cambridge.

J. Hardy and A. Frost (eds), 1989, *Studies from Terra Australis to Australia*, Australian Academy of the Humanities, Canberra.

Richard Hough, 1994, *Captain James Cook*, Hodder & Stoughton, London.

K. R. Howe, 1984, *Where the Waves Fall*, George Allen & Unwin, Sydney.

Russel Ward, 1987, *Finding Australia*, Heinemann, Melbourne.

G. Williams, '"Far more happier than we Europeans": reactions to the Australian Aborigines on Cook's voyage', *Historical Studies*, October 1981.

G. Williams and A. Frost (eds), 1988, *From Terra Australis to Australia*, Oxford University Press, Melbourne.

3

'A LAND

SEEN FOR

THE FIRST

TIME'

ollowing Cook's voyage, there was little to excite British interest in New South Wales. Moreover, Cook's assertion of a legal claim over the eastern coastline of the southern continent was no stronger than the claims of the Dutch, who could assert a competing claim to its western, northern and southern coastlines based upon their 'discovery' of most of it. The Spanish also could mount a claim based upon a mixture of discovery and the Papal division of the world between the Spanish and Portuguese which had been designed to stop them squabbling over the unclaimed spoils. That division had placed the east coast of Australia within the Spanish half of the world. If the British were to properly secure New South Wales for themselves, they would have to occupy it, thereby buttressing Cook's assertion of a legal claim with a claim of effective proprietorship based upon invasion, dispossession of the original inhabitants and their supplanting by British inhabitants.

Cook's subsequent voyages to the Pacific helped to provide the British with compelling reasons to do so. As a result of his failure to find the great south land on his first voyage, Cook was sent back to the south Pacific in 1774 to settle the question once and for all. This time he did so, tracking across the most southerly reaches of the Pacific Ocean where geographers had speculated the great south land was situated. But there was only Antarctica. On the same voyage, he discovered Norfolk Island, an uninhabited island off the east coast of

New South Wales that grew flax and tall pine trees. Both were immensely important as strategic materials for a naval power, pine trees as masts and spars and flax for sails and ropes. He also proved a new British route into the Pacific by way of the southern reaches of the Indian Ocean, Van Diemen's Land and New Zealand, which would avoid the more difficult, Spanish-controlled route around Cape Horn. Landing at Van Diemen's Land and New Zealand to replenish his stores of wood and water, Cook also pointed to the advantages of a port being established in those parts if the route was to be developed and made secure for British trade. By 1787, the British government had decided to equip a fleet of ships to establish a settlement at Botany Bay.

Until about 50 years ago, the reason for settling Australia seemed obvious—it was a place to dump convicts who could no longer be sent to the United States following the outbreak of the American Revolution of 1776. In the 60 years preceding that revolution, some 50 000 British convicts had been sent to the American colonies to work on plantations. At one stroke, the system had helped to secure the North American colonies and their important produce for Britain while at the same time ridding Britain of its prison population. Following the American Revolution, convicts sentenced to transportation accumulated in British county gaols and in hulks, decrepit ships anchored in English estuaries, exciting scare stories of disease and vice. The convicts had been sentenced to transportation for seven, 14 or 21 years and their numbers were growing dangerously, particularly in the gaols of 'middle England'. Attempts to send them to North America or to find alternative places of transportation on the west coast of Africa had been unsuccessful.

The botanist Joseph Banks was the first to sing the praises of Botany Bay as a suitable place for these British felons, suggesting to a committee of the House of Commons in 1779 that it was 'best adapted' for the purpose. But his suggestion was ignored since Britain was not yet convinced that it had lost the American option. Four years later, after Britain finally acknowledged defeat in North America, another crew member on Cook's voyage, the New York-born James Matra, suggested that Botany Bay might be a suitable place to send the thousands of American loyalists thrown out of the American colonies after the revolution and living in poverty in England. In New South Wales, suggested Matra, these loyalists might recover their fortunes through working the land and trading with India, China and Japan. When it seemed that the government was more disturbed by the convicts than the loyalists, Matra changed tack to press the case for Botany Bay as a suitable place for convicts.

Matra's view was supported in 1785 by Admiral Sir George Young who proposed that Botany Bay be used as a place both to settle the loyalists and dump the convicts. Being so far from England was its attraction, since it would ensure that the convicts would be got rid of 'for ever'. However, when the government finally acted, it was only the convicts who were included in the plan announced to parliament in January 1787. And they were being sent there to relieve the congestion in English gaols. According to the prime minister William Pitt, 'no cheaper mode of disposing of the convicts could be found'. So there it is, the 'dumping ground' theory of Australia's settlement. As an explanation of the English occupation, it satisfied historians for more than a century.

In 1952 a little-known historian, Ken Dallas, published an article in an obscure Tasmanian historical journal which opened up a debate that will probably never be concluded. Dallas argued in his article, and in a subsequent slim book, *Trading Post or Penal Colony*, that Australia was settled as part of a wider commercial expansion by Britain into the Pacific. He argued that it was the fur trade of the north Pacific, the trade opportunities in China and South America, and the possibilities in the Pacific for whaling and sealing that combined to make a British settlement at Botany Bay a profitable proposition. The convicts were merely the means to this wider end.

There was evidence to support Dallas's contention. Many of the ships in the First Fleet, once they had landed their convicts, set sail for China to fill their holds with a cargo of tea for the return voyage to England. Moreover, the Industrial Revolution in Britain was producing a big demand for whale and seal oil and the whaling ships were having to go further in search of it. Many of the early so-called convict ships to New South Wales, from the Second Fleet onwards, were whaling ships converted to carry a human cargo that were then reconverted once they reached Sydney and headed off in search of whales, often partly crewed with convicts.

The early proposals for settling Botany Bay had extolled its commercial opportunities, the possibilities for trade with China and with the Aleutian Islands of the north Pacific which had become an important source of furs. Botany Bay could not only act as a supply base for such trading routes in the Pacific but also supply an alternative to the present Dutch-dominated route to China via the East Indies. It had also been pointed out that New South Wales could supply crops ranging from tropical to temperate.

Dallas's arguments were taken up and added to by other historians. In *The Tyranny of Distance* (1966), Geoffrey Blainey emphasised the naval stores aspect, suggesting that the flax and pine trees of Norfolk Island combined to make a powerful argument for British settlement. Blainey argued that these essential requirements for an 18th century naval power—providing sails and spars—was akin to the strategic significance of an oilfield in today's terms. Like Dallas, he pointed out how Captain Phillip, within days of arriving at Port Jackson, had also laid claim to the uninhabited Norfolk Island.

In the same year that Blainey argued forcefully against the 'dumping ground' theory, the noted Australian historian A. G. L. Shaw restated in his book *Convicts and the Colonies* the arguments for New South Wales being settled mainly as a convict colony. Others also joined the fray in an argument that seemed to have no end. One of the most dogged participants in the debate has been the Melbourne historian Alan Frost, who has made three substantial contributions. First, in his book *Convicts and Empire: A Naval Question* (1980), Frost suggested that Sydney was settled mainly as a naval base for possible use in a war with France for control of the eastern trade. He argued that its advantage to Britain was the supposed ability of Botany Bay to shelter a fleet of ships and the capacity of the flax and pine trees of Norfolk Island and New Zealand to supply and refit such vessels with sails, cordage and timber.

In a subsequent book, *Arthur Phillip: His Voyaging* (1987), Frost has shown that Phillip was not an ordinary naval officer plucked out of semi-retirement for this thankless task, but was an officer who had served as a spy in France for the British Admiralty and had spent time with the Portuguese navy. According to Frost, Phillip was chosen for the governorship of New South Wales precisely because he was likely to appreciate the strategic significance of it. He pointed out that Phillip's two successors as governor were also naval officers. More recently, Frost returned to the fray with his book *Botany Bay Mirages: Illusions of Australia's Convict Beginnings* (1994), which brings forward more documentary evidence gleaned from British archives to rebut some of the major arguments put forward by adherents of the 'dumping ground' theory. The accumulating evidence in these books has made clear that Australia was settled as more than a dumping ground for convicts.

It is likely, as in most human affairs, that there was a mix of motives. By deciding on Sydney, the government satisfied those calling for the convicts to be expelled from England; it satisfied the whaling firms who wanted a replenishment base in the Pacific; it satisfied the trading firms who wanted a secure route to China; it satisfied the imperialists who were anxious to repair the damage to Britain's fortunes caused by the American Revolution by creating a new trading empire in the East; it satisfied those wanting to forestall the territorial ambitions of the French and to undercut the claims of the Spanish and the Dutch; and it did it all with convict labour that was expected to free the colony from reliance upon the British exchequer. In other words, it seemed to be an economical way for the British politicians of the time to earn kudos from everyone.

The voyage of the First Fleet of 11 ships, holding some 1000 convicts and marines, officials and officers, together with some of their wives and children, was a credit to the professionalism of Arthur Phillip. Leaving Portsmouth on 13 May 1787, he headed west across the Atlantic to Rio de Janeiro, where he remained for a month replenishing his stores before heading south-east to the Cape of Good Hope, the last port of call before Botany Bay. At each place he took on supplies together with plants and animals with which to stock a settlement. They would not only provide food but also gradually tame the Australian 'wilderness' by imposing a European sense of order upon it. Oranges from Brazil were probably the most important addition to his supplies, ensuring that scurvy, the dreaded scourge of a sailor's life, would be kept at bay.

The vessels arrived at Botany Bay on 18 January 1788, having lost just 48 people from the rigours of the eight-month voyage over some 19 000 kilometres. Considering its length and the nature of the human cargo, it was a remarkable achievement. But then things started to go wrong. Botany Bay at the height of summer did not reveal itself to be as pleasant as Banks had claimed following his visit in the autumn of 1770. They looked in vain for the fresh water and fertile soils while their anchored ships bucked in the relatively unsheltered waters of the wide and shallow bay. Surgeon John White complained of not being able to see the 'fine meadows talked of in Captain Cook's voyage' although he 'took some pains to find them out'. Cook had arrived off Botany Bay primed by Dampier's vivid account of the barren west coast and was pleasantly surprised by the contrast, and perhaps disposed by his prior disappointments over the great south land to dress his discovery in colours more attractive than it deserved. In turn, the officers of the First Fleet had arrived off Botany Bay primed by the overblown, autumnal accounts of Cook and had been as bitterly disappointed as Cook had been pleasantly surprised.

A resourceful Phillip took a party of men by small boat to check the inlet just to the north that Cook had noticed and named Port Jackson but had not entered. He found a harbour that an admiral's dreams might be made of, capable of sheltering a thousand ships and easily defendable from a hostile fleet, together with a more promising place for a settlement. With the convicts still confined aboard ship, he moved his vessels to Port Jackson without delay and landed on the shores of one of its many small inlets, which he named Sydney Cove, where a stream provided fresh water and the soil appeared fertile.

Had he not been so pressed for time, Phillip might have explored the harbour more thoroughly and discovered the Parramatta River which ran into its upper reaches and whose banks provided more extensive areas of fertile soil. Parramatta was a more suitable site for a settlement and a subsequent city. As it happens, Sydney has since expanded to more than encompass Parramatta. If Phillip had even more time at his disposal, he might have decided to settle his convicts about 80 miles north of Sydney, where the valley of the Hunter River provided more extensive agricultural land and easier access into the interior. But it was necessary for the success of the settlement and the health and temper of the convicts that a landing be made without delay. He was also anxious to claim New South Wales for Britain before a rival French expedition could do so first.

Just as Phillip was transferring his ships to Port Jackson, his officers were disconcerted to see two strange sails appear off the entrance to the bay before they had had a chance to land and lay claim to New South Wales. Some feared that they were 'Dutch ships com'g after us to oppose our landing'. But closer inspection revealed that they were French vessels under the command of the explorer Jean François de La Pérouse. The French were not there by accident. La Pérouse, who had been exploring in the north

25

Pacific, had received instructions from Paris to visit Botany Bay and report on the activities of the British. He was also instructed to visit New Zealand to see if the British had made any claims there. Fortunately for the success of the British enterprise, La Pérouse was gathering intelligence about their intentions and the prospects of the place rather than establishing a rival claim. Not then being at war, the British cordially welcomed the French into Botany Bay while they continued their own move north to the adjacent Port Jackson.

With the French in Botany Bay, Phillip lost no time in reinforcing the claim to New South Wales that Captain Cook had made 18 years earlier on Possession Island. On 26 January 1788, the day after the French arrived, Phillip assembled his officers and the marines on a space freshly cleared by European hands on the shores of Sydney Cove. Phillip then ran up the flag to reassert the legal claim over New South Wales and its adjacent islands in the Pacific. Not content with doing it once, Phillip did it again that evening when the second echelon of ships arrived from Botany Bay.

Phillip's claim had considerably expanded on the rather vague claim made by Cook, who had been concerned to include within the ambit of his claim only that part of the coastline that he had 'discovered' together with its rivers, bays and adjacent islands. This left rather indeterminate the extent of Cook's claim over the continent. Phillip clarified this uncertainty by claiming all the territory west to the line of longitude at 135 degrees east of Greenwich, encompassing within this claim about half of the continent. This line of longitude was the line accepted by the Spanish as marking the limit of their control in the Pacific. To the west were the Portuguese and their imperial successors, the Dutch, who had divided the island of Timor between them. As the historian Bill Gammage has pointed out, while trampling on the historic claims of the Spanish, whose power to dispute it was waning, the British were careful to keep clear of the Portuguese and Dutch who they were keen to have as allies in Europe.

There was also a lingering doubt as to whether New South Wales and New Holland were part of one continent or whether they were separated by a channel running south from the Gulf of Carpentaria. Dampier had entertained this possibility and failed to disprove it. And the doubt would remain until the circumnavigation of the continent's entire coastline by Matthew Flinders in 1801. When Flinders approached Spencer Gulf in South Australia, he half expected to find a passage north to New Guinea. It was not until he had charted the northern reaches of that extensive gulf that Flinders finally confirmed that Australia was a single continent.

By limiting his claim, Phillip was also acknowledging that the Dutch had established a claim over the western coastline by right of first discovery. In the words of one of his officers, Watkin Tench: 'By this partition it may be fairly presumed, that every source of future litigation between the Dutch and us will be for ever cut off, as the discoveries of English navigators alone are comprized in this territory.' This was rather disingenuous, since Phillip had included within the British orbit the claim made by Tasman in Van Diemen's Land and the Gulf of Carpentaria. Nevertheless, Tasman's legal claim, made in passing, had not been followed up by a Dutch occupation, thereby leaving it open to be challenged by a rival power such as Britain which was prepared to go to the trouble of invading and settling it. By brushing aside Tasman's claim, the British were also perhaps testing the resolution of the Dutch. If the Dutch failed to react, then it left open the possibility of the remainder of the continent being claimed by the British in due course.

In making his claim, Phillip was not only asserting British sovereignty over New South Wales but also claiming the ownership of all its land on behalf of the Crown. This latter assertion would bedevil European–Aboriginal relations for the next two centuries. The claim of British sovereignty over New South Wales assumed that the Aborigines did not constitute a nation that was capable of exercising sovereignty over the continent they had occupied for perhaps 120 000 years. Or even of constituting, as they did, a large number of 'nations' each exercising sovereignty over their separate territories. Similarly, Phillip's claim of ownership of the land within that continent assumed that the supposedly nomadic Aborigines had no legally enforceable interest in the land, that they could be shifted aside. The British were relying upon the accepted legal principle of *terra nullius* which allowed unowned land to be claimed and owned by the first person who 'finds' it. It was only in 1992, in the landmark Mabo case in the Australian High Court, that this legal fiction was finally set aside and the traditional land rights of the Aborigines acknowledged.

The British may have made some attempt to acknowledge these rights earlier had they not been operating under several crucial misunderstandings about the Aborigines. As a result of the reports by Cook and Banks, the British wrongly believed that the Aborigines were few in number, that they lived only along the coast in an almost animal-like condition and that they were nomadic with no sense of land ownership. Banks had assured the British government that the Aborigines would mount little resistance to a British invasion and could be easily shifted aside to allow the establishment of a British settlement. He also claimed from his brief observations at Botany Bay, during which he failed to notice any campfire smoke far inland, that the interior of the continent was totally uninhabited. It was considered sufficient compensation for the supposedly scattered and primitive Aborigines to come under the protection of the British king and to be exposed to the uplifting experience of European civilisation. Phillip was more concerned about a challenge from the French.

Raising a flag, firing off a few salutes and drinking a toast to the king does not make for an effective claim over half a continent—especially when the French were occupying a fortified encampment on the shores of the adjoining bay and busily exploring its hinterland. Within three weeks of landing at Sydney Cove, Phillip split his meagre force by sending off a contingent of convicts and marines to claim Norfolk Island, with its supposedly rich resources of pine trees and flax plants, for the British king before the French could do so first. Although it would be some years before they would discover it, both the pine trees and the flax plants would prove to be unsuitable for naval purposes. And the island's usefulness was hampered by the lack of a sheltered landing place for ships. Norfolk Island was then used instead as a dreaded place of secondary punishment, an isolated prison for convicts sentenced for offences committed in Australia. Its name vied with that of Van Diemen's Land as a place of infamous cruelty. Later, it became a haven for the descendants of the men who mutinied against Captain William Bligh on the *Bounty*.

The settlement at Sydney and its outlier at Norfolk Island could not constitute for long a meaningful claim to the possession of half a continent. But the feared challenge from the French did not eventuate. La Pérouse, who six years earlier had captured British settlements in North America, was now intent on gathering information, both scientific and strategic, rather than dislodging them or establishing a rival settlement in New Holland. Although reports based on his six-week sojourn in Botany Bay, and sent back to Paris courtesy of the British, may have inspired the French king to counter the British move, La Pérouse never returned to Paris to reinforce them. Fortunately for Phillip, the two ships of the French expedition foundered in a storm soon after departing from Botany Bay and its men perished. Moreover, the outbreak of the French Revolution the following year and the subsequent war in Europe distracted French attention from their wider ambitions in the Pacific. Although a Spanish expedition visited Sydney Cove in 1793 to investigate the scope of Britain's imperial designs in the Pacific, its warnings of the threat posed by the new British port were not acted upon due to political rivalries in the Spanish court. As a result, the British enjoyed a breathing space of 14 years before the French challenge reappeared in the form of a scientific exploring expedition in two ships under the command of Nicholas Baudin, sent by Napoleon to chart the coasts of New Holland so that they might know the 'entire coastline' of what he called 'the great south land'.

After surveying much of the west and south coast, Baudin ended up in Sydney in June 1802 with a crew largely disabled by scurvy. For five months the French rested at Sydney, Baudin striking up a friendship with the then governor, Phillip Gidley King, as Baudin's artists and scientists took their measure of the British settlement and its plants and animals. Despite their friendly reception, the French arrival alarmed the authorities in both Sydney and London, arousing fresh suspicions as to the French intentions, particularly when Baudin sailed off to Bass Strait to chart the southern coasts and islands off New South Wales.

When rumours spread through Sydney that the French planned to settle in Van Diemen's Land, King sent a small party of marines in pursuit.

They caught up with the French party on King Island in Bass Strait where the French were camped. The marines delivered a letter from King asserting British sovereignty. To drive the point home unmistakenly, they flew a British flag from a tree sheltering the French tents. The polite Baudin declined to point out that the ignorant marines flew the flag upside down, a signal of distress. As for King's assertion of sovereignty, Baudin acknowledged the British claim while nevertheless wondering at the 'justice or even fairness on the part of Europeans in seizing, in the name of their governments, a land seen for the first time, when it is inhabited by men who ... were still only children of nature ...' The gout-ridden governor was not troubled by such philosophising. Nor was the British government, which was even then intent on securing its claim over that southern region of New South Wales and its strategic southern strait.

In July 1801, it despatched Matthew Flinders to chart the entire coastline of the continent so that the British might make a better claim for it. In an epic voyage, Flinders charted the southern coastline on his way to Sydney, meeting Baudin at Encounter Bay in South Australia. In the process, he found and surveyed Port Phillip Bay, at the head of which the city of Melbourne would be established three decades later. Flinders then sailed north from Sydney to survey the coast of what is now Queensland and continued along much of the northern coast. In the process, he chanced upon a fleet of fishermen from Macassar who had descended upon the tropical northern coastline to gather their annual harvest of sea slugs. These were cured onshore before being taken home for trading with China where they were used in soups and as an aphrodisiac. The British had 'occupied' New South Wales for 13 years before they discovered this annual visitation which had been going on for several centuries.

With his ship rotting beneath him, Flinders set sail for Timor and then back to Sydney via the west coast, becoming the first person to circumnavigate the continent. When he then attempted to return to England with his charts and specimens, his vessel was shipwrecked. Returning again to Sydney, he set out in a vessel of just 29 tons. Stopping at the French island of Mauritius, where Baudin had also called just three months earlier before dying soon after, Flinders found that the intermittent war with France had flared up again. He was arrested and imprisoned for a harrowing six years that broke his health. During that time, Baudin's fellow officers published the results of their exploration, thereby beating Flinders into press and claiming for the French parts of Australia's southern coastline, stretching roughly from present-day Adelaide to Melbourne, naming it Terra Napoleon.

Upon his release, Flinders worked feverishly to retrieve the situation by belatedly publishing in 1814 an account of his voyages. It finally appeared, according to the *Quarterly Review*, on the same day the world 'released from its cares and vexations their unfortunate and injured author'. Flinders was dead, but the publication of his journal made an important contribution to the British claiming of the continent. Now that it was clear from his voyage that New Holland and New South Wales were part of a single entity of continental extent, it seemed appropriate that it should have a single name. Flinders proposed a name for the entire continent that would 'do justice to the discovery rights of Holland and England', while deliberately ignoring any rights the rival French might care to claim. At first, he suggested calling it 'Austral-land or Australia'. Then, when publishing the charts of his epic voyages, he titled a map of the continent, Terra Australis or Australia, the former name having been commonly applied to the southern continent for centuries past and the latter name being a misspelt derivation of the Spanish name applied to the New Hebrides by de Quiros in 1605. In a burst of inspiration, the latter name was seized upon in 1817 by that nation-building governor, Lachlan Macquarie, who henceforth addressed his despatches to England with that name. It was a name that fitted well with the names of the other continents and it quickly came into common usage to describe both the continent and its people. Despite the name, there was no such political entity as 'Australia' until the federation of the colonies in 1901. Until then, they were known by their individual names or collectively as the Australian, or more often, the Australasian colonies so as to include New Zealand and sometimes Fiji.

As 'Australia' was adopted, so the name 'New Holland' soon slipped off the maps, taking with it any residual claim the Dutch may have had to the continent's western half. To ensure that no other nations sought to make claims in their place, particularly the French, the British established outposts of settlement at strategic points around the coast of the continent. In 1802, Lieutenant John Murray had been sent south from Sydney in the brig *Lady Nelson* to explore the Bass Strait coastline, entering and charting a large bay that he named Port King in honour of the governor, who promptly renamed it Port Phillip Bay. Before leaving the bay, Murray's party was attacked by Aborigines as they were seeking to befriend them. The spears were thrown to no effect and answered with a European musket fired over their heads. When this did not have the desired effect, Murray reported that 'our party were obliged to teach them by fatal experience the effect of our walking sticks'. Murray later took possession of the bay in the name of his Sacred Majesty George III, flying the new Union Jack on shore and on ship for five hours before three volleys were fired at 1 p.m. and a double issue of grog was given to the crew. Murray then went ashore with 'an armed party and passed the remainder of the day about and under the colours flying on shore' before hauling them down at sunset and departing. In British eyes, the Aborigines thereabouts had now been legally dispossessed.

The next step in the process of supplanting the indigenous inhabitants was quickly taken when, in April 1803, a mixed convoy of convicts and free settlers set sail from London for Port Phillip Bay to establish a British claim by occupation over those parts. The attempt failed. Although two sizeable rivers emptied their waters into Port Phillip Bay, the commander, David Collins, chose to land near the heads of the bay in a dry and rather barren area that was selected more for exercising strategic control of Bass Strait than for settling the shores of the bay. With his convicts running off and the settlers complaining, the short-sighted Collins concluded that Port Phillip Bay 'cannot, nor ever will be, resorted to by speculative Men'. The narrow entrance to the bay had dangerous currents that jeopardised its safe use by sailing ships, while the Aborigines had proved troublesome and were feared to be cannibals.

Although Governor King suggested that Collins move his disgruntled charges to the north coast of Van Diemen's Land, from where strategic control of the strait could still be asserted, Collins went instead to its south coast, joining his settlers to the settlement at Hobart which King had established in September 1803. Collins also had been meant to establish a presence on King Island at the western entrance to the strait so that a British stranglehold could be maintained on that strategic waterway between Europe and the Pacific. But Collins ignored those instructions. It was left to Governor King to send a second expedition from Sydney to establish a settlement in 1804 at the mouth of the Tamar River on the north coast of Van Diemen's Land, where it might also exercise an effective claim over the adjacent strait and its windswept and snake-infested islands.

No more claims were made until 1824 when an expedition was sent to Melville Island off the north coast of Australia, near present-day Darwin. Being west of the 135 degree line of longitude, the British simply extended the boundary of New South Wales westwards to 129 degrees to encompass it. This distant lodgment was meant to assert a British claim of effective proprietorship over those northern parts. It was also meant to tap into the trade of the Dutch East Indies, as Singapore had been doing since 1819, to act as a replenishment port for the shipping that plied through the Torres Strait to China and to trade with the Macassan fishermen on their annual hunt for the sea slug. But it failed miserably in all its objects. It could not compete with Singapore, the approach to its harbour was difficult for vessels to enter and the Macassans came nowhere near it. Another port established 200 miles to the east was more successful in attracting the Macassans but the expense of supplying it from Sydney also spelt its early doom. By 1829, both of them had been abandoned.

The abandonment of those northern ports did not signal a lack of interest by the British in extending their original claim over New South Wales to encompass the entire continent. In fact, by the time those northern ports had been abandoned, the British had shifted their attention to the south-west coast of the continent. In 1826, an expedition was sent from Sydney to stake a claim at King George's Sound, site of the Western Australian town of Albany. The region had been visited previously by the British captain George

Vancouver in 1791. Vancouver had claimed it then on behalf of the king but the government had declined to recognise the claim, presumably for fear of unnecessarily antagonising the Dutch. The settlement in 1826 made clear that Britain's ambitions were continental in scope, although it was still concerned more with controlling the sea routes that swept past Australia to China and the Pacific than with occupying its largely unexplored interior. Indeed, when the first free settlement was founded in 1829 at Swan River, site of Perth, the British government was unwilling to bear any responsibility for the cost.

With the British claim to the western half of Australia, the original claim of legal proprietorship by Captain Cook to the eastern coast of Australia had been extended to encompass the whole continent and the offshore island of Van Diemen's Land. This legal claim needed to be buttressed by a claim of effective proprietorship over the continental expanse if it was to be secured for the long term. It required the British to do what they believed the Aborigines were not doing—to invest the land with the industry of man. By the 1820s, they were already doing that. As the ring of British outposts laid legal claim to the continent, the original colony at Sydney was spreading out from its limited agricultural hinterland to lay a claim of effective proprietorship across wide swathes of the interior. It would be the bleating of sheep that would signal the coming of this British army of occupation.

Recommended Reading

Frank Crowley (ed.), 1980, *A Documentary History of Australia*, Vol. 1, Nelson, Melbourne.

K. M. Dallas, 1969, *Trading Posts or Penal Colonies*, Fullers Bookshop, Hobart.

Alan Frost, 1980, *Convicts and Empire*, Oxford University Press, Melbourne.

Alan Frost, 1987, *Arthur Phillip, 1738–1814: His Voyaging*, Oxford University Press, Melbourne.

Alan Frost, 1994, *Botany Bay Mirages*, Melbourne University Press, Melbourne.

Bill Gammage, 'Early Boundaries of New South Wales', *Historical Studies*, October 1981.

Robert J. King, 1990, *The Secret History of the Convict Colony*, Allen & Unwin, Sydney.

Ged Martin, 1981, *The Founding of Australia*, Hale & Iremonger, Sydney.

Anon., 'Flinders' voyage to Terra Australis', *Quarterly Review*, Vol. 12, London, 1814–15.

A. G. L. Shaw, 1966, *Convicts and the Colonies*, Faber, London.

Watkin Tench, 1979, *Sydney's First Four Years*, Library of Australian History, Sydney.

4

'THEY MUST ALWAYS CONSIDER US AS ENEMIES'

Although Britain had by 1826 extended its claim of legal proprietorship to include the entire continent, it required the application of human industry to buttress that legal claim with a claim of effective proprietorship. The British had to deal with the Aboriginal possessors of the continent while also demonstrating to the outside world that they were making more fruitful use of the continent in ways that their God intended. This meant that buildings had to be erected and the soil tilled. Tilling of the soil also began the creation of a claim to the moral proprietorship of the continent. The British settlers could then argue that they were doing what the Aborigines during their long occupation had clearly failed, or been disinclined, to do. As a British paper assured its readers in 1787, New South Wales was 'formed of a Virgin Mould undisturbed since the Creation'. In disturbing that 'virgin mould' for the first time, the British would ensure their survival while also establishing their moral authority for supplanting the Aborigines.

By April 1788, just three months after the convicts had first landed at Sydney Cove, the settlement was well on its way to staking a claim of effective proprietorship, at least over its immediate surrounds. The grandly titled Governor's Mansion had been erected and a nine-acre farm laid out and fenced on the slopes above the appropriately-named Farm Cove. By July 1788, a plan of the settlement reveals an attempt to lay out a town along broad avenues fit for an empire rather than the haphazard, contour-hugging arrangements following the first landing. Provision was already made for a church, for government offices and a courthouse—all the signs of civilisation that Manning Clark celebrated in his history—although the rather irreligious Phillip made no move during his four years in Sydney to actually build the church.

Phillip was conscious of imposing European order on what he persisted in seeing as a wilderness:

> *There are few things more pleasing than the contemplation of order and useful arrangement, arising gradually out of tumult and confusion; and perhaps this satisfaction cannot any where be more fully enjoyed than where a settlement of civilized people is fixing itself upon a newly discovered or savage coast.*

Phillip took quiet satisfaction from observing the process of 'settlement', whereby 'large spaces are opened, plans are formed, lines marked, and a prospect at least of future regularity is clearly discerned'. This future regularity would not be along the lines of Phillip's initial imperial design. The necessity to ensure sheer survival for the first few years would force the grandiose town plan to be abandoned and Sydney to grow as best it could within the relatively cramped lines of the original settlement.

The benefit of hindsight has allowed us the luxury of viewing Phillip's act of settlement as the first act of an ongoing European invasion that would sweep across much of the continent within a century of the First Fleet's arrival. But such a view was not clear at the time, either to Phillip and his officers or to the Aborigines, whose initial degree of resistance to the newcomers does not suggest that they looked upon them as invaders. For his part, Phillip could hardly view himself as an invader while at the same time believing that the Aborigines had no sense of attachment to the land over which they appeared to roam.

While failing at first to notice the abiding attachment the Aborigines had to their land, the Europeans also looked upon the alien landscape without appreciating the ways in which it had been fashioned over millennia to meet Aboriginal needs. They described the relatively fertile Cumberland Plain west of Sydney, with its widely spaced, tall trees and luxuriant grasses, as being like an English deer park without acknowledging the part Aborigines may have played with their use of firestick farming in creating it for their own purposes. In their ignorance, British surveyors imposed grid lines and county boundaries over countryside that was already intersected with Aboriginal boundaries. Although not acknowledging the Aboriginal impact on the landscape, they followed Aboriginal pathways through the tall grasses and underwood, turning some of them into European tracks and then roads, and they seized upon the lightly treed grasslands for their livestock and crops.

Tilling the soil proved more difficult than Phillip had anticipated when making the move to Sydney Cove. He had chosen the position in haste, attracted by its fresh water, the capacious harbour and a cove whose deep water close to shore allowed jetties easily to be constructed at which large ships could unload their cargoes. The site was also set on rising land to allow for the movement of air through the settlement and thereby prevent the presence of miasmas that were believed to promote disease. Phillip had been misled by his European experience into believing that the presence of the tall eucalypt trees and ample grasses was an indication of the soil's fertility. Only after landing did they discover that the soil thereabouts was as indifferent as that of Botany Bay. So jaundiced did their view of Sydney Cove become that one junior officer suggested in July 1788 that it was 'the opinion of every body here that the Government will remove the Settlement to some other place for if it remains here this country will not be able to maintain its self in 100 years ...' As a naval man of wide experience, Captain Phillip had been well-chosen to ensure the safe passage of his convoy to New South Wales. In his civilian role as a Hampshire farmer, he was well equipped to set the settlement on its way to a secure agricultural and pastoral future. Which he did, but only after two years of hard times.

The early history of the United States has examples of settlements that were defeated by the rigours of their alien environment. Such a calamitous ending almost occurred in Sydney. Because of delays in their departure from England, the First Fleet arrived at the height of summer, in stark contrast to the pleasant autumn weather Banks and Cook had experienced 18 years previously and to the spring weather Phillip had planned to arrive in. Despite Banks's promise of New South Wales growing a wide range of crops, Phillip found that their hastily planted seeds failed to germinate in the unmanured soil, or the green shoots were burnt by the summer sun, or the unsuitable season led to premature fruiting. The surgeon George Worgan was puzzled that 'nothing seems to flourish vigorously long, but they shoot up suddenly after being put in the Ground, look green & luxuriant for a little Time, blossom early, fructify slowly & weakly, and ripen before they come to their proper Size'. Phillip had been forced to plant as soon as they arrived, instead of awaiting the following spring, so that the health of his company could be restored by fresh vegetables and other vitamin-rich plants. When the European plants largely failed to thrive, although they would do so from the following spring, they looked for native plants to take their place and found some that were at least partly suitable. A convict woman described how 'there is a kind of chickweed so much in taste like our spinach that no difference can be discerned. Something like ground ivy is used for tea.'

At first, they had few animals to provide manure to boost the fertility of the soil. There were only seven horses, seven cattle, 29 sheep, 19 goats and 74 hogs. Many of these animals wandered off into the bush or were killed to provide food for the increasingly desperate settlement. Later, after Phillip had had a chance to explore the surrounding area and discovered the river flats along the Parramatta River, and along the Hawkesbury River which emptied into Broken Bay just to the north of Port Jackson, farming activity shifted to those areas. Although the first settlers had some trouble adapting their farming implements and methods to the new environment, Alan Frost has demonstrated conclusively in his book *Botany Bay Mirages* that they were well equipped to impose European horticulture on what they saw as virgin soil. Contrary to popular belief, Frost has shown that there were several ploughs sent with the First Fleet, although the tilling of the soil was mainly to be done by the intensive labour of the convicts who would earn redemption from their crimes through hard work. There was a spade, a shovel, a felling axe, a hatchet and three hoes for each convict. These short-handled hoes were the weapons used by the English to claim the soil of New South Wales.

Many of the convicts did not realise that their survival depended upon their labour. Some deliberately broke their tools to avoid the arduous labour, while Phillip's officers thought it below their dignity to remonstrate with shirking convicts. To make matters worse, the convicts were mainly drawn from urban areas and were unused to agriculture. It was later estimated by the superintendent of convicts that it took two to three years to turn such a convict into a useful farm labourer. Phillip could not wait that long if he was to stave off starvation and secure the British claim on New South Wales. Although he sent the colony's ship, *Sirius*, to Cape Town for a cargo of flour, Phillip was relying upon the labour of his convicts and the timely arrival of the next fleet to provide relief.

It was not until April 1788 that Phillip explored the headwaters of the harbour and came upon the Parramatta River and the fertile land thereabouts. He established a second settlement on the banks of the river, which he named Rose Hill. By the end of 1789, as the settlement subsisted on rationed food, the convicts of Rose Hill harvested some 200 bushels of wheat and 60 bushels of barley, along with smaller quantities of other grains. It was not sufficient to stop the famine, which did not end until the Second Fleet arrived in June 1790. An earlier supply ship from England had come to grief when it had hit an iceberg out of Cape Town.

For 18 long months, the lookout on Sydney's South Head had scoured the seas in vain for the sign of a sail and the succour it would bring. When at last it was sighted, a party of officers was rowed out to meet the newcomers. What a miserable sight met their eyes. The captains of these vessels had made such poor provision for the convicts that more than a third died either *en route* or soon after they crawled ashore in Sydney. Whereas there was a profit motive in ensuring the survival of slaves, no such consideration applied in the case of convicts. The more convicts that died *en route*, and the earlier in the voyage they did so, the more rations would be preserved for sale by the captains in Sydney. To curb the incidence of such brutal exploitation, the British government introduced stricter supervision of the convict convoys.

While the emaciated and sickened convicts of the Second Fleet added little to the labour force of Sydney, the supplies aboard ship lifted the threat of starvation from the struggling settlement. Although food shortages occasionally recurred, they never again reached the desperate depths of those early months when the land was slow to respond to the convicts' grudging industry and the supply ships failed to arrive. In April 1792, Phillip was able to report: 'All our fruit trees thrive well, & I have this year gathered about three hundred weight of very fine grapes ... we have now vegetables in abundance. At Parramatta they are now served daily to the Convicts'... By the end of that year, there were 1400 acres of grain being grown, 400 of those acres by private farmers. Convicts with expired sentences and former marines who chose not to return to England were given grants of land on which to farm, thereby establishing the basis for a free society of agriculturalists. Before he left for England in December 1792, Phillip had granted some 6000 acres to 112 emancipated convicts and 55 marines who had left the service and chosen to remain in the colony.

While the hand of industry was making its mark on the land, children were being born who would have no direct experience of any other home but Australia. On 25 January 1788, as the First Fleet was being moved from Botany Bay to Sydney Cove, the first of these European Australians was born to the wife of Thomas Whittle. Four years later, young Whittle had been joined by another 300 children who would know only New South Wales as home. These children would gradually help to lay the basis for a society of free colonists born in an environment that was not alien to them. As such, many would develop links to the landscape that some of their parents would find difficult to share. Some of the convicts were so desperate to escape from their situations in New South Wales that they took to the bush in the hope of finding salvation but found only death. One group, including a man, his wife and their two young children, stole away in Governor Phillip's cutter and sailed it all the way to Timor, enduring great privations and dangers *en route* before the remnants of the group posed as survivors of a shipwreck. However, their ruse was discovered and they were returned to England where the woman became a *cause célèbre* and was eventually pardoned. Others, though, found their salvation in their alien surroundings.

In March 1791, just nine months after her arrival at Sydney Cove, Elizabeth Macarthur, the young and inquisitive wife of the paymaster of the New South Wales Corps, wrote with delight about the native landscape while at the same time decrying its soil as the 'most wretched and totally unfit for growing any European productions'. Despite this, she was still able to see great beauty in the bush, describing it as 'flourishing even to luxuriance; producing fine Shrubs, Trees, and Flowers which by their lively tints, afford a most agreeable Landscape'. Her initially bleak view of the soil's fertility was transformed by experience and hard work until, within seven years, she was celebrating the 'many luxuries' provided by what she now described as the 'fruitful soil'. Unlike the convicts or the children, she was there by choice and New South Wales had replaced England as her home. When, in an ironic turn of fate, her husband was later exiled for a time to England and suggested she sell their extensive properties and join him, she refused. Instead, she continued with their development and lived out her days in her antipodean home.

Although the British government did not have a clear sense of the possibilities of New South Wales, it had made some provision for the future population of the settlement. Among the convicts of the First Fleet, there were 188 women, or just under a quarter of the 736 convicts. When the women finally splashed ashore from the convict transports on 6 February 1788, their arrival unleashed what more than one officer described as scenes of 'Debauchery and Riot' as the pent-up passions of the convicts, marines and sailors, fuelled by alcohol, made the beginnings of a native-born population. The whole licentious panorama was played out under the thunderous symphony of a Sydney thunderstorm that eventually drenched the participants.

Phillip knew better than to interfere. However, the following day he assembled the convicts and had his commission as governor read out. In a speech to the convicts as they sat upon the grass, Phillip called upon his charges to abandon their former pursuit of wickedness and to follow instead the path of righteousness, earning redemption through honest labour. They were urged to embrace the institution of marriage and warned that sentries would shoot at any men found entering the female tents after dark. The following Sunday, 14 couples were married by the Reverend Richard Johnson, perhaps as a way for the women to fend off undesired attention or for the men to avoid being shot. One of the officers, David Collins, suggested that it was motivated by the notion 'that married people would meet with various little comforts and privileges that were denied those in the single state'. Other women lived as the mistresses of officers and marines.

While the fertility of the soil proved a disappointment, the fertility of the women proved a surprise. In the relatively healthy conditions and climate of Sydney, and with women receiving a full ration even as men had theirs cut back by a third, they bore children at a greater rate than would have been expected in England. According to Watkin Tench, 'Women, who certainly would never have bred in any other climate, here produced as fine children as ever were born.' Similarly, a convict midwife, Margaret Catchpole, wrote: 'It is a wonderful country for to have children, even very old women have them that never had none before.' Later observers embellished this early description by attesting to the above-average physique of the native-born population.

Moreover, these earliest European Australians benefited from the isolation that had kept so many diseases from the Aborigines. Many diseases that devastated urban populations in Europe could not survive the long sea voyage to New South Wales, with crew and passengers forced by necessity into close contact. Even if picked up at Cape Town, such diseases would usually be burnt out by the time the vessel anchored in Sydney Harbour. Later, as the voyages became progressively faster and vessels less cramped in their accommodation, the diseases might still be active but the evidence of their presence would usually ensure that quarantine measures could be taken to ensure the health of the Australian population. This natural immunity helped to embellish the idea of Australia being a pristine island untouched by the debilities of the old world.

Phillip had been instructed to supplement the female convicts with women recruited from the islands of Polynesia. These women were intended to provide wives for those members of the marines and the convicts who might decide to settle in New South Wales, in the same way as they had in the past provided congenial companions for British seamen exploring the Pacific. Based upon a misinterpretation of his experience as a junior officer aboard the *Endeavour* at Tahiti, James Matra had assured a parliamentary committee in 1785 that these women were 'more partial to Europeans than to their own Countrymen'. However, the plan to fetch the women to Sydney was abandoned by Phillip in view of the straitened times with which the settlement was faced. With the dreaded scurvy appearing among the poorly nourished settlers, there was no point bringing such women 'to pine away in misery'. The plan was never resuscitated. As for Aboriginal women, they were not considered suitable as mothers for the new settlement, although they were widely used as sexual outlets for the men, with some being kept aboard the ships in the harbour.

Just as Joseph Banks had been wrong about the suitability of Botany Bay, so too was he wrong about the Aboriginal population which he had suggested was sparsely scattered along the coast and cowardly in temperament. Far from being sparse, the Europeans of Sydney Cove sometimes encountered groups of armed Aborigines numbering some 200–300 strong. And far from being cowardly, Phillip was so impressed with the 'manly undaunted behaviour of a party of natives' seen on a northern harbour beach upon their 'taking possession of the country' that he named the area Manly. It was soon clear from their expeditions into the countryside that the Aborigines were not restricted to the coast or to a meagre diet of mainly fish.

Although Phillip had blithely robbed the Aborigines of their land, he had been instructed to treat the Aborigines with every kindness and consideration. As Watkin Tench observed, the English intention was first 'to win their affections, and our next to convince them of the superiority we possessed'. Their military superiority was demonstrated by shooting a musket ball through an Aboriginal bark shield placed against a tree. The later use of

39

muskets against the Aborigines themselves reinforced the message. By December 1788, a party of around 50 Aborigines had appeared at the brick kilns apparently intent on attack but had been frightened off by the convicts 'pointing their spades and shovels at them, in the manner of guns'. By February 1790, Phillip was able to assure the British government that free settlers would 'have nothing to apprehend from the natives, who avoid those parts we most frequent, and always retire at the sight of two or three people who are armed'. Similarly, Elizabeth Macarthur claimed the following year that the Aborigines were 'under such terror of our firearms that a single armed man would drive an hundred natives with their spears'.

Initially, though, relations between the two groups were cordial. Both were curious about the habits and possessions of the other. At an early stage, Phillip was impelled to restrain the Aborigines' curiosity when their presence proved a nuisance as the Europeans made their dinner. Phillip marked out a circle in the sand, indicating to the Aborigines that they were not to cross it. They complied, sitting 'very quiet' outside the white man's boundary. Tench saw it as a significant acknowledgment by the Aborigines of Phillip's authority. But the idyllic days could not continue.

Although a colony of convicts, Sydney was a gaol without walls. Only convicts convicted of further offences were actually gaoled or forced to work in leg irons. This meant that unsupervised convicts were able to commit depredations against the Aborigines without the knowledge of Phillip or his officers. It became commonplace for the convicts to steal Aboriginal goods left lying about which they then sold to the crews of the convict transports for shipment back to England as curios. This created ill-feeling which resulted in several attacks on isolated convicts. Aboriginal women were also abused by the convicts.

Initial relations with the Aborigines were complicated by the simultaneous presence of the French at Botany Bay. Their presence must have exacerbated in the minds of the Aborigines the effect of the English arrival. Phillip was careful to conciliate the Aborigines, but the French built a temporary stockade for their visit and had occasion to shoot at Aborigines for various transgressions. It is unlikely that the Aborigines discriminated between the two settlements. Whatever the complications, conflict between the two societies was inevitable as the European lifestyle increasingly impinged upon that of the Aborigines.

Fishing with nets by the Europeans depleted an important Aboriginal food stock, although this was alleviated somewhat by part of the catch being given to Aborigines who may have helped with its landing or simply been in the vicinity at the time. At times, some Aborigines exchanged some of the fish they continued to catch for the rations of the Europeans, particularly bread and, later, rum. In mid-1791, Aborigines at Parramatta 'found it in their interest to sell or exchange fish', receiving in exchange 'a small quantity of either bread or salt meat'. Although the trade was encouraged by the officers, it ended when convicts destroyed the canoe of an Aboriginal man who retaliated by spearing a convict.

The clearing of land for agriculture and the hunting of animals with guns reduced the number of animals the Aborigines could hunt for their food. When Spanish explorers visited Sydney in 1793, they remarked on the 'great consumption' of kangaroos by the Europeans, noting that 'there were very few times that it was missing from our table'. Although five years of hunting them with muskets and greyhounds had not seemed to affect their numbers, the Spanish observer predicted that 'a consumption so excessive and the progress of Population must winnow them'. Perhaps of more importance, the gradual clearing and fencing of grasslands for crops would rob the kangaroos of their choicest habitat. Just as the Europeans killed native animals, so the Aborigines sometimes killed the settlers' animals, thereby adding to the fluctuating tensions between the two groups. The disruption of traditional food sources caused some Aborigines to become dependent on the settlers for food and others to fight against their presence.

By early February, within a week of their landing at Sydney Cove, the first signs of serious tension were experienced when Aborigines fled at the approach of a party surveying the harbour and later caused the surveyors to flee in turn when they were confronted with 'an astonishing number of the Natives all armed' with spears. The reason for the sudden change in relations remains a matter for speculation. It is likely the Aborigines realised by that time that these visitors were not temporary. The extensive felling of trees and clearing of ground would have suggested as much. The netting of fish in the harbour might also have been seen as a threat by this time, while the demonstration of the European weaponry would have made any sensible Aborigine apprehensive about approaching any armed Europeans. One of the surgeons observed that 'from the first, they carefully avoided a soldier, or any person wearing a red coat'.

Friendly exchanges still occurred, but they were increasingly interspersed with instances of defiance and hostility. When Aborigines stole some European tools on 19 February, perhaps in response to the theft of their own property, they found themselves 'well pepper'd with small shot'. In March, one of the officers came upon an Aborigine who had been beaten about the body by some unidentified men. By May, Phillip admitted that the Aborigines were avoiding contact with the settlers because of the conflict with the French and the 'bad behaviour' of the sailors and convicts. Before he could retrieve the situation, an Aborigine was killed in a fight with convicts. They apparently responded by killing two convicts cutting rushes. Since it was believed that the convicts brought their fate upon themselves by abusing the Aborigines, no retaliation was attempted.

It was just as well. When Phillip took a dozen armed men to attempt a reconciliation he encountered a group of more than 200 armed Aborigines.

As a result of this and subsequent experiences, Phillip reassessed his view of the native population, rejecting Banks's estimation of them being sparse and suggesting instead that perhaps 1500 lived in the vicinity of Port Jackson. The warriors probably outnumbered the marines by at least two to one. This was a sobering thought when reinforcements were more than a year away.

While Phillip still hoped that he could encourage some Aborigines to live side-by-side with the settlement, the marine commandant, Major Ross, was urging that defence works should be built to stave off any massed attack. Both groups were now very much on their guard, the British tending to fire as soon as they felt the slightest threat while the Aborigines maintained a state of what Tench described as 'petty warfare'. By the end of 1788, however, only four convicts were known to have been killed by the Aborigines. Phillip sought to break through this state of armed stalemate by capturing an Aborigine who they could indulge with every kindness so that, when released, he might convince his fellows of the Europeans' good intentions. No-one seemed to consider that kidnapping was hardly the best way to demonstrate good intentions.

On 31 December 1788, an Aborigine by the name of Arabanoo was kidnapped and submitted to the civilising influence of his English captors. He found himself washed, his hair cut, and clothes put on him before being chained to a convict with handcuffs. The last 'gift' of civilisation— smallpox—killed him. Striking with sudden severity in April 1789, the disease also quickly killed perhaps half of the Aborigines living in the vicinity of Sydney, despite attempts by Phillip to care for some of the sufferers. How it arrived in Sydney remains a matter of debate.

Some historians have speculated that it came from the Macassans who passed it to the Aborigines during one of their annual visits to Australia's northern shores. From there, it spread slowly across the continent until finally appearing, opportunely, in Sydney at a time when the British were feeling hard-pressed by the increasing hostility of the Aborigines. However, because of the nature of smallpox and the relatively low population density in northern Australia, such a timely coincidence is extremely unlikely. The historian Noel Butlin suggested instead that the smallpox came from a jar of variolous material, effectively smallpox scabs taken from victims of the disease, that had been brought from England by surgeons of the First Fleet to use for vaccination purposes. Knowing the vulnerability of unprotected native populations to smallpox, one must ask why the variolous material was not used to inoculate the Aborigines of Port Jackson before the disease appeared among them.

Rather than inoculating the Aborigines, Butlin has argued that this material was spread, deliberately or accidentally, among the Aborigines with immediate and devastating effect. Although Butlin's surmising has been dismissed by Alan Frost in his book *Botany Bay Mirages*, there remains considerable circumstantial evidence to suggest that officers other than Phillip, or perhaps convicts or soldiers angered by Aboriginal attacks on their fellows, deliberately spread smallpox among the Aborigines.

The outbreak occurred at a time when the unfortified settlement was thought to be in danger of attack from the Aborigines. The latter half of 1788 had seen what Tench described as 'unabated animosity' between the Aborigines and the British, with isolated parties of convicts being subject to attacks. Although deaths were uncommon, the fear engendered in the settlement was considerable. When a party of some 50 Aborigines gathered near convicts working at brick kilns about a mile from Sydney, terrified convicts fled to Sydney with stories of 2000 marauding savages. Three months later, a party of convicts at the brick kilns who had set out to steal from the Aborigines were instead ambushed by their quarry and forced to flee, with one of their number being killed and seven wounded.

Marine officers like Major Ross who were concerned at the possible threat posed by the Aborigines may well have felt impelled to take decisive action to end this uneasy stalemate in which the Aborigines were becoming increasingly assertive. A female convict wrote in November 1788 of how 'the savages still continue to do us all the injury they can, which make the soldiers' duty very hard, and much dissatisfaction among the officers'. With Phillip disparaging the need for fortifications and refusing to arm the convicts who necessarily had to work at a distance from the protection the settlement afforded, it is possible that Ross may have seized upon the variolous material as the most effective way to deal with the Aborigines. He would have been conscious of the ravages that smallpox could wreak on a susceptible population that had not been exposed to it. He also would have been aware, from his previous service in North America, that smallpox had been used there by the British army to devastate a hostile Indian population. Then again, it may have been either convicts or soldiers, or a combination of them, that spread the material among the Aborigines. While Frost has surmised that the variolous material was kept in secure conditions, just days before the disease first appeared among the Aborigines a number of marines were found to have duplicated keys to the public stores and to have robbed them of 'flour, meat, spirits, tobacco, and many other articles'. Six of them were hanged for their offences. It is possible that this may have been the route by which the Aborigines became infected.

With Arabanoo dead from smallpox and his fellow Aborigines devastated by the disease, two survivors were kidnapped later that year, one of whom, Bennelong, was quick to learn the habits and language of the Europeans. But they both escaped within months. In September 1790, following the arrival of the Second Fleet and the consequent doubling of the settlement's numbers, Phillip came across Bennelong and a large group of Aborigines feasting on a beached whale. As he approached the group, Phillip had a ten-foot spear thrown through his shoulder. The 51-year-old governor survived, learning later, as if he needed to be told, that the Aborigines were aggrieved 'at the number of white men who had settled in their former territories'.

Phillip did not retaliate for the attack and Bennelong was soon encouraged to return to the settlement along with some of his fellow Aborigines who seem to have acknowledged their growing dependence upon the settlement by turning to it for food whenever they were hungry. On the point where the Sydney Opera House now stands, a hut was built for the tamed Bennelong. But the dependence of some of the depleted Aborigines was countered by the defiance of others. In December 1790, Phillip's gamekeeper, the convict John McIntyre, was speared by an Aborigine from Botany Bay called Pemulwuy. No-one in the settlement doubted that McIntyre had been involved in shooting Aborigines. But Phillip responded to the man's slow death by ordering the first official punitive expedition against the Aborigines, instructing that ten adult males be killed and their heads hacked off and returned to Sydney.

The force of some 40 marines and a succeeding one, both burdened by their equipment and hampered by the swampy terrain, proved complete failures with hardly a single Aborigine even being sighted. Pemulwuy survived for another decade during which he harassed the settlers in a form of guerrilla warfare before he was finally killed and his pickled head sent to England in a barrel. They were the first serious clashes in the competition for control of the continent. As one of Phillip's officers, David Collins, observed, the conflict was inevitable despite the relatively good intentions of Phillip. So long as the Aborigines 'entertained the idea of our having dispossessed them of their residences, they must always consider us as enemies; and upon this principle they made a point of attacking the white people whenever opportunity and safety occurred'. But their attacks were in vain.

After just four years, the British were too numerous and too well-armed for the Aborigines to recover their lands. The rate of natural increase among the convict women, together with the additional convicts brought aboard the Second and Third Fleets, meant that Sydney and Norfolk Island numbered some 4000 British souls by the end of 1792. There were now many more Europeans than Aborigines in Sydney and its surrounds, allowing Phillip to feel confident of having secured a claim of effective proprietorship over it.

Perhaps as a sign of this new-found confidence, in June 1791 Phillip ordered that the name of Rose Hill be changed to its original Aboriginal name of Parramatta. The change was not an acknowledgment of Aboriginal ownership. Rather, it was a way of securing more certainly the British claim on this landscape that many found so alien. A modern map of Australia will reveal a discordant arrangement of Aboriginal and transplanted European names scattered across the continent. The colonial capitals were all given European names, usually of royalty or politicans, to connect them with their imperial protector and the land in which so many of the colonists had been born. Similarly, the colonies were given loyal British names, as in the case of Victoria and, not to be outdone, Queensland. Or they were given unimaginative, descriptive names, as in the case of Western Australia, South Australia and the Northern Territory. Only Van Diemen's Land was different, acknowledging the original Dutch act of 'discovery'. When the name was changed in 1855, the colonists preserved the distant Dutch link by calling it Tasmania rather than imposing a British name upon it or adopting an Aboriginal name.

Adopting European names was a way of making familiar that which was starkly alien. Cook had begun it with his naming of New South Wales, which allowed British readers to develop an immediate mental picture of the exotic landscape while also asserting by the name a British claim over the eastern part of the continent that would contrast with the Dutch name of New Holland. Phillip continued it with his naming of Sydney Cove. Adopting Aboriginal names for some secondary settlements (and later for the Commonwealth capital of Canberra) and for geographical features, was not simply the last resort of Europeans unable to think up their own names, although that consideration was sometimes involved. Rather, it was a subtle way of partially satisfying the need to claim moral proprietorship over an alien land with pre-existing occupiers.

By renaming Rose Hill with its Aboriginal name of Parramatta, the Europeans were taking the Aboriginal name for their own just as they had previously taken the land for their own. Tilling the soil of Parramatta fulfilled the physical need for food while at the same time fulfilling the need to morally justify the act of supplanting the Aborigines. By tilling the soil, the Europeans were fulfilling their God's injunction in a way that the Aborigines were disinclined to do. By working this virgin and foreign soil, Europeans became familiar with its ancient rhythms and developed links to the landscape that would, in some cases, come to outweigh the links to the landscapes from which they had come. Similarly, the taking of Aboriginal names deepened those links to the new landscape while at the same time according a superficial respect to the Aborigines whose name it was.

Although Phillip had come to New South Wales with the intention of maintaining cordial relations with the few inhabitants the continent was believed to contain, relations between the two groups broke down as they increasingly competed for the resources around Sydney. The subsequent history of the colony would be one of continuing conflict on the moving frontier of settlement as Phillip's original claim was gradually extended to cover the entire continent and the Aborigines were steadily dispossessed. However, before the forlorn continent was to be occupied effectively, an economic rationale had to be found for doing so. And Phillip had not found such a rationale by the time he took his leave of Sydney in 1792.

Recommended Reading

Graeme Aplin (ed.), 1988, *A Difficult Infant: Sydney before Macquarie*, New South Wales University Press, Sydney.

Noel Butlin, 1983, *Our Original Aggression*, George Allen & Unwin, Sydney.

Frank Crowley (ed.), 1980, *A Documentary History of Australia*, Vol. 1, Nelson, Melbourne.

Alan Frost, 1994, *Botany Bay Mirages*, Melbourne University Press, Melbourne.

Alan Frost, 1987, *Arthur Phillip, 1738–1814: His Voyaging*, Oxford University Press, Melbourne.

John Hardy and Alan Frost (eds), 1989, *Studies from Terra Australis to Australia*, Australian Academy of the Humanities, Canberra.

Frank Horner, 1987, *The French Reconnaissance: Baudin in Australia 1801–1803*, Melbourne University Press, Melbourne.

Portia Robinson, 1993, *The Women of Botany Bay*, Penguin, Melbourne.

Watkin Tench, 1979, *Sydney's First Four Years*, Library of Australian History, Sydney.

John Molony, 2000, *The Native Born: The First White Australians*, Melbourne University Press, Melbourne.

Glyndwr Williams and Alan Frost, 1988, *From Terra Australis to Australia*, Oxford University Press, Melbourne.

5

'THE CULTIVATION AND IMPROVEMENT OF WASTE LANDS'

When Captain James Cook summed up his impressions of New South Wales, he conceded that the continent did 'not produce any one thing that can become an article of trade to invite Europeans to fix a settlement upon it'. The settlement of Botany Bay went ahead nonetheless for reasons that have been discussed. The British government was attracted partly by Cook's suggestion that 'most sorts of Grain, Fruits, Roots, &c of every kind would flourish here'. Which they did, after the first few years of hard times. However, while the flourishing of agriculture helped to establish Sydney Cove as a replenishment port, it did not provide the answer to the colony's long-term economic future. If the land was to be occupied, and a claim of effective proprietorship asserted over it, an 'article of trade' had to be found to provide for the growing population of existing settlers and to encourage the immigration of free settlers.

The arguments for establishing a settlement at Botany Bay had been based upon an understanding that it would soon pay for its own upkeep rather than remain as a burden upon the British treasury. This hope was quickly dissolved. In April 1790, as the colony faced the threat of starvation and waited anxiously for relief, the embittered chief surgeon, John White, described the country as being 'so forbidden and so hateful, as only to merit execrations and curses', claiming that 'there is not a single article in the whole country, that in the nature of things could prove of the smallest use or advantage to the mother country or the commercial world'. White's letter, which was later published in London, was written during the depths of the so-called hungry years and was one of the more extreme reactions to the privations that had to be endured as Governor Phillip worked to establish farming on a firm footing. But it raised a crucial point: even if agriculture managed to secure the colony from starvation, it could not secure the commercial viability of the colony, which depended on it developing an export of sufficient value to be shipped profitably across the world for sale in Europe or elsewhere. It would take the colonists many years to find one.

When Phillip left Sydney in 1792, he left the settlement in the temporary charge of the recently arrived Major Grose who was commander of the New South Wales Corps, an army unit specially raised to garrison the convict colony in place of the former marines. Among his officers was the young and ambitious John Macarthur who, even before Phillip had taken his leave, had chartered a ship on behalf of his brother officers to bring a speculative cargo of goods, mainly rum, from the Cape of Good Hope. As paymaster of the Corps, Macarthur had access to the regiment's funds with which to finance his ventures. When a visiting ship called, this access to negotiable funds allowed him and his colleagues to be better placed than most to monopolise the purchase of its stores. The officers' authority also allowed them to be first on board the ships.

Even in a convict colony, there was a lucrative market for imported produce, particularly alcohol. The soldiers bought it with their wages, the convicts bought it with their labour, and the free settlers and emancipated convicts bought it in exchange for their grain or their animals, and sometimes in exchange for their land itself. Within a very short time, with the continual shortage of coinage in the colony, rum became the colony's *de facto* currency and the enterprising officers of the Corps have since been widely disparaged by historians as the Rum Corps. More recently, their pursuit of private profit has been seen in a better light, with their entrepreneurial efforts in farming and their trading activities helping to build a solid economic foundation for the struggling colony in ways that government-directed convict labour was unable to do.

The officers not only sponsored speculative voyages but also bought from visiting whaling and convict ships. They let it be known that Sydney not only had supplies of fresh produce for their onward voyages but also had a market for rum and other goods that might make the first leg of their voyage profitable. They also had labour, both convict and ex-convict. It made whaling voyages even more economical if they could sail to the Pacific with their vessels lightly crewed and then take on extra men at Sydney prior to the actual whaling.

Through their trading activities, and through the land grants which were permitted following Phillip's departure, many officers quickly became wealthy landowners. Although grants were made to time-expired convicts and marines, the success of such small farmers was hampered by inexperience and indebtedness to the officers. At the same time, the population of the colony was slowly increasing as more convicts arrived from Britain. They joined a small number of free settlers with farming experience who were sent from England at the suggestion of Phillip. Some were intent on making their fortune and returning to England, but an increasing proportion of the inhabitants of New South Wales, both bond and free, were content to live out their days in this new world. By 1798, John Macarthur's resourceful wife, Elizabeth, was extolling its delights to a friend in England: 'We enjoy here one of the finest Climates in the world—The necessaries of life are abundant, & a fruitful soil affords us many luxuries. Nothing induces me to wish for a change.' She remained true to her word, living out her days in the comfortable, and increasingly familiar, confines of New South Wales.

The economy in the period up to 1800 was based upon the limited trade monopolised by men like Macarthur as well as a steady expansion of government-financed agriculture to feed the growing number of convicts. This expansion could only continue until the colony became self-sufficient in food. Then some alternative product, of sufficient value to be exported, would be required to generate the hard currency that could in turn pay for the increasing imports demanded by the growing colony. Only by developing such a staple export could the colony become economically viable and thereby partially relieve the treasury of the burden of supporting it. With such a staple export attracting additional population, the colonists would also have some hope of eventually claiming the continent's wide interior.

The early prospects for a staple export were not promising. One suggestion was to use the surplus grain to distil spirits for sale within the colony and for export. But this was blocked by a British government anxious to restrict the supply of alcohol in a convict colony. In fact, of course, it simply led to the illegal distillation of alcohol, both from grain and from the peaches and other fruits now being grown with great success around Sydney. The discovery of coal near the present site of Newcastle looked promising for a time, but several attempts at exporting cargoes of coal to India and the Cape of Good Hope failed to establish an ongoing trade. The coal was used instead to warm the houses of Sydney. By 1798, Joseph Banks, who continued to take a proprietorial interest in the colony, was forced to conclude that British expectations had been dashed by subsequent experience. 'We have now possessed the country of New South Wales more than ten years', wrote Banks, 'and no one article has hitherto been discovered, by the importation of which the mother country can receive any degree of return for the cost of founding and maintaining the colony.' Their aim of a self-funding, convict colony had failed.

As it happened, at the same time that Banks was making his gloomy prognosis for New South Wales, the first free trader had been attracted to Sydney as a place of future profit. The young Robert Campbell arrived from Calcutta in 1798 after having first sent out in 1797 a speculative cargo mainly of rum. The ship sprang a leak in Bass Strait and was beached on what the crew gratefully named Preservation Island. Seventeen of them set off for Sydney in a longboat which also foundered, forcing them to continue on foot along the coast for some 200 miles. Only three of the men survived the epic trek to Sydney, where they reported their experiences to Campbell. Their ordeal in Bass Strait and along the coast had alerted them to the large number of seal colonies in the region. Apart from establishing a mercantile base at Sydney, Campbell was now also determined to exploit this seal fishery.

By 1802, Governor King was able to report to London that seal skins were 'the most considerable among the very few natural productions of this country that can be esteemed commercial'. More importantly, sealing provided one dimension in the increasingly multifaceted Pacific trading economy that came to be centred upon Sydney. A typical operation by Campbell or his officer competitors might involve the charter of a ship to drop off a party of sealers on a Bass Strait Island along with perhaps six months' supplies. The men would turn that island's beaches into a killing field of dead seals which were stripped of their skins. While the men went about their work, the ship might go on to the islands of the south Pacific to gather a cargo of sandalwood that would be taken to China in exchange for tea and other goods for the colonial market. After landing them in Sydney, the vessel would then pick up the sealers and the skins they had collected in Bass Strait, taking the cargo to Sydney for storage before shipment to London or China. More than 100 000 skins were landed in Sydney between 1800 and 1806. Others would have been collected from Australia's offshore islands and gone direct to London or China for making into shoes or hats. In 1804, 11 Sydney-based ships were engaged in the Bass Strait sealing trade. Apart from exploiting the seals, others went into whaling, particularly bay whaling which was easier and cheaper than deep sea whaling.

By the early 1800s, there were four main types of economic activity in New South Wales, often overlapping. Agriculture and grazing was now producing enough food to feed the growing colony, with larger landowners predominating over the government's goal of encouraging yeoman farmers. Many of these larger landowners were also engaged in mercantile activities, importing speculative cargoes in competition with merchants such as Campbell. They were joined by an increasing number of emancipated convict merchants who the gentleman officers had employed to sell alcohol so that their own hands would not be stained with trade. These emancipated convicts quickly became traders on their own account and grew to rival in wealth their officer patrons. Although often lucrative, this speculative trade was marked by gluts and scarcities. It was possible to make huge profits but also to sustain considerable losses if several cargoes arrived simultaneously. The period up to 1820 was marked by several instances of wealthy merchants finding themselves suddenly insolvent when their speculative cargoes had to be unloaded into a glutted Sydney market.

Many of the merchants, often operating their own vessels, also engaged in maritime endeavours, both whaling and sealing, together sometimes with collecting pearl shell and sea slugs from tropical waters. They also used their vessels for collecting salted pork from Tahiti and Norfolk Island for sale in Sydney, and for trading Pacific island sandalwood in China. A complex web of trading relationships was built up based on Sydney and crisscrossing the Pacific. Although it infringed the East India Company's monopoly of trade in the region, governors were often willing to turn a blind eye to such breaches for the sake of the local economy, and sometimes their own pockets. As these trading and farming activities steadily increased, and Sydney became a popular replenishment port for Pacific whalers and China traders, more scope became available for the development of a wide range of local industries in Sydney, from brewing to flour milling, boat building and repair.

Of all these alternatives, it seemed that whales held the most promise, despite official British restrictions on local boats engaging in the trade and a prohibitive British duty being imposed on the import of colonial whale oil. When these were rescinded, the duty being reduced in 1828, the local industry boomed, pushed along by a surge in the price of sperm oil. The number of deep sea whalers operating out of Sydney rose from five in 1827 to 76 in 1835. Between 1826 and 1835, the value of fishery products passing through Sydney reached £950 000. But the industry was gradually strangled by its own success.

Seals were wiped out by the mid-1830s from their previous safe havens on the islands of Bass Strait. Conservation was impossible as colonial sealers competed with crews from Britain, America and France. The whalers also killed without thought of tomorrow, slaughtering the vulnerable bay whales after calving, while the pressure on sperm whales increased from the fast expanding fleet of boats. In 1849, there were 37 boats based in Hobart employing 1000 seamen. As well as the impact from such fleets, the 1840s saw a slump in the price of sperm oil. Although this later recovered, the gold rushes in California in 1848 attracted whaling ships into transporting gold-seekers only to have the ships abandoned by their crews who also made off for the goldfields. Much of the colonial whaling fleet was left to rot in San Francisco's crowded harbour. At the same time, the market for whale oil and sperm candles was being undermined by the growing use of gas for lighting and, from 1859, by the use of kerosene after the development of oilwells in the United States.

The maritime dimension to the economic life of early New South Wales saw the colonists looking outward from coastal settlements as they sought to garner wealth from the surrounding seas rather than looking inwards to the interior for wealth from the continental expanse. This was partly a practical problem, with the Great Dividing Range hemming the colonists into the narrow coastal plain. But it was also an economic problem since it seemed as if there could be nothing worth producing on the land that would bear the cost of transporting to outside markets.

On surveying the ample fodder of Botany Bay in 1770, Banks had predicted that New South Wales would be able to provide enough feed to support large numbers of grazing animals. But Phillip encountered serious problems in his efforts to establish livestock in New South Wales. The animals were either killed by the convicts or the Aborigines, or they ate native plants that killed them, or they simply wandered away. Despite these setbacks, and although there had only been 29 sheep on the First Fleet, successive convict fleets added to the flocks and herds and the numbers quickly expanded by natural increase. By 1805, there were 500 horses, 4000 cattle, 5000 goats, 23 000 pigs and hogs, and 20 000 sheep.

Initially, sheep were raised only for their meat. But their increasing numbers soon gave the colony more meat than the colonists could eat. Given the great interest in the scientific improvement of animals through selective breeding, it was inevitable that the increasing number of large landowners would seek ways in which their burgeoning flocks could be used for more than just meat. This led to the import of different breeds to improve the standard of local flocks. Prominent among these breeders were the 28 officers of the New South Wales Corps who in 1800 had an average landholding of 434 acres.

In 1802, after he had reported to London on the commercial possibilities of whaling and sealing, Governor King also mentioned, almost as an afterthought, that the 'introduction of some half-bred Spanish rams among the increasing flocks of individuals, and the consequent improvement of their fleeces, will in the course of a few years produce sufficient wool to cloath the inhabitants'. But what then? At the rate at which sheep were breeding in the colony it was necessary for them somehow to be converted into a commercially viable export. And the only viable export that seemed capable of absorbing the costs of transport across the world and still returning a profit would be, not the coarse wool of the early flocks, but the fine wool developed by the officer farmers.

As it happened, even as King was writing, the entrepreneurial John Macarthur was in London urging the government to grant him an extensive acreage upon which he could prove the value of raising fine wool for the mills of northern England. Although Macarthur got his way, he found a serious obstacle to his plans back in Sydney. Governor William Bligh had arrived in 1806 to replace the gout-ridden Governor King. Bligh was a man with a volatile personality whose foul language could whip men into acts of armed rebellion, as he had done most famously with Fletcher Christian on the *Bounty*. According to Joseph Banks, who had been instrumental in securing his appointment, Bligh was 'firm in discipline, civil in deportment and not subject to whimper and whine when severity of discipline is wanted'. But Bligh met his match in the equally volatile and determined John Macarthur.

Bligh had squandered much of his moral authority soon after landing when he concluded a corrupt deal with the departing Governor King. Since governors could not grant land to themselves, King granted 1345 acres of land to Bligh before handing over his office to the newcomer. Bligh then responded by granting 790 acres to Mrs King, who named the ill-gotten property, 'Thanks'. With his authority eroded, Bligh then lost the backing of the officers by supporting the small landholders along the Hawkesbury River and elsewhere who railed against the often rapacious commercial practices of the officers. Then, in a direct challenge to the officers' economic supremacy, Bligh cracked down on the importation and sale of alcohol and seized an imported still which Macarthur intended using to make his own alcohol. He then seized one of Macarthur's ships which had taken an escaped convict to New Zealand. When Macarthur resisted Bligh's authority, his arrest was ordered.

With another shipload of his alcohol about to arrive in Sydney, Macarthur called on his former fellow officers to free him and arrest Bligh instead. Fearing their own imminent arrest by the irascible governor, the officers led a revolt against constituted authority, marching on the governor's residence to arrest him and end his reign. The celebrating populace were supplied, appropriately, with roasting sheep and liberal supplies of alcohol by Macarthur and the well-satisfied officers. For the next two years until a replacement governor could be sent out, the rebellious officers ruled supreme and the interests of the pastoralists prevailed over those of the small farmers as more than 80 000 acres were granted to the supporters of the regime.

Bligh's replacement as governor, Lachlan Macquarie, returned both Bligh and the leading rebels to London so that their respective cases could be argued before the British government. In fact, Macarthur was already on his way to London to plead the case of the rebels. The subsequent trial saw the rebels treated lightly for the crime of mutiny by judges who recognised that Bligh was at least partly to blame for inciting it. In a reversal of the order of things, Macarthur was exiled to England in a move that indicated perhaps the changing perception of the colony in British eyes. It had become a punishment to be kept in England rather than be sent to New South Wales. Macarthur used his years of exile to press for further government assistance for the wool industry while, in New South Wales, his wife Elizabeth continued with his sheep breeding experiments to produce fine merino wool. The efforts by the Macarthurs and the rest of the large landowning fraternity resulted in a dramatic change in the export statistics, with the weight of wool being exported rising from just 167 pounds in 1811 to 175 433 pounds in 1821.

The Cumberland plain west of Sydney became the preserve of these large landholders concentrating on pastoral pursuits, while the smallholders around Parramatta and on the fertile banks of the frequently flooding Hawkesbury River persisted with agriculture, growing grain for the government store with which to feed the convicts. Given the economic circumstances of the time, with grains being uneconomical as an export commodity, the supremacy of the large landholders, who increasingly looked to pastoralism for their economic salvation, was inevitable given the nature of the Australian landscape, with its relatively infertile soils and absence of many large rivers suitable for transporting the bulky products of intensive agriculture to distant markets.

Many small settlers also flourished in their own way with the guaranteed market provided by the government store, grants of land, cheap labour of the convicts and favourable climate. Mary McDonald, an ex-convict who married a former marine-turned-settler, was able by 1806 to write effusively to her daughter in England encouraging her emigration to New South Wales:

> Here my Dear is the most healthful country in all the Globe for there is nothing that grows in a hot or Cold Country but comes to the Greatest perfection here, for Instance one acre of wheat will produce from Forty to Fifty Bushels of wheat—and as to fruit no country can equal it, and our Cattle is farr beyond in size and meat to your finest cattle in England. So my Dear do not loose a moments time when you receive this but use all your Interest and endeavours to come to the Garden of the World.

Despite such encouragement, the daughter appeared not to have gone, having been sentenced to imprisonment herself. As for Mary, she seemed to prosper until, at the age of 73, she was drowned in a boating accident with her husband and a neighbour while drunk and quarrelling. Mary's was not an isolated success. As a sign of the opportunities to be had, more than half of the men of the New South Wales regiment chose to remain in New South Wales rather than return to England when given the option in 1810 by Macquarie.

Likely as not, these men were attracted by the offer of land that would be theirs if they stayed. As in England, wealth was commonly measured in terms of land which provided the necessaries of life and which, in New South Wales, was granted in small lots to ex-convicts, ex-marines and soldiers, and immigrants of limited means. It was granted in larger lots to the officers and civil officials and to immigrants with capital. Even ex-convicts could occasionally accumulate large lots through their endeavours, as Simeon Lord did with his trading activities, amassing some 18 000 acres. Those without land could also do well, measuring their living standards in terms of food and wage rates, both of which were much better than standards applying in England. One contented convict reported to his wife that he was treated 'as a free man' and was provided with 'plenty of good meat and clothes with easy work'. So satisfied was this man, that he judged himself 'better off this day than half the people in England, and I would not go back to England if any one would pay my passage'. It was not an uncommon experience.

With the natural increase of the colony's flocks and herds, the available grazing land on the coastal plain around Sydney was soon filled to capacity. It was an indication of the colony's original orientation to seaward, as much as the ruggedness of the mountain range that hemmed them in, that it took until 1813 for a way across the mountains to be found. Once across, the three successful explorers, Gregory Blaxland, William Charles Wentworth and William Lawson, and their Aboriginal guide looked out upon a lightly forested expanse that stretched to the horizon. With the land around Sydney enduring a drought, it offered a fresh source of fodder for their livestock. Although it would be sheep with their fine wool that would come to occupy these ancient hunting grounds of the Aborigines, Wentworth initially saw it as 'an invaluable acquisition to persons possessing large herds of Cattle'. He also extolled the natural defence advantages offered by a settlement beyond the ranges. Whereas Sydney was relatively vulnerable to the sorts of attacks the British often mounted against Spain's seaboard settlements in South America, the pass to this newly discovered territory provided easy access for cattle but at the same time went 'through a country so strong as to be easily defended by a few against the efforts of Thousands'. It would thereby hold out the prospect of profitable grazing while also offering the colonists the prospect of extending and securing their claim of effective proprietorship over New South Wales. Within three years, a road had been built by convicts to connect these plains with Sydney and land grants given out around the new inland settlement of Bathurst.

As the possibilities of wool became apparent, people rushed to reap a quick profit. The Australian Agricultural Company was formed in London in 1824 'for the cultivation and improvement of waste lands in the colony of New South Wales'. Under a special Act of parliament, the company was given one million acres in return for investing £1 million to develop the agricultural, pastoral and mineral resources of New South Wales. Although the company proposed to cultivate the soil and grow such crops as grape vines, olives, tobacco, hemp and opium, the potential profits from sheep were so great that its activities were predominantly pastoral. People of more moderate means simply purchased a flock and moved with their convict shepherds onto the 'empty' lands of the interior, grazing their sheep as they went until the natural increase of their flock and the growth of their wool turned a handsome profit within several years.

With the crossing of the Blue Mountains and the breeding of fine merino wool, the colony had a potential staple export and the limitless land on which it could be produced. The remaining ingredients for a successful staple export industry were labour and markets. Fortunately for the future of the colonists, there was a renewed surge in both convicts and free settlers arriving in New South Wales following the end of the war with France in 1815, such that its European population more than doubled in the six years from 1815 to 1821, from 13 000 to 30 000. Macquarie had used much of this convict labour on schemes of civil construction, including an extensive road system linking Sydney to its hinterland and a stone hospital so grand that part of it still serves as the New South Wales legislature. Although the road system helped to ensure the economic viability of the pastoral industry, complaints about the ballooning costs of his administration led the government to order the release of many more convicts for the use of pastoralists, thereby freeing them from government expense. After Macquarie's departure in 1822, government policy became one of turning convicts *en masse* into shepherds.

Just as they were provided with ample labour, so the pastoralists secured the market in Britain for their wool following the British decision not to increase the penny per pound weight duty on colonial wool to threepence in 1823 and sixpence in 1826, a move that would have priced it out of the London market. As a result of these factors, the products of the pastoral expansion were overtaking in export value the formerly supreme maritime products. By the late 1830s, the expansion of pastoralism was so great that the value of its exports was twice those of the whale and seal fisheries. And the most valuable of these products was fine merino wool.

The growing wealth from wool helped to transform both Sydney and Hobart into Georgian towns of some distinction. The building efforts of Macquarie had left a very visible mark of European civilisation on the port towns, while the growing flocks of sheep were steadily occupying the interior and sending the wealth from their backs to the merchants of Sydney. By his civic building, Macquarie had strengthened the British claim of both effective and moral proprietorship over the continent. He had improved its defences against an external attack while also improving the public infrastructure on which the profits of pastoralism, and thereby the hold of the colonists on the continent, depended.

The claim of moral proprietorship was strengthened by the extent to which colonists could now loudly proclaim their success in imposing 'civilisation' upon the former 'wilderness'. A convict writing home in 1818 described the 'very prepossessing' government house that overlooked the harbour, while the new hospital was 'a most excellent building exceeding all possible expectation for so infant a colony as this'. The whole settlement, he claimed, 'commands the attention of a stranger for its neatness even in the poorer orders of society,... most gardens being stocked with the peach tree, which thrives abundantly and gives a most delightful countenance to nature in her cultivation and improvement by art.' Foreign visitors confirmed this impression, often contrasting the orderly farms, gardens and buildings of Sydney with comparable supplanting settlements in other continents. And none was so orderly and so extensive as that of John Macarthur who returned to Sydney from his exile in England in 1817 to take over the running of his extensive acreage outside of Sydney.

Through grant and acquisition, the Macarthur family's land had grown by 1838 to encompass more than 27 000 well-developed acres which were worked by some 110 employees in circumstances reminiscent of the grand houses of England, save that half the workers were convicts. To complete the transplanted vision, the Macarthurs built a village complete with church for their workers. A visitor in 1842 remarked on how 'the house, the park, the water, the gardens, the style of everything and of every person, master and servant, resembled so much what one meets with in the old country'. While transplanting many of the features of English life, such that one visitor to Sydney in 1827 was 'scarcely to be sensible that I was out of England', the colonists also incorporated into their lives many of the features of their adopted land, from pet kangaroos to wattle blossom, such that their combining of the familiar and unfamiliar became a composite creation that was, simply, 'home'. As one emancipated convict who had done well informed Commissioner Bigge in 1819, he was 'a Colonist and [had] a young Family growing up whose Country this is'. But where did that assertion leave the Aborigines?

As early as 1820, Russian explorers visiting Sydney were impressed by the extent to which the British had managed to transform the former 'wilderness' with the industry of man. While this confirmed their claim of proprietorship over New South Wales, the Russians also noted that the British had been less successful in imposing their civilisation upon the Aborigines. Their ship was visited by Boongaree, an Aborigine who had accompanied Flinders on his circumnavigation of Australia which had done so much to extend the British claim over the continent. However, as the Russians observed, Boongaree remained adamant that his pre-existing land rights endured despite the British presence. Pointing to the north shore of the harbour, he proclaimed, 'This is my Land.' The Russians concluded:

> *The natives remember very well their former independence. Some expressed their claims to certain places, asserting that they belonged to their ancestors. It is easy to understand that they are not indifferent to having been expelled from their former localities. Despite all the compensation offered to them, a spark of vengeance still smoulders in their hearts.*

The British claim of proprietorship could hardly be secure while the prior inhabitants proclaimed the primacy of their own proprietorship over the continent. The problem would be solved by muskets rather than by concessions.

Recommended Reading

G. J. Abbott and N. B. Nairn (eds), 1969, *Economic Growth of Australia 1788–1821*, Melbourne University Press, Melbourne.

Patricia Clarke and Dale Spender (eds), 1992, *Life Lines: Australian Women's Letters and Diaries 1788 to 1840*, Allen & Unwin, Sydney.

David Day, 1992, *Smugglers and Sailors*, Australian Government Publishing Service Press, Canberra.

M. H. Ellis, 1955, *John Macarthur*, Angus&Robertson, Sydney.

B. H. Fletcher, 1976, *Landed Enterprise and Penal Society*, Sydney University Press, Sydney.

D. R. Hainsworth, 1968, *Builders and Adventurers*, Cassell, Melbourne.

D. R. Hainsworth, 1981, *The Sydney Traders*, Melbourne University Press, Melbourne.

John Hardy and Alan Frost (eds), 1989, *Studies from Terra Australis to Australia*, Australian Academy of the Humanities, Canberra.

John Ritchie, 1986, *Lachlan Macquarie*, Melbourne University Press, Melbourne.

Margaret Steven, 1965, *Merchant Campbell, 1769–1846*, Oxford University Press, Melbourne.

6

'THEY CLEAR THE LAND OF A DETESTED INCUBUS'

The British had made no explicit provision for recognising the sovereign rights of the Aborigines as the prior occupants of the continent and owners of its land. This made Australia unique among British supplanting societies. The British colonies in North America, New Zealand and South Africa all recognised in some way, albeit often inadequate, the pre-existing rights of the prior inhabitants. Treaties were made with the indigenous peoples of those places to admit an assumption of British sovereignty and to allow for settlement. Although these treaties were often broken and derisory in their compensation, they did allow for later legal redress, as has happened in New Zealand and North America. In New South Wales, it was thought sufficient, given the perceived primitive state of Aboriginal society, to simply bring the indigenous people under the legal protection of the British Crown.

Unlike in New Zealand and other places, the Aborigines had not presented a sufficiently formidable threat to the Europeans to make a treaty imperative. Their primitive military technology allowed their rights to be ignored. As Banks had assured a House of Commons committee in 1785, the Aborigines were armed merely with primitive spears and would, in the face of a settlement of 500 Europeans, 'speedily abandon the country to the newcomers'. Although the Aborigines did not bear Banks out by readily abandoning their land, neither could they capture back those parts occupied by the British. The military technology of the Aborigines, limited mainly to spears and waddies, was well suited for hit and run attacks on small parties of Europeans, particularly if they could be taken unawares. But it was incapable of defending their territory in a sustained way against European attacks using guns and horses. The Aboriginal use of such guerrilla tactics helped to undercut any sympathy that their plight evoked among the Europeans. It painted them as treacherous savages who did not merit the respect they might otherwise have conceded to foes adopting more conventional methods of warfare.

As well, the apparent nomadism of the Aborigines, and their lack of cultivation of the soil, suggested to many Europeans that the Aborigines did not have a fixed interest in the soil. It was believed that the Aborigines enjoyed the land rather than occupied it, that they ranged over it rather than resided upon it. As the Scottish philosopher Henry Home argued in 1761, a piece of land might be considered to belong to nomadic people while they were actually 'in possession' of it, 'but the moment they removed to another quarter, there no longer subsisted any connection betwixt them and the field that was deserted'. Experience soon showed that many Aboriginal groups were much less nomadic than was supposed by Banks and Cook, and for a time by Phillip. As they learnt more about the Aborigines, it gradually became clear to the invaders that the Aborigines had links akin to ownership over particular areas of land. But by then the die had been cast.

The invaders believed they had a divine right of dispossession based upon the apparent nomadism of the Aborigines and the supposed superiority of their own civilisation. They believed that European civilisation was a gift to be conferred upon the Aborigines. As he indicated prior to his departure from England in 1787, Phillip had planned to encourage several of the Aborigines 'to settle near us, and who I mean to furnish with everything that can tend to civilize them'. The fact that the Aborigines were regarded as being uncivilised, almost to the extent of being less than human, helped to overcome any qualms Europeans might have had about dispossessing them. These qualms were further overcome by their experience at Sydney Cove when the Aborigines mostly declined the 'gift' of European civilisation that was being foisted upon them. Increasingly, the Aborigines were seen as being uncivilisable. Like the Irish, they were beyond the pale of British civilisation.

When Phillip arrived back in London in 1793, accompanied by Bennelong, the *London Times* informed its readers that the Aborigines 'appear to be a race totally incapable of civilization', that they were on a level 'with the beasts of the field' and 'form a lower order of the human race'. Despite every inducement, nothing could 'draw them from a state of nature'. This view of the Aborigines allowed the argument to be made that, since the Aborigines lived in such a state of nature, no such thing as private property could be said to exist. According to the philosopher John Locke, private property was created by the combination of what nature provided and the labour of man. Therefore, a person going into a wilderness and creating a farm would have a right of property over that land. The Aborigines, on the other hand, seemed to European eyes not to have added their labour to the land and therefore not to have established any property rights over it.

This gulf in perceptions was seen most graphically during an incident in the early 1800s when a small group of Aborigines, walking with their customary firesticks, passed close to the stacked corn of a Parramatta farmer. The anxious farmer rushed out to remonstrate with them for imperilling his harvest. But the Aborigines were unconcerned, pointing out to the alarmed farmer: 'You know we must have our fire; the country is *ours, you* must take care of your corn.' Of course, as far as the British were concerned, both the country and the corn were theirs and the Aborigines would have to adjust to their gradual dispossession as best they could. With two such disparate societies both claiming proprietorship of the same country, conflict was inevitable.

Until recently, historians tended to play down the extent of the conflict, suggesting that the Aborigines were easily overwhelmed by the greater technology of the white man. However, just as Aborigines were demanding land rights in the late 1960s, and the 'white Australia' policy was being dismantled, academics began reassessing the nature of race relations in the colonial period. The impetus came first from the anthropologists. In 1968, W. E. H. Stanner spoke of what he termed 'the Great Australian Silence' in which Aborigines had largely disappeared from the work of 20th century historians, while C. D. Rowley in his landmark three-volume study, *Aboriginal Policy and Practice*, detailed the history of massacre and disease that decimated the Aborigines. At the same time, white Australians were focusing on the dismal Aboriginal experience on the margins of Australian society through such novels as Nene Gare's *The Fringe Dwellers* (1961) and Tom Keneally's *The Chant of Jimmie Blacksmith* (1972), while Aboriginal writers such as Kath Walker, Kevin Gilbert, Jack Davis and Colin Johnson began making an impact, both on the self-esteem of their own people and on the outlook of white Australians.

Then came the historians, the most prolific of them being the Townsville-based Henry Reynolds who has examined various aspects of the conflict on what Reynolds calls the Australian frontier. From his *Aborigines and Settlers* (1972) to *The Other Side of the Frontier* (1981), Reynolds popularised the concept of the frontier in Australian discourse, emphasising the extent of Aboriginal resistance to European encroachments. In *The Law of the Land* (1987), Reynolds has shown how, contrary to legal opinion at the time of his writing, British authorities in the 1830s and 1840s did set aside the doctrine of *terra nullius* and acknowledge Aboriginal land rights, albeit to little effect at the time. More recently, his book *With the White People* (1990) has examined the other side of this question by showing the ways in which Aborigines accommodated themselves to the European presence and, by providing men for the native police and workers for the cattle industry, were even partly instrumental in ensuring the dispossession of their people. The Queensland native police, in particular, under the guidance of their European officers, 'played a decisive role in crushing Aboriginal resistance, and preparing the way for untrammelled development of pastoralism, mining and agriculture'.

Reynolds has been accompanied by a growing legion of historians who have largely concentrated on regional studies that have helped to fill in the detail of the conflict and to emphasise its complexity. Among the many valuable studies that have appeared are Noel Loos's study of north Queensland, *Invasion and Resistance* (1982), Marie Fels's examination of the Port Phillip Aboriginal police, *Good Men and True* (1988), Jan Critchett's study of Victoria's Western District, *A Distant Field of Murder* and Gordon Reid's book on the early days of the Northern Territory, *A Picnic with the Natives* (1990). And Reynolds returned with a regional study of his own, *Fate of a Free People* (1995), which re-examined the conflict in his native Tasmania. More recently, an outpouring of oral histories has provided Australians with Aboriginal memories of the conflict.

Although there were differences in the scale and intensity of the conflict as it erupted across the continent, from the time of the First Fleet's arrival in 1788 there was a fairly common pattern that gave an air of tragic inevitability to it. As in other supplanting situations, it was on the ruins of the Aboriginal society that the colonial civilisation was to be constructed. Aborigines would have to either reconcile themselves to their dispossession and be blended into the lower levels of the supplanting society until they disappeared, or resist its encroachments and be swept away by the overwhelming force that would be brought against them. Well-meaning colonial officials, anxious to avoid the inevitable bloodshed caused by Aboriginal resistance, sought to incorporate the Aborigines within the supplanting society. Phillip had some initial success with this, managing to attach the remnants of the Guringai people from around Port Jackson to the margins of Sydney's social and economic structure. They had been devastated by smallpox and overwhelmed by the firepower and increasing numbers of the Europeans. Their British-appointed 'chief', Bennelong, who accompanied Phillip home to England in 1792, returned to take up residence in his hut at the head of Sydney Cove from where he could survey the dissipation of his people.

In largely accommodating themselves to the European invasion, the Guringai were ensuring a continuing association with their traditional territory and avoiding the probable annihilation that would face them if they were expelled by the European presence beyond the boundaries of their territory and forced to compete for possession of land held by hostile neighbours. By associating with the Europeans, the Guringai remnants were also able at times to enlist the potent power of the Europeans in their ongoing intertribal conflicts. It was Bennelong who identified Pemulwuy from the neighbouring Botany Bay tribe as the killer of Phillip's gamekeeper, McIntyre, and thereby unleashed a punitive expedition, albeit unsuccessful, against their southern rivals.

Other expeditions proved more successful in their intended purpose of instilling fear and dependence in the Aborigines. A Spanish visitor to Sydney in 1793 observed how the local Aborigines

> ...keep generally good harmony with the Europeans: punishment has made them cautious in this regard; there are very few tribes which do not maintain a strict subordination to the English, and the inequality in arms has extinguished or removed the discontented.

Despite this, because of their apparent susceptibility to European diseases, he predicted the 'destruction rather than the civilisation of these unhappy people'. Propelling them towards destruction was the spread of venereal diseases and the adoption of certain deleterious dietary habits from the British. Fish caught in the harbour by Aborigines were exchanged for bread, wine or spirits, while their labour on menial tasks around Sydney was paid for similarly. Their former varied diet changed to a more monotonous one based on bread and alcohol. 'It was no uncommon circumstance', reported David Collins in 1793,

> ...to see them coming into town with bundles of firewood which they had been hired to procure, or bringing water from the tanks; for which services they thought themselves well rewarded with any worn-out jackets or trousers, or blankets, or a piece of bread. Of this latter article they were all exceedingly fond, and their earnest prayer was for bread, importuning with as much earnestness and perseverance as if begging for bread had been their profession from their infancy.

Begging was hardly the sort of European habit that Phillip had been so anxious to inculcate, but their increasing dependence on European foods held out to some observers the hopeful prospect of the Aborigines being weaned from their wandering ways and adopting a settled existence.

As the European expansion continued during the 1790s to occupy the coastal plain around Sydney, the embattled Aborigines of surrounding tribes were forced, like the Guringai, to make some semblance of accommodation. However, this was invariably undercut by the conflict that erupted sporadically as the cultures and lifestyles of the two societies proved increasingly abrasive. Much of this conflict occurred over competition for food supplies.

In the first few years after their arrival, the British had found that maize did better than wheat in the unmanured soil and proved easier to store. It also proved much more attractive for the hungry convicts to steal. Aborigines also became aware of the meals that were there for the taking in the ripening fields. When farms were established for 30 miles along the banks of the Hawkesbury River in 1794, the often unarmed farmers were beset with Aborigines intent on plundering their harvests after being increasingly deprived of their traditional food sources. By the following year, some 400 Europeans had moved there and conflict with the Aborigines intensified. When five of the Europeans were killed, 60 soldiers were sent to drive the Aborigines from the area, in the process killing some seven or eight Aborigines and capturing five who were taken to Sydney to be detained until they realised 'that it is not in their interest to do us injuries'. But the conflict continued.

In 1799, three Aboriginal boys were captured and two of them tied up and killed by a party of five white men. The men had been acting in retaliation for the killing of a European farmer, although the boys they caught were innocent of that crime. When the men were put on trial for murder and found guilty, the court shrank from the prospect of hanging white men for the murder of Aborigines, referring the matter to London from where the men were granted a pardon. Although Governor King was careful to warn that future acts of wanton murder would be dealt with harshly, he conceded that the Europeans had a right to use 'effectual' means of resisting Aboriginal attacks. But the only effectual means that seemed to work were massive reprisals against any Aborigines in the vicinity, killing sufficient of them and so terrorising the survivors that further Aboriginal retaliation was stifled. While distant officials might mouth humanitarian platitudes about the sanctity of Aboriginal lives, the unofficial reality on the frontier, sometimes sanctioned by officialdom, was one of wreaking terror against Aboriginal resistance.

For 30 years, the impact of the British invasion had been largely restricted to the territory around Sydney and the island of Van Diemen's Land. The successful crossing of the Blue Mountains in 1813 allowed the confident invaders, with their new-found pastoral pursuits, to break out of the coastal strip and spread across the interior. As one of the explorers later proclaimed, their expedition across the forbidding bulk of the Great Dividing Range 'changed the aspect of the Colony, from a confined insulated tract of land, to a rich and extensive continent'. Surveyors followed the path they had marked and explored further west into the lightly treed grasslands beyond. Within two years, convicts had constructed a road across the mountains, spurred on by a promise of freedom when they had finished. Governor Macquarie rode along its length in 1815, founding the site of Bathurst, while the expanding herds of cattle and flocks of sheep followed close behind to occupy the abundant native grasslands around the new inland sheep capital.

Governor Lachlan Macquarie (1810–21), who did more than any other person to establish the signs of European civilisation in New South Wales, was also the governor who came closest to Arthur Phillip in his civilising mission towards the Aborigines. Macquarie was eager to incorporate the Aboriginal remnants onto the lower rungs of European society, establishing a school in 1815 to teach their children, setting aside land where Aborigines were encouraged to adopt British farming practices and providing rowing boats to encourage them to fish commercially. However, the school managed to attract few students and was closed soon after Macquarie departed the colony; the farming experiment was of even shorter duration, being abandoned within months; while the fish were often bartered for rum. As an implicit admission of his failure to incorporate Aborigines within British society, Macquarie proposed shortly before his departure for England the establishment of a 10 000-acre reserve for the protection of the remaining Aborigines from the ill-effects of European contact. However, nothing came of this proposal.

The need to protect the Aborigines from Europeans, rather than to incorporate them into European society, arose from the increasing tension between the two societies under Macquarie. His administration witnessed a rapid increase in British arrivals following the end of the Napoleonic Wars in 1815. As shipping became more available, convicts were sent out in greater numbers along with free settlers. After taking 27 years to reach some 13 000 people by 1815, the British population of New South Wales more than doubled to nearly 30 000 by 1821. This explosion in population filled the available lands along the cramped coastal plain around Sydney and led to a movement across the mountains to the beckoning grasslands of the interior. As Aboriginal attacks against the invaders of their land increased, Macquarie resorted to methods of massive retaliation to deter them. A punitive expedition by his troops in 1816 succeeded in killing at least 14 Aborigines in order to try and deter future attacks on isolated farms. The idea, argued Macquarie, was to 'eventually strike Terror amongst the Surviving Tribes'. Henceforth, Aborigines would be prohibited from moving in large groups near European settlements and forbidden from carrying their weapons near them. Offenders were liable to be shot, either by the soldiers or by the increasing number of farmers resorting to firearms for protection and revenge. This terrible pattern of conflict spread across the mountains.

By 1820, there were more than 100 Europeans living west of the Blue Mountains with some 30 000 sheep and cattle. Four years later, the number of Europeans had increased to more than 1200, with more than 100 000 head of livestock grazing across nearly 100 000 acres around Bathurst. With no accommodation of the land rights of the local Wiradjuri people, and little or no attempt to incorporate them into the enveloping pastoral expansion, conflict was inevitable. Initially, it was the warriors of the Wiradjuri who had the upper hand, using guerrilla tactics to attack the isolated shepherds and kill them and their stock. But it did not take long for the Europeans to organise hunting parties that retaliated against any Aborigines they encountered. Hundreds of the Wiradjuri were killed, although their exact numbers were never counted, while as many as 20 Europeans were killed.

After one shepherd was wounded by a spear in May 1824, a punitive expedition of seven of his fellow shepherds set off in search of Aboriginal targets. Coming across a party of some 30 Aborigines, they fired at them, killing three females. When news of the killings reached Sydney, some were sufficiently outraged to cause five of the men to be put on trial. Although they were acquitted, the trial put frontier settlers on notice that their massacres must go unreported if they were not to risk being hanged for them. For their part, the Wiradjuri people maintained their resistance to the invaders, driving squatters to embrace genocide as the 'most certain way of getting rid of this pestilent race'. They must 'learn by terror', urged one correspondent to the *Sydney Gazette*. Governor Sir Thomas Brisbane obliged by declaring martial law in the Bathurst region in August 1824, allowing an officially sanctioned open season on the Wiradjuri as soldiers joined in the slaughter. Countless numbers were massacred. From one massacre alone, 45 severed heads were souvenired, boiled down and the polished skulls sent to England.

The killings and other acts of degradation brought upon the Aborigines caused some observers to question the costs of the pastoral expansion. What will future generations think, one correspondent asked in 1826, 'when they find recorded that our proprietorship of the soil has been purchased at such a costly sacrifice of human happiness and life'? The invaders had consoled themselves with their faith in their civilisation, particularly their religion, believing it to be a gift they were bestowing on the Aborigines which would lift them out of their primitive existence. Instead, 'strange to say, Civilisation has been the scourge of the Natives; Disease, Crime, Misery and Death, have hitherto been the sure attendants of our intercourse with them'. Unless something could be done to avert it, the end result of the spread of settlement would be 'the total annihilation of the Natives of New Holland'. However, rather than calling for an end to the spread of settlement, the writer simply called for 'some reparation for the wrongs we have done them'. But most colonists would have denied such wrongs, suggesting instead that it was the Aborigines who were responsible for their own downfall.

Largely ignoring these isolated calls for reparations, the natural expansion of the flocks allowed the pastoralists to spread quickly across the temperate grasslands of the south-eastern interior, often too quickly to reach an accommodation with the Aboriginal inhabitants who were effectively dispossessed of their land by the coming of the sheep. Since Aborigines were not necessary for labour, their presence was seen at best as a nuisance, at worst as a threat that had to be dealt with. In some places, the resulting conflict took on the appearance of organised warfare across a fairly clear frontier. At other times and places, the conflict was much more sporadic and more in the nature of retaliation by the Aborigines for wrongs suffered rather than organised resistance to European occupation. Perhaps the most serious challenge to their dispossession was in Van Diemen's Land where the Aboriginal resistance, combined with attacks by roving bands of escaped convicts, threatened the economic viability, and often the lives, of the supplanters.

There were an estimated 3000 to 8000 Aborigines in Van Diemen's Land when the British first established their settlements at opposite ends of the island in 1803–04. In May 1804, the first large-scale killing of Aborigines took place when some 40 were shot by nervous soldiers with muskets and cannon when several hundred were seen advancing on the camp at Risdon Cove. They were later thought to have been engaged in a kangaroo hunt. This killing established a pattern that made that island a byword for infamy and genocide. Over the following two decades, death by disease and killing reduced the Aboriginal population to perhaps as few as 1000. On the other side of the frontier, just five Europeans were recorded as having been killed by Aborigines during those first two decades.

Initially, Van Diemen's Land was an agricultural settlement that spread quickly from both north and south along the two river systems, the Derwent and Tamar, along the banks of which wheat was grown to feed the local inhabitants and to supply the sister settlement at Sydney. Easy access to water transport made wheat an economical venture, even when shipped as far as Sydney where it sold in competition with wheat from Parramatta and the Hawkesbury River. Such was the success of the settlements in Van Diemen's Land, originally established simply to forestall the territorial ambitions of the French, that the years 1810–20 saw the island come to rival the mainland in wealth. Sheep were added to wheat and the process of settlement quickened. In 1820, 181 young merino rams from Macarthur's flock were brought from Sydney for sale by the government to Van Diemen's Land farmers in an effort to improve the quality of their wool such that it could be exported. This, together with the increasing population, helped to push the boundaries of settlement into more distant reaches of the colony. However, it could not last since there was only so much good arable land on the island and most of it was soon taken up. Naturally, this was also the land most desired by the Aborigines.

The build-up to the slaughter followed a similar pattern to that on the mainland. Early attempts to 'assimilate' or conciliate the Aborigines were mixed with violent incidents with occasional deaths on both sides of the frontier. Retaliation by Aborigines for wrongs committed against them, together with increasing competition for food resources, particularly kangaroos, was met with massive reprisals. The Aboriginal threat in the early years was complemented, and sometimes outweighed, by the depredations of bushrangers. As the tempo of the conflict with the Aborigines increased in the 1820s, the British view of the Aborigines changed dramatically and for the worse. Whereas the *Hobart Town Gazette* had called in 1817 for 'charity and humanity' to be extended to 'these much lamented Heathens', in 1826 it described the Aborigines as 'this savage and vindictive race'. Their mere presence in an area aroused suspicion. In 1824, a farmer who came upon four Aboriginal women on his land feared that they were

> ...*spies for the men who ... take every opportunity to spear a white man when it is in their power. I even saw one of the women, at a time when she thought herself unobserved, using violent gestures, and, as I thought, cursing the ground, but it might all be imagination. No doubt, however, they look upon us as intruders.*

In a barefaced reversal of the situation, farmers appealed to the governor to save their 'very towns and inmost sanctuaries' from the threatened Aboriginal 'invasion'.

Tasmania's early historian, the Reverend John West, recorded with a broad brushstroke the changing relations between the Aborigines and the supplanters. Firstly, wrote West, the colonists were 'charmed by their simplicity', but this changed under the impact of Aboriginal attacks and intensifying competition for the island's resources:

> *Passing from censure to hatred, they speak of them as improvident, importunate, and intrusive; as rapacious and mischievous; then as treacherous and blood-thirsty—finally, as* devils, *and* beasts of prey. *Their appearance is offensive, their proximity obstructive: their presence renders everything insecure. Thus the muskets of the soldier, and of the bandit, are equally useful; they clear the land of a detested incubus.*

A desperate struggle for possession of the island ensued, concentrated in the years 1827–30. In contrast to the mainland experience, the Europeans were often defeated in a struggle that was played out across a landscape of narrow valleys and wooded hills that was more suited to the guerrilla tactics of the Aborigines than the lumbering response of the British soldiers.

Proposals were made to isolate the Aborigines, either in a containable region of the island or remove them altogether to one of the Bass Strait islands where they could be 'compelled to grow potatoes, wheat, etc., catch seals and fish, and by degrees, they will lose their roving disposition, and acquire some slight habits of industry, which is the first step of civilisation.' Either way, it would allow the Europeans to secure their claim of effective proprietorship over the island. But Governor George Arthur opposed such plans, at least initially. As he argued, the Aborigines 'already complain that the white people have taken possession of their country, encroached upon their hunting grounds, and destroyed their natural food, the kangaroo'. If they were then banished to a distant island, they were hardly likely to accept attempts to force British civilisation upon them.

Instead, as the conflict intensified, George Arthur established a line of military posts in 1828 enclosing those parts of the island supplanted from the Aborigines and forbad Aborigines from entering it, claiming that it was as much to protect the Aborigines as to protect the British. When that failed to work, Arthur resorted to martial law, making Aborigines liable to be shot if found within the wide boundaries of settlement. Soldiers, convicts and settlers could now do legally what they had been doing for years—massacre the original inhabitants. The death toll is unrecorded in detail as it mounted into the hundreds. And the comparative Aboriginal advantage in the Van Diemen's Land bush was increasingly neutralised by the use of other Aborigines, either accommodating locals or Aborigines recruited from the mainland, to hunt them down.

In an attempt to slow the carnage, in 1830 Arthur offered rewards of £5 for the capture of adult Aborigines and £2 for children. This certainly encouraged settlers and convicts to hunt down the survivors, with the reward encouraging them, if necessary, to kill some Aborigines in the process of capturing others. John Batman used the services of Aborigines from Sydney to track one group to their camping place. After firing at the sleeping figures, Batman's party was able to capture two men, a woman and a child. However, the men were then shot when it was found that their wounds slowed them up and impeded the progress of the party. During the conflict, it has been estimated that 200 Europeans and perhaps 800 Aborigines were killed. This represents the highest ratio of Europeans killed on the frontier. Elsewhere in Australia, it has usually been calculated, probably conservatively, that ten Aborigines were killed for every one European.

Van Diemen's Land was different because of the nature of the landscape which allowed Aborigines the opportunity to adopt guerrilla tactics, attacking the isolated farms and then retreating to the wooded hills where pursuit and capture was difficult. Just how difficult was graphically demonstrated when Governor Arthur tried to bring the conflict to an end by organising a moving line of 2200 soldiers, convicts and civilians, stretching 120 miles across the inhabited parts of the island, to force the Aborigines into captivity. Each man in the line was within sight of the next one as they moved south towards Hobart hoping to capture within their human net all the remaining Aborigines. For a cost to the government of £30000, they ended up with one old man and a boy, together with two others shot in the final stages.

The unsuccessful Black Line was followed up by the self-appointed missionary George Robinson who went out among the Aborigines from 1830 to 1834 at considerable personal danger and convinced them, with the help of several Aborigines, including Trucanini, that they would be better off being shifted to a place of safety where the government would undertake to take good care of them. It was intended in their isolated island exile that 'every endeavour should be made to wean them from their barbarous habits, and progressively to introduce civilised customs amongst them'. The remnants of the island's Aboriginal population responded by following Robinson into Hobart.

In 1832, more than 200 Aborigines were transferred to the windswept wilds of Flinders Island where, within a decade, 150 of them had died. The survivors, Robinson was pleased to report in 1836, had abandoned spear-making for cricket and marbles. But still they died. In 1847, 44 survivors were shifted to a disused penal station near Hobart. In May 1876, the Aboriginal woman Trucanini, long commemorated as the last of the original Tasmanians, albeit wrongly, died in Hobart. Fearing that her body would be mutilated after death in the interests of science, as had happened to others, she was buried in a prison yard. This did not save her from the attentions of the Royal Society which had her body exhumed and the skeleton taken. Although it was long believed that the Tasmanian Aborigines had disappeared with the death of Trucanini, their heritage lived on with Aboriginal women who survived with sealers on the offshore islands and whose descendants today proudly proclaim their Aboriginality.

When he wrote his history of Tasmania in 1852, West was anxious to escape the opprobrium that was even then being attached to his fellow citizens for their treatment of the Aborigines. By the radical expedient of killing and deportation, the Vandemonians had secured a claim of effective proprietorship over the island but had lost any claim they might have been able to make to the moral proprietorship of the island. It was this claim that West was keen to recover in writing his history. Admitting that there was guilt to be apportioned, West argued that it should only be apportioned to those involved in the acts of killing and forcible dispossession and that it 'cannot contaminate those who were helpless spectators, or involuntary agents'. Moreover, West argued that the original occupation of Tasmania 'necessarily involved most of the consequences which followed' and, in a familiar recitation of European thinking from North America to southern Africa, claimed that the act of original occupation was 'just'. According to West:

> The right of wandering hordes to engross vast regions—for ever to
> retain exclusive property in the soil, and which would feed millions
> where hundreds are scattered—can never be maintained. The laws
> of increase seem to suggest the right of migration: neither nations
> nor individuals are bound to tarry on one spot, and die.

Such logic would return to haunt Australians as they increasingly worried about their own insecure claim of proprietorship over the vast regions of the continent.

Even Governor Arthur, the official most responsible for the expulsion of the Aborigines, realised the enormity of his crime, regretting in 1835 that a treaty had not been signed with the Aborigines providing compensation for 'what they surrendered'. He warned the British government, as Vandemonians spread across Bass Strait with their sheep to the beckoning grasslands of the Port Phillip District, later Victoria, that an understanding needed to be reached with the Aborigines of that district 'to prevent a long continued warfare' during which both sides 'will destroy each other'. However, his warning failed to halt the carnage.

Recommended Reading

Frank Crowley (ed.), 1980, *A Documentary History of Australia*, Vol. 1, Nelson, Melbourne.

Bruce Elder, 1988, *Blood on the Wattle*, Child & Associates, Sydney.

John Hardy and Alan Frost (eds), 1989, *Studies from Terra Australis to Australia*, Australian Academy of the Humanities, Canberra.

Robert J. King, 1990, *The Secret History of the Convict Colony*, Allen & Unwin, Sydney.

Sharon Morgan, 1992, *Land Settlement in Early Tasmania*, Cambridge University Press, Cambridge.

Henry Reynolds, 1982, *The Other Side of the Frontier*, Penguin, Melbourne.

Henry Reynolds, 1990, *With the White People*, Penguin, Melbourne.

Henry Reynolds, 1995, *Fate of a Free People*, Penguin, Melbourne.

John Ritchie, 1986, *Lachlan Macquarie*, Melbourne University Press, Melbourne.

7

'THEY UNDERSTAND THE SYSTEM OF REPRISALS'

In making his claim of legal proprietorship over New South Wales, Arthur Phillip had also claimed ownership on behalf of the Crown of all the land contained within its borders. Early governors were given the power to make grants of this land to ex-convicts and immigrants with capital at nominal quit rents. This system was changed in 1831 when the British government, taking fright at the disorderly invasion of the interior, introduced regulations providing for the sale at a minimum price of five shillings per acre of so-called Crown land within the limited, government-approved boundary of settlement. As the colonial secretary Viscount Goderich advised, it was intended to prevent the present situation whereby 'large tracts of land' were being taken up by people 'unable to improve and cultivate them' and who were instead roaming across those lands with their flocks, often beyond the reach of authority and the civilising effects of a settled existence. A British claim of proprietorship over the continent could not be based upon such shifting foundations.

The proceeds of the land sales were to fund the immigration of labourers and their families, along with single women, in order to build up the market for agricultural produce. It was all intended to promote closer settlement and, according to the London *Times*, 'to make a new country as like as possible to an old one'. But the Australian interior was mostly unsuited to intensive agriculture along English lines, at least until means could be found to economically transport bulky agricultural produce to coastal ports for export. Nevertheless, the new land regulations were successful in boosting immigration as the prospect of easy wealth that pastoralism promised, and of becoming members of a new landed gentry, attracted many men and women of capital along with thousands of immigrants wanting to work for them. Between 1832 and the eve of the gold rushes in 1850, more than 200 000 British immigrants poured into and across Australia. While most were detained by the opportunities offering in the coastal towns, many followed the paths of explorers who trekked across much of the relatively well-watered, south-east corner of the continent.

By 1835, the economic supremacy of pastoralism was beyond dispute, with exports of fine wool increasingly dominating the colonial trading figures. The success of pastoralism was achieved at the cost of the British government's efforts to slow the invasion of the interior. Its success was a fortuitous circumstance for the far-off colonies, saving them from possible economic stagnation or even decline. It was a success built upon the unique circumstances of the colonies which had cheap land taken from the Aborigines and cheap labour in the form of convicts, and sometimes Aborigines, who were able to supervise large flocks over the extensive, unfenced grasslands of the interior. And it was a success that would be threatened by any official recognition that Aborigines might have a pre-existing and superior claim of proprietorship over the continent.

Following the debates in Britain about slavery that resulted in it being made illegal in 1833, there was much debate about the right of Europeans to occupy Australia. While voices were raised in support of the Aborigines, ready rejoinders were usually at hand to justify their dispossession. Some claimed that Cook's discovery of the east coast of Australia and his claim of British sovereignty at Possession Island gave Britain good title to the land. Others claimed that the title of discovery had been made good by the subsequent occupation. By the 1840s, as it was realised through exploration that there was no part of the continent that was not occupied and claimed by some group of Aborigines, some argued that the British claim over the continent was justified on the basis of conquest. As a settler in Western Australia proclaimed in 1847, rather than 'right of occupancy',

> Why not say boldly at once, the right of power? We have seized upon the country, and shot down the inhabitants, until the survivors have found it expedient to submit to our rule. We have acted exactly as Julius Caesar did when he took possession of Britain.

But this sat uneasily upon those colonists anxious to disown the image of ruthless invaders that such a justification necessitated.

Some looked to the Bible as a way of solving their dilemma. As the radical Presbyterian clergyman, J. D. Lang, assured a concerned meeting of the Moreton Bay Friends of the Aborigines in 1856, the British had not 'done anything wrong' in dispossessing the Aborigines.

> *God in making the earth never intended it should be occupied by men so incapable of appreciating its resources as the Aborigines of Australia. The white man had indeed, only carried out the intentions of the Creator in coming and settling down in the territory of the natives. God's first command to man was 'Be fruitful and multiply and replenish the earth'. Now that the Aborigines had not done, and therefore it was no fault in taking the land of which they were previously the possessors.*

The killing was an inevitable result, albeit regrettable, of following God's injunction. Similar arguments echoed through the pages of the colonial press and the private correspondence of those with the wit to reflect on such matters. While the arguments proceeded, the killing went on regardless.

While few questioned that the Aborigines were predestined, or even deserved, to be dispossessed, there were some who were concerned that it not be done by annihilating the Aborigines. Governor Arthur had presided over the near annihilation of the Aborigines of Van Diemen's Land and had warned of a similar occurrence across Bass Strait as Vandemonians and their flocks rushed to claim the land around Port Phillip Bay while other squatters rushed overland from Sydney with wagons, livestock, shepherds and supplies to claim their own corner of the continent. The episode is noteworthy for being the only serious attempt to acknowledge the pre-existing proprietorship of the Aborigines, when one of the leading Vandemonians, John Batman, conscious of the almost ruinous resistance mounted by the Aborigines in claiming that island and anxious to steal a march on his competitors, claimed to have concluded a treaty with the Aboriginal 'chiefs' of the Port Phillip District. Batman exchanged European trade goods for 600 000 acres of grassland centred upon the present site of Melbourne.

Batman's treaty was a calculated commercial transaction designed to establish his claim over choice land that lay beyond the government's declared boundary of location. It was this that drove him to make the unique gesture of a treaty that recognised, however inadequately, the prior rights of the original inhabitants. The goods handed over to the Aborigines under this treaty helped to ensure that early relations were amicable in the absence of an official government presence. The invaders could hardly believe their good fortune. In May 1836, Batman's rival as founder of Melbourne, John Fawkner, lauded the advantages of the district with its 'fine plains, beautiful rises, and the land free from underwood, except in small patches near the rivers, and [which] contains a great many native wells, ponds, and lagoons, all of which the natives are willing to show.' As a further inducement for others to follow his example, Fawkner described the Aborigines as 'a quiet, and … cowardly race' who 'perform little offices for the whites, such as showing the country, hunting, and fishing, and bringing in wood and water for provisions or clothes'. In return, Fawkner and his associates had given them 'a large quantity of blankets, clothes, tomahawks, knives, and provisions'.

Batman's treaty was dismissed by Governor Richard Bourke in Sydney, and Batman himself was accused of trespassing on what the governor described as the 'vacant lands of the Crown'. The government in London agreed, noting that Batman's treaty would 'subvert the foundation on which all proprietary rights in New South Wales at present rest, and defeat a large part of the most important Regulations of the Local Government'. In other words, if land rights were accepted in one part of New South Wales, they could be claimed with equal force in other parts. The existing title of all European property would become suspect. Moreover, as the British also suggested, it would strike at the heart of government administration which was financed by the sale of what it liked to claim as Crown land. Such sales were used to finance the immigration schemes upon which the prosperity of the colony depended.

But the pastoral tide could not be stopped by government edict. To try and do so, argued Governor Bourke in October 1835, would be 'a perverse rejection of the Bounty of Providence'. Instead, suggested Bourke, the government should sell the land in order to diminish the 'evils of dispersion' by financing the establishment of 'centres of Civilization and Government, and thus gradually to extend the power of order and social union to the most distant parts of the wilderness'. This advice was initially rejected in favour of imposing an annual licence of £10 for squatters spreading beyond the official limits, thereby ensuring at one stroke the success of the Port Phillip squatters and the doom of the Aborigines whose land they were determined to seize. Bourke had notions of mixing the lower class Europeans with the Aborigines and thereby 'civilising' the latter, although the official who was first sent south to preside over the process dismissed the Aborigines as being beyond the 'pale of civilisation'.

Following a visit he made to the new settlement of Melbourne in mid-1837, Governor Bourke predicted 'that the intercourse between the natives and the white Population of Port Phillip will be carried on with greater benefit to the former than has hitherto been experienced in other parts of the Colony'. Although the early indications around Melbourne seemed promising, they were sadly deceiving. Initial good relations were smoothed by the use of an escaped convict, William Buckley, who had fled from the camp at Sorrento in 1804 and had lived with Aborigines on the western shores of Port Phillip Bay for more than 30 years. When Bourke ceremoniously founded the city of Melbourne, Buckley told the 200 or so watching Aborigines in their own language that the government would 'feed and clothe and care for them' so long as they stayed 'peaceable and well behaved'. The familiar pattern of supplantation would be played out in the Port Phillip District as it had been elsewhere in Australia, with the original inhabitants being either subjugated and incorporated on the bottom rungs of the supplanting society or exterminated. There was no middle way.

Officials were sent south from Sydney to oversee the orderly transfer of the district from its Aboriginal owners and to ensure that the sovereignty of New South Wales was firmly asserted over these southern parts so as to ward off the possible territorial ambitions of the Van Diemen's Land government. Within five years, there were 10 000 Europeans in the Port Phillip District. Among the officials was George Robinson, the man who oversaw the end of the Aborigines in Van Diemen's Land and who was now appointed in 1838 as Chief Protector of the Port Phillip Aborigines. Together with his four protectors sent from London, Robinson could do little to prevent the killing that accompanied the swift dispossession of the Aborigines over the following decade. As in Van Diemen's Land, his role was to encourage the Aborigines to abandon their traditional ways and adopt the civilised ways of the Europeans, specifically to cultivate land and adopt a settled existence. They were to be encouraged to do so by issuing rations to those prepared to abandon their lifestyle. When the ration depots became scenes of disease and inter-group conflict, Robinson and others despaired of saving any but those willing to embrace Christianity, which they saw as the surest path to a sedentary existence and physical salvation.

While adopting the name of Melbourne for the capital of the Port Phillip District, and later naming the self-governing colony Victoria, was a reflection of their British roots and allegiances, the founders of Melbourne adopted a derivation of the Aboriginal name, Yarayara, for the river that flowed through their settlement and which subsequently was known as the Yarra Yarra and, later, simply the Yarra. Initially, it had been known as Batman's River. The Aboriginal name was also preserved in Yarraville, which became the name of one of Melbourne's suburbs but not of the city itself. Like Parramatta, this was a reflection of the generally good relations that existed between the Aborigines of the Port Phillip District and the new arrivals during the first years after their arrival. With the Aborigines living amongst them, it was natural and easier for the new inhabitants to adopt the name that the Aborigines used. In fact, one of the tasks allotted to the protectors of the Aborigines was to collect a list of Aboriginal place names.

In contrast to the situation around Melbourne, when pastoralists invaded the Gippsland district of eastern Victoria, relations with the Aborigines were sometimes marked by trenchant resistance and retaliatory massacres which reduced the opportunities for peaceful communication with the local inhabitants. Particularly in east Gippsland, which was further from the view of officials in Melbourne, the Aboriginal names often died with their users, leaving a void that the supplanters filled with transplanted names just as they transplanted European trees and shrubs around their homesteads. Names in that region tended to be overwhelmingly European, with the town of Stratford on the river Avon being the epitome of this. At the same time, even in Gippsland, named after a British governor, there remain a considerable number of Aboriginal names scattered across the modern map, the proportion increasing as one approaches Melbourne. In many cases, the Aboriginal names preserved on the map would become the main memorial to peoples who had otherwise been wiped from it.

The situation on the more open grasslands of the western district of Port Phillip was little different for the Aborigines in its end result. Jan Critchett's recent study of the western district of Victoria, *A Distant Field of Murder*, has detailed the course of the conflict on that rich pastoral expanse. Again, the European reaction to instances of Aboriginal resistance was usually one of massive retaliation, killing any Aborigines who could be brought within range of their guns and swords. As the Victorian pastoralist Niel Black coldly observed after having come across a mass grave containing the remains of some 20 Aborigines: 'A Settler taking up a new country is obliged to act towards them in this manner or abandon it'. As Black indicated, the ferocity of the European reaction was partly explained by the fact that the killing of their sheep meant ruin. Their wealth resided in their livestock not in the land, which they did not own.

The nature of pastoralism, with flocks scattered over wide areas and tended by isolated, often unarmed convict shepherds, pushed the invaders towards murderous methods of what they called 'dispersal', a euphemism for genocide. It was only by the annihilation of the Aborigines that the invaders could be assured of their security. Also, the permanent removal of the Aborigines from the landscape helped to absolve Europeans of any remorse or guilt they might feel about their dispossession of the Aborigines. Their apparently inexorable disappearance, whether through murder, disease or some other cause, gave their demise a sense of tragic inevitability.

Conflicts arose over the misuse of Aboriginal women by shepherds, many of whom were convicts or ex-convicts, over the Aboriginal killing of livestock, or simply over their presence on the land which the Europeans were determined to make their own. In one massacre, the Whyte brothers led a party of nine men, five on horseback and four on foot, in search of Aborigines who had stolen some 50 sheep. When they came across them, together with the dead sheep, they allegedly shot all the men except one. In three different reports of the incident, the number of casualties varied from 25 to 41 to 51 and the bones of the Aborigines, intermingled with those of the sheep, were left to bleach in the sun.

Sometimes officials tried to prevent the atrocities. Following a massacre in the Western District of three sleeping Aboriginal women and a child in 1842, Governor Gipps threatened to close the district to pastoralists and turn it into an Aboriginal reserve unless the perpetrators of the outrage were turned in. Matters were not as simple as they appeared from Sydney. As the Superintendent of the Port Phillip District, Charles La Trobe, observed, there was no 'well-defined frontier or neutral ground ... between the civilised and the uncivilised'. Instead, 'the savage tribes are not only upon our borders, but intermingled with us in every part of this wide district'. Given such attitudes, together with the acquisitive drive of the squatters and the brutality of their convict shepherds, there was little that Gipps could do to moderate the violence. Moreover, the successful prosecutions of Europeans depended upon European witnesses testifying as to the atrocities, since the heathen Aborigines were not legally able to testify in a court of law.

With the indiscriminate use of massive terror, and the operation of the white-led native police, together with the insidious spread of diseases, the surviving Aborigines were reduced to a state of submission and dependence. By 1844, a squatter was able to write of them being 'not very troublesome', suggesting that they did not dare raise their hands against the Europeans 'as they understand the system of reprisals'. Four years later, a visitor to the Western District observed that the settlers 'lived in as great security as any other country in the world—never locking the doors at night or indeed in many instances possessing locks'.

During the course of the conflict, just 40 Europeans were listed officially as being killed by Aborigines between 1836 and 1844. Thirty-three of them were employees, mainly shepherds and hutkeepers. Others went missing and were presumed also killed. As for the recent picture of Aborigines engaging in deliberate warfare to defend their land, Jan Critchett has questioned the extent to which the Aborigines in the Western District were resisting the Europeans, suggesting that they often were simply retaliating to individual breaches by Europeans of Aboriginal law and customs. As she has observed, there were no instances in western Victoria of large-scale Aboriginal attacks and only one confirmed instance where more than one European was killed in a single incident. Moreover, only ten Europeans were killed in 1842, the year of greatest violence, and only 35 up to 1848.

On the Aboriginal side, Critchett has estimated from an examination of the documentary evidence that some 350 Aborigines were shot or killed in the Western District during the 16 years prior to 1850. Only five Europeans were ever charged over the killing of an Aborigine in the Port Phillip District and only one was ever found guilty. He served a two months' gaol sentence on a charge of causing grievous bodily harm. The real level of killing may well be much higher than Critchett suggests. While the European deaths can be listed with some certainty since they were usually recorded, that was not true in relation to the Aborigines who were killed often out of hand and usually out of sight of officials. The records are necessarily sketchy and the estimates of the dead, where they were recorded, are often vague and even contradictory. Many doubtless died unrecorded. In 1839, one of the Aboriginal protectors was alarmed when Aborigines at a special feast prepared for them by the protectors suddenly refused to eat the proffered food for fear it was poisoned. He noted stories of 'many' Aborigines 'up the Ovens and Broken River' having been 'put aside in this way'.

The Aboriginal population declined from an estimated pre-contact figure of some 8000 to just 645 by 1863. Most of this decline was due to disease. Moreover, some of the killing of Aborigines was done by other Aborigines as their traditional patterns of life were increasingly disturbed by the European intrusion. Aboriginal groups that were traditionally hostile to each other were brought together to receive rations, or were simply attracted to central locations in search of European goods for which they had quickly aquired a taste—particularly sugar, tobacco, bread and alcohol. Their proximity produced incessant conflict between them. The population also declined due to a sharp drop in the birthrate, caused partly by the high incidence of venereal disease and partly through infanticide. A Victorian protector was informed by an Aboriginal 'chief' in 1845 that he could not prevent the infanticide, that the blacks remarked, 'no country, no good have it pickanineys'. Among later generations of British Australians, some blamed the Aborigines for their own demise. Thus, Henry Gyles Turner argued in his history of Victoria in 1902 that the 'costly and continuous efforts' made to protect and civilise the Aborigines failed because of the 'absolute incompatibility of the native character with even primary conditions of civilization'. To argue otherwise—to admit that the invaders were responsible for the demise of the vanquished Aborigines—would call into question the claim of moral proprietorship that the descendants of the invaders, and Turner in particular, wished to assert.

Despite the best intentions of the British government, the 'settlement' of South Australia in 1836 produced a similarly tragic result. Established by a private land company, the British government prevented the settlers' departure until arrangements had been made regarding the rights of the Aborigines. The South Australian Land Commissioner instructed that no land was to be sold until it had been acquired from its native owners who were not to be 'disturbed in the enjoyment of the lands over which they *may* possess proprietary rights'. This apparent acknowledgment of Aboriginal land rights was hedged by the conditional clause—'lands over which they *may* possess proprietary rights'. In fact, the South Australians did not recognise that Aborigines possessed such rights anywhere. So there was no purchase of land from the Aborigines and there was no compensation paid for the loss of their lands. According to the commissioner, the ownership of land was 'utterly unknown' to Aborigines. When the British government objected, he pointed to their own Act establishing the colony in which the land was described as being 'wasteland and unoccupied'.

Rather than seeking to accommodate their presence to the pre-existing Aboriginal presence, the Aborigines would be forced, as elsewhere in the colonies, to accommodate themselves to the invaders. The founding governor of South Australia, John Hindmarsh, told local clans around Adelaide, that they

> ... *cannot be happy unless you imitate white men. Build huts, wear clothes, work and be useful.*
> *Above all things you cannot be happy unless you love God who made heaven and earth and men and all things.*
> *Love white men. Love other tribes of black men. Learn to speak English.*

There was implicit in this scheme an acknowledgment that the coexistence of two such disparate cultures claiming to occupy the same territory was ultimately impossible. The Aborigines would have to become resigned to their dispossession and become incorporated within the dispossessing society.

Some recompense was attempted by the British government when it established a system of Aboriginal reserves, insisting that 15 per cent of the revenue raised from the sale of land be devoted to Aboriginal welfare. It also provided for Aborigines to enjoy their traditional rights to hunt across unfenced leasehold land. This right was also conceded in Western Australia. In practice, this did not amount to much at the time as they were often shot or shooed away, but it has since come to be of potentially great importance after the decision in 1992 of the Australian High Court in the Mabo case which decided that Aborigines exercising their traditional links to unalienated Crown land were judged to have native title to that land. More importantly, where such links were maintained to leasehold land, it was possible for those Aborigines to purchase the leases and convert the title to the newly defined native title under which they could hold it in perpetuity. This has the potential of promising Aborigines a much brighter existence in the 21st century than they suffered in the 19th.

For all the thousands of Aborigines murdered at the hands of vengeful Europeans, there are only two cases where colonists were executed for the murder of Aborigines. The most notable case was at Myall Creek in northern New South Wales. On Sunday, 11 June 1838, a party of 11 white men rode up to a stockman's hut on Myall Creek. The hut was occupied by two assigned convicts working as stockmen. Camped nearby were 40 to 50 Aborigines, some of whom were away at the time. The Aborigines were working on the property and also providing sexual services to the stockmen. The party of white men, apart from one colonial-born, were either convicts or ex-convicts, who had been hunting down Aborigines in the area following the killing of a shepherd. Twenty-eight of the Myall Creek Aborigines, mostly old men, women and children, were roped together and taken a little way down the creek where the 11 white men and one of the stockmen butchered the Aborigines with guns, knives and swords. A hunt ensued the following day for the Aborigines who had escaped the slaughter before the men returned on the Tuesday to burn the bodies. Later, the remaining evidence was removed from the site as news of the massacre filtered out.

Initially, the men had appeared unconcerned by their acts which were in keeping with the ethos of the bush thereabouts. Earlier that same year, a punitive expedition under the command of the mounted police commandant, Major Nunn, had ranged across the region massacring many of the Aborigines they had encountered. Nunn was responding to appeals from local squatters worried by the depredations committed to their livestock, and occasionally their shepherds. He was advised by the acting governor of New South Wales, Lieutenant Colonel Snodgrass, that there were 'a thousand Blacks there, and if they are not stopped, we may have them presently within the boundaries'. With such a hysterical summons, Nunn set forth intent on suppressing this apparent threat to the European hold on the continent, or at least that part of the continent.

It cannot be known how many Aborigines Nunn and his men killed, but it may have amounted to several hundred. Reporting back to Sydney, he was confronted by the unsympathetic figure of the newly arrived governor, George Gipps, who was expected by London to bring such massacres to a close. However, rather than arresting the head of his mounted police, Gipps seized instead upon the fortuitous circumstance of the Myall Creek massacre to prove his humane bona fides to London while at the same time sending a stern message to the squatting community that the unofficial killing of Aborigines would not go unpunished. At the time, he was being pressed by delegations of squatters, who were alarmed at an outbreak of multiple killings of European shepherds and surveyors across the length of the colony, to raise a militia force for the purpose of 'levying war' against the 'untutored savages'. Gipps refused, setting up instead a series of military outposts on the road between Yass and Melbourne along which the squatters trekked their livestock while also augmenting the strength of the mounted police.

The calls for urgent action to be taken against the Aborigines allowed Gipps to sidestep the issue of inquiring into the alleged atrocities by Nunn and his men. He argued that such an inquiry would tie up men of the mounted police as witnesses who were required urgently to respond to an Aboriginal attack in the Port Phillip District in which eight shepherds were killed. It would also threaten the morale of the police, who were all military men on voluntary secondment and able to leave their police positions if dissatisfied with their treatment. Such a walkout would leave the interior of the colony dangerously vulnerable. So the Myall Creek murderers provided Gipps with a fortuitous distraction to satisfy London and preserve his police. As he conceded to a delegation of squatters, the hand-wringing in London over the dispossession of the Aborigines was half a century too late: 'After having taken entire possession of the country, without any reference to the rights of the Aborigines, it is now too late for the Government to refuse protection to persons who have come hither, and brought with them their flocks and herds.' So the police would continue their killing while Gipps would earn kudos in London by bringing the convict killers of Myall Creek to justice.

The perpetrators of such massacres had escaped justice in the past because Aborigines were unable to give evidence in a court of law. Not being Christian, they could not swear to tell the truth and no reliance could therefore be placed on their evidence. In this case, though, the overseer of the Myall Creek property, who had been absent during the killings, reported the massacre to a police magistrate who in turn informed the authorities in Sydney. On the orders of Gipps, the killers were duly arrested and brought to trial in Sydney, apart from the colonial-born man who supposedly escaped to Van Diemen's Land but was really hidden by supporters nearer to home. The case caused an uproar in the colony, not because of the massacre, but because white men were being tried for their lives over the murder of Aborigines. Defence funds were set up by sympathetic squatters and the men were visited by a magistrate who advised them to stick together and not turn Queen's evidence since there was insufficient evidence for a conviction.

The first jury found the men not guilty. Four of them were released in the hope they would give evidence against the other seven who were tried on another count of murder. Although the four remained silent, the seven were this time convicted and hanged, protesting that it was 'extremely hard that white men should be put to death for killing blacks'. Ironically, the result of the trial was not to protect the Aborigines but to hasten their demise as acts of retribution, particularly using poison, multiplied and the notorious native police were established to bring 'order' to the frontier.

It was the frontier in northern Australia that saw the most sustained and deadly attacks by Aborigines. In 1857, 11 Europeans on a sheep station on the Dawson River, inland from the Queensland port of Maryborough, were killed by Aborigines. Unusually, the women and a girl were raped and a man castrated. The killings shocked the colonies, not least because the family were believed to be kindly disposed towards the Aborigines. However, the symbolic nature of the attack suggests the nature of the Aborigines' intentions. It seems that, prior to the massacre, Aboriginal girls had allegedly been raped and beaten by the sons of the family. But few Europeans were prepared to read any such implications into the nature of the attack. Instead, the massacre was used to justify successive massacres of Aborigines across the continent, with the Queensland native police being issued with a standard instruction which remained in place for 38 years, to 'disperse'—that is, fire upon—all assemblies of Aborigines. Even those seeking refuge in the coastal towns were not immune from unprovoked attack.

The methods of the native police were revealed to the townsfolk in Maryborough when, under the command of a Lieutenant Bligh, they rode into town and commenced to kill those Aborigines camped thereabouts. An outraged citizen reported:

> *Mr. Bligh, with a party of the police, rode into town early, and fired several shots at a few blacks encamped near Cleary's; then came into East Maryborough, charged a camp near Mr. Melville's, drove the poor creatures from it—some through the town, some into the river—and commenced butchering them forthwith.*

One Aborigine, described as 'an excellent and industrious black', tried to swim to freedom only to be pursued by bullets and then by Bligh in a boat who, when he caught up with him, 'lowered his carbine, and shot the defenceless, tired, unresisting wretch, in the back'. An old Aboriginal man was led from the town in handcuffs and reportedly killed some miles away. 'Thus terminated the foulest deed—and shall I say, the foulest day—Maryborough ever witnessed.' The official killings prompted further Aboriginal retaliation.

In October 1861, a squatter with 18 members of his family and employees were killed at a recently established sheep station on the Nagoa River in central Queensland. The squatter had only just arrived in the district and was well-disposed towards the Aborigines. The district was only newly opened up, and relations with Aborigines had been good until the arrival of the native police. With their orders to disperse any Aboriginal gatherings, the police made their first attack in March 1861, just seven months before the Aborigines retaliated. A squatter complained to the government about the police action, claiming that the Aborigines were 'dreadfully excited and accused me and all the Europeans, with complicity in what they rightly termed treachery'. When the government ignored the protest, the Aborigines eventually retaliated with a massacre of their own, apparently mistaking the innocent squatter for a neighbour who had attacked them in the past. In the wake of the massacre, a politician proclaimed that Queenslanders were 'at open war with the Aborigines'.

In time, outrages by the native police became more difficult to perform in the coastal townships. In 1867, a resident of Maryborough observed that the Aborigines 'know they are safe in town where it is next to impossible to catch them, and dispersing is not permissible'. By then, any danger from Aborigines in such towns, where Aborigines were required, and often forced by police wielding whips, to be out of the town centres between sunset and sunrise and all day on the Sabbath, had been reduced largely to nuisance value. As the European frontier spread across the continent, the remnants of the vanquished Aborigines left behind were collected into 'reserves' for their protection or allowed to remain in so-called fringe camps on the outskirts of country towns where they could be drawn upon for menial labour and the women for their sexual services.

The murderous retaliation went on unabated in the interior. As an anonymous correspondent to the *Queenslander* asked in 1880, 'Is there room for both of us here? No. Then the sooner the weaker is wiped out the better, as we may save some valuable lives by the process.' In 1928, a party set out from Alice Springs under the command of a mounted policeman with orders to arrest the murderers of a white man who apparently had been killed for abducting Aboriginal women. The expedition arrested two Aborigines who were subsequently acquitted. At the same time, the party seems to have killed some 70 Aborigines, including women and children. A board of inquiry was appointed which effectively covered up the deed. It may have been the last large-scale massacre, although the killing of individual Aborigines, often by police, continues to the present day. Massacres, though, were no longer possible. Although Aborigines continued to pose an occasional nuisance when spearing cattle, they had become simply too valuable as cheap labourers on these economically-marginal cattle stations to be exterminated.

Throughout the 150 years' war, the initial conflict was often sparked by competition for resources as Aborigines sought to pursue their traditional lifestyles in ways that conflicted with the untrammelled pursuit of pastoralism. In the Australian interior, that often meant access to water or the native grasslands. Not surprisingly, the places where Europeans chose to settle, perhaps beside a waterhole or on the banks of a creek, were those that Aborigines also found desirable and were almost invariably already occupying. As the explorer Edward Eyre observed, 'the localities selected by Europeans, as best adapted for the purpose of cultivation or grazing, are those that would usually be equally valued above others, by the natives themselves'. An observer in western Victoria recorded in 1840 how 'a regular Aboriginal Settlement' of 20 to 30 huts had been established on the banks of a creek along which sheep stations had also been claimed. On a day when the Aborigines were absent, the village was set ablaze and destroyed by the Europeans. There is a suggestion that the Aboriginal inhabitants were subsequently hunted down or otherwise dispersed. Similarly, when one of the squatters in the Western District came across an Aboriginal hut, he ordered it to be destroyed and a sign left that it had been done by white men so that it would be clear 'we did not want them near us'. The consequent disruption to the normal patterns of their traditional lifestyle exposed the Aborigines to illness and dietary inadequacies.

The ability of Aborigines to mount a sustained campaign of attrition was hampered by their need to gather food each day. At one point, Aborigines threatened settlers in a Queensland town that they would be attacked when the fruit of the bunya pine was ripe, since only then would there be sufficient food to attract and supply a sizeable contingent of Aborigines. As well, while it was possible for Aborigines to drive Europeans off their land, they could not defend their gains in the way the Maoris in New Zealand could do with their formidable system of forts and their adept use of European weapons. The Aborigines were also hampered in their ability to mount sustained resistance by their custom of 'pay-back' killings for transgressions against them. When they killed a white man, or stole his livestock, in retaliation for a wrong committed, the Aborigines expected that it would end the matter and that friendly relations could resume. The Europeans usually regarded such attacks by Aborigines as proof of their innate treachery and took it as a signal for unleashing massive terror, wiping out whole groups regardless of age or sex or involvement in the act being avenged. The Aborigines were unable to respond in kind. Their social organisation did not allow for large-scale, organised assaults, while the massacres obviously reduced their ability to mount any sort of reprisal at all.

One such act of massive reprisal was led by the governor of the Swan River colony of Western Australia, Captain James Stirling, who in 1834 led a mixed party of mounted police, soldiers and civilians in search of Aborigines who had been involved in the spearing of several Europeans and their livestock at the new settlement of Pinjarra on the Murray River, 80 kilometres south of the Swan River settlement. Coming across a group of some 70 Aborigines, among whom were the perpetrators of the recent 'outrages', the Europeans caught them in a withering crossfire that killed about half of them, including some women and children. Two of the Europeans were wounded. Some of the surviving Aborigines were captured and later released after being warned that, if they attempted any retribution for the massacre, 'four times the present number of men would proceed amongst them and destroy every man, woman and child'. They had to submit to the invaders and abandon their traditional ways, thereby being culturally annihilated, or try to persist with their traditional ways and face the prospect of being physically annihilated. A successor to Stirling, Governor Hutt (1839–46), urged that Europeans and Aborigines at Swan River should be 'encouraged to mingle as one people'. He tried to force the pace of Aboriginal submission implicit in such 'mingling' by instructing that Aborigines could not enter Perth unless they wore a woollen shirt 'earned by labour'.

The conflict lasted longest where geographical features provided Aborigines with a secure place of retreat, such as the wooded hills that sloped down to the relatively narrow river valleys of Van Diemen's Land. In contrast, the conflict on the open grasslands of New South Wales was swift and brutally decided by the superior firepower and mounted speed of the Europeans. Aborigines tended not to use European methods of killing, guns and horses, but sometimes adapted European goods, such as making iron spears which were better for killing cattle. Although guns were sometimes stolen by Aborigines from farms in Van Diemen's Land, it was not to use them against Europeans but to deny their use by Europeans against Aborigines. When an Aborigine who had been living among the Europeans went back to his people and taught them the ways of the enemy's firepower, a price was placed on his head. Even then, his intention seems to have been to teach his people ways in which they could use their traditional weapons while minimising the risk of being shot. Although guns were sometimes used by Aborigines in Victoria, there are few reports of them being turned against Europeans. Instead, they were used for hunting or even, when inoperable, as signs of status. Initially, their technological handicap was less important since convict shepherds were often unarmed and a well-thrown Aboriginal spear could often be effective against the cumbersome and unreliable muskets. But as the use of guns became more common, and their effectiveness increased, the conflict became increasingly uneven.

The use of native police, or other Aborigines consorting with the settlers, hastened the end of Aboriginal resistance by neutralising the Aboriginal advantage in bushcraft and by providing deadly but silent accomplices to the slaughter. Because their evidence could not be accepted in a court of law, the native police could kill indiscriminately in the knowledge that they would never be brought to account for it. Henry Reynolds has estimated that a quarter of the Aborigines killed on the Queensland frontier, scene of the most prolonged and bloody conflict, were killed by Aborigines in the service of Europeans.

Aboriginal society was further disrupted by the increasing conflict between different groups of Aborigines whose normal relations were disturbed by the European presence. Distant Aborigines, from different cultural and linguistic groups, were regarded as 'wild blackfellas' and were liable to be killed if caught intruding upon another group's land. But the pressure of the European encroachments caused some Aborigines to move into areas where they had no protective kinship ties. Aborigines believed that such distant people were 'dangerous or less than human or both'. Their evil magic was blamed for natural disasters, deaths and diseases. As an official at Port Phillip was informed, distant Aborigines were 'foreign in speech, they are foreign in countenance, they are foreign altogether—they are no good'. When an Aborigine from Port Fairy was taken to Melbourne on a charge of stealing that was later dismissed, he was released and put with local Aborigines who promptly killed him as a 'wild blackfellow'.

It has been estimated by Henry Reynolds and others that some 20 000 blacks and 5000 whites were killed during the course of the conflict as it rolled across the continent for a century and a half. The number of whites killed is likely to be much more accurate than those of the Aborigines. They were known as individuals and could be listed as such. On the other hand, the Aborigines were often nameless and their casualties uncounted. They left no records of their own other than through oral accounts which are only now being collected. European reports speak in euphemisms, of 'collisions' with the blacks where a 'large number' were 'laid low'; other reports speak of unspecified 'outrages' being perpetrated upon unidentified blacks.

Contemporary estimates of the deaths by violence varied enormously. One squatter who took a close interest in the Aborigines of Victoria estimated that between 15 per cent and 25 per cent died violently at the hands of Europeans. George Robinson estimated at one stage that perhaps 40 Aborigines were killed for every white person killed. Some squatters suggested that between ten and 20 Aborigines were killed for every European. This figure seems borne out in the Bathurst massacres of 1824 when somewhat more than 100 Aborigines were killed following the killing of seven shepherds. But it is impossible from the fragmentary and inconclusive evidence that remains to determine precisely the ratio of Aboriginal to European deaths. And how do we deal with those Aborigines killed by other Aborigines as an indirect consequence of the European encroachment on their territory?

Looking at the decline in the overall population figures provides another way of approaching the problem. It was estimated that there were just 60 000 Aborigines remaining in Australia by 1888. The estimates of the Aboriginal population in 1788 vary from 300 000, which was the accepted figure for many years, to the more recent estimates of between 750 000 and 1 500 000. To suggest that, of this dramatic drop in population, only 20 000 were killed by Europeans seemed to stretch credulity to its limits. A more reasonable, even conservative, 'guesstimate' would be somewhat more than 50 000 Aborigines killed during 150 years of sporadic conflict. This is taking the low estimate of ten Aborigines killed in retaliation for every white casualty. Such a figure would approach that of Australians killed during the First World War.

Sixty years after Governor Phillip had legally dispossessed them, the subsequent conflict on the colonial frontier, together with the diseases and other effects of European contact, had nearly destroyed the Aboriginal population. Across the south-east of the continent, in a wide swathe of the interior stretching from Brisbane to Adelaide and on the island of Van Diemen's Land, Europeans through their physical occupation of the land had largely supplanted the Aborigines as the effective proprietors of those parts of the continent. By 1860, some 4000 pastoralists with their 20 million sheep had occupied 400 million hectares of inland Australia. The gold rushes, by boosting Australia's population and increasing the European hunger for land, had only hastened the continuing dispossession of the Aborigines who had remained beyond the reach of the spreading, supplanting society.

Recommended Reading

Michael Cannon (ed.), 1982–83, *Historical Records of Victoria*, Vols 2A & 2B, Victorian Government Printing Office, Melbourne.

Jan Critchett, 1990, *A Distant Field of Murder*, Melbourne University Press, Melbourne.

Frank Crowley (ed.), 1980, *A Documentary History of Australia*, Vol. 1, Nelson, Melbourne.

Andrew Markus, 1990, *Governing Savages*, Allen & Unwin, Sydney.

Roger Milliss, 1992, *Waterloo Creek*, McPhee Gribble, Melbourne.

Gordon Reid, 1990, *A Picnic with the Natives: Aboriginal–European Relations in the Northern Territory to 1910*, Melbourne University Press, Melbourne.

Henry Reynolds, 1982, *On the Other Side of the Frontier*, Penguin, Melbourne.

Henry Reynolds, 1987, *The Law of the Land*, Penguin, Melbourne.

Henry Reynolds, 1990, *With the White People*, Penguin, Melbourne.

C. D. Rowley, 1972, *The Destruction of Aboriginal Society*, Penguin, Melbourne.

8

'BURIED IN A COUNTLESS THRONG OF CHINAMEN'

Pastoralism spread sheep across the temperate, south-eastern and south-western interior of the continent, dealing a multitude of blows to Aboriginal groups who sought vainly to retain their separate parts of the continent. By the sale of land, immigration was fostered on such a scale that immigrants and the colonial-born came to outnumber the convicts and emancipists. By 1840, Australia had become in the eyes of many Europeans a land of opportunity rather than a land of exile. This change in perception was crucial in allowing the colonists to increase their numbers so that they might more securely establish their still tentative claim across the broadest reaches of the continent.

The growth in population was spectacular. New South Wales grew from 76 845 European inhabitants in 1836 to 187 243 in 1851. Growth in the Port Phillip District was even more spectacular. From having just 224 European inhabitants in 1836, it had grown to 97 489 in 1851. South Australia had a similarly rapid growth, increasing threefold in just six years, from 22 460 in 1845 to 66 538 in 1851. And by 1841 more than half the male population of New South Wales was colonial-born or immigrant rather than convict, while convicts and emancipists comprised just over one-third of the total population. Males still outnumbered females roughly two to one. And this declining proportion of convicts was set to continue as they stopped being sent to New South Wales in 1840, although a short-lived attempt to resuscitate the convict labour trade to New South Wales in the late 1840s saw some 2000 being dumped onto the colonial labour market before popular protest threatened a break with Britain over the issue. The supply of convicts to Van Diemen's Land was stopped in 1853, which celebrated by reinventing itself as Tasmania, and to Norfolk Island in 1855. But it was not the end of convict labour. While the people of New South Wales were holding them at bay, Western Australia was appealing for them to be sent there to solve the chronic labour shortage and help correct their financial problems. It was not until 1868 that the trade finally ended, bringing to a close a system that had seen 160 663 convicts exiled to the Australian colonies.

While pastoralism transformed Australia into a land of opportunity, allowing a person of limited capital to become a person of considerable capital and labouring men and women to be assured of a reasonable standard of living and a chance to aspire to become landowners themselves, many Europeans continued to opt for the opportunities closer at hand in the United States and Canada. Moreover, while a minor government official could proclaim from the security of his position in Melbourne in 1845 that Australia was 'a Land flowing with Milk and honey', as well as having 'the finest Beef and Mutton @ 1½d per pound', some of his fellow colonists found the 1840s to be a more difficult decade. A combination of drought and a drop in wool prices caused a contraction of credit from London, while the simultaneous ending of transportation and a decrease in official land sales caused a revenue crisis for the government. Some squatters responded to the difficult times by importing non-European labourers, thereby embedding in the memory of the labour movement the spectre of non-European labour constituting a threat to living standards. Even with cheap labourers imported from India or the islands of Melanesia, who mostly proved unsuited to shepherding, some pastoralists were ruined by a series of spectacular bankruptcies while others boiled down their sheep. In 1850, 95 boiling-down works in Sydney turned some 500 000 sheep and 50 000 head of cattle into tallow. This was not the disaster it seemed at first sight, since it provided a minimum price for sheep that might otherwise have been unsaleable.

As if the economic depression was not enough to dim the allure of Australia, the discovery of gold across the Pacific in 1848 caused California to be hailed as 'that fortune making country', prompting many gold-seekers from Australia to sail there in search of it. Others, taking advantage of Sydney being closer to San Francisco by sea than was New York, did well for a time by shipping speculative cargoes to the American goldfields. Immigrants from Europe, who might have intended to go to Australia, now turned their attention to the United States. If the partially secured claim of effective proprietorship over the continent was not to be rolled back, it was imperative for Australia's reputation as a land of opportunity to be resuscitated.

As it happened, it was resuscitated by one of the Australian gold-diggers who returned disappointed to New South Wales. The corpulent Edward Hargraves arrived back from California in January 1851 with experience of alluvial goldmining, albeit unsuccessful, and an ample capacity for self-promotion. He had an inkling that his old stamping ground around Bathurst could be similarly gold bearing and convinced a Sydney businessman to finance his efforts. He quickly found the desired gold and rushed to Sydney to divulge his find to the government. When it was officially announced in May 1851, it sparked a minor rush to the Bathurst area by which time hundreds of ounces had been discovered. Then a massive nugget weighing ten pounds was discovered by an Aboriginal shepherd. Although he was rewarded by his employer, it was the squatter who kept the nugget. When news of this find was broadcast, the rush turned into a stampede.

Once it was widely known that it was possible to find gold in Australia, people seemed to find it practically everywhere. In fact, samples of gold had been found as early as 1823 but no rush had developed. People pointed to the Aborigines not displaying or otherwise using gold, thereby concluding that there was not much to be found. Moreover, the ownership of any gold resided in the Crown, so there was little incentive to look for it. And colonial governors worried at the mayhem that might be caused if gold was discovered in a convict colony. Even when 38 ounces was brought to Melbourne in 1849 after being discovered up-country, the short-term rush that it prompted was dispersed by the native police who had been instructed to assert the ownership rights of the Crown. However, in the wake of the Californian discoveries, it was now in the interests of the Crown and the economic future of the colonists for the hungry-eyed gold-seekers to be unleashed. When Hargraves' discovery was announced, it sent satisfied smirks across the faces of Sydney merchants as they mentally counted the profits to be made while their counterparts in Melbourne faced ruin as their labourers deserted their positions to seek gold in New South Wales.

The Port Phillip District was preparing for its imminent separation from New South Wales when the news of gold was reported in May 1851. The optimistic celebrations planned for July 1851, as the district prepared to take on the name of Britain's young Queen for their new colony, were cast under a pall of pessimism. Melbourne merchants and other public-spirited citizens combined to offer a reward for the discovery of gold in their nascent colony. By mid-July, two genuine finds had been made but they did not prove to be extensive. However, in the following month, gold was discovered in greater quantities at Buninyong, 16 kilometres from Ballarat, and then at Ballarat itself. In September, the Cavanagh brothers proved the riches that were waiting to be found when they arrived in Geelong with 60 pound weight of gold worth some £3000. By October, £75 000 worth of gold had been taken to Melbourne from Ballarat.

Despite the efforts of historians to paint the succeeding years as a golden age, the immediate effect of the discovery of gold was to bring poverty to many people. It was estimated that, in the wake of Hargraves' announcement, 500 families were added to the list of the destitute in Sydney as inflation of prices, partially fuelled by speculation, combined with the desertion of wage-earners to the goldfields. Overall, gold caused Australia to experience its greatest ever bout of inflation, with prices increasing by about 200 per cent over three years. Only gradually, and unevenly, did the increase in the wealth of the community wrought by gold compensate for the inflation and other adverse effects of the social and economic upheaval.

Squatters were hard hit in the early days of the gold rushes when much of their labour deserted to the diggings. Some responded by amalgamating their flocks into one great flock which they moved about their property with as much labour as they had left. Others turned to Aborigines, who they had previously used for more menial duties, and encouraged them to become shepherds and stockmen. Despite these short-term difficulties, the squatters' long-term prospects were good, particularly if situated near the goldfields where their livestock fetched good prices to feed the hungry diggers rather than being boiled down to make tallow. And their land increased in value as the increased population, enriched by gold, sought land on which to settle.

The diggings were along creeks where the gold-bearing clay and gravel was washed to reveal the gold. As hundreds, even thousands, of diggers camped along these creeks, the sanitary conditions were abysmal. Ironically, Aborigines were sometimes employed to use their skills to construct shelters for the diggers. Disease was rife, and drinking water had to be carted in at great expense. Diggers had to make a quick strike in order to remain on the field and to pay for further provisions. Later, as various of the goldfields endured, permanent buildings were constructed and sizeable towns grew up almost overnight on former sheep runs. The central Victorian gold capital of Ballarat had a population of 50 000 inhabitants in 1854 and boasted all the facilities of a European town—theatres, libraries, churches, a newspaper and hotels. The luxuriant grasslands of south-east Australia, which had only recently been lightly sprinkled with squatters and their demanding sheep, were now awash with a flood of gold-diggers dragging the encumbrances of European civilisation into the bush.

It was common for diggers to rush from one field to the next as rumours spread of lucky strikes. Sometimes squatters spread such stories to attract miners to their land on which they were ready with stores stocked with provisions. Such storekeepers were often the most wealthy at the end of the day. There were diggers who did well and used their gold to buy property, build solid houses and establish businesses. But most of the wealth went to men and women of existing capital, while much of the gold found its way back to Britain, paying for the shiploads of imports that saw Australian colonies increase their share of British exports from around two per cent prior to the gold rushes to nine per cent afterwards.

The miners were able to stake a claim—sometimes limited to as little as 64 square feet—which they registered with the resident gold commissioner and on which they could dig for gold. Some of these mines went down for perhaps 100 feet in search of a nugget that would set them up for life. At Ballarat in 1853, a nugget weighing 136 pounds and worth perhaps £7000 was found in one such mine. But few miners were so fortunate. The diggers at Bathurst who proved unlucky in the first weeks after Hargraves' discovery were reported to have 'faced starvation or hiring of their labour which was reported to be common'. Similarly at Ballarat in October 1851, 'plenty of men' were reported to be offering themselves for hire at the diggings for a guinea a week plus rations.

The diggings have been portrayed by historians as breeding grounds of an Australian egalitarianism, a place where small groups of diggers worked cooperatively and where the master–servant relationship was absent. There was much truth to it. Where a goldfield was producing ready supplies of the mineral with relatively little effort, such cooperative methods were common since one person alone could not work a claim. However, it was also common for hired labour to be used. In July 1851, an Aborigine employed to make a shelter for an aspiring digger gave up this work to try his hand at digging for gold. Rather than hiring out his labour to the diggers, this Aborigine said that 'he intended to employ blackfellows himself'.

As was often the case, where success was more sporadic and required greater effort, more miners exhausted their resources before striking gold. It was these men who gave up independent digging to hire out their labour, perhaps only until they could start again on their own account, or perhaps to earn the money for their return to town. It has been estimated that one-third of miners were disappointed at the diggings. An observer on the Ballarat goldfield surveyed 567 miners who reported an average return of more than an ounce of gold a day. Amongst those men, four had worked for four days and dug just one ounce of gold; they could have got much more by hiring out their labour. On the other hand, a party of seven men had worked for six days and dug 560 ounces—perhaps a year's wage earned in less than a week.

Contrary to popular myth, the common experience on the goldfields was probably one of independent digging interspersed with varying intervals of wage-labour. The egalitarianism that was present on the goldfields was caused by the dropping of gentlemanly pretensions in the primitive conditions as all scrambled for their piece of gold. As so many observers noted at the time, the goldfields were no place for people reluctant to roll up their sleeves and swing a pick. And it was those more adept at such labour who often showed the best returns. One visiting English gentleman described the situation on the goldfields as a 'hairystocracy' in which 'every servant in this Austral Utopia thinks himself a gentleman, and really is far more independent than his employer for the time being'. As this observer suggested, the egalitarianism was promoted by the nature of the labour market in which workers could demand their own rates of pay during much of the 1850s and walk out if unsatisfied.

The requirement to buy a gold licence at 30 shillings a month had the effect of sorting out the successful from the unsuccessful. The licence was introduced as a means of asserting the Crown's historic ownership of gold but was regarded as an onerous tax by the miners. It was often those unable to finance the monthly licence who would have to hire out their labour or desert the diggings altogether. Alternatively, they could work on illegally in the hope of striking gold and buying a licence before the police found them out. It was partly resentment caused by the licence system that sparked the most serious armed rebellion by Europeans in Australia's history. Many of the rebels were non-English in background which, together with a coincidental influx of Chinese miners, raised fears that the British would lose their claim of proprietorship over the gold-rich continent.

Concerned about keeping order on the goldfields, with diggers on some fields combining to defy authority and refusing to buy their gold licences, the Victorian governor sent troops onto the diggings in October 1852 to support the hard-pressed police. Troops had previously been deployed in the countryside to 'disperse' the Aborigines and thereby assert British proprietorship over their land. Authorities now feared that the goldfields would experience the sort of lawlessness that had occurred on the Californian goldfields, with armed vigilantes usurping legitimate authority. Their fears were heightened by having politically-aware miners fresh from the revolutionary turbulence of late 1840s Europe; Irish miners fresh from the famine that was devastating that island and increasing their resentment against the English; and American miners proud of their war of independence and committed to republicanism and democracy.

The Victorian government had been warned in August 1852 that a large number of American diggers were on their way to Australia, or already there, intent on campaigning for a republican form of government. It took the warning seriously. Initially, native police had been used to enforce the gold licence, a ploy which was hardly calculated to amuse the miners. Although the native police were replaced by white troopers, more often than not they were ex-convicts who were paid a reward for every digger caught. This encouraged them to use methods of trickery and brutality to entrap miners. And the government's mounting financial crisis, which saw public expenditure soar from £75000 in 1851 to £1225000 in 1854, put increasing pressure on the gold commissioners to enforce the licence system rigorously. The arrival in Melbourne in June 1854 of a new governor completed the preconditions for the coming upheaval.

Sir Charles Hotham was a naval martinet in the mould of Governor Bligh. He was met in Melbourne by 60000 citizens under a triumphal arch proclaiming, 'Victoria welcomes [Queen] Victoria's choice'. Before his term expired, he would unintentionally convert many of them into republicans. Almost immediately, he left for the goldfields where he met with an enthusiastic response and saw for himself the riches that could be dug from the soil. Just outside Bendigo, where the anti-licence agitation had begun, the horses of his carriage were unyoked and a huge crowd of welcoming miners, estimated by Hotham as 25000 strong, pulled his carriage into the town. At Ballarat, he saw the deep shafts that were being sunk in search of gold. These shafts might take six months to reach the level at which gold could be found. But instead of his visit evoking some sympathy for the diggers and their industry, he only saw the potential for enforcing the licence system and collecting what he called the 'trifling sum' from each miner that was so essential for rescuing the colony's finances. Hotham believed the diggers' investment would make them supporters of order and authority, which essentially they were. However, as events would prove, they were also determined opponents of despotism.

Only 43000 of the estimated 70000 Victorian diggers had bought a licence, despite it being reduced to just £8 for 12 months. If they all could be forced to pay, the government's financial problems would be solved. In September, Hotham instructed that the hated licence hunts be carried out twice a week, thereby creating the political fuel that would soon fire a rebellion. The spark came with the killing of a drunken Scotsman, James Scobie, on 7 October 1854, when he and a friend tried to get a drink after hours at the rather grand Eureka Hotel owned by James Bentley, an ex-convict from Van Diemens Land, who had done well and was said to be well-connected with corrupt police and magistrates. A judicial inquiry at Ballarat exonerated Bentley, prompting a protest meeting of diggers who burnt down his hotel and forced Bentley to flee for his life. In the wake of the protests, Bentley was arrested for Scobie's murder while two diggers were arrested for the burning of his hotel. The officials were anxious to reassert their tarnished authority by bringing on a conflict with the diggers.

Goldfields commissioner Robert Rede proposed to send out his police on the next day to 'test the feelings of the people', while also arresting another digger for the burning of the hotel. Reinforcements of police and British soldiers arrived from Melbourne as the local magistrate appealed for 'loyal and respectable inhabitants' to be sworn in as special constables. Only three turned up out of some 23000 adult males at

Ballarat. Hotham tried to appease the miners with an inquiry, but the demands of the diggers' newly formed Ballarat Reform League escalated to encompass manhood suffrage and other democratic political reforms, ominously repeating the American refrain that taxation without representation was tyranny, and threatening to push for a republic if Queen Victoria continued to rule through obnoxious laws and dishonest ministers. More immediately, they demanded an end to the goldfield commissioners and the hated licences.

Some of the heat might have been removed by the gaoling of Bentley for three years' hard labour on the road gang, but that was balanced by the gaoling of the three diggers for burning his hotel, albeit for lesser terms. When the miners appealed for Hotham to release their comrades, the governor responded by sending yet more troops to Ballarat. One group of reinforcements bringing wagonloads of guns and ammunition was set upon by the diggers, the wagons were overturned and looted, and a drummer boy was killed. That night, Commissioner Rede attended a Thanksgiving dinner of American miners where he refused to be taken in by their protestations of loyalty, confiding later to Hotham that the American miners were intent on 'Americanizing this Colony'. After all, the English could not be made to rebel, argued Rede. So the ferment had to be inspired by the Americans, or the Irish, or the Germans or even the Italians. Or perhaps it was the drunken Scots. All were aliens of varying shades in the eyes of the English and all were intent on dispossessing Queen Victoria of her golden colony at the same time as she was locked in a struggle with the Russians over the Crimean peninsula. The threat of a Russian naval attack in late 1854 was regarded so seriously that it prompted several invasion scares in Melbourne. While concerned officials took defensive measures against the threat of a foreign incursion, purchasing a warship for Victoria, they attempted simultaneously to subdue the foreign-inspired turmoil on the diggings which seemed set to come to a head.

On Wednesday, 29 November, a mass meeting of about 10 000 miners at Ballarat met to hear the report from their delegates to Governor Hotham. They rejected appeals for a conciliatory approach and cheered the Italian Raffaello Carboni when he called upon them to salute the Southern Cross flag as the 'refuge of all the oppressed from all countries on earth'. The Irish nationalist Peter Lalor then moved that another meeting be held on the following Sunday to elect a new and more radical committee for the Ballarat Reform League. Many of the diggers then burnt their licences. The authorities, who had spies and provocateurs among the diggers, were determined to bring things to a head. They decided to have another licence hunt the next morning, hoping that it would bring on a conflict that would drive most of the 'decent diggers' into the camp of the government and leave the radicals isolated.

Instead, the diggers threw rocks at the police, prompting Rede to read the riot act and have eight diggers arrested. In response, the diggers built a stockade at Eureka intending to 'resist force with force', while a police spy urged them to mount an immediate attack. Over the stockade flew the flag of the Southern Cross. Later that day, some 500 men swore by the Southern Cross 'to stand truly by each other, and fight to defend our rights and liberties'. A last-minute bid for peace was made by a delegation of diggers but Rede was in no mood for compromise, being convinced that the diggers' protests about the licence fee were 'a mere cloak to cover a democratic revolution'.

By Saturday, some 800 soldiers and police were in the government camp. That same afternoon, the diggers at the stockade were joined by some 200 men of the self-styled Independent Californian Rangers, armed with revolvers and knives and under the command of an American, James McGill. He was immediately made second in command under Lalor. So an Irishman was in charge supported by an American, an Italian and a German. All the alien fears of Hotham and Rede seemed to be confirmed. That night, about 120 diggers armed with rifles, pistols and pikes, stayed in the stockade while in the government camp Rede prepared his men for an early morning attack, writing off to Hotham that the rebels had formed themselves into separate companies—French, Swedish, German, Irish and Vandemonian— 'the greatest scoundrels in the colony'.

Out of the early Sunday morning gloom, 200 soldiers and 100 police emerged to attack the sleeping defenders. In the fighting, four soldiers and a captain and perhaps 50 diggers were killed, many of them innocent men cut down by the police who swarmed over the surrounding diggings attacking anyone in sight. Peter Lalor, who had been shot through the shoulder and left for dead, escaped capture or worse by the police. Rescued by supporters, his arm was amputated and he remained hidden from the police until the trials were over.

With the rebellion suppressed, and with British troops still fighting in the Crimea, Hotham persisted in portraying the rebels as being 'principally Foreigners', while a government proclamation called them 'foreign anarchists and armed ruffians'. From London, Karl Marx thought it was a revolutionary movement of the workers. Men of substance in Melbourne combined to form a volunteer force to defend the city against an army of foreign diggers that was reported to be marching against it. A second meeting of Melbournites, however, condemned the murderous and illegal acts by the troops. Not everyone was buying the foreign threat.

Of the 114 arrested miners, just 13 were singled out to be tried for their lives on a charge of high treason. They included a black American, the Italian Carboni, five Irishmen, one Scot, a Jamaican, a Dutchman, a Dane, an Irish Australian and one Englishman who was presumably led astray. Although they were tried in Melbourne where the juries were thought to be more sympathetic to authority, they were all acquitted. Hotham caught a chill soon after and died on the last day of 1855 a broken and discredited man, while the political demands of the diggers were largely conceded by a subsequent inquiry. The hated licence was replaced by a miner's 'right' costing just £1 a year, while the government's finances were protected by the introduction of an export duty on gold. The British claim of effective proprietorship over Victoria had been made safe by guns and then by political concessions.

To Peter Lalor, it had been a move for independence. But this Irish patriot did not mean independence from Britain but financial independence for the aspiring miner and shopkeeper. Despite the fears of the officials, perhaps the most important aim of the diggers was to release the stranglehold the squatters had on the land. As Lalor recalled, he only took charge of the movement when he 'saw brave and honest men who had come thousands of miles to labour for independence. I knew that hundreds were in great poverty, who would possess wealth and happiness if allowed to cultivate the wilderness which surrounded us.' To emphasise the point, meetings of his supporters raised money to buy Lalor a farm and elected him to represent them in the Victorian parliament.

While the diggers used their new-found political power to attack the hold the squatters had over the land, they also directed it against the rising tide of Chinese miners which threatened to swamp them before their political aims could be realised. Between July 1853 and August 1854, some 4200 Chinese men arrived in Victoria in search of gold. The Chinese had appeared in large numbers just as the Eureka rebellion had concentrated the official mind on the perceived threat from foreigners. The presence of the Chinese had also figured as one of the grievances of the miners and they provided an easy scapegoat for the government to satisfy the rebels. There was also a fear of the Europeans losing their claim of effective proprietorship over the continent to the increasing numbers of Chinese arrivals. In its report of 1855, the inquiry into the Eureka rebellion warned of 'an unpleasant possibility of the future, that a comparative handful of colonists may be buried in a countless throng of Chinamen'. This warning, expressing deepseated fears that were already becoming embedded in the colonial psyche, was penned in the city of Melbourne which had grown to substantial size but was still less than 20 years old.

A publican from Castlemaine had given evidence to the commission of a conversation with a Chinese man who had told him that 'in the course of a few years we might expect either one or two millions. He says they are all coming.' This fear of dispossession was buttressed by resentment at the Chinese for not bringing out their wives, for not wanting to till the soil, for smoking opium, for gambling, for speaking Chinese and for just generally being alien. So, in June 1855, when there were some 17 000 Chinese on the

Victorian goldfields, the government imposed a poll tax of £10 per head on each Chinese arrival while also restricting their numbers to just one Chinese for every ten tons of a vessel's tonnage. In a petition to the legislators in Melbourne, a local Chinese merchant extolled the virtues and accomplishments of his countrymen, claiming they would be an asset to the growing colony. Among them were 'fine agriculturalists who know how to till both good and bad soil', observing that 'a vast area of land lying beyond this town has never been cultivated'. This was hardly calculated to appeal to colonists concerned at the possibility of being dispossessed and the bill was signed into law. The Chinese avoided the impost by landing at Robe in South Australia and slipping across the nearby Victorian border. In April and May 1857, 16 ships offloaded Chinese passengers at Robe. Nearly 15000 Chinese men and one woman set out from Robe that year for the Victorian goldfields. When the South Australians emulated the Victorians with restrictive legislation at the end of 1857, the Chinese landed in New South Wales instead, before many crossed into Victoria. Further measures were taken by Victoria, this time to encourage those already in the colony to leave through the imposition of heavy import duties on their consumables, particularly rice and opium, and a residence tax of £1 a month on the Chinese.

Despite the restrictions, the numbers continued to climb, reaching 35000 by the middle of 1857. In May of that year, Chinese miners discovered a rich gold deposit at Ararat in central Victoria but were dispossessed of it by the European miners. In June there was fighting between the races at Daylesford. That same month, John Fawkner urged his colleagues on the Victorian legislative council to prevent the goldfields 'from becoming the property of the Emperor of China and of the Mongolian and Tartar hordes of Asia'. Despite the great influx of European gold-seekers which did so much to strengthen the colonists' claim of effective proprietorship, the influx of the Chinese, and the prospect of much greater numbers following them, raised the awful spectre of the colonists being dispossessed by the Chinese in the same way they had dispossessed the Aborigines. Some argued against the Chinese because of the lack of women among them. But the radical Presbyterian, J. D. Lang, rebutted such arguments: 'We don't want the flat faces, the pug noses, the yellow complexions, the small feet, and the long tails multiplied a thousand-fold amongst us, as they would very soon be if the Chinese ladies came to us as well.' Echoing Fawkner's fearful refrain, Lang warned that 'a few years of unlimited Chinese immigration' would 'swamp the whole European population of these colonies' and 'obliterate every trace of British progress and civilisation'. So began Australia's enduring obsession with the 'yellow hordes'.

On 4 July 1857, at a new gold rush at the Buckland River in north-eastern Victoria, the first serious conflict between the white miners and Chinese occurred when 500 white miners determined to toss out the

Chinese for 'robbing us of our gold fields' and did so with considerable violence, driving off more than 2000 of the Chinese, killing several of them, beating up the European wife of one Chinese man and destroying all the Chinese property. The fact that it occurred on American Independence Day suggested that the involvement of American miners was probably significant. Chinese miners in California had been subject to such treatment and worse, with 82 being murdered there in 1853–54. Although the police, under Robert O'Hara Burke, arrived belatedly on the Buckland to stop the violence, arrest the ringleaders and allow the Chinese to return, the Chinese wisely stayed away and only four of the diggers were convicted. Later that year, the Victorian government introduced tougher restrictions on the entry of Chinese which had the effect of stabilising the population at about 40 000, before many of these began drifting away under the pressure of the regulations and the attraction of gold rushes in New South Wales.

It was in New South Wales, at the rich Lambing Flat goldfield near the town of Young in 1860–61, that perhaps the worst anti-Chinese rioting took place. In November 1860, some 500 Chinese were forcibly ejected from their camp and had their property plundered or destroyed. The turmoil died down for a time under the watchful eye of troops until in June 1861 the diggers, now formed into a Miners Protective League, called on all white miners to combine in a struggle for their race. They marched in procession behind a German band, chanting:

Rule, Britannia!
Britannia rules the waves!
No more Chinamen
In New South Wales.

Under English, Irish, American and Southern Cross flags, they proceeded to lay into the Chinese in the usual manner, beating them, cutting off their cues and destroying their property. Police later arrested three diggers and, when a riotous crowd tried to free them, one digger was killed and many wounded. The police then fled the field for fear of being overwhelmed by the enraged diggers. Troops eventually arrived from Sydney to restore order. It is unclear how many Chinese, if any, were killed during the rioting. Eric Rolls has recently rebutted stories of up to 14 Chinese being killed. Certainly, the newspapers of the time reported no bodies having been found, although many Chinese were grievously injured. Again, only two diggers were convicted over the incident while the government responded with restrictive legislation against the Chinese.

It was the sheer numbers of Chinese on the goldfields that provoked such intense fear-driven hostility, particularly as they arrived in Australia as the easily recoverable gold was beginning to decline. To the frustration of the

Europeans, the Chinese managed to get gold from the tailings, the clay and gravel that the Europeans had already gone over. They were also wasteful of the water that was so essential for alluvial mining, but which was often in short supply. By the late 1850s, the Chinese comprised more than ten per cent of the adult male population in Victoria and a much higher proportion on certain goldfields. For a time on the Buckland River, they outnumbered Europeans by five to one. They also competed for the very limited number of white women.

The gold rushes had confirmed the view of all those boosters who spoke of a Terra Australis with great mineral wealth. During the 1850s, Australia produced 40 per cent of the world's gold production. This wealth, and the gold-seekers who came in search of it and stayed on, made possible a drive to industrialise the overwhelmingly pastoral economy. The lure of gold brought workers for the factories of the cities and customers for their products. The inrush of population, nearly trebling Australia's population during the 1850s, from 400000 to 1100000, diluted the rising ascendancy of native-born Australians and also to some extent the British predominance in Australia. By 1862, only 92.5 per cent of non-Aboriginal Australians were born in the British Isles or Australia. Previously, the figure would have been close to 100 per cent. The newcomers also helped to wash away much of the convict stain.

The experience of the gold rushes made the now self-governing colonists wary of alien invasion and laid the basis for the later 'white Australia' policy. Just when the threat from the Aborigines had been largely dealt with in that boomerang of settlement that swept across south-east Australia, the colonists suddenly found in their midst thousands of alien Chinese men. Thus was sown the seeds of a deepseated fear that the colonists would in their turn be dispossessed by the people of Asia just as surely as they had previously dispossessed the Aborigines.

Despite this fear, the influx of immigrants attracted by the heady allure of gold had made the effective occupation of the continent more assured. Towns and even cities sprang up almost overnight on the diggings, peopled with increasing numbers of women and children. While many towns withered away as the gold ran out, others remained as solid concentrations of European population scattered across an interior that had previously seen little more than the lonely slab huts of the occasional shepherd. As well, in the wake of the gold rushes, a new surge of exploration in search of fresh grazing lands sent expeditions crisscrossing the continent, particularly over northern Australia. Apart from opening up stretches of territory previously unseen by Europeans, the gold rushes increased calls for settling the existing soil more intensively and for transforming the large pastoral holdings of absentee squatters into smaller agricultural allotments on which permanent habitations would be built and its soil tilled.

Recommended Reading

Geoffrey Blainey, 1969, *The Rush that Never Ended*, Melbourne University Press, Melbourne.

Raffaello Carboni, 1993, *The Eureka Stockade*, Melbourne University Press, Melbourne.

Andrew Markus, 1979, *Fear and Hatred: Purifying Australia and California 1850–1901*, Hale & Iremonger, Sydney.

John Molony, 1984, *Eureka*, Viking, Melbourne.

Bob O'Brien, 1992, *Massacre at Eureka: The Untold Story*, Australian Scholarly Publishing, Melbourne.

C. A. Price, 1974, *The Great White Walls Are Built*, Australian National University Press, Canberra.

Eric Rolls, 1992, *Sojourners*, University of Queensland Press, Brisbane.

Geoffrey Serle, 1977, *The Golden Age*, Melbourne University Press, Melbourne.

9

'INTO THE BOSOM OF UNKNOWN LANDS'

As the gold rushes died away in the late 1850s, and mining companies took over from individual miners to pursue the deeper leads, there was a renewed interest in exploring the interior of the continent. The pastoralists were able to quickly follow up the explorers with their sheep and cattle because the 1850s had also seen the opening up of the extensive Murray–Darling river system to steamboats. Grazing land that would have been too far from the sea to make the transport of its wool economical now became financially viable. From the 1860s, the development of railways provided a similar boon to the pastoralists, allowing them to extend the ambit of their operations across more and more distant swathes of the interior. An index of their success was provided by the sheep population which had remained around 17 million during the 1850s, but rose sharply to 104 million by 1891.

The exploration of the interior of the Australian continent occurred in two major bursts of activity. The first came in the wake of the crossing of the Blue Mountains in 1813 as pastoralists shifted their flocks in search of feed beyond the officially approved limits to settlement and government-sponsored expeditions explored the extent and potential of the grasslands beyond. Much of the potential of such grasslands hinged on their access to water, both to sustain livestock and as the most economical means of shifting produce to market and of supplying any sheep runs that might be established there. These early explorers of the inland plains found a succession of sluggish rivers that all trailed off westward. Some postulated that they must empty into a great inland sea, much like the great seas of central Asia or the lakes of North America. Such theories gained substance from Aborigines who reported the existence of 'large waters to the westward, on which the natives had canoes, and in which there were fish of great size'.

Charles Sturt, military secretary to Governor Darling, showed this to be wrong in two expeditions from 1828 to 1830 when he proved that the rivers discovered draining off the western slopes of the Great Dividing Range in southern New South Wales all joined together into the Murray River rather than draining into a great inland sea. In the first expedition, he traced the Murrumbidgee River to its junction with the Murray and also discovered the Darling River. On the second expedition, he followed the Murray to its termination in a small lake, which he named Alexandrina, on the east coast of South Australia. The usefulness of his discovery was limited by the Murray not having a navigable mouth that might otherwise have allowed the easy and economical occupation of the Australian interior. Despite proving that the Murrumbidgee did not empty into an inland sea as speculation had suggested, Sturt did not abandon his search for the inland sea. It merely spurred him to look elsewhere for it, striking out north from Adelaide in 1844 in a further fruitless search that found instead a stony desert which was named after him. Moreover, Sturt's earlier failure to find a river equivalent to the Mississippi or the Nile, that would be capable of promoting the British occupation of the interior, did not stop others from speculating as to its existence.

Prior to Sturt's expeditions, there was also a theory that the rivers west of the Blue Mountains could be tributaries of a great river that drained most of the continent before emptying into the sea off the Kimberley coast on the far north-west of the continent. Such a possibility was proposed in a speculative book, published in 1827, along with detailed plans for exploring the interior. Despite Sturt disproving such speculations in the case of the Lachlan, Murrumbidgee, Darling and Murray rivers, the stories persisted of a great river flowing north-westward across the continent. This seemed to be borne out by the discovery of rivers north of the Lachlan that trended to the north-west, and by reports from an escaped convict. Sturt's great rival in exploration, Major Thomas Mitchell, the surveyor general of New South Wales, proved these stories to be baseless when he showed that the rivers were tributaries of the Darling. But that still left unexplained how some two-thirds of the continent to the west and north could exist without a sizeable river reaching into its interior.

Commonsense seemed to dictate that this continent, like all the others, would contain rivers sufficiently ample to drain its wide expanses. Reports from sailors touching along its northern and western coasts suggested that it might empty into those tropical seas. But arduous efforts by a young army officer, George Grey, sent there by the Colonial Office in 1837, failed to find anything more than several rivers of no great extent. One of Grey's companions, John Lort Stokes, continued until 1843 with Admiralty-sponsored efforts to find the elusive river, again without success. Instead of a great river or an inland sea with verdant shoreline, the lands beyond appeared to become progressively arid, raising questions as to their usefulness. Stokes was convinced from his travels that the interior was occupied by a great desert rather than an inland sea.

Undeterred, Mitchell tried in 1845 to find such a river emptying into the southern waters of the Gulf of Carpentaria. He found instead the upper reaches of a considerable river that flowed north-westward to the horizon across 'downs well covered with grass, and redolent with the rich perfume of lilies and strange flowers'. He regarded it as a 'reward direct from Heaven for perseverance' in his efforts 'to solve the question as to the interior rivers of Tropical Australia'. Mitchell believed he had found the river sought by Grey and Stokes, a river 'leading to India; ... the grand goal ... of explorers by sea and land, from Columbus downwards'. Naming it Victoria River after his Queen, because it deserved a 'great name', Mitchell returned to Sydney with news of his discovery. Only later was it found that the river, which was renamed Cooper's Creek, ran fitfully into the interior with the waters of the northern wet season before disappearing into the salt pans of the continent's centre.

As far as the people of New South Wales were concerned, there was now little economic incentive to explore beyond the lands drained by the Murray-Darling river system. The land further west was too distant to be economically supplied or to transport their produce to market. Mitchell had led an expedition to a point on the upper reaches of the Darling River in 1835 and the following year he had traced the Darling River south from Fort Bourke until it joined the Murray River. He then proceeded to explore the country south to the coast where he was surprised to find a settlement already occupying the fertile ground on the shores of Portland Bay and supplying passing whalers. Mitchell's exploration of this land south of the Murray prompted him to dub it 'Australia Felix' to signify its pastoral potential. Already, Batman and Fawkner had established their own pastoral properties on the shores of Port Phillip Bay, and Mitchell's reports of the land's potential prompted pastoralists from New South Wales to shepherd their flocks overland to compete for its choicest swathes. In the wake of his expeditions, Mitchell published a map showing what he called the 'natural limits' of settlement that were largely confined to the east of the Darling River and its tributaries. It was within these limits that most attention was turned in the period prior to the gold rushes as pastoralists sought to claim their various territories.

Following the gold rushes, and financed by the wealth that the discovery of gold provided, the second burst of exploration activity occurred as the colonies competed against each other to explore those regions of the continent that had not yet felt the feet of Europeans. There were also expeditions sponsored from London as the Royal Geographical Society combined its scientific inquiries with the more pragmatic purposes of the British government, much as the Royal Society and the Admiralty had earlier combined to sponsor Cook's first voyage to the Pacific. In 1855, the Western Australian surveyor Augustus Gregory was appointed by the British government to explore a route from the Kimberley district of Western Australia across the tropical north to Brisbane. Accurately mapping the water courses and grasslands as he went, Gregory laid out a trail that pastoralists from Queensland would follow in reverse when they came to occupy the Kimberley district with their cattle.

The most well-known expedition was that of Burke and Wills in 1860. It was first suggested in 1857 in the wake of the Gregory expedition, when the Victorian Philosophical Institute set up an exploration committee to plan an expedition from east to west along the Tropic of Capricorn so that the now most populous and wealthy colony of Victoria could take 'a share in the labors of revealing the unexplored portion of the interior of Australia'. It was not just for curiosity's sake that the Victorians were willing to finance such an expedition. The launching of steamboats on the Murray–Darling river system during the 1850s had the potential of capturing much of the inland trade of New South Wales, and even Queensland, for the merchants of Melbourne. By 1859, a riverboat had travelled as far as Fort Bourke on the upper Darling. An expedition along the line of the Tropic of Capricorn could open up new grasslands that would provide an economic outlet for the colonists of Victoria and an expanded trade for its merchants. In the event, advice from Gregory dissuaded the committee from following the east–west route and pushed them instead to adopt a south–north route, striking out from Melbourne to the southern coast of the Gulf of Carpentaria. The expedition was placed under the command of an Irish-born officer in the Victorian mounted police, Robert O'Hara Burke, and was paid for by public subscription and by a belated contribution from the Victorian government. It was intended to give the confident but cramped colony of Victoria dominion over the interior, to find new grasslands for their increasing flocks of sheep and to establish an overland link between Melbourne and the countries of Asia. It was to be an expedition on a grand scale with no expense spared. Camels were brought from India and much of Melbourne gathered to watch the men depart.

The expedition is etched on the national memory because, like the Eureka Stockade, Ned Kelly and Gallipoli, it was a tragic failure. Yet, of all the expeditions that set out across Australia, this one should not have failed. Burke was a Galway man who had served in the Austrian cavalry before fetching up in Australia as a superintendent of police. He had sailed to London during the Crimean War in an effort to secure a commission and prove his heroism on the battlefield. He failed to get one and returned disappointed to Victoria, while his brother was killed in Crimea. Back in Victoria, Burke's efforts to prove his heroism and derring-do would instead cause him to perish. Frustrated at the slow progress of his over-equipped expedition, Burke and three of his men struck out from a base camp on Cooper's Creek to reach the Gulf of Carpentaria, 3000 miles from Melbourne. While achieving this feat, their return ended in disaster when they arrived back at Cooper's Creek just hours after the rest of the expedition had abandoned it and retreated towards Melbourne, leaving behind a buried store of food. Too exhausted to follow them, Burke dug up the food and set off slowly along Cooper's Creek hoping eventually to reach Adelaide. Although his retreating companions returned to check whether Burke had arrived at the base camp, they saw no signs of him having been there and gave him up as lost. Meanwhile, Burke, Wills and the other survivor, King, decided to remain on Cooper's Creek, where Aborigines managed easily to sustain themselves. Spurning assistance from the Aborigines until it was too late, Burke and Wills died of starvation while King was kept alive by the Aborigines until he was finally rescued by a search party.

Despite his tragic ending, Burke had blazed a trail that pastoralists were quick to follow. The many search parties looking for the explorers, sometimes blazing a trail with their guns, found extensive areas of native grasslands that would soon be grazed by sheep. While leading a search party of three Europeans and five native police, Frederick Walker was ordered by a large party of Aborigines to leave a waterhole near Hughenden in western Queensland. Walker's party charged the Aborigines, killing 12 and wounding a similar number without a spear being thrown. In the 30 years after 1860, more land was occupied by the sheep and cattlemen, often resorting to such murderous methods, than had been occupied in the 70 years up to 1860. All along Burke's trek to the Gulf, sheep or cattle were soon grazing on the native grasses, while the settlement of Burketown was established on the shores of the Gulf itself. Undeterred by Burke's tragic end, explorers and pastoralists crisscrossed much of the remaining mysterious interior in the three decades after Burke's demise, establishing tracks across its tropical parts along which pastoralists herded their cattle from Queensland clear to the Kimberley in Western Australia, completing the physical occupation of a continent in the shortest time the world had ever witnessed.

The claims of the explorers and the explorer–pastoralists were reinforced by naming the geographical features as they went. The ambitious Scot, Angus McMillan, struck out from the Monaro district of south-east New South Wales in 1839 in search of 'fine country' said by Aborigines to exist to the south-west. When he found it, he called it Caledonia Australis, although the name 'Gipps' Land', which was given to it by the subsequent Polish explorer, Paul Strzelecki, was the one that stuck when Strzelecki's report reached official notice first. While pastoralists were usually content to report their 'discoveries' in letters and newspapers accounts, alerting those who might want to come in their wake, the official explorers recorded their results in journals that were often published in England to reach a wide audience among an inquiring public eager for stories of the exotic. The journals, together with their accompanying maps, laid out the alien landscape as seen for the first time by European eyes, etched in its curious wildlife and described the Aboriginal customs and languages they encountered. The passage of the explorers through the untramped wilderness transformed it by their physical passage, and the subsequent publication of their journals, into known parts of the spreading British Empire. The journals, with their illustrations of British men flourishing British flags from mountain tops, on distant beaches or from the stern of their boats as they rowed along the snaking rivers of the interior, provided confirmation of the continuing British conquest of the continent.

Although the entire continent had been legally claimed at various points around its coastline, explorers of its interior clearly felt impelled to reassert this legal claiming procedure when achieving their goal, whether it was to cross the continent or to reach its centre. When Lieutenant George Grey was sent by the Colonial Office in 1837 to search for a great river emptying into the sea off the continent's north-west coast, he began his expedition by reasserting the British claim to that part of the continent. At the time, some maps still called the continent New Holland and called separate parts of the Western Australian coastline by the names given to those parts by the Dutch discoverers. Doubtless conscious of this, soon after Grey landed at Hanover Bay in December 1837, he 'hoisted the British flag and went through the ceremony of taking possession of the territory in the name of Her Majesty and her heirs for ever'. The Dutch claim of legal proprietorship over that territory was thereby expunged and a British claim overlaid in its place.

When John McDouall Stuart reached the geographical centre of Australia in April 1860, he 'marked a tree and planted a British flag there'. But this was clearly not sufficient to mark such a significant moment in the claiming of the continent. So he climbed a mountain a couple of miles off centre, on top of which he

> built a large cone of stones, in the centre of which I placed a pole with the British flag nailed to it. Near the top of the cone I placed a small bottle, in which there is a slip of paper, with our signatures to it, stating by whom it was raised. We then gave three hearty cheers for the flag, the emblem of civil and religious liberty, civilization, and Christianity is about to break upon them . . .

It was an affirmation of ownership, that the British had asserted dominion even over the harsh interior. In recognition of Stuart's achievement, the Royal Geographical Society conferred upon him its gold medal.

Stuart later crossed the continent from Adelaide to the northern coast and back again. When he reached the sea opposite Bathurst Island on 24 July 1862, he recorded that he dipped his feet and washed his face and hands in the sea before cutting his initials on a large tree. He then pressed on towards the mouth of the Adelaide River where he planned to raise the flag. *En route* he noticed many paths and camps of the Aborigines but did not see any inhabitants. Failing to reach the mouth of the river, Stuart 'had an open place cleared, and selecting one of the tallest trees, stripped it of its lowest branches, and on its highest branch fixed my flag, the Union Jack, with my name sewn in the centre of it'. Hoping that 'this may be the first sign of the dawn of approaching civilization', the party gave three cheers for the Queen and three more for the Prince of Wales before burying a tin near the tree recording the fact that the South Australian Great Northern Exploring Expedition had reached there 'having crossed the entire Continent of Australia from the Southern to the Indian Ocean, passing through the centre'. He returned to Adelaide with the news that he had found country 'well adapted for the settlement of an European population'.

Even when they did not perform this formal claiming ritual, the explorers were implicitly asserting a claim based upon conquest, whether it be conquest of distance, or of the arid environment or even of the Aborigines who might have resisted their passage. In seeking to cross the continent from central Australia to the Western Australian coast in the 1870s, Ernest Giles wrote that his object 'was to *force my way* across the thousand miles that lay untrodden and unknown'. After losing one of his party on the second attempt, Giles abandoned his attempt to reach the coast, noting that he 'had pitted myself against Nature and a second time I was conquered'. Three times he was defeated by the desert until finally achieving his goal.

Later, the published accounts of their expeditions acted as records of conquest, confirming that they had broken the supposed 'virginity' of the continent's interior spaces and had thereby established a claim of effective and moral proprietorship over them. There was a strong sexual undercurrent coursing through much of the exploration literature. When attempting to cross from central Australia to the Western Australian coast, Giles wrote of his desire 'to be first to penetrate into this unknown region'. Similarly, John Lort Stokes, when exploring the upper reaches of the Victoria River in 1839, recorded his joy at being able 'to dart your eager glance down unexplored valleys, and unvisited glens; to trace the course of rivers whose waters no white man's boats has ever cleaved, and which tempt you onwards into the bosom of unknown lands ...'

The descriptions of the country they crossed, previously unseen by Europeans, together with their maps and pictorial representations, allowed

Australia's mainly urban populace to construct a mental map of those distant parts of the continent they would likely never see for themselves but which they could now encompass within their claim of proprietorship. To emphasise the act of possession that had taken place during his passage over these distant parts, the map accompanying the published account of Stokes's expedition has the names of the Dutch discoveries, which predated the British occupation, shifted off the continent and listed instead off the coast as an historical fact rather than a legal claim. On land, the continent was simply divided into Western Australia, South Australia, New South Wales and North Australia.

By exploring across lands untravelled by Europeans, and by performing acts of possession, the explorers were reasserting the British claim of legal proprietorship while also buttressing the claims of effective and moral proprietorship by demonstrating to the colonists and the outside world that they had conquered the landscape. At the same time, they acknowledged that the act of exploration was insufficient in itself to secure a claim of proprietorship over these new-trod territories. Most of the explorers set out with the intention, or at least the expectation, of drawing in their wake the spreading tide of conquering civilisers. When Major Thomas Mitchell looked out across the Western District in 1836, 'the first European intruder on the sublime solitude of these verdant plains', he claimed to have been 'conscious of being the harbinger of mighty changes; and that our steps would soon be followed by the men and the animals for which it seemed to have been prepared'.

When Grey chanced upon a fine river flowing through fertile country on the Western Australian coastline in 1839, he named the river Gascoyne after a friend, noting that he was

> *conscious that within a few years of the moment at which I stood there, a British population, rich in civilization, and the means of transforming an unoccupied country to one teeming with inhabitants and produce, would have followed my steps, and be eagerly and anxiously examining my charts.*

Even Ernest Giles, when crossing the deserts of central Australia, had hopes that his steps would be dogged by settlers. Coming upon a spring in the otherwise waterless wastes, he named the surrounding desert Great Victoria Desert and the spring Queen Victoria's Spring in the hope that in 'future times these may be celebrated localities in the British monarch's dominions'.

The act of naming the geographical features was an important part of the claiming process. They did not have to be European names. Aboriginal ones would do just as well. Just as supplanting societies in other continents and at other times have assumed the pre-existing names for geographical features, so too did the explorers in Australia on the understanding that they were not thereby acknowledging any rights to the land by the Aborigines but perhaps, if they thought about it, were making a more complete act of dispossession.

Where an explorer could discover the name that the local Aborigines used for a particular feature, whether it be a river or hill, that name was usually adopted. At one stage during his exploration north from Sydney in 1846, Major Mitchell found himself 'at a loss for names' for the surrounding mountains since 'no more could be gathered from the natives'. So he named the remaining features 'after such individuals of our own race as had been most distinguished or zealous in the advancement of science ...' He later named two rivers by what he believed to be their Aboriginal names but then came across a river for which no Aboriginal name could be learnt. He named it Victoria, after the Queen. It was later renamed by Edmund Kennedy with its Aboriginal name, the Barcoo, before later assuming its present name, Cooper's Creek.

The adoption of the name 'Barcoo' was not meant as a concession to the Aborigines, whom Kennedy was intent on dispossessing. Instead, on the explorers' maps they became names largely divorced from their Aboriginal origins while simultaneously conferring a heightened air of legitimacy to the European occupation by providing a potent link connecting European settlements such as Parramatta and Gundagai to the soil of the ancient continent. It also had a practical purpose, as Mitchell readily conceded: 'The great convenience of using native names is obvious ... so long as any of the Aborigines can be found in the neighbourhood ... future travellers may verify my map. Whereas new names are of no use in this respect.' There was also a competitive element in such naming, as Paul Carter pointed out in *The Road to Botany Bay*, noting that Mitchell mostly resorted to Aboriginal names when traversing country already covered and named by rival explorers. By overlaying what he understood to be their Aboriginal names onto geographical features that have been named already by previous explorers, Mitchell removed his rivals' presence from the map and helped to 'authenticate his own passage'. Elsewhere, many of the non-Aboriginal names were borrowed from British royal, political or military personages, perhaps as a way of connecting the distant colonies to their powerful protector on the other side of the world, and sometimes of connecting the explorers to powerful patrons. Other names were descriptive, many of them helping by their description to encourage settlement, act as silent advisers as to routes or fording places, or to warn against a particular route.

The exploration impulse had several roots. There were the obvious ones of establishing their reputations, preserving their names for posterity or perhaps laying claim to a fortune through the claiming of new lands. But there was also a sense in which explorers like young Wills were engaging in a sort of rite of passage for the imperial manhood, performing acts of derring-do in the 'wilderness' of the far-flung empire. The former postal clerk Ernest Giles, who successfully crossed from central Australia to the Western Australian coast in 1875 after three previously unsuccessful attempts, wrote of having been a 'delighted student of the narratives of voyages and discoveries'. Giles claimed to have been attracted by the thought that the unexplored expanses of the continent contained 'room for snowy mountains, an inland sea, ancient river, and palmy plain, for races of new kinds of men inhabiting a new and odorous land, for fields of gold and golcondas of gems, for a new flora and a new fauna, and, above all the rest combined, there was room for me!'

The unknown drew them on. After exploring parts of the Kimberley region of Western Australia in 1841, John Lort Stokes suggested using camels to explore into 'that land of mystery, Central Australia'. Few could credit that such an expansive continent would not offer, as all the other continents did, large fertile areas or spectacular geographical features that might immortalise their feats.

Another root of the surge in exploration has been connected with the need to know and to name all the major geographical features of this continent that had been claimed on their behalf. As Stokes argued: 'When we consider that Australia is our own continent, and that now, after sixty years of occupation, we are in total ignorance of the interior,... it seems not unreasonable to expect that so important a question should at length be set at rest.' Even after numerous exploring expeditions answered this call over the succeeding decades, the botanist Ferdinand von Mueller could still write to the Royal Geographical Society in 1875, urging that they 'ought not to rest until all the wide inland tracts of Her Majesty's Australian territory are mapped'. By overlaying the continent with the regular grid lines of the geographers, Europeans would inch closer to securing their claims of effective and moral proprietorship over it.

The explorers helped to establish a claim of proprietorship over even the most distant and elusive parts of the continent. They did on land what Cook had done at sea. They trod on ground 'where all was new'. Or so they confidently believed, dismissing from their calculations the pre-existing claims of the Aborigines whose ancestors had trod that ground for countless millennia. In June 1836, when Major Thomas Mitchell climbed Pyramid Hill to look out over what became western Victoria, he exulted at the sight of grasslands 'shining fresh and green in the light of a fine morning ... A land so inviting, and still without inhabitants!' Naming the country Australia Felix, to emphasise its pastoral possibilities in the same way as John Lort Stokes later named the southern coast of the Gulf of Carpentaria the Plains of Promise, Mitchell made only the most scant reference to the Aboriginal inhabitants, despite noticing that they 'were very generally scattered over its surface'. The Aborigines were disregarded for their quiescence in allowing Mitchell's passage across their lands and for their apparent lack of civilisation. They were regarded with 'indifference', wrote Mitchell, 'so harmless were these natives, compared with those on the Darling', while their ancient living space was pronounced by Mitchell as being 'open and available in its present state, for all the purposes of civilized man'.

Like Mitchell, many explorers observed with some surprise the presence of Aborigines even in the most inhospitable reaches of the continent. The explorers laid to rest the claim made by Banks following his cursory visit to Botany Bay, and suggested by Dampier before him, that the Aborigines were restricted to the coastline. It was this claim that had helped to persuade the British that they could legitimately occupy a continent that appeared to be otherwise virtually uninhabited. Their belated appreciation of the extent of Aboriginal occupation did not cause them to alter their original claim over the entire continent, although as we have seen it may have influenced the British to make some acknowledgment, albeit still a token one, of an Aboriginal right to the land when extending their occupation to South Australia and the Swan River.

Like many of the explorers, Mitchell was a former army officer who saw his role as an explorer in military terms. He was asserting European superiority in terms of civilisation, asserting their sovereignty over the continent and ownership of its lands. As such, it was more satisfying than the glory to be won from battle since he was now spreading 'the light of civilization over a portion of the globe yet unknown'. While he was conscious of the necessity, where possible, to move across the land by conciliating the Aborigines, he was not above overawing them or even killing them where necessary. What he would not do was acknowledge any right the Aborigines might have had to their land. In May 1835, when exploring along the upper reaches of the Darling River, he stopped in a position that he considered suitable for a future township. Rather than seeking out and conciliating the Aborigines, Mitchell recorded that their 'first care was to erect a strong stockade of rough logs, that we might be secure under any circumstances; for we had not asked permission to come there from the inhabitants, who had been reported to be numerous'. He adopted the military name of Fort Bourke for the camp, 'the better to mark the progress of interior discovery'.

Later, when confronted with a party of Aborigines who 'used the most violent and expressive gestures, apparently to induce us to go back', Mitchell was sufficiently sensitive to view the incident through Aboriginal eyes, acknowledging that the explorers 'were rather unceremonious invaders of their country'. But that insight did not cause him to submit to the Aboriginal claim of sovereignty. Similarly, John Lort Stokes, when exploring the Victoria River, understood that the Aborigines looked upon them as the 'invaders of a peaceful country'. But he did not shrink from the possible implications of his role. He was merely thankful that the Aborigines 'seemed impressed with some sort of respect either for our appearance,... or our position, and forbore any nearer approach' so that 'no appeal to force was necessary'. The young Jardine brothers had no compunction about appealing to force when they set out in 1864 to drive a herd of cattle from Rockhampton along the west coast of Cape York Peninsula to the new port of Somerset at its tropical tip that jutted into the Torres Strait. Encountering repeated resistance from the Aborigines whose land they crossed, the party shot perhaps as many as 72 Aborigines in 11 separate incidents without incurring a single casualty themselves.

When Peter Warburton, who had served in the British navy and army in India before becoming police commissioner in Adelaide, crossed from Alice Springs to the Western Australian coast in 1873, he found that 'the blacks all avoided us as though we had been plague-stricken'. This was potentially disastrous since most of the explorers crossing the interior relied upon intelligence from the Aborigines to point out sources of water. Undeterred, he captured a young Aboriginal woman who was kept 'a close prisoner', until 'the creature escaped from us by gnawing through a thick hair-rope, with which she was fastened to a tree'. They then captured 'a howling, hideous old hag' who was secured 'by tying her thumbs behind her back, and haltering her by the neck to a tree'. After several days they 'let the old witch go' when they realised that the wily woman had, 'under pretence of leading us to some native wells', been leading Warburton's party 'backwards and forwards over heavy sand-hills, exhausting the camels as well as my small stock of patience'.

The explorers justified their invasion of Aboriginal land in the same terms as their fellow colonists, noting that the Aborigines lacked the familiar signs of civilisation—cultivation of fields, construction of permanent housing, the wearing of clothes and the belief in a supreme being. While describing the Aborigines along the Darling River in 1829 as 'a clean-limbed, well-conditioned race', Charles Sturt also considered that they were 'at present, at the very bottom of the scale of humanity'. Similarly, the Aborigines along the Murrumbidgee were described by Sturt as being 'a quiet and inoffensive people' and evidently related to the Aborigines of the Darling River who together he described as 'the savage and scattered inhabitants of a rude and inhospitable land', although he believed European civilisation was capable of lifting Aborigines up the scale of humanity.

Later, the spread of Darwinian ideas mixed with Christianity to provide a justification for the dispossession of the Aborigines that at the same time absolved the explorers of any personal responsibility. In 1873, on one of his unsuccessful forays across the interior, Giles came across a valley that provided a veritable oasis in the arid wastes. Promptly naming it Fairy Glen, he concluded from the presence of Aboriginal huts that it was 'an old-established and favourite camping ground' and that his chancing upon it would lead in time to their bloody dispossession from it.

Giles argued that the inexorable process of evolution, ordained by God, made the dispossession inevitable:

> *Progressive improvement is undoubtedly the order of creation, and we perhaps in our turn may be as ruthlessly driven from the earth by another race of yet unknown beings, of an order infinitely higher, infinitely more beloved, than we. On me perchance the obloquy of the execution of God's doom may rest, for being the first to lead the way, with prying eye and trespassing foot, into regions so fair and so remote; but being guiltless alike in act or intention to shed the blood of any human creature, I must accept it without a sigh ...*

When later faced in 1875 with a massed attack by Aborigines who 'looked like what I should imagine a body of Comanche Indians would appear when ranged in battle line', Giles described them as 'reptiles', thereby dehumanising them and effectively negating any claim this disciplined force might have had to the land they were protecting.

So rapid and extensive was the expansion of pastoralism in the decades after the gold rushes that a run of good seasons in the 1880s saw dairy cattle being grazed as far inland as the Simpson Desert while so-called overlanders herded cattle clear across Australia from north Queensland to the Kimberley district in the north-west of Western Australia. The expansion was at the expense of the Aborigines who again found themselves being either 'dispersed' or sometimes partially incorporated into the pastoral economy. And the expansion was legalised by way of pastoral leases that allowed large areas to be controlled by a small number of pastoralists at a time when there was much political pressure to have the squatters' estates broken up for more intensive farming by people aspiring to a life on the land.

Recommended Reading

G. C. Bolton, 1958, *Alexander Forrest*, Melbourne University Press, Melbourne.

G. C. Bolton, 1972, *A Thousand Miles Away: A History of North Queensland to 1920*, Australian National University Press, Canberra.

Paul Carter, 1987, *The Road to Botany Bay*, Faber & Faber, London.

J. H. L. Cumpston, 1964, *The Inland Sea and the Great River: The Story of Australian Exploration*, Angus&Robertson, Sydney.

Geoffrey Dutton, 1970, *Australia's Last Explorer: Ernest Giles*, London.

Stephen Martin, 1993, *A New Land: European Perceptions of Australia 1788–1850*, Allen & Unwin, Sydney.

Ann Millar, 1986, *I See No End To Travelling*, Bay Books, Sydney.

Charles Sturt, 1982, *Two Expeditions Into the Interior of Southern Australia*, Vols. 1 and 2, Doubleday, Sydney.

E. M. Webster, 1980, *Whirlwinds in the Plain: Ludwig Leichhardt—Friends, Foes and History*, Melbourne University Press, Melbourne.

Mona Stuart Webster, 1958, *John McDouall Stuart*, Melbourne University Press, Melbourne.

10

'A HOME
IN THE
VAST
WILDERNESS'

One of the principal demands of the rebellious diggers at the Eureka Stockade had been for the 'unlocking' of the land. Those intending to remain in the colonies, and those looking for a future after gold, looked to the land as the place where their economic salvation could be secured. But they saw it in the hands of squatters who leased it at minimal rents from the government and did little to occupy it effectively. Squatters also offered little in the way of employment for miners wishing to leave the goldfields.

In the eyes of the landless settlers, the squatters were almost akin to the Aborigines. They did not till the soil, nor, because of their relatively insecure tenure, did they build solid houses to assert their possession and their conquest of the 'wilderness'. Moreover, many of the squatters lived in grand houses in Melbourne or Sydney or one of the other colonial capitals and employed managers to watch over their interests.

The British government had tried for decades to prevent the unregulated dispersal of squatters across the interior but without success. As Governor Gipps remarked, it was like trying to 'confine the Arabs of the Desert within a circle, traced upon their sands'. Moreover, trying to confine them threatened the prosperity of the colony. Far better, urged Gipps, for the government to wait until the time arrived naturally for the squatter to improve his properties. The implications of the gold rushes changed the government's calculations and brought unbearable pressure for a direct assault on the squatters' landholding monopoly.

The gold rushes had brought European women and children into the interior and promoted the establishment of many small towns and even cities in the bush, such as Ballarat and Bendigo, that were built on gold. While this solved the labour problem of the squatters in the absence of convict labour, it also brought widespread, popular demands for the squatters' holdings to be broken up for closer settlement. If the new-found towns and cities were to survive as the gold was gradually depleted, and European civilisation was to take permanent root in the bush, people had to be encouraged to establish themselves on small farms where before only the flocks of the squatters had wandered across their indeterminate, leasehold properties.

A ballad in 1864, titled *Hurrah for Australia*, summed up this popular hunger for land:

> *... Our dearest and greatest ambition*
> *Is to settle and cultivate land:*
> *Australia's thousands are crying*
> *For a home in the vast wilderness,*
> *Whilst millions of acres are lying*
> *In their primitive wild uselessness.*
> *Upset squatterdom's domination,*
> *Give every poor man a home,*
> *Encourage our great population,*
> *And like wanderers no more we'll roam ...*

Influential newspapers like the Melbourne *Age* agreed, arguing that squatting was making poor use of the land and spelt 'slow death ... to the very existence of this colony, as a self-sustaining community'. As the New South Wales Land League argued in 1859, 'the only legacy' of a departed squatter was 'a crop of thistles and burrs, and the dilapidated remains of a few miserable huts'. According to the league, the practice of squatting was 'the most primitive, the most wasteful, and the most imperfect of all modes of occupying a country which professes to be civilised'. It was the antithesis of a 'settled society', which alone was capable of securing an enduring claim over the interior.

With adult male suffrage in Victoria, New South Wales and South Australia in the late 1850s, the land-hungry populace were able to get their way. So-called Selection Acts were passed in most of the colonies in the 1860s to answer this popular demand for the unlocking of the land. They provided for Crown land leased by squatters to be surveyed and sold in small lots of up to 640 acres on condition that the selector fenced it, cultivated at least one acre in ten and built a house upon it. In other words, that they established a claim of moral proprietorship over that land in a way the squatters were generally disinclined to do. Moreover, a proportion of the income raised from the sale of this land would be used to finance immigration schemes, thereby helping further to secure the effective proprietorship of British Australians over the continent. Pastoralism was to give way to agriculture and the interior of the continent would be populated.

By 1869, a speaker in the Victorian parliament was able to claim that, through the Selection Acts, 'some of the best classes of colonists have been attached to our soil, who would otherwise have been wanderers up and down upon the face of the earth'. Their attachment to the soil was proclaimed on the surveyors' maps, where the names of the successful selectors were enclosed within the solid grid lines of the surveyors, overlaying the land's geographical features and obscuring the faint claims of the prior Aboriginal occupiers. Some of the selectors were Irish immigrants who established viable potato farms on patches of well-watered soil around towns such as Kilmore, north of Melbourne. And it was estimated that perhaps a hundred Aborigines were working as independent farmers in New South Wales by the 1880s, some having obtained land by purchase while others obtained it through the Selection Acts. While some 20 000 Victorian selectors had settled on around three million acres by 1878, many of them were faced with unbearable financial burdens and hamstrung by ignorance of Australian farming methods and distance from markets.

In time, most of the land ended up where it had begun, in the hands of squatters who had used a variety of unscrupulous stratagems to secure their holdings, or at least the choicest parts of those holdings without which the adjoining land was valueless, or who bought back land from unsuccessful selectors. Moreover, across much of northern Australia this was the time when squatters spread out across broad swathes of the semi-arid interior. The Queensland *Land Act* of 1860 allowed properties up to 100 square miles to be leased by pastoralists for as little as ten shillings a square mile per year. Some were joined together to make virtual pastoral principalities, with one property in western Queensland amounting to more than 25 000 square kilometres. Although these were whittled down by subsequent laws, a Queensland property in 1891 still managed to shear more than half a million sheep drawn from its 11 000 square kilometres.

Despite the intentions of the legislators being thwarted in such a barefaced manner, their aim of strengthening the effective claim of proprietorship over the continent was partially achieved. Although a royal commission in 1878 warned of the selected land reverting to 'pastoral wilderness', squatters now had the pressure of legislation, the competition from selectors and the certainty of their tenure to encourage them to fence their land and build substantial houses upon it. Moreover, the gold-induced expansion of population and the extension of railways and river transport made agricultural production economical where it had never been so before. As the law demanded, many squatters could profitably mix agriculture with pastoralism. They could till the soil and thereby establish moral proprietorship over these former 'wastelands'. Between 1860 and 1900, the number of acres being cropped across Australia increased nearly eightfold to more than 8.5 million acres.

Some of it was on the irrigated land along the Murray River where the Victorian government gave a quarter of a million acres on good terms to the Chaffey brothers on the understanding that they develop a new centre of population in the colony's north-west. Officials optimistically predicted that the land, once irrigated, might support a population of half a million people growing grapes, fruit and vegetables for the tables of Australian cities and even for export, as wine and dried fruit, to Britain and Europe. Other vine growers had been established earlier along the upper Murray, where cheap Chinese labour did much of the work. It would not be the first time that non-European labour would be used to help secure the European claim over a continent from which non-Europeans were even then being excluded. Chinese fencing gangs, cutting up the red-gum forests along the Murray, also helped to secure the properties of squatters across the Riverina district now that they had a legislative requirement to enclose their land.

Those selectors who were successful in securing blocks of land found that the laws of the parliament were often overruled by the laws of the economy. It was no good cultivating what could not be transported economically to a market; it was no good grazing on land that was too small to return a livable income; and the isolation of the bush failed to provide the necessary amenities of civilised life—schools, shops, churches, people to talk to—all the complex tapestry of daily life common in closely settled, rural Europe that both constrained and sustained the individual. So, despite the ongoing political pressure to closely settle the land, relatively few colonists wanted to live in the bush. As Beverley Kingston observed, the widespread desire in the 1860s to own 'a small farm in a fertile valley' had been transformed by the 1880s into a desire to own 'a small cottage on its own block of land not too far from a suburban railway line'. As a result, Australia became one of the most urbanised nations on earth, huddling mainly in towns and cities along the eastern seaboard.

By 1891, two-thirds of the Australian colonists lived in towns and cities, a higher proportion than anywhere else in the world. Another remarkable feature of Australia's population distribution was the primacy of her capital cities. Not only did the colonists cluster in urban areas, but they overwhelmingly clustered in the capital cities of each colony. Not only were these cities bigger than their nearest rivals, but they were all on the coast.

Moreover, once established the capitals stayed where they were regardless of other developments such as gold rushes or the development of inland transport by railway and riverboat. This left the relatively ludicrous position of Brisbane and Perth remaining the capitals of colonies which stretched more than 1000 miles to their north.

There were a number of reasons why these seaboard capitals were able to dominate the subordinate settlements so overwhelmingly. They were ports of entry to rich hinterlands while the growth of alternative ports was hampered by customs regulations. Vessels with cargoes for Geelong had first to call at Melbourne to clear at the Customs House before proceeding to Geelong. Similarly, on their return voyage to Britain, a ship taking wool from Geelong had to clear from Melbourne's Customs House before leaving Australian shores. By the time this regulatory impediment was removed, Melbourne had established itself firmly as the colonial capital and attracted many of the maritime industries.

Being the colonial capital, the organs of government gave such settlements a decided advantage over their rivals, providing a solid core of employment that built up an inertia against change. The erection of government buildings also provided a powerful argument against shifting the capital. Such arguments were used at different times against robbing both Hobart and Adelaide of their status as colonial capitals. The development of railways, mainly in the 30 years from the 1860s to 1890, also militated against changing the often chance location of the capitals, cementing their dominance as they spread out like a spider web to snare much of the colony's trade.

As for the relatively high rate of urbanisation, that was largely a reflection of the economic realities of the continent, with its relatively poor soil dictating large properties supported by small, widely scattered towns. The first settlements were looking outwards, to trade and to the exploitation of the maritime resources of the Pacific. When the interior was unlocked by the crossing of the Blue Mountains, the pastoralism that was practised was not labour intensive. To be economically competitive with European pastoralists, colonial shepherds had to mind many more sheep. Each shepherd in early New South Wales cared for perhaps 800–1000 sheep, and sometimes up to several thousand, compared with perhaps 100 in Europe. So pastoral properties were widely scattered with relatively few workers, thereby failing to foster the growth of many towns as intensive agriculture would have done. Moreover, they employed overwhelmingly single male workers rather than married couples with children. This restricted the rural population, along with the demand for such services as shops, schools and churches.

It was in the seaboard cities where most British subsidies and investments were concentrated, creating artificial wealth centres that set up a self-sustaining cycle that attracted yet more population. The continent's limited river systems made inland transport largely reliant upon the more expensive roads, thereby increasing the cost of living in rough relation to the distance from the coast. Most of the immigrants to Australia, both bond and free, were urban dwellers from Britain or elsewhere who preferred to take the chance of finding familiar work in the towns rather than the certainty of finding unfamiliar work in a countryside that many viewed as hostile. Unlike North America, there was no imperative to 'go west' to fertile land accessible by broad rivers and lakes and to a western coastline sprinkled with gold. In Australia, the land became more arid and difficult to access the further people moved from the east coast. And when gold was discovered in Western Australia and the Northern Territory in the 1880s and 1890s, it was easier and cheaper to reach it by sea rather than overland in the manner of the American '49ers'.

Ironically, the work of the explorers, which had been meant to open up the interior, deterred urban dwellers from trying their luck in the bush. The statue of the ill-fated Burke and Wills stared down on Melbournians with its silent message of despair and death that awaited intruders into the interior. It was not only the aridity of the interior but the whole gamut of climatic disasters that threatened those who ventured forth. In June 1852, torrential rains caused the Murrumbidgee River to burst its banks and sweep away the towns of Gundagai and Wagga Wagga along with many of their inhabitants. The previous year, a horrendous bushfire swept across Victoria, destroying hundreds of homes, thousands of head of livestock and some ten inhabitants. The smoke from the fires blocked out the sun across Bass Strait in Tasmania. Many Victorians thought the 'Great Day of Wrath was come', while the artist William Strutt left the urban dwellers of Melbourne a dramatic, 3.3-metre-wide painting of the conflagration, providing them with a permanent reminder of the perils to be faced in the bush. Life on the land was also imperilled by the occurrence of droughts, when the lack of rain for years at a time left the interior parched, its livestock dead and its inhabitants ruined. And then there were the snakes and insect plagues, and the rogues and villains who haunted the bush tracks.

A common complaint of newcomers to Australia was that of a female immigrant passing through Hobart who protested at the presence of the 'great many fleas and bugs; and many mosquitoes that bite worse than bugs'. A visitor to New South Wales also noted that the mosquitoes there were 'so thick as almost to make us mad with their bites', while there were also

> ... numerous nests of Ants which are inch long, and whose bites are dangerous; centipedes and spiders as big as a man's hand. But, what terrifies us most is that the country abounds in many kinds of dangerous serpents, the bites of which are instant death.

To try and repel them, the Irish exile Sir Henry Brown Hayes imported 500 tons of supposedly 'snake-repellent turf' from his serpentless homeland to surround his Vaucluse house in Sydney, employing 'only genuine Irish convicts' to dig it in. If such dangers and annoyances were not enough to deter people from venturing into the bush, the lack of civilised amenities helped to tie many people to the towns and cities. In contrast, Australian cities had become by many standards the equal of those in Europe.

Following the gold rushes, Melbourne had become the second largest city in the Southern Hemisphere and its wide streets boasted shops, offices and public buildings that would have done credit to their counterparts in Europe. The colonies were shrouding their rough, convict days behind the civilised constructions of their coastal cities. While a large crowd had gathered in 1854 to watch a convict drop to his death on a scaffold outside Adelaide gaol, the execution of Malachi Martin in 1862 was done decently out of sight behind the gaol walls. The colonial crowds went instead to the new stone-built cathedrals of knowledge, the public libraries, art galleries and museums that were set imposingly on wide city streets, or to the suburban mechanics institutes where weighty matters were discussed in a general spirit of optimism. At work, these urban dwellers enjoyed conditions that were sometimes the envy of Europe while, back home, they managed to supplement their wages by growing fruit and vegetables and raising poultry on their domestic allotments. They industriously tilled their patches of suburban soil in ways that allowed them to feel a real sense of proprietorship over the tamed landscape while the surrounding houses promoted a comforting sense of community that was largely absent in the bush. Detached cottages in Sydney were described as having 'verandahs in front, and enclosed by a neat wooden paling' with 'a commodious garden attached, commonly decked out with flowers, and teeming with culinary delicacies'. This description dated from the mid–1820s, but it held good for all Australian cities during the 19th and much of the 20th centuries.

The hostility of the Aborigines, potential or real, also deterred urban dwellers from venturing forth up-country. Stories of cannibalism by Aborigines chilled the blood of urban newspaper readers, while the pitch darkness of the bush concealed the source of such myriad fears, as George Carrington revealed when recalling his first night as a shepherd in north Queensland in the late 1860s:

> *All the horrible stories I had ever heard thronged to my recollection of men attacked by savages and murdered, of ghastly corpses subjected to frightful mutilations, of dead men lying unregarded and found days after in lonely huts. Then I began to picture to myself the dreary bush outside, and the forms that might even then be creeping up in silence shortly to be broken by unearthly yells. I lay now broad awake, and the perspiration streamed from every pore. My hearing seemed unnaturally sharpened ... all around the hut I fancied I heard the crackling of dry sticks, and the rustling of grass ...*

The increasing concentration of Australians in seaboard cities during the last four decades of the 19th century was occurring as the last of the Aboriginal resistance was being broken in northern Australia, allowing the colonists more or less uncontested occupation of the continent.

From the landing of the First Fleet in 1788, white men had been determined to pacify the bush, to invest what they saw as nature in its wild state with the labour of man. To many of these early European observers, the bush was seen as alien and forbidding. Early Australian paintings were mostly of the bush subdued, along with its Aboriginal inhabitants, with the painter having his back to the bush and painting where the stamp of man had imposed itself on the landscape. Aborigines were often placed peacefully in the foreground, in order to locate the scene for the viewer, but the Aborigines were usually dominated by the signs of European settlement. Where the Aborigines were specially featured, it was often to contrast their lack of civilisation, or their succumbing to alcohol or other degradation, with the civilised signs of English settlement.

As the interior was opened up by pastoralism, possession was established by guns and poison and confirmed by government leases as the straight lines of the surveyors carved up the countryside for European occupation. Paintings of the squatters' properties helped to confirm their proprietorship, invariably providing proof on canvas that the squatters had fulfilled their God's injunction to make the earth fruitful by investing it with the hand of human industry. The paintings were not of sheep wandering in the wilderness but of a wilderness tamed by the hand of man, with the bush usually being cleared and pushed to the margins of the painting while the fine house of the squatter occupies the centre of the painting, surrounded by fenced land. They were paintings of the bush conquered by man, and usually they were done for the person who had done the conquering and were destined to hang on the wall of the self-same house. With the coming of photography in the 1850s, paintings were supplemented by photographs and later by a succession of colonial cyclopaedias that recorded among other things the major pastoral properties and their owners, complete with photographs of the physical improvements they had imposed upon the wilderness.

Towards the end of the 19th century, with the gentrification of Australian society wrought by sheep and gold, the bush was pacified in the minds of the mainly urban colonists by the soft brushstrokes of the so-called Heidelberg School of artists. They were generalised scenes of 'typical' bush characters—the digger, the shearer, the small selector, the bushranger—and were painted to be hung in art galleries or fine city houses. They were not sold to the selector or the shearer or even stolen by the bushranger. They were a means by which urban Australians connected themselves to the bush, in the same way as they moulded Australian animals onto their urban architecture where live native animals no longer scrambled. Plaster possums stared sightlessly down upon suburban gardens which featured rose bushes and deciduous English trees, while Sydney's Zoological Society organised the 'introduction and acclimatisation of [European] songbirds and game'.

In the same way, readers of the proudly nationalistic *Bulletin* could read stories of the bush, chuckling at the humour and wondering at the heroism told in these stories as they sat crammed in their seats on the new cable trams. With a few notable exceptions, such popular evocations of the bush genre as 'Banjo' Paterson's *Clancy of the Overflow* and *The Man from Snowy River* tended to romanticise bush life and thereby help to pacify the bush in the minds of the city clerk. In Paterson's view, having consorted with the squattocracy, the bush was the place where real men lived virile lives in clean surroundings as opposed to the sapping tedium and filth of the city. A more gloomy view of the bush was provided in the short stories of Barbara Baynton who had lived as a selector's wife only to have her husband run out on her. In Baynton's view, the bush was a place of tedium and filth and horror rather than heroics. She emphasised the terror of the bush, with the isolation and brutality of its male-dominated society where the bushmen were idiots or rogues, or both. As a result, all except one of Baynton's stories were excluded from the pages of the *Bulletin*. As its literary editor observed, Baynton's 'truthful glimpses of Australian life, graphically expressed, could not (would not) have been printed in any Australian paper'.

The Christmas 1899 edition of the Baynton-less *Bulletin* carried the usual bush stories and poems, while claiming that the colonists were developing 'a nostalgia for the breadth of the bush and the breath of the gums' which more than equals their nostalgia 'for the green turf and the hawthorn-buds in pleasant Warwickshire lanes'. In the same issue, the Victorian and New South Wales railways ran full-page advertisements extolling the joys of taking a Christmas excursion into the countryside. However, nowhere was the 'bush' mentioned by name in these advertisements. That might conjure up the wrong images for the pleasure-seekers of Sydney and Melbourne. Instead, the delights were extolled of boating on the Hawkesbury River—scene of so many massacres and floods in the not too distant past—and of alternating that with 'delightful rambles among the ferns and flowers of the surrounding country'. Or the 'holiday-maker' could escape from the 'routine of city life' by climbing Australia's highest mountain, Kosciusko, to enjoy the 'refreshing coolness of an Alpine climate during the hottest months of the year' and possibly take silent comfort from the fact that, after just over a century of occupation, they were master of all they surveyed from its lofty heights.

By 1900, much of the Australian continent had felt the impact of the European invasion. The Aboriginal population of perhaps one million people in 1788 had been reduced by 1900 to just 60 000. Most Europeans were convinced that the Aborigines were a dying race, that their days on the continent were numbered. Some Australians noted it with regret, others with a sense of smug satisfaction. Few felt guilty about the expected passing of the Aborigines from the landscape. They believed it was ordained by Darwinism and the Bible, and was beyond the power of Europeans to avert. By 1880, the *Bulletin* was writing with a sense of resignation that largely set the tone for the next 50 years about the Aborigines being 'doomed' and beyond 'preserving'. 'All we can now do', it suggested, 'is to give an opiate to the dying man, and when he expires bury him respectably'. Accordingly, the Aborigines largely passed from beneath the threatening shadow of the native police rifles to the comforts of the Bible and the protective strictures of government regulations as missionaries and government protectors took over their care and supervision in isolated reserves.

As British Australians accepted that the Aborigines seemed doomed to disappear, the supplanters began to take over their symbols. In 1887, a Queensland workers' newspaper took as its name the Aborigines' weapon, the boomerang. According to the fevered view of its editor, William Lane, Australians were the apex of the white man's evolutionary development and it would be 'in Australia that the battle against Nature's brutal laws will be fought out; it is here in Australia that human society will develop itself, and that the yet-unanswered riddles of the Sphinx will be finally solved'. Five years later, this passing Australian patriot ended his antipodean interlude without solving the riddles, taking 200 of his followers to establish what he dubbed as 'New Australia' in the wilds of Paraguay, a socialist nirvana for 'those who long to be manly'. It was a miserable failure.

Before departing disillusioned from Australia, Lane had been of that crowd who had taken comfort from the apparent remorseless demise of the Aborigines. Their removal would leave the continent free for the white civilisation that would arise from its sturdy sons and comely daughters. His faith in this outcome was shattered by the apparent crushing of the labour movement following several unsuccessful strikes. But it was also tested by the presence of Chinese Australians who sullied his social Darwinist view of how a 'pure' Australian race would progress to a new nirvana. Along with many other Australians, Lane feared that millions of Chinese might invade the continent to supplant the British Australians as they had done to the Aborigines.

The Chinese who had arrived in search of gold, and the Pacific Islanders who had been brought to Queensland to work on sugar plantations, combined in the minds of British Australians to pose a double-edged threat to their occupation of the continent. They held out the prospect of Australia being overrun by alien invaders and they reminded the colonists that they would never succeed in achieving the moral proprietorship of the continent unless they could show the overcrowded populations of Asia that they were effectively occupying the entire continent. That meant occupying and tilling the tropical soil as well as the soil of the more temperate regions. However, it was widely believed that the tropics were an unsuitable environment for Europeans, that the climate would sap their strength and virility.

Looking north from their comfortable south-eastern cities, Australians saw instead that the tropics was being populated by Pacific island labourers, Japanese and Malay pearl divers, and Chinese goldminers on the Palmer River goldfield near Cooktown in north Queensland and at Pine Creek in the Northern Territory. The surveying of some 600000 acres to encourage settlement near Darwin had simply led to a brief frenzy of land speculation in London and little in the way of population. By 1877, Chinese men outnumbered European men on the Palmer River goldfield by 17000 to 1500. In the Northern Territory, administered by South Australia, there were 3500 Chinese in 1879, mainly on the Pine Creek goldfield, compared with just 460 Europeans. Some of these Chinese were imported by the South Australian government. As the gold ran out in the late 1880s, some of the Chinese walked across into Western Australia to seek work on the cattle properties of the Kimberley district or drifted south towards Perth, partly defeating that colony's restrictions against the entry of Chinese just as their compatriots had defeated Victorian restrictions in the 1850s. However, the Western Australian restrictions were more comprehensive than those in Victoria, effectively denying the Chinese the right to participate in a range of economic activities from mining to fishing. As a result, their numbers remained low, just 1000 in 1891. They were joined in the north-west by Malays and Japanese brought as indentured labourers for the pearl fishing industry around Broome, which had the appearance of being an Asian township. Supplying the isolated pastoralists of the hinterland with goods were Afghan camel drivers who dominated the transport industry across arid Australia.

Not only were the Chinese in large numbers in the tropics, but those in rural areas in the southern colonies were moving into thriving Chinese quarters in the cities of Sydney and Melbourne, where they set up furniture factories and competed directly with European tradesmen. Between 1871 and 1891, the number of Chinese in Sydney increased more than tenfold, from 336 Chinese comprising 4.7 per cent of the Chinese population in New South Wales, to 3465, comprising 26 per cent of the state's Chinese. Moreover, there were fresh arrivals of Chinese into New South Wales, with 2000 stepping ashore in 1880 and 3500 in 1881.

In 1879, when the first intercolonial workers' congress met in Sydney, the most heated discussion was on the subject of the Chinese. One delegate suggested that Chinese entry had to be stopped to prevent the 'supplanting of Europeans by Chinamen' since, he claimed, there were 400 million Chinese people who 'would come here readily enough if they saw a chance'. Another warned of the polluting of young white girls by Chinese men such that 'he did not know what colour the population would be by and by'.

Another likened Chinese people to apes: 'The smell and presence of them were alike offensive.' It was not just racism that motivated these union leaders. They were also motivated by the desire to protect hard-won living standards. The Chinese had been used as strike-breakers at a goldmine in Clunes in 1873, of which the Eureka rebel Peter Lalor was a director, and to reduce the wages of firemen in 1878.

The colonies reacted to the popular pressure by erecting an even higher legislative barrier, mainly by way of the poll tax on the entry of Chinese and tightening the restrictions on the number of Chinese that could be brought in any one vessel. But the laws varied widely between the colonies, from one Chinese for every 100 tons of a vessel's tonnage in Victoria to one for every ten tons in Queensland. To prevent them moving between colonies, customs officers along the Murray River and on other inland borders charged the poll tax there as well. In 1882, a Chinese man with a wooden leg going from southern New South Wales to Melbourne to get a new one was arrested when he tried to cross back into New South Wales. He was fined £20 or 12 months in gaol.

Such draconian laws caused Chinese numbers to stabilise at around 10 000 each in Queensland, New South Wales and Victoria, 4000 in the Northern Territory, and 1000 each in Tasmania and Western Australia. As such, they comprised just over one per cent of the European population. Despite stabilising their numbers, the agitation against them increased. An intercolonial congress in 1888 agreed to increase restrictions still further by raising the tonnage limit and poll tax and preventing their naturalisation. Even Western Australia and Tasmania eventually complied, thereby creating a continent-wide barrier to the entry of Chinese and to their movement across colonial borders.

At the tiny Queensland border settlement of Camooweal in 1898, the local police constable intercepted ten impoverished and exhausted Chinese who had walked overland from Darwin, leaving behind debts and the exhausted goldfield as they sought work in Queensland. The succeeding days brought another 17 Chinese straggling into the tiny settlement. Several others had died *en route*. With just £8 and three old horses between the lot of them, the men were arrested and fined £50 each for crossing into Queensland without a permit. They were then walked a further 200 miles to Cloncurry to catch a stagecoach to Hughenden and then a train to Townsville where they served out their six months' gaol sentence. At the end of it all, the government considered arresting them again and starting the cycle over, but instead put them on a ship to Darwin, escorted by the constable from Camooweal.

The official persecution took its toll on the Chinese population, which declined through deaths and departures to just 30 000 by 1901. To many colonists, the experience with the Chinese and the difficulties of agreeing on a common approach proved the benefit of a federation of all the colonies that could then ensure what everyone wanted, a white Australia. Such a creation would allow the society of mainly British Australians to secure itself from being supplanted by Chinese or other Asian immigrants while also allowing such a cohesive society to better defend itself against a more direct threat of invasion.

Recommended Reading

Barbara Baynton, 1990, *Bush Studies*, Angus&Robertson, Sydney.

Graeme Davison, 1979, *The Rise and Fall of Marvellous Melbourne*, Melbourne University Press, Melbourne.

Shirley Fitzgerald, 1987, *Rising Damp: Sydney 1870–90*, Oxford University Press, Melbourne.

K. S. Inglis, 1974, *The Australian Colonists*, Melbourne University Press, Melbourne.

Beverley Kingston, 1988, *Oxford History of Australia*, Vol. 3, Oxford University Press, Melbourne.

Andrew Markus, 1979, *Fear and Hatred: Purifying Australia and California 1850–1901*, Hale & Iremonger, Sydney.

Patrick O'Farrell, 1987, *The Irish in Australia*, New South Wales University Press, Sydney.

C. A. Price, 1974, *The Great White Walls Are Built*, Australian National University Press, Canberra.

Eric Rolls, 1992, *Sojourners*, University of Queensland Press, Brisbane.

Geoffrey Serle, 1977, *The Rush to be Rich: A History of the Colony of Victoria, 1883–1889*, Melbourne University Press, Melbourne.

C. T. Stannage (ed.), 1981, *A New History of Western Australia*, University of Western Australia Press, Perth.

Gavin Souter, 1991, *A Peculiar People: William Lane's Australian Utopians in Paraguay*, University of Queensland Press, Brisbane.

11

'THE TIME
FOR UNION
IS
COME'

While explorers were conquering the physical landscape of the continent, mapping its features into a continental unity, the political landscape was fracturing into separate colonies. One of the most important ways for Europeans to secure a long-term claim to the continent was to create, as the founding prime minister Edmund Barton later phrased it, 'a nation for a continent', to forge the separate colonies, each laying claim to different parts of the continent, into a single nation that would lay claim to the lot. But the initial impulse in Australia was to divide the continent up for easier digestion by inhabitants clamouring for their separate places in the sun. It made administrative sense, and there were only occasional external threats impelling the colonists to band together in a defensive union. Even then, the power of the British navy generally reassured them as to the sanctity of their separate existences.

For a time, as British settlements were established from Moreton Bay to the Derwent River, political control remained firmly in the hands of the governor at Sydney. In fact, a succession of governors could hardly control Sydney's hinterland let alone distant outposts such as Van Diemen's Land or Westernport Bay. With the inexorable spread of settlement, there were calls for separation from Sydney's control. Van Diemen's Land was hived off from New South Wales in 1826, the same year the Swan River settlement was set up from London. In 1836, the settlement of Adelaide was established as the capital of a new colony of South Australia, while the Port Phillip District was separated from New South Wales in 1851 to become the new colony of Victoria. Eight years later the settlement at Moreton Bay, renamed Brisbane, became the capital of a new colony that stretched northwards to Cape York Peninsula. With a few minor changes, the internal political boundaries of Australia were now established.

The colonial boundaries mostly followed unseen lines of latitude and longitude, overlaying ancient Aboriginal boundaries and pathways and helping to confirm the fact of their dispossession. The colonists gradually realised that, if they were not to be dispossessed in their turn, they would have to combine into a single political unit in order at least to coordinate their economic and defence policies. In 1850, when the British government extended self-government to the Australian colonies, except for Western Australia, it had originally included plans for a federal council. But the proposal, which was criticised as being unworkable, was omitted from the Act before it was passed. The idea for such a council had been suggested from Sydney in 1846 when the colonial secretary, Deas Thomson, had proposed a central authority to connect the colonies and coordinate policies on such matters of common concern as migration and customs duties. Although it found favour in London, it was not imposed upon the colonies since it was believed that it would come naturally. But it was not to be.

Until the gold rushes, the colonies were largely separate coastal communities linked mainly by sea and with little contact by land. The gold rushes changed all that. Apart from diluting the rising sense of nativism, they increased the population in the border regions, particularly along the upper reaches of the Murray River between New South Wales and Victoria after gold was discovered in the vicinity. Cross-border trade became an important issue, as each colony had a different rate of import duty on such essentials as spirits. To protect their particular interests, the colonies set up customs posts along their borders.

When the first riverboat managed to navigate its tortuous way along the twisting Murray River from South Australia to Albury in 1854, its captain was met by a newly appointed New South Wales Customs officer who interrogated him about cargo that had been off-loaded *en route* on the New South Wales side of the river without the required import duty being paid. Such impediments to the free flow of colonial trade were not only established along the Murray but also far inland at such isolated places as Birdsville, on the edge of the Simpson Desert. It is not surprising in this competitive atmosphere that a call by the radical Presbyterian minister John Dunmore Lang for an independent Australian republic was not answered. Although a committee of the Victorian Legislative Assembly subsequently reported in 1857 on the prospects for federal union, suggesting that 'the time for union is come', it had not. Not by a long shot. Instead it was a time for jealousies and protecting one's individual interests.

Not only did the colonies impose different import duties but, to further protect their interests, they established railways that sought to drain trade towards their own seaboard capitals rather than have it leak to neighbouring colonies. New South Wales, whose border started on the Victorian side of the Murray River, also resisted moves to build bridges across the Murray so as to impede its citizens in the Riverina from trading with Melbourne. Instead, railways were built radiating out from Sydney to capture the trade of its own interior as well as some of the river trade of the adjoining colonies. In an act of short-sighted folly, each of the colonies built their railways using different gauge tracks in a deliberate attempt to contain their trade within their own borders.

The differing tariff policies, particularly between protectionist Victoria and free trade New South Wales, were a major factor militating against the federation of the colonies. Victoria used its highly protective tariff as the main source of government revenue and to build up its industrial base. The number of factories in Melbourne increased from 400 in 1861 to 3000 in 1891. In contrast, New South Wales' much greater area allowed it to raise much of its government revenue through the sale or lease of Crown land, while import duties were imposed principally as a revenue measure, rather than a protective measure, on a limited range of goods such as spirits and tobacco, and generally at a lower rate than in Victoria. This created powerful commercial and industrial bodies who saw federation, which would involve a common tariff policy, as a threat to their interests.

But technology was drawing the sanguine citizens of the various colonies together. Distance between them was shortened by the telegraph wires which had connected Sydney and Melbourne by 1861, and later joined Adelaide and Perth to the eastern colonies, while a transcontinental wire was strung across the continent to connect with the telegraph that linked the rest of Britain's eastern empire to London. From the 1850s, an increasing number of steamships brought speed and regularity to maritime communications around the continent, while railways did the same across the interior. Melbourne and Sydney were connected by train in 1883, albeit with a change of train on the border at Albury to accommodate the change of gauge. Although newspapers retained a provincial focus, national magazines like the influential *Bulletin*, established in 1880 with its cry of 'Australia for the Australians', crossed colonial borders to cater for an increasingly educated readership. The combined effect of these influences, together with the perceived need to implement a common policy towards Chinese immigrants, prompted talk of federation to resurface in 1881 when the New South Wales politician Henry Parkes suggested that a Federal Council be established to pave the way for federation.

The son of a Warwickshire tenant farmer, Parkes had left for Australia in 1839 at the age of 24 seeking the opportunities it seemed to offer for himself and his young wife who bore him a daughter as the ship sailed into Sydney. Although an ivory turner by trade, and a poet by inclination, he went into the bush, albeit just outside Sydney, to work in the vineyard of one of the colony's wealthiest landowners. Parkes had been convinced that the bush would provide opportunities for men such as him, allowing them to 'get rich there in no time', but found himself instead living on indifferent rations and sleeping on an 'old door and a sheet of bark'. He left after six months to seek his future in Sydney where he got a sinecure in the Customs department. By 1849, he made his first political speech at a mass meeting called to protest at the arrival of convicts at Sydney, beginning a political career that would take him from budding poet to newspaper editor to premier of New South Wales by 1872. While he pursued affection in the arms of a succession of women, he was pursued in turn by his creditors. His main claim to fame prior to his advocacy of federation was the introduction of a free, compulsory and secular education system for children aged between six and 14. But it is as the 'father of Federation' that Parkes is best known.

In 1882, Parkes had travelled to London by way of the United States. He was fêted in San Francisco as the senior Australian political leader, and he looked the part with his flowing white hair and long white beard. But when he arrived in Washington to meet with the American Secretary of State, the British ambassador interrupted the talks when Parkes raised matters of trade since no instructions had been received from London on the subject. It was an object lesson for Parkes on the limitations of his position and prompted him to call in London for a new relationship of equality between Britain and the colonies. He did not want independence; rather, he wanted the colonies, with their people 'attached to the soil of their birth', to be 'parts really and substantially of the Empire'. He also spent time in Germany, where he visited a torpedo factory and saw this rising rival to the British Empire at first hand.

On his return to Australia, Parkes was hailed as a conquering hero. He was toasted at a banquet in Melbourne from where a special train took him to Wodonga. There a horse-drawn coach carried him beneath a triumphal arch erected on the Murray River bridge. Eight thousand supporters welcomed him home to Sydney and another banquet. Ironically, he lost the election for his Sydney seat soon after but was put forward as the member for Tenterfield, just south of the Queensland border, by a candidate who stood down in his favour. It was an electorate that would have felt the aggravation of the customs duties exacted by the roving band of inspectors protecting the revenue of their respective colonies.

In 1883, an intercolonial conference was called because of fears of French moves in the New Hebrides and a desire by the colonists to prevent the south-west Pacific resuming as a repository for convicts, whether Chinese criminals exiled from Hong Kong by the British, or French convicts exiled to New Caledonia and the New Hebrides. The colonies tried to assert their own

Monroe Doctrine for the south Pacific to prevent any European power claiming additional territory south of the equator, just as the United States' Monroe Doctrine attempted to prevent European powers from interfering in the affairs of North and South America. Queensland had already annexed southern New Guinea in 1883 to forestall the Germans and to promote the commercial interests of the Queensland premier, Sir Thomas McIlwraith. The annexation was not recognised by Britain, concerned at how Queensland would treat the native inhabitants, which agreed instead in 1884 to divide eastern New Guinea between itself and Germany.

A federal council of the various colonies met in 1886 but had no power and limited influence. Although it had originally been suggested by Henry Parkes, New South Wales did not attend. Neither did New Zealand, although Fiji did before it too dropped out. It was not a very propitious beginning for closer cooperation between the colonies. And yet it was a harbinger of bigger things as the federation movement began to gather pace. But there could be no nation without a sense of nationhood. And that was continually being diluted by fresh infusions of immigrants whose loyalties tended to remain fixed to the land from which they had come. Only slowly did links of attachment to their adopted land cause their old links to be attenuated. Those born in the colonies, and who therefore knew no other land but Australia, provided the basis for a resurgent Australian nationalism.

Although his subsequent conservatism damned him in the eyes of radical historians, William Charles Wentworth was the first to give voice to a sense of Australian nationalism. Wentworth was the son of a well-connected father who had been sent into exile to New South Wales to avoid being tried for highway robbery and became a wealthy landowner. Like generations of well-to-do Australian children, young William was sent to London to complete his education, studying at Cambridge where in 1823 he submitted a poem, *Australasia*, for a university competition just six years after Macquarie had adopted Australia as the name for the continent. Wentworth's poem looked forward to the day when Australasia would

> *float, with flag unfurl'd*
> *A new Britannia in another world.*

Although his poem came second, Wentworth returned to Sydney as a hero of the colonial-born and promptly started the radical newspaper, the *Australian*, to propagate his nativist views.

Wentworth's poem expressed a fairly common feeling that has waxed and waned with each succeeding decade – that Australia had the potential to emulate the United States and eventually to take over the leadership of the empire from a declining Britain. But such grand visions, together with the sense of nationalism that gave birth to them, required that there be a majority of native-born Australians who acknowledged the links that united them to one another and which distinguished them from outsiders, even Britons. Such a majority proved elusive as fresh infusions of convicts and immigrants enveloped the growing core of colonial-born Australians, largely smothering the incipient nationalism.

It was not until 1871 that the Australian Natives Association was formed in Melbourne with its call for Australians to 'be as proud of their fair country as any Scotchman, Englishman, or Irishman was of his'. By 1880, the proportion of native-born, white Australians had become a majority of the population. When this was confirmed in the census returns of 1882, a Melbourne businessman took satisfaction from the inexorable ascendancy of the colonial-born over what he called the 'foreigners', by which he meant the British-born, who were being removed by 'Death's remorseless fingers'. Not only would these colonial-born be more nationalistic, but they were generally believed to be finer physical specimens than the British, such that they might give rise to a new superior race. The English writer Anthony Trollope claimed after a visit to Australia, 'The best of our workmen go from us, and produce a race superior to themselves'. In other words, the British emigrants were superior by self-selection, while the native-born Australians were superior by breeding in the Antipodes. This was taken up by other writers such as the Irish MP Michael Davitt who thought that an Australian 'born of British or Irish parent, is the best physically developed man of either of these races'. This was seen as a cause for celebration, holding out hope that Britain's relative decline as a great power, and the apparent declining 'vigour' of its people crammed into industrial cities, could be arrested by the development of its extensive colonies. Ironically, they were writing just as the colonists were increasingly becoming urban-dwelling factory workers and clerks.

Of course, being native-born provides only a rough measure of national feeling. Many native-born Australians, even recently, scorned their birthplace by regarding Britain or elsewhere as 'home'. In contrast, many Britons arriving in the colonies, grateful for the economic opportunities and political freedoms they offered, became committed Australians as they established links to the land and its rhythms. While this growing sense of national identity provided the opportunity for federation, it was the practical needs of the colonists that made it imperative. The mechanisation of factories allowed for economies of scale, leading Victorian manufacturers to seek markets outside their own colony only to find themselves held back by colonial tariffs that protected the small and inefficient manufacturers in each colony. Such tariffs were also a constant irritant to people in the border areas. The severe economic depression of the 1890s, exacerbated by a prolonged drought, prompted people to look to federation as something to invigorate businesses and to provide federal regulation of banks in order to prevent a repetition of the disastrous closures caused by the depression.

The rise of trade unions during the 1880s, and a series of bitter strikes in the early 1890s, led conservatives to fear that an inexorable socialist tide would sweep away conservative governments and even private property itself. The strikes, involving some 50 000 workers, began in the maritime industries in a great test of will between bosses and workers against a background of worsening economic conditions. The bosses were backed by the armed power of the colonial state, with Colonel Tom Price notoriously instructing the men of the Mounted Rifles in Melbourne, if confronted by protesting strikers, to 'fire low and lay them out so that the duty will not have to be performed again'.

In 1891, shearers had struck across Queensland in protest at attempts by pastoralists to erode their hard-won wages and working conditions and to force the introduction of shearing machines. They were also protesting against the use by pastoralists of 'Chinese and coloured aliens'. The Chinese were now seen as a greater threat than the Aborigines and almost equalled them in numbers. What was worse, the Chinese were increasing in numbers while the Aborigines seemed set on the path to extinction. Accordingly, 'pure-bred Aborigines' were admitted to membership of the shearers' union while 'coloured Asiatics, South Sea Islanders, Kaffirs or Chinese' were all rigorously excluded. Gathered together in camps outside towns in western Queensland, the striking shearers practised rifle drill with sticks beneath the rebellious flag of the Southern Cross and warned darkly of an 'Australian Revolution'. Some stole out at night to burn down the shearing sheds of the squatters. For their part, the authorities warned darkly of dispersing these 'nomads of the far West' in the manner of the Aborigines and, in an operation that smacked of Eureka, sent several thousand mounted troops, police and volunteers, armed with artillery and machine-guns, to combat the strikers. Although the violence was minimal, 13 unionists were gaoled for three years on charges of conspiracy and rioting. With the suppression of the strikes, the trade unions switched their attention to political organisation, hoping to achieve their objectives through parliamentary means.

By 1899, the first labour party government in the world took power in Queensland, albeit for just six days. By creating a federal parliament with a conservative constitution, the establishment hoped this tide of reform might be kept at bay. They were right. The new federal parliament had two houses, with the states electing an equal number of members for the upper house or Senate, with senators being elected for six-year terms rather than three years as in the lower house, or House of Representatives. Every three years, only half the Senate had to face election. The relatively unrepresentative Senate usually played the conservative, blocking function that the writers of the constitution intended for it. Only rarely was the Labor Party able to have a majority in both houses of parliament. More recently, the rise of smaller parties, such as the Greens and Australian Democrats, has meant that neither Labor nor the conservative coalition parties has been able to count on control of the Senate. Even when the reformist Labor Party was able to control both houses, the constitution, rigidly interpreted by the High Court, remained as a usually reliable, fall-back position for the conservatives. In this, the court reflected the innate conservatism of the Australian people who almost invariably rejected radical changes to the constitution when it was put to them at referendum.

The combination of tariffs, defence and the restriction of non-European immigration provided the main impetus for federation. They were issues that went to the heart of white Australians' fears about their ability to secure their claim of effective proprietorship over the continent. In 1885, Parkes had opposed sending men to avenge the death of General Gordon in the Sudan, arguing that it was better for them to stay home and 'subjugate the soil'. Otherwise it might be the Chinese, or the Japanese or the Pacific Islanders who would do so. Although the colonies finally agreed in 1888, the centenary of the British invasion, to restrict the entry of Chinese immigrants, there was no agreement as to other races. Queensland still allowed Pacific Islanders to work on sugar plantations, and Japanese, Malays and Filipinos to work in the pearling industry. A federal parliament was needed to ensure a continental approach to this question.

The colonies were also increasingly nervous about their defence. During the 1870s, Britain had withdrawn its armed forces from Australia leaving the colonies responsible for their own local defence. When the telegraph cable to London was accidentally cut in 1888, it caused a brief invasion scare, with the Victorian government sending gunboats to Port Phillip Heads to mount a minuscule guard against the anticipated Russian attack. While each colony developed a token naval force, the 1890s saw the emergence of the modern battleship as the decisive weapon of naval warfare. No single colony could hope to afford one. Together, they might be able to construct a respectable naval force. And there were an increasing number of external threats forcing the Australian colonists to look to their defences.

Competition between the European empires was spilling over into the Pacific. Russia spread into Manchuria, while China was carved up by the European powers. The Japanese had scored decisive victories against China in 1894 and had concluded a commercial treaty with Britain. The United States also began to loom large in the Pacific, demanding an 'open door' policy in China to allow entry for her trade and annexing the Philippines in 1898 after its victory over Spain. Closer to Australia were the French in New Caledonia and the New Hebrides, while the Germans shared a border with the British Empire in New Guinea. Colonists began to realise that their combined population of less than four million trying to occupy an entire continent left them vulnerable to the territorial ambitions of these powers and that Britain was not necessarily able to guarantee their security.

For all these reasons, federation was an idea whose time had come. But it still depended upon political leaders to fly the federal banner and argue its merits against the persistent opposition that it encountered from those fearing that it would erode their economic advantages. Although Parkes was convinced of the sense of federation, he pushed the idea of a federal council only to see his colleagues retreat at the perceived threat to their cherished policy of free trade from protectionist Victoria. When he was returned as premier in 1887 at the age of 72, he introduced measures to restrict Chinese immigration and proposed to celebrate the centenary of Governor Phillip's landing at Botany Bay by renaming New South Wales as Australia. Although he dropped the latter idea in the face of vociferous Victorian protests, he spoke grandly at a centennial banquet of the coming federation. Three thousand of Sydney's poor were also treated to food and tobacco at government expense, although Parkes dismissed a suggestion that Aborigines should also be included, remarking that it would 'remind them that we have robbed them'.

In 1889, Parkes was again returned as premier, this time with federation as part of his platform. Several months later, he boasted to the British governor that he could federate the colonies in 12 months if he wanted to. 'Why don't you do it—it would be a grand finish to your life', riposted the governor. Parkes took up the challenge while also bringing some order to his private life, following the death of his wife, by marrying his long-time mistress. Although his renewed call for federation was rebuffed by Victoria, it met with a more favourable reception in Brisbane. Returning from there by train, Parkes stopped off in Tenterfield where he made his famous speech publicly calling for a convention to devise a federal constitution. He brandished an alarming report by visiting British general Bevan Edwards on the state of the colonial defences which called for federal control of the separate colonial forces, a federal military college and a uniform railway gauge as the best security for the colonies. Otherwise Australia was 'in great danger'.

A subsequent meeting of colonial representatives in Melbourne secured agreement in principle to work for federation. At the subsequent banquet, Parkes proposed a toast to a united Australasia, proclaiming that the

crimson thread of kinship runs through us all. Even the native-born Australians are Britons, as much as the men born within the cities of London and Glasgow. We know the value of their British origin. We know that we represent a race ... for the purposes of settling new colonies, which never had its equal on the face of the earth.

The proposed act of federation would ensure that these 'settled' colonies could be more securely held against the rising races of Europe and Asia who might be inclined to challenge the British hold. Although elected president of the second convention held in Sydney in 1891, he took little role in it after badly breaking his leg when a horse-drawn cab in which he and his wife were travelling overturned in a Sydney street. That same year, he lost power as premier and in 1895 lost his seat in parliament. He also lost his second wife but was remarried within months to his 23-year-old servant. Although the marriage caused consternation in the best circles of Sydney, as a *Bulletin* cartoon observed when asking why Parkes remarried so soon: 'At 80 one cannot afford to wait!' Five months later he was dead. Other politicians took up the banner of federation and carried it through to fruition. They were mostly colonial-born and all were of British origin. 'Amongst the fifty names of the members, not one is of foreign derivation', historian Ernest Scott huffed with satisfaction.

They created on 1 January 1901 a Commonwealth of Australia, a self-governing federation of the former colonies that fell short of being an independent nation. As the Victorian politician Alfred Deakin observed, the federation was not a nation but simply 'preludes the advent of a nation'. It had no control over its foreign policy, which was decided in London, and it had little control over its defence. British laws continued to take precedence over Australian laws. And the states remained very powerful, retaining control of such areas as police, education, health, railways, ports and immigration schemes while also receiving a guaranteed three-quarters of the income raised by the new federal tariff. As a representative of the Melbourne Chamber of Commerce told a London audience in 1901:

> *We sometimes talk of a new nation under the Southern Cross. This is scarcely correct; we are not a new nation — we don't want to be — but in reality we are only part of a nation [meaning greater Britain], a large and growing part … [and] desire nothing better than to be part of the great people from whom we have sprung.*

The new nation had come into existence without its own flag, and a competition to design an Australian flag had as its essential condition that the Union Jack must appear on it. It all proved, according to the *Bulletin*, that Australia was still 'Britain's little boy'.

Most supporters of federation believed its effect would be minimal and mainly economic, with the lowering of tariffs along with the introduction of continental-wide restrictions against the entry of non-European immigrants and the expulsion of those already within the continent. Nevertheless, Australians ushered in the new commonwealth with widespread celebrations, perhaps because it also signalled the start of a new year and a new century. The biggest celebration was at Centennial Park in Sydney where military units from throughout the empire allayed concerns about Australian defence while thousands of schoolchildren, drawn up in ranks and dressed in virginal white, provided a misleading picture of Australia's faltering fecundity. Throughout Australia, every city and town had its own celebration with children figuring large in all of them. The children were the future of the nation and they were called upon to display the physical prowess of the new Australian race in countless athletic meetings where races were run and games were played, followed by a distribution of sticky buns and ginger beer and a special federation medal.

Wherever there was a significant population of non-European Australians, they also joined in the celebrations by contributing triumphal arches across city streets or, in Darwin, hanging the main street with lanterns and setting off fireworks. Aborigines were notable for their absence, having been pushed outside the margins of white society. In Darwin, where Aborigines persisted in camping within the town limits, the local police expelled them in the wake of federation. It was 'the only solution to the black problem', observed the local paper.

As these events indicated, the new commonwealth was designed to cement the European ascendancy. Under the bipartisan 'white Australia' policy, the Chinese and Japanese residents of Darwin and elsewhere would be pushed, like the Aborigines, beyond the margins of white society. The almost universal support for 'white Australia' was an indication of the fears that surged beneath the surface of Australia's often confident exterior. British Australians had a brash feeling of hope that they could create a prosperous and relatively egalitarian society if they were given the time to do so. But they also were conscious of being increasingly hemmed in by the rising nations of Asia, and of being caught up by the imperial competition that was besetting the nations of Europe.

Recommended Reading

Hugh Anderson (ed.), 1977, *Tocsin: Radical Arguments against Federation 1897–1900*, Drummond, Melbourne.

Scott Bennett (ed.), 1971, *The Making of the Commonwealth*, Cassell, Melbourne.

Alfred Deakin, 1995, *The Federal Story*, Melbourne University Press, Melbourne.

John Eddy and Deryck Schreuder (eds), 1988, *The Rise of Colonial Nationalism*, Allen & Unwin, Sydney.

A. W. Martin, 1980, *Henry Parkes*, Melbourne University Press, Melbourne.

Bede Nain, 1989, *Civilising Capitalism: The Beginnings of the Australian Labor Party*, Melbourne University Press, Melbourne.

Stuart Svenson, 1989, *The Shearers' War*, University of Queensland Press, Brisbane.

Luke Trainor, 1994, *British Imperialism and Australian Nationalism*, Cambridge University Press, Cambridge.

David Walker, 1999, *Anxious Nation: Australia and the Rise of Asia 1850–1939*, University of Queensland Press, Brisbane.

12

'UNTIL THE LAST COLOURED MAN HAD DISAPPEARED'

With less than four million white Australians occupying an island
continent the size of Europe, it became an urgent necessity for the
federation of former colonies to boost its population before it had
to face the widely feared threat to their right to hold that continent. British
Australians were motivated by an anxious mixture of hope and fear. They
hoped that their young nation would be able to breed a new race freed from
the historic quarrels and class struggles of the old European nations. At the
same time, white Australians feared that their nation was already becoming
a 'polyglot' society like the United States, with various groups of non-
Europeans appearing as blemishes on the national visage. As a result, the new
commonwealth was determined to expel from its continental shores all those
inhabitants who did not comply with its strict racial requirements. The
national ethos for more than half a century would become bound up with the
'white Australia' policy.

Central to the 'white Australia' policy was the *Immigration Restriction
Act*, the first Act passed by the new federal parliament in 1901, which was
designed to prevent the entry of non-European immigrants. But the 'white
Australia' policy was more than that. It was meant not only to prevent the
entry of non-Europeans but also to bleach the existing Australian society
white. Aborigines were thought to have been taken care of. They would

continue to die out until their eventual extinction, as they had been doing ever since the arrival of the First Fleet. That still left, as the liberal Alfred Deakin pointed out in 1901, some 70 000 to 80 000 'aliens ... who have found their way into our midst'.

In fact, other figures suggest there were just 50 000 non-Europeans, apart from some 60 000 remaining Aborigines, in an Australian population of 3 377 000. Of those 50 000, about 30 000 were of Chinese origin, some of them having arrived during the 1850s' gold rushes while others came in the subsequent decades to follow other gold finds or, increasingly, to work in the market gardens and factories of the cities. Apart from the Chinese, there were 9800 Pacific islanders, most of them working in the sugar fields of Queensland and northern New South Wales. A further 4600 were of Indian origin and 2000 were Syrians. Lastly, there were 3500 Japanese, mainly working in the tropical pearl fishery at Broome, Darwin and Thursday Island. The 'white Australia' policy was a two-pronged attack to prevent new arrivals and remove or reduce the numbers of those already within Australia 'at the earliest time, by reasonable and just means'.

Some of the more guileless proponents of 'white Australia' were open about the racist underpinning of the policy. They wanted to keep what they saw as the new Australian race 'pure', believing that any mixing of races would produce a less virile people with the worst qualities of both races. Many pointed to the example of the United States, and that nation's apparent inability to assimilate black Americans. The founding Australian prime minister, Edmund Barton, tried to reconcile the racism of the 'white Australia' policy with the idealism that motivated much of the political debate as they established a new nation at the opening of a new century. Barton denied that the 'doctrine of the equality of man was really ever intended to include racial equality', stating that it was 'never intended to apply to the equality of the Englishman and the Chinaman'.

Some of this racist thinking had a quasi-scientific basis, with social Darwinism suggesting that societies were engaged like species in a competition in which the fittest would inevitably triumph. This tended to absolve Australians of any qualms they might have had about the dispossession of the Aborigines which was seen as being sadly inevitable, as the apparently inexorable extinction of the Aboriginal remnants seemed to confirm. Social Darwinism provided Australians with a new strand to their claim to the moral proprietorship of the continent. And it was a strand that was all the stronger for being based on science. Whereas colonists in the 19th century had largely relied upon religion to justify their dispossession of the Aborigines, now they turned to science for the same purpose. Not that the remaining Aborigines posed much challenge to their claim of moral proprietorship. Instead, it was the peoples of Asia who now posed a potential challenge. Australians could not be sure that the workings of social

Darwinism would not see them being overtaken in their turn and dispossessed of the continent by the rising races of Asia.

Australian bookshops displayed invasion novels that had as their theme an invasion of the Australian continent by Chinese or Mongol 'hordes'. Similar invasion novels were produced in Britain around the turn of the century, predicting an invasion of the imperial capital by a European power, most commonly the French or the Germans. The appearance, beginning in 1896, of a new standard edition of Edward Gibbon's multi-volume *History of the Decline and Fall of the Roman Empire* focused attention on the relative decline of Britain's power in the world, prompting people to wonder whether the British might go the way of the Romans. Taking a world view, some began to predict that 'white' people as a whole would eventually face a global challenge from the fast-increasing peoples of Asia. And there were growing doubts as to whether the increasingly urbanised race of white people could defeat such a challenge. If it was to be 'survival of the fittest', there were worrying signs that the British might not survive.

Australians' physical prowess had been remarked upon for much of the 19th century and it was feared that it would be put at risk if a non-restrictive immigration policy allowed non-selective breeding. Also placed at risk would be the sanctity of white women, bearing in mind that most of the non-Europeans landing in Australia were male. There was a deepseated unease in the minds of Australian males about male Chinese market gardeners and other traders who toured the towns, suburbs and bush with their wares, calling on European women alone in their houses. Australians had to prepare for the coming conflict between the 'white' and 'yellow' races, that many saw as inevitable, by ensuring the 'purity' and strength of their race. Victory in the coming cataclysm required the expulsion of the non-Europeans living among them.

Some argued that the 'white Australia' policy was essential to protect the relatively high living standards that Europeans enjoyed and for Australia to fulfil its promise of becoming a highly progressive and democratic society. Non-Europeans had been used in the past as strike breakers and had shown themselves willing to work longer hours for less wages. Underneath it all, though, was the fear of not having secured their claim of effective proprietorship over the continent and of possibly having to face an alien challenge to that possession before they were capable of warding it off. The irony was that the strict criteria for entry under the 'white Australia' policy made it harder for Australians to achieve the effective occupation of the entire continent, since it was unlikely that enough immigrants from Britain could be attracted to fill its sparsely populated spaces.

One lone voice in parliament spoke against the Immigration Restriction Bill, pointing out that the Chinese and Japanese were more 'pure' than the British, that the bill went against everything the British Empire stood for, and that it would define Australians adversely in the eyes of the world. But such prescient warnings were ignored in the rather hysterical atmosphere in which the bill was debated. As the debate proceeded, the MPs were informed that 80 Afghans had landed in Melbourne, almost within sight of their debating chamber, and that other non-Europeans were infiltrating themselves into Victoria from Western Australia and Queensland. Speed was of the essence if 'white Australia' was to be saved from this 'invasion'. But how could a bill be drafted that would satisfy the concerns of the British government, whose imprimatur was required before Australian Acts could become law, and which would not unduly offend the Japanese who were taking a close interest in the debate?

The main weapon for preventing unwanted immigrants was a dictation test, adopted from the South African province of Natal, which had to be passed by any immigrants considered by a customs officer to be undesirable. Initially, it was proposed that the test be done in English, but that would have obvious drawbacks since it was not intended that the test be one that could be passed. Non-Europeans with a good command of English would be able to thwart the intentions of the parliament. While the Japanese were prepared to countenance a test in English, they were greatly offended by the ultimate Australian decision to set the test in any European language. This would allow the customs officer to discover which European language was unknown by the applicant and then set the test in that language. Some MPs argued for the Act to be more direct, to proclaim without the subterfuge of the test that Australia simply would not admit 'coloureds'. The Labor MP, W. G. Spence, argued that Asian governments like Japan should be informed 'that no matter what their people do they will not be admitted'.

The government declined this opportunity to be so direct, not out of any racial sensitivity but simply because such a bill would not have been approved by the British government. At the same time, it snubbed Japanese sensitivities by specifying that the test could be set in any European language of the customs officer's choosing. The Act was still carefully written so that its real intention, to prevent absolutely the entry of non-whites, was not specifically spelt out. It was left to the bureaucrats to ensure that the will of parliament was enforced.

At first, there was some confusion. Customs officers whose own language was English set the test in that language rather than use the opportunity to set it in a language unknown to the applicant. This allowed four Indians to pass the test in Sydney, while Italians in Fremantle failed it. This was the direct opposite to the intention of parliament and caused a furore in the press. Customs officers were quickly informed as to how they were to apply the test so that it acted as 'an absolute bar to admission'. Those considered to be 'undesirable immigrants' were 'persons of coloured races; persons likely to become a charge on the State; and persons suffering from diseases of certain classes'. Unless one of these last two categories applied, Europeans would not normally have to sit the test, while non-Europeans were to be given the test in a language 'with which the immigrant is not acquainted'.

Despite the passing of the Act, reports were still splashed across the pages of newspapers about the Australian continent being taken over surreptitiously by non-Europeans. There were alarming instances of Chinese men being smuggled by ship into Australian ports, and disappearing into the Chinatowns of the inner cities or finding employment in outlying market gardens. Between 1902 and 1910, 182 Asian stowaways were found aboard ships calling at Australian ports while others managed to land undetected. Raids by police and customs officers found a number of such illegal immigrants who were subjected to the dictation test before being gaoled to await deportation. The authorities were under continual pressure to complete the process of racial bleaching by ruthless means rather than wait for the various laws to take their effect over time and for the ageing population of Chinese men to die out. To back its case for radical action, the Sydney *Worker* pointed to the opium dens of Sydney's Chinatown where the 'womanhood of Australia is prostituted on the unclean couches of the cheap imported Chinaman, and the manhood of Australia stoops to the blackening of the Chinaman's boots'. In this one sentence, the *Worker* succeeded in including the idea of compromised European womanhood, the threat to living standards and the sapped virility of Australian manhood. According to the *Worker*, 'either Australia had got to fire out the mongrel herd of Chows, Japs, Hindoos, and Assyrians, or else the white Australian will in time be fired out himself'.

With considerable numbers of Chinese stowaways being discovered aboard ships, and an unknowable number managing to slip ashore, the government shifted more of the responsibility for detecting stowaways onto the shipping companies. From 1908, they were liable for fines of £100 for each stowaway found to be aboard. This gave the companies a powerful incentive to search their ships for stowaways before leaving Asian ports, often fumigating their holds to force them from their hiding places. The law was welcomed by the *Worker* as having closed 'a serious gap in the Commonwealth's defence against surreptitious invasion by the coloured man'.

Official figures showed a slow but steady reduction in the numbers of non-Europeans. From Thursday Island, the government resident and former Queensland premier John Douglas reported in 1903 that the European population of the island had increased to 736 while the Asian population had declined from 614 to 595, most of whom were employed in the pearl fishery. The Torres Strait Islanders and Aborigines were not counted in Douglas's figures. He was particularly pleased to report an increase in the number of white children which suggested, contrary to popular belief, that Europeans could procreate and thrive in the tropics. It all went to show that the 'absolute ascendancy of the white Race' was assured. Other official figures from around

Australia supported such a reassuring suggestion but they were not believed. Every young Chinese face seen in the streets of Australian towns and cities prompted doubts in European minds and sensational stories in the press. Such young faces contradicted the easy assumptions about the gradual extinction of the ageing remnants of the mainly male Chinese community.

The other main arm of the 'white Australia' policy was provided by the *Pacific Island Labourers Act* which was passed that same year and described by Barton, together with the *Immigration Restriction Act*, as constituting 'a handsome new year's gift for a new nation'. Whereas British Australians could assume that the mainly male and increasingly elderly Chinese in their midst would die out over time, they could not make such a comforting assumption about the Pacific Islanders. Many of them had wives in Australia or had married locally. They had been brought to Australia from 1863, originally to grow cotton in Queensland and later to work in the sugar plantations. After some early atrocities committed by recruiters, regulations were introduced to control the trade and ensure that proper contracts were drawn up for these indentured labourers.

The system was attacked during the late 19th century by missionary interests in London and by increasingly vocal trade unions in Australia who saw such labour as a threat to their living standards by monopolistic companies such as the powerful Colonial Sugar Refineries. Some were also concerned that it seemed to confirm that British people were unable to live and work in the tropics, thereby calling into question whether a large part of the continent was to become dominated by non-European inhabitants. To allay such concerns, 350 Italians were brought out in the 1890s to try and wean the sugar industry off its dependence upon Kanaka labour and to populate northern Australia with sturdy European stock. Measures were also introduced to break up large company plantations and encourage small sugar farms on which little or no extra labour would be needed. The Italian labourers were meant to follow this route onto the land when their contracts expired. But it would not necessarily rid Australia of the Pacific Islanders, since some had gone to work on inland pastoral properties while many of the Italians abandoned the back-breaking work of cane-cutting for the lure of the goldfields.

Under the *Pacific Island Labourers Act*, all the Pacific Islanders were to be expelled. No more were allowed to be introduced to Australia after March 1904, and any in Australia after December 1906 were to be repatriated to their islands. After protests, the measure was relaxed to allow 1600 long-term residents to remain, while 4269 were deported to their home islands or to work in Fiji. An appeal for them to be allowed to live on a reserve in the Northern Territory where they could grow tropical produce was denied out of hand, as this would have symbolically conceded the tropics to non-Europeans.

The deportion of Pacific Islanders was buttressed by a sugar bounty which made it economically advantageous to use only European labour. A high duty was placed upon imported sugar to protect the local industry, while a lesser excise duty was placed upon the local product with a large part of that duty being refunded to growers who used only white labour. This not only removed any remaining Pacific Islanders from the sugar industry but also any Chinese or even Aborigines. The cost was astronomical, both to the government and to the consumers, who paid one-third more for Australian sugar than consumers in Britain. But the cost was insignificant compared with the aim Australians had in mind. When the bounty was debated in 1909, the leading Labor MP, Andrew Fisher, pressed for it to remain 'until the last coloured man had disappeared'. The figures continued to decline thereafter until, by 1912, only four per cent of sugar was grown by non-white labour, while the following year Queensland banned the use of such labour in the sugar industry altogether. In Australia, white sugar would have a double meaning, despite bans on its import into Asian countries affronted by Australia's racist legislation.

It proved more difficult to rid the pearlshell industry of non-European labour. The isolation and danger of their diving work discouraged European participation, while the Japanese and Malays were more adept at it. When it was suggested in 1907 that Japanese influence in the industry should be reduced, it was decried by one MP who claimed that the proponents wanted to 'whitewash the bottom of the ocean'. Although a Royal Commission in 1908 urged that white divers be recruited, when ten British divers were brought to Broome in 1912, three soon died from the 'bends' while others left the industry for an easier life ashore. The government resigned itself to the non-white participation in this industry, taking comfort from the extreme isolation of the pearling ports where the non-European workers could be effectively quarantined from the distant Australian cities. They would be brought in on temporary contracts, and be prevented from leaving the pearling ports and from cohabiting with the local population. It was a plan that went rather awry as contracts were repeatedly renewed, creating semi-permanent communities of non-European men, some of whom managed to cohabit with local women despite official attempts at preventing this. The other visitors to Australia's northern shores—the Macassan fishermen who had been coming for centuries to gather and process sea slugs for the Chinese market—were also effectively deterred from making their visitations after federation.

The new federal tariff was also used as an essential part of the 'white Australia' policy. By replacing the different colonial tariffs with a continental-wide tariff barrier, the entry of cheap consumer goods from Asian countries was impeded while the development was promoted in Australia of labour-intensive industries, such as the shoe, clothing and textile industries, that might otherwise not have been economically viable. Just as the *Immigration Restriction Act* protected Australian jobs by preventing the entry of cheap, indentured labour, so the tariff protected Australian jobs by hampering the entry of cheap,

Asian imports. The government also turned to the tariff to encourage the departure of Chinese Australians, imposing a high duty on their common consumables such as rice and opium. The duty on opium was replaced by an outright ban on its importation in 1905 to force Chinese addicts out of Australia. In fact, it simply promoted the smuggling of opium, an activity that was now much more lucrative, beginning a 'war on drugs' that would be carried on to little effect but at enormous cost to the Australian community.

The 'white Australia' policy was not only concerned with bleaching the existing population, and preventing non-European arrivals from landing, but also with building up the white population of Australia. Historically, this had been done with immigration, but this had dropped away during the 1890s' depression and the labour movement was loath to see it re-started after federation for fear of exacerbating unemployment. Australia's ability to attract immigrants was also complicated by immigration schemes remaining the responsibility of the states, with each maintaining agents in Britain to recruit likely applicants and pay for their passage. Such schemes had been abandoned during the 1890s when the economic depression dried up the pool of potential immigrants while also reducing the colonial revenue available for assisted immigration schemes.

Anyway, the best new Australians, according to a succession of government ministers, were those born to Australian parents. As late as 1888, there seemed to be no doubt that Australians could meet the challenge of populating the continent. The Victorian statistician predicted that year from the prevailing birth and immigration rates that the population would reach 30 million by 1950, while a Methodist minister in South Australia drew on prevailing social Darwinist theories to proclaim that Australians, being 'the pick of the most energetic and superior races of mankind', would have no trouble securing the occupation of the largely temperate continent:

> *If it be true that dwelling in a temperate climate tends to the improvement of the race, the ascendancy of Australians over all other people in their own part of the world seems assured ... as also is their ability to manfully hold their own against all comers.*

However, with the onset of the 1890s' depression, Australians began showing a declining inclination to procreate. The average number of children born to Australian women slumped from eight in the 1880s to just four in the early 1900s. It called into question the new nation's hopes for achieving greatness, or of even being able to hold on to the continent, and seemed to suggest 'a weakening national vitality', wrote a worried *Bulletin* writer in 1899. Two years later, as the first federal parliament was meeting in Melbourne, the *Age* noted the worldwide 'rebellion against maternity' that had become evident in Britain, the United States and particularly France which would cause 'a loss of national power, a decline of national influence and an arrest of national progress'. Most worrying, Britain's rival, Germany, and Australia's Asian neighbours showed no signs of joining this rebellion against maternity. The portents seemed ominous for the new federation.

The publication of the 1901 census figures, and a pamphlet in 1903 by the government statistician on the decline in the birthrate, confirmed the worst fears of the national Jeremiahs. Alarmist headlines in the Sydney press screamed that New South Wales was losing population. They were right. Immigrants abandoned the depressed economic conditions of New South Wales for more promising foreign parts or returned home to Britain or elsewhere. The decline was exacerbated by an internal shift in population from Victoria and New South Wales to Western Australia as thousands impoverished by the depression left for the new gold discoveries at Kalgoorlie and Coolgardie. In 1903, Australia experienced a net loss from migration of 10 000, compared to an average net annual gain of 36 000 during the 1880s. Similarly, the average annual population increase of more than three per cent in the 1870s and 1880s was only 1.07 per cent in 1903.

What was worse, of course, was that the decline in the birthrate was more marked among the middle class and, presumably, among those of Protestant background than of Irish Catholic background. Thus, middle-class Protestant Australians were confronted with the twin fears of not being able to hold the continent against a possible Asian onslaught while also facing the prospect of being relatively overwhelmed by the largely Irish Catholic working class. These fears presumably helped to prompt the Anglican rector of All Saints' church in the salubrious Sydney suburb of Hunter's Hill to call upon his female parishioners to procreate to stop Anglo-Saxons being swamped by inferior races. 'If, through love of ease and luxury', intoned the rector, 'they refused to accept the trust, they were false to the higher interests of the race and to God.'

A royal commission, set up by the New South Wales government in 1903 to inquire into the birthrate, agreed with the rector, largely blaming the selfishness of women, and their ability though birth control devices and information to control their own fertility, for the decline in the birthrate. It was a potential calamity for Australia's hopes of claiming the continent before they were dispossessed in their turn. As a doctor warned the royal commission, 'With Russia, Germany and France becoming Pacific powers, and the yellow peril looming up again as a possibility of the future, a population sufficiently large to discount any thought of invasion is a vital necessity.' While much of the decrease in the birthrate was concentrated among the middle class, working-class women were also having fewer children as they were drawn increasingly into the industrial work force. To keep their jobs, women put their newborn babies into so-called baby farms where they were artificially fed in primitive conditions that caused high rates of mortality.

Part of the royal commission's solution was to keep women in ignorance by having the federal government ban the import of contraceptive devices and birth control information. For the next half-century, Customs officers watched on the wharves for anything that could be used to reduce the Australian birthrate. The government also introduced a baby bonus of £5 to be paid on the birth of every white child as an incentive against abortion and also to help pay for doctors to be in attendance at the birth. This measure, together with the establishment of infant welfare centres and women's hospitals, was successful in cutting the infant mortality rate in Australia until, by 1926, white Australians and New Zealanders had the lowest infant mortality rates in the world. The impact of these measures, along with the gradual return to economic prosperity which provided people with greater confidence to procreate, saw the rate of natural increase gradually recover.

Apart from blaming women, the apparent decline in the national fertility was laid at the door of cities, which were depicted as 'huge cancers' spreading their disease into national life. This seemed to be confirmed by the outbreak of plague in Sydney's inner suburbs at federation, which spread by ship to other states. Doctors providing evidence to the royal commission recommended that people be sent from these diseased cities to populate small farms in the bush. They argued that such marginal farmers would abandon birth control methods as they would have an economic incentive to have large families to provide themselves with cheap and compliant farm labour. Such arguments were borne out by the observation of an Irish immigrant to Western Australia who observed in 1900, after establishing a small farm and reflecting on the possibility of beginning a family, that there was 'very little trouble here in bringing up youngsters. They earn their tucker ... as soon as they can ride and muster stock'. But the trend was mostly in the other direction as people slowly seeped from the bush to the cities.

The supposed selfishness of women was not the only factor believed to play a part in the declining birthrate. Many also feared that Australian men were emulating their urban counterparts in Britain and suffering from declining strength and virility as a result of city living. The experience on the Boer War battlefield had raised questions about the physical prowess of the colonial soldiers compared with the South Africans. The British soldier, believed to be a product of urban slums, was also seen to have done badly. With another war in the offing, and Germany as the likely enemy, moves were made to increase the physical prowess of the British race and to encourage them to breed. Movements such as Baden-Powell's Boy Scout movement in 1907, with its quasi-military organisation, encouraged bush skills and physical agility for boys while such organisations as the Girl's Realm Guild encouraged girls to believe that their future lay in the home as the breeders and nurturers of the race. The medical profession supported such sentiments, with the *Australian Medical Gazette* extolling the 'breeding of a stronger and sturdier race'.

The Australian concern with their perceived physical debility was seen when the German physical culturalist Eugene Sandow toured the new federation in 1902. Sandow, who had developed a muscle-building program of exercises and diet, was proclaimed as 'the most perfectly developed man the world has ever seen'. His visit caused a sensation. He was fêted by Melbourne dignitaries who were given a private viewing of his physical attributes, while he later held the Melbourne Opera House spellbound as he twirled on a revolving pedestal clad in leopardskin trunks and sandals. A newspaper described how 'people stood open-mouthed to see standing up in sharp relief muscles that they did not know existed'. In his introduction to a book that was published to propagate Sandow's methods in Australia, an Adelaide minister claimed that it could 'have a lasting effect on the Australian race'. Another of Sandow's works, the *Book of Strength*, was allowed into the country free of duty so that it might reach a wider audience.

A member of the New South Wales royal commission and father of 13 children, Octavius Beale, was so concerned about the apparent declining vitality of the Australian race that he financed his own royal commission in 1907 into 'secret drugs' which he believed were having a deleterious effect on the Australian race. Drugs such as opium and cocaine were common ingredients of various patent medicines that promised to cure every manner of affliction from childhood teething pains to geriatric aches, while also being used in manufactured food and drink. Coca-Cola really was the real thing, with cocaine as its most active ingredient. Strict rules were introduced to ensure proper labelling of patent medicines in the wake of Beale's commission, while the publication in 1910 of his book *Racial Decay* continued his personal crusade against 'interferences with the sexual function'. His campaign was supported by such publications as the popular monthly magazine, *Lone Hand*, which was established in 1907 by the publisher of the *Bulletin* with its platform of 'an Honest, Clean, White Australia' and a proclaimed intention to 'take a militant interest in the people's health'. For its part, the government introduced compulsory military training for boys aged from 12 to 20. This was done in the wake of the Japanese victory over Russia in 1905 and was the culmination of a long campaign by Labor MP Billy Hughes who had extolled the physical and moral benefits of such a scheme. Labor leader Andrew Fisher also argued for compulsory physical inspection of all youths to ensure they developed 'physically, morally, and mentally'.

Despite the royal commission's recommendations to try and stem the decline in the birthrate, and these later attempts to restore the vitality of the Australian race, there was a general acceptance that it was largely beyond the power of government regulation or religious exhortation to prevent the use of birth control devices. Although the import of devices was banned, there was no ban on their local production and there was little that could be done to stop the spread of information about birth control. Attention increasingly turned to immigration schemes as providing the best answer to the population dilemma. As a Sydney businessman observed in 1905, 'Babies are all very well in their places, but for us to wait for the country to be populated as fully as it ought to be by the Australian born only, would be for us to wait a very long time indeed.' Immigrants provided ready-made labourers and consumers.

As economic conditions improved, the states began to renew their immigration schemes from 1905 onwards. Much of it was directed into closer settlement schemes, and the construction of railway lines to service them, which saw large areas of Western Australia put under the plough for wheat, while the eastern states saw a similar breaking-up of large pastoral properties for agricultural purposes. A new strain of rust-resistant wheat was developed for Australian conditions, allowing wheat farmers to spread onto land that was previously rejected as too arid, while irrigation schemes were developed on both sides of the continent. In Victoria, the American head of the newly formed Water Commission predicted that irrigation would allow the population of the state to be increased to perhaps 100 times its present level. By 1913, more than 1200 small farms had been established on newly irrigated land across Victoria, allowing farmers to till the soil of extensive pastoral properties where previously only sheep had wandered.

In New South Wales, the government announced in 1906 the construction of a huge dam at Barren Jack to irrigate land along the lower Murrumbidgee River on which some 50 000 people were expected to settle. Acknowledging that 'in the interior of this country, the isolated existence is terrifying to most people', the government planned 'villages at various points' to 'afford all the conveniences of civilisation'. While the name 'Barren Jack' was hardly calculated to encourage such settlement, the Public Works minister thought it was 'a mistake to depart from well-known names'. This principled attachment to the existing name was soon overtaken by pragmatism, with the dam being renamed Burrinjuck to remove any adverse connotations that might deter wary farmers. Despite this, the inflated hopes for intensive settlement in English-style villages were never achieved.

While the labour movement usually agreed with closer settlement schemes, it was always equivocal about immigration schemes which it feared might swamp the labour market and threaten wage rates and working conditions. Rejecting the New South Wales scheme of assisted immigration, Labor MP W. A. Holman chanted the familiar mantra that 'the best of all immigrants is the Australian baby'. For its part, the federal Labor government introduced regulations in 1912 to restrict working-class migrants who might flood the job market. As a way of curbing cheap passages for migrants, the government decreed that passenger ships had to have proper bathroom facilities. 'Other nations are apt to think it somewhat arrogant', suggested the *Argus*,

... that 4 000 000 Australians should claim the right to possess this vast continent in the teeth of all the powers which are hungry for territory. Will the world be wrathful or merely amused when it learns that our fear has reached such a pitch that before we admit a newcomer we inquire whether he has been careful to wash regularly on the voyage!

Despite these regulations, 400 000 British migrants arrived in Australia in the period up to the First World War, most of them in the period from 1910 to 1914. They added more than ten per cent to the Australian population, helping by their presence to further the physical occupation of the continent.

The bush had been largely pacified by the rifles of the native police and the pens of the writers, by the poison of the pastoralists and the paints of the Heidelberg School artists. But the bush remained relatively unpopulated, particularly in the north. In 1911, the federal government had taken over from South Australia the responsibility for the Northern Territory after South Australia had singularly failed to populate it with white people or to provide it with a viable economic future. Apart from the particular problems of developing its tropical potential, there were simply not enough white Australians to occupy and defend adequately all of the continent. There had been some suggestion that this might be done in the marginal cattle country of the Northern Territory by bringing indentured labourers from Asia, but this was no longer feasible given the all-party support for 'white Australia'. One MP suggested importing Scandinavians who were 'immigrants of a very virile type' who would 'insure that the Territory will remain in our undisturbed possession for all time'. Southern Europeans, on the other hand, would not be suitable, he argued, since 'their physical stamina is not up to the necessary standard to insure a robust race in the future'. By 1914, with little to show for three years of federal administration of the territory, the *Sydney Morning Herald* conceded that even Italians would be acceptable as settlers for northern Australia.

The previous year, Billy Hughes had helped to lay the foundation stone to mark the site for the new national capital of Canberra. Hughes extolled Canberra, a name purloined like the land itself from the Aborigines, as a symbol of the nation. It was more than that. It was the first Australian capital not to be sited on the coast. Instead, it was set securely behind the imposing bulk of the Great Dividing Range and roughly in the centre of the settled south-east corner of the continent. Its location was partly to appease the competing claims of Sydney and Melbourne to be the national capital. But it was also a dramatic assertion of the claim of effective proprietorship by British Australians over the bush, with Hughes taking comfort from the fact that there was no sign at the ceremony 'of that race we have banished from the face of the earth'. Nevertheless, he warned that British Australians might go the way of the Aborigines if they did not use the succeeding decades to occupy the continent.

Meanwhile, as the tension between Britain and Germany increased, Australia worried about the sanctity of its northern shores from Chinese who were reported to be landing illegally in large numbers. Brisbane's *Daily Standard* caused a furore when it published a string of stories in April 1914 about this 'Yellow Menace'. A Queensland senator fuelled the storm by claiming that illegal Chinese immigrants could be seen in the alleys of Queensland's Chinatowns 'wearing sandals, loose robes, and flying pigtails, and can be noticed walking up and down, jeering in their own lingo at white men and women'. Not only that, but their employment on banana plantations had led to a deterioration in the quality of Queensland bananas. The reports prompted suggestions that a destroyer be sent to patrol the nation's northern waters to guard against such Chinese incursions. But it was the Germans, not the Chinese, who within months were at war with the British Empire, and hence with Australia.

Recommended Reading

F. K. Crowley, 1973, *Modern Australia in Documents*, Vol. 1, Wren, Melbourne.

David Day, 1996, *Contraband and Controversy*, Australian Government Publishing Service Press, Canberra.

Tom Griffiths, 1996, *Hunters and Collectors*, Cambridge University Press, Melbourne.

Patricia Grimshaw, Marilyn Lake, Ann McGrath and Marian Quartly, 1994, *Creating a Nation*, McPhee Gribble, Melbourne.

Neville Hicks, 1978, *'This Sin and Scandal': Australia's Population Debate 1891–1911*, Australian National University Press, Canberra.

M. J. Knowling and A. T. Yarwood, 1982, *Race Relations in Australia*, Methuen, Sydney.

William J. Lines, 1991, *Taming the Great South Land*, Allen & Unwin, Sydney.

Stuart Macintyre, 1986, *Oxford History of Australia*, Vol. 4, Oxford University Press, Melbourne.

John Mordike, 1992, *An Army for a Nation*, Allen & Unwin, Sydney.

Patrick O'Farrell, 1984, *Letters from Irish Australia 1825–1925*, New South Wales University Press, Sydney.

G. Souter, 1992, *Lion and Kangaroo*, Sun, Sydney.

Richard White, 1981, *Inventing Australia*, George Allen & Unwin, Sydney.

Myra Willard, 1967, *History of the White Australia Policy to 1920*, Melbourne University Press, Melbourne.

A. T. Yarwood, 1982, *Attitudes to Non-European Immigration*, Methuen, Sydney.

13

'NOW WE KNOW WHAT NATIONS KNOW'

Australians had waited anxiously outside newspaper offices for the latest news from London of the European situation. When Britain declared war on 4 August 1914 following the German invasion of Belgium, crowds of Melbourne larrikins roughed up anyone of Germanic appearance before smashing all the windows in that city's Chinatown. Things were quieter in Sydney where the *Sydney Morning Herald* warned against 'racial feelings asserting themselves'. Although Australians had long feared being caught up in a war that would test their resolve to hold their continent, their fears had largely focused upon an Asian enemy rather than a European one. Asia had replaced the bush as the source of mystery and danger to white Australia. The 1890s and early 1900s had seen shelves of books published, both fiction and non-fiction, with an Asian invasion of Australia as their central theme. Events were suggesting that such fears were well justified.

The Anglo-Japanese alliance of 1902 and the subsequent Japanese defeat of Russia in 1905 had ended forever the comforting idea of the white races standing together to resist the encroachments of the yellow races. In an implicit acknowledgment of its waning power relative to the rising powers of Germany and the United States, Britain looked to the alliance with Japan to shore up British interests in the Pacific, particularly in China, and also to indirectly protect the north-west frontier of India from possible Russian expansion by creating a potential Japanese threat to Russia in Siberia.

Australia expressed grudging satisfaction that Japan was neutralised as a threat to Australia because of its alliance with Britain. At the same time, Australian governments became more forthright in building up their own defences and were suspicious of the value of British defence guarantees. In a break with the country's dependent past, Prime Minister Alfred Deakin unilaterally invited the American fleet, on a tour of the world in 1908 at least partly designed to overawe Japan, also to visit Australia. The fleet of 16 battleships was dubbed the Great White Fleet, partly because it was painted white, but also in recognition of its purpose in deterring Japan and its perception in the minds of Europeans perched precariously around the Pacific Rim that they were engaged in a climactic struggle between the white and yellow races. When the fleet steamed into Sydney, it was greeted with great celebration.

The following year, Australia's Labor government decided to build its own navy rather than continuing to contribute money to build up the Royal Navy. It also ended popular suggestions that Australia should contribute a dreadnought to Britain's navy as it scrambled to keep ahead of Germany's naval building program. The Australian squadron, built in Britain and manned largely by British sailors, assembled in Australia in 1913. It was comprised of a battle cruiser, three light cruisers and three destroyers. It was a respectable force designed mainly for the protection of trade routes and to deter hit-and-run cruiser raids on Australian cities. It was not sufficient to deter or prevent a major invasion of the continent. That still depended, as always, on the strength of the Royal Navy and the willingness of the British government to station sufficient forces in the Pacific. But Britain discounted the possibility of a Pacific threat, being intent instead on obtaining Australian forces in Europe for the expected war against Germany. In 1911, when attending the imperial conference in London, Australia's defence minister, Senator Pearce, was quietly informed that Britain was preparing for a war with Germany and that Australia should prepare itself to supply an expeditionary force for use in the European theatre. Labor man though he was, Pearce returned to Australia determined to prepare the dominion's forces for involvement in such a war.

Despite Pearce's planning for war, many in the labour movement were organising to stop its outbreak. As war became ever more likely in Europe, socialist and anti-war movements across the world joined together to try and prevent it. Trade unions were urged to uphold ideals of international working-class solidarity by undertaking to strike immediately war was declared, thereby making its prosecution impossible. A large number of Australian trade unions and other organisations pledged their support for such action. In one of many anti-war tracts printed prior to the war, working-class readers of Victoria's Labor newspaper, *Labor Call*, were warned: 'The war trenches are yawning for your lives — a gulf in which the hopes, the happiness, the blood and the tears of your class will be swallowed. Refuse.' But they did not refuse, not in Germany, not in France, not in Britain and not even in far distant Australia.

When news of the war's imminent outbreak reached Australia, Labor leader Andrew Fisher uttered the immortal words, pinched from a Boer War exhortation by British politician Austen Chamberlain, about Australia standing by Britain 'to the last man and the last shilling'. Or, as his colleague Billy Hughes put it, 'this indeed is the occasion when none shall be for the party, but all be for the state'. Even the formerly anti-war *Labor Call* caved in to the patriotic fervour, explaining that it was 'possible to bitterly denounce war as a barbarous, brutal and uncivilised expedient, and yet be willing to fight to the death when one's country is threatened'. Such sentiments were in tune with popular feelings. The anti-war voices were largely swamped by this fervour that saw 50000 men respond to a call for 20000 volunteers for the Australian Imperial Force (AIF). This allowed the army doctors to choose the finest physical specimens for the first echelon of expeditionary troops.

As an integral part of the British Empire, there seemed to be no question of Australia standing aside. It was convinced that its fate rested on Britain's. Even had it been possible to know the awful cost that Australia would pay for this dependence, it would be unlikely to have deterred them. Australian identity was so intermingled with that of a grander British imperial identity, that sentiment alone would have impelled most Australians into battle. Set at the antipodes of the 'mother country', Australians took confidence from their membership of an invented British race, which they believed to be self-evidently superior, and of an empire they proclaimed to be the most powerful in the world. The survival of 'white Australia' demanded that it be so.

Australia was tied to Empire by more than sentiment. Its export-oriented economy was dependent upon British purchases of its primary products and on the City of London for its capital. Middle-class Britons who dined on Australian beef raised by the exploitative Vestey company in the Northern Territory were financing the occupation of the continent's more marginal cattle country and thereby helping Australians to solidify their claim of effective proprietorship over the entire continent. By ignoring this vital economic link, Australians would be placing their very existence at peril. And, of course, Australian security still depended on the power of the British navy.

Neutralism was never an option. Even the growing number of Australian nationalists were anxious to prove themselves on the battlefield in competition with the more experienced, martial nations of Europe. Australians would not be fighting in Europe so much to defend poor Belgium as to defend their cherished vision of white Australia. 'Australia's fate is going to be decided on the continent [of Europe] and not out here', observed one recruit in justification of his enlistment. Success on the battlefield would lay to rest the niggling doubts about the virility of Australian manhood. Had he not enlisted, one recruit felt that he 'would never have been able to hold my head up and look any decent girl in the face'. He died of wounds in 1917. An Irish Australian recruit thought it was 'every young fellow's duty' to enlist. He was dead by August 1916.

More prosaically, individuals were attracted by the excitement, the wages and the travel, anticipating that the expeditionary force was destined for training in England prior to service in Europe. For some, it was an escape from unemployment brought on by a severe drought. 'We haven't had any rain for months so I thorrt [sic] I would join the army', wrote one early recruit. Others were recent immigrants from Britain and eager to fight for the mother country from which they had come. Some Australians even travelled to England to enlist in British units rather than suffer the perceived social stigma of joining a colonial unit. Most Australians, though, were more than content to take the six shillings a day they would earn overseas with Australian forces, compared to the one shilling a day paid to British soldiers.

After fearing an Asian invasion for so long, Australian soldiers on their way to war now watched from the decks of their troopships as Japanese cruisers provided part of their escort. Judging it 'the most adventurous period' in his life, a taxidermist from Mosman exulted at having at last 'really began the game in deadly earnest'. Meanwhile, the new Australian navy became a subsidiary component of the Royal Navy. It had gone to war stations on an order from the Admiralty in London, rather than from the government in Melbourne, and it was handed over to the control of the Admiralty for the duration of the conflict. There was not much danger close to home after the German Pacific fleet was destroyed by ships of the Royal Navy during the battle of the Falkland Islands. Moreover, the lightly defended German colonies in the southern Pacific were quickly seized by Australian forces in September 1914, although the Australians moved too slowly to prevent Japan from seizing the German islands north of the equator. Prior to federation, some of the Australian colonies had dallied with the notion of having their own Pacific empire. Now, as federated Australia, they had such an empire, adding to their existing control over Papua. The Melbourne *Age* celebrated their capture, suggesting that they would lay the 'foundation of a solid Australian sub-empire in the Pacific Ocean'. It was the first satisfying taste of a war that would become increasingly bitter.

In a curious sideshow to the battles in the European theatre, two Turkish nationals from the New South Wales mining town of Broken Hill engaged an unsuspecting party of Australians in their own battle on New Year's Day, 1915. A holiday crowd of some 1200 citizens of the town were packed into the open trucks of an ore train which shunted them to a reserve outside the town for a miners' union picnic. From a hill overlooking the track, and with their ice-cream cart defiantly flying the Turkish flag, the two men shot 11 of the party-goers, killing four of them, before they in turn were hunted down and killed. In the isolation of the bush, and fearing enemies everywhere, the frustrated townspeople marched that night on the German club, loyally burning it down, before turning their attention on the camp of Afghan camel drivers who luckily were protected by police and soldiers with bayonets fixed.

Due to the Turkish entry into the war, the first echelon of the AIF landed in Egypt for training in the shadow of the pyramids. These 'six bob a day tourists' also visited the sights of nearby Cairo, fighting their first battle on Good Friday, 1915, when they rioted through Cairo's red light district, throwing into the street and burning the beds on which so many of them had caught venereal disease. Their first real battle came against the Turks. After the tedium of training in the Egyptian desert, where there was 'sand, sand, sand in your tucker, in your ears, eyes, nose, everywhere, and anywhere' and where they had been 'marching, skirmishing and digging for weeks and weeks', the call to action came as a relief. 'It was like putting a bit of roast meat to a starving man—we sprung to it', wrote a recruit from Western Australia who would be killed the following year.

In a grand strategy to knock Turkey out of the war and open up the Black Sea route to Russia, a combined Anglo-French force together with Australians and New Zealanders were organised into an Australian and New Zealand Army Corps (ANZAC) which landed on the beaches of the Gallipoli Peninsula on 25 April 1915. Due to the tide, the Australian troops were swept past their designated beach to land on an adjoining one. With the Turkish cliffs in sight, a former tram conductor from Sydney described in his diary how his fellow soldiers were 'talking like a lot of school kids ... but they have got their rifles clean and their bayonets have been sharpened in a very business manner'. The lives of around 500 Australians were brought to an abrupt close during those first hellish 24 hours. The former enthusiasm among the untried troops was diluted by all the spilt blood. After being forced to use 'a dead mans legs for a pillow' on his first night ashore, one young disillusioned soldier was looking forward to the war's finish, since the experience of battle was 'enough to drive a fellow mad' with 'your pals shot down beside you and the roar of the big 15-inch naval guns the shrieks of our own artillery and the clatter of the rifle fire'. Australia was unused to war on such a scale, but it was child's play compared with what was to come.

Back home, the complete lists of dead and injured were slow to make their appearance in the columns of the newspapers for fear of alarming the public. Instead, Australians read stirring reports by the British journalist Ashmead-Bartlett of how the untested Australian troops

> ... sprang into the sea, and, forming a sort of rough line, rushed at the enemy's trenches. Their magazines were not charged, so they just went in with cold steel. It was over in a minute. The Turks in the first trench were either bayoneted or they ran away ...

The second Turkish trench was set into the cliffs above the beach. Ashmead-Bartlett reported breathlessly how 'this race of athletes proceeded to scale the cliffs without responding to the enemy's fire. They lost some men but did not worry.' Again the Turks were either bayoneted or fled. Instead of staying to secure their hard-won beach-head, the Australians kept on going, 'rushing northwards and eastwards, searching for fresh enemies to bayonet'. The fact that these first reports, with their glowing admiration for Australian fighting prowess, were written by a British journalist gave them added credibility in Australian eyes.

There were few prisoners taken in those early days. Stories of Turkish atrocities, apparently untrue, had incited Australians to seek retaliation. As C. E. W. Bean, Australia's official correspondent at Gallipoli, observed in his diary, the Australians would not 'if they can help it take prisoners'. Bean tried to put a good gloss on this, arguing that 'the Australian when he fights, fights all in'. He contrasted this with the New Zealand soldier fighting alongside who 'has not the devil of the Australians in him; the wild pastoral independent life of Australia, if it makes rather wild men, makes superb soldiers.' It was the battle for which Australians had been mentally preparing for so long. In Australian eyes, the Turks were akin to the coloured foe of their recurring national nightmare. Moreover, some of the Australian soldiers were drawn from the pastoral frontier where punitive expeditions were still being organised against the Aborigines in places like the Kimberley district of Western Australia and the cattle country of the Northern Territory. At the same time, there were several hundred Aborigines who enlisted with the expeditionary force. For white Australians, there were also the historical and religious associations at Gallipoli with the Crusades, with Christians once more being set against Muslims. The Melbourne *Punch* thought it 'peculiarly fitting that it should be the sons of a new land, nurtured in the atmosphere of freedom, who should have the task of driving the unspeakable Turk at long last from Europe'. They would not succeed.

Ironically, the experience of battle forced the Australian soldiers to examine their racial prejudices. In the first rush of the landing, one soldier exclaimed after shooting a Turkish opponent: 'Take that you black b—s.' However, within a month of the landing, Bean observed with some surprise that the Australian troops reacted to the close fighting against the Turks, and the slaughter on both sides, by taking a more respectful attitude towards them. According to Bean, they were now 'quite friendly with the Turks; anxious to get in the wounded if they can — give them cigarettes'. They had been impressed by the unexpected courage of some 40 000 Turkish soldiers who on 19 May had charged *en masse* into a fierce fusillade of fire from the Australian trenches. Thousands of Turks died uselessly for the loss of just 160 Australians killed. While they had come to Gallipoli with preconceptions about the Turks being a coloured foe, their close proximity forced them to reassess their racial assumptions. The Australian predeliction for sunbathing on the Gallipoli

beaches left them 'much darker than Turks' while Bean's observations of the
Turkish prisoners at their latrines gave him 'excellent grounds for saying that
many Turks, are as white as Europeans'. The Australian soldiers often mistook
Turkish officers for Germans because of their light complexion. In a remark
that respected the bravery of the Turks while also, perhaps, reflecting a
reconsideration of their colour, an Australian officer described the Turks in
August 1915 as 'the whitest fighters that ever fought'.

As the awful scale of the death toll began to reach Australia, the press
ensured that the enthusiasm of their readers for war would not be put off by
the early casualty lists which were completely outside the experience of
Australians formerly innocent of such carnage. One newspaper counselled its
readers to maintain 'all the high patriotism and self-control of a ruling race'.
It reminded them, based on the reports of Ashmead-Bartlett, that their troops
had 'proved themselves worthy representatives of their race' as Australia made
her 'European debut as a fighting unit of the Empire'. This was important,
since the earlier fighting in the Boer War had raised serious doubts about
Australian military prowess.

Stories of gallantry at Gallipoli erased these doubts. Australians read
overblown accounts of their wounded troops being happy 'that they had been
tried for the first time and had not been found wanting'. The rate of recruiting
soared in the wake of the Gallipoli landings. It seemed that everyone wanted to
be in it. A bank clerk from Kyneton in Victoria was moved to enlist, believing
that 'it is the greatest opportunity for a chap to make a man of himself, those
that come back from this war will be men of the right sort that anybody would
be proud of'. But he did not come back, being killed instead in October 1917,
by which time the Gallipoli campaign had long ended in defeat. Despite
repeated offensives, the Allies failed to move far off the beaches until, in
December 1915, they began to withdraw altogether. In a triumph of sorts, they
managed to evacuate all the Australian forces for the cost of just two casualties.
They left behind the bodies of nearly 9000 dead Australians and evacuated
during the eight-month campaign some 20 000 others.

Although the ANZACs comprised a minority of the mainly Anglo-
French force, and the campaign had failed, Gallipoli became an Australian
legend. It was popularly believed that Australia was forged as a nation on the
cliffs of Gallipoli in 1915 rather than in Sydney's Centennial Park in 1901. 'It
was there that our young and untried troops ... quitted themselves as men',
observed the Melbourne *Argus*. Australians defined themselves, and were
defined by others, in comparison with British soldiers. They came out of the
comparison well. As Bean observed in his diary on seeing the British in action
at Gallipoli, 'after 100 years of breeding in slums, the British race is not the
same ... as in the days of Waterloo'. The Australians were all volunteers,
compared with the partly-conscripted British troops who Bean dismissed as
'puny narrow-chested little men'. Their 'only hope', wrote Bean, was 'if they

come out to Australia or N.Z. or Canada' where they could 'within 2 generations breed men again'. The Australians also looked with disfavour on the upper-class British officers who were blamed for the Gallipoli debacle and similar failures in France. 'The British staff, British methods, and British bungling have sickened us', wrote a former mining engineer from Rutherglen in Victoria, now a major in France. Many had similar feelings when on leave in London, where they were confronted with the hidebound reality of the class system and the slums. Observing the English at close quarters in London, a former clerk from Thebarton in South Australia thought they

> *...all bore the hall mark of the Cog. Pale faced and undersized, they appeared quite passionless, these people who work year in and year out beyond the reach of sunshine and out of touch with nature. They seem to have been moulded to a definite pattern by a machine-like, artificial existence.*

It all went to instil a feeling of being Australian, rather than of being British living in Australia. 'I hardly realized what a great country Australia is untill [sic] I left it', was a common response. The subsequent publication of the official history by Charles Bean added to the legend, as Bean transformed the image of the typical Australian from the egalitarian bushman into the relatively undisciplined but brave and resourceful digger. The day of the Gallipoli landing was commemorated with a holiday, dubbed Anzac Day, and memorials were erected in practically every town, suburb and city recording the lost generation that had saved 'white Australia' by attacking Turks in Gallipoli, and later in Palestine, and engaging in the slaughter of the Western Front in Europe. Australia's national poet, 'Banjo' Paterson, commemorated it in verse in his poem, *We're all Australians now*:

> *The mettle that a race can show*
> *Is proved with shot and steel,*
> *And now we know what nations know*
> *And feel what nations feel.*

It engendered a national feeling of self-confidence, not seen since the 1880s. As a Sydney University economist exclaimed, the example of the Australians at Gallipoli had justified 'our optimism in the future of the British race'. But the war was not yet won.

Across Australia, German clubs were closed down, partly for the protection of their members, as anyone found in the streets of German appearance was liable to be beaten up. Thousands of German Australians, along with others of enemy origin, were rounded up into detention camps while others were subjected to the strict control over the movement of aliens introduced under the draconian provisions of the *War Precautions Act*. British ethnicity, as much as race, became the new measure of acceptability in loyalist Australia.

Those Australians cramped in the tortured trenches of the Western Front were too obsessed with surviving their ordeal to ponder deeply on such matters. Although they were fighting as one unit under the capable Australian general, John Monash, and despite the great casualties they incurred as some 50 000 young Australians perished, their efforts made less impact on the national psyche. Unlike Gallipoli, there was little opportunity for individuals to shine in battle. It was slaughter on a massive scale that cut a swathe through a generation of Australians, as it did through all the other nations who threw their men into the mire of mud and blood. 'Fighting here is just simply massacre', wrote a 38-year-old corporal from Melbourne after his first taste of France. At the battle of Fromelles in July 1916, the first major Australian engagement in France, a machine-gunner from Sydney described how one of their lieutenants, as the German shells exploded all around, 'literally cried like a child' while others 'carried down out of the firing line were struggling and calling out for their mother'. More than 5000 Australian casualties were suffered during the course of that brief, fruitless battle. 'It was like a butcher's shop', wrote one soldier in his diary. Later that month, at Pozieres, more than 22 000 Australian casualties were suffered, for no great gain. They rationalised it as best they could, with a bank clerk from Katanning in Western Australia informing his wife of five months that it was 'better to die for you and Country than to be a cheat of the empire'. He was dead before Christmas.

So great was the slaughter and so concerned was Prime Minister Billy Hughes for Australia to play her full part in it and to share in the spoils of war that he pushed for conscription to be introduced. Australian men were no longer coming forward in sufficient numbers to maintain reinforcements for the divisions already in the field let alone the new ones that Hughes wished to form. When he was opposed by many of his Labor Party colleagues, acting out of principle against conscription for overseas service, Hughes went to the people in a referendum in October 1916 certain that he would win. The referendum unleashed the most divisive and bitter political debate that Australia had seen. And it was race, or rather the protection of the 'white Australia' ideal, that was used in the debate by both sides. Anti-conscriptionists argued that conscription of white males would necessitate the introduction of coloured labour into the factories and farms of Australia, thereby signalling the death knell of white Australia. For their part, the conscriptionists argued that such a drastic measure as conscription was necessary to win the war and therefore preserve white Australia. Hughes pointed to the 'teeming millions' of Asia who were 'jostling each other for space, striving virtually for a foothold on the earth's surface'. While the 'white Australia' policy had kept them at bay from Australia's shores, a defeat for the Allied armies would cause them to 'come in their millions'.

To try and neutralise the arguments of his opponents, Hughes promised that 'no coloured or cheap labour would be allowed to enter Australia' during the war. Then, just as the 1916 referendum was about to be voted upon, a vessel carrying 214 Maltese men intent on seeking work in Australia appeared off Fremantle. The news of its arrival was censored during the days prior to the referendum, which was narrowly lost by the time the ship had reached Melbourne. Hughes maintained his commitment to their exclusion, lining the wharf with police and customs officers who subjected the Maltese to a dictation test in Dutch. They all failed and were sent on to Noumea. Despite the bipartisan support for 'white Australia', the treatment of the Maltese caused considerable controversy, mainly by conservatives, in favour of the Maltese. It was pointed out that they were British subjects, that many of them had fought at Gallipoli and that Malta was even then where wounded Australian troops from Gallipoli were being treated. More importantly, these men did not pose a threat to Australia's narrowing, national identity. They were not a 'black race' but men of 'good physique, possessed of great energy'. They were as Caucasian as the next white man, observed the *Sydney Morning Herald*, which also pointed out that they were not drawn from an overpopulated nation with the potential to swamp Australians.

The admission of the Maltese, argued the *Sydney Morning Herald*, would help to secure Australians' claim of moral proprietorship over the continent. While the power of the British Empire ensured Australians of the legal title 'to these millions of square miles composing a practically empty land', their continuing enjoyment of that title required Australians not to be 'sitting on them instead of developing them'. In the face of such arguments and appeals, when the men returned from Noumea to Sydney to await a Malta-bound ship, Hughes relented and allowed all but a few to land provided they had guaranteed employment and promised to join trade unions.

The 1916 referendum had followed the Easter Uprising in Dublin where the sight of British troops executing wounded Irish rebels tarnished the image of the British Empire, particularly in the eyes of Irish Australians. Melbourne's Catholic archbishop, Daniel Mannix, was drawn into the conscription debate when he questioned the rationale for the war, likening it to a trade war. His participation increased the temperature of the campaign and deepened the sectarian divide in Australian society in a way that would take several generations to bridge. It also divided the Labor Party as Billy Hughes led his supporters to join with the conservatives in a new Nationalist Party. Their choice of name was some recognition of the growing nationalist feeling in Australia, although it was a misnomer, the party being intent on keeping Australia integrated into the empire rather than fostering any sense of independence.

The failure of the conscription referendum, together with a further one in December 1917 in which Mannix took an even more prominent part, did not prevent thousands of Australian soldiers from continuing to distinguish themselves on the battlefields of Europe and Palestine. Some recruits still came forward to join them as the government successively lowered the enlistment requirements to take men as short as five feet and as young as 18 without their parent's permission. Men in their fifties were also accepted into the ranks. General Monash showed that his countrymen could direct strategy from divisional headquarters as well as they could fight in the trenches. And the men of the Australian Light Horse Brigade, many of whom were bushmen, spent the war fighting to topple Turkey's Middle Eastern empire. In a decisive battle when the Allied advance into Palestine was stopped at Gaza in October 1917, the brigade managed to turn the Turkish flank at Beersheba. As night fell, troops of the Light Horse Brigade charged the Turkish trenches armed only with bayonets, overwhelming the defenders and taking the town. A captured German officer exclaimed that the Australians were 'not soldiers at all; they are madmen'. Gaza fell soon after and the Allies pushed on to take Jerusalem before Christmas in a renewed crusade against Mohammedanism.

Australia had offered up 330 000 men for service overseas, 40 per cent of those eligible to join, of whom some 59 000 did not return while another 167 000 were wounded, returning broken in mind or body to a nation transformed by a war that had barely touched its shore. They had left bouyed up with the juvenile imperialism of W. H. Fitchett's popular book, *Deeds That Won the Empire*, but found in the trenches that 'War is not a thing of Romance and wonderful adventure, [as] we imagined it in day's gone by'. Nevertheless, many took solace that their ceaseless sacrifice had helped to defeat the German army and prevented the British Empire from going under. As such, they felt they were defending Australia from their trenches in France and Belgium. 'The more the Germans get of France the closer they are getting to Australia', observed an English-born compositor from Sydney in July 1918. 'God knows what they would do if they became masters of the world', wondered a young railway signalman from New South Wales who survived the slaughter. And certainly there would have been forfeits to pay in Australia if the Kaiser had emerged victorious from the European maelstrom. Who can know today whether the terrible sacrifices suffered by Australians were worth incurring to avert possible postwar demands on Australia from the victorious Germans. But few doubted it then, at least in the early years of the war.

According to Billy Hughes, their sacrifice also had a deeper significance. Hughes had been a long-time campaigner for military training before the war, partly to ensure the physical fitness of Australian youths. Now, in words reminiscent of advertisements for patent medicine, Hughes proclaimed that the experience of war had stopped Australia 'from slipping into the abyss of degeneracy and from becoming flabby ... war has purged us, war has saved us from physical and moral degeneracy and decay'. In the eyes of Hughes, and the many Australians who reflected the new national self-confidence borne of battle, the virility of their manhood had been confirmed by killing and being killed and their hopes of securing their claim over the continent were consequently strengthened.

Recommended Reading

E. M. Andrews, 1993, *Anzac Illusion*, Cambridge University Press, Melbourne.

C. E. W. Bean, 1993, *Anzac to Amiens*, Penguin, Melbourne.

David Day (ed.), 1998, *Australian Identities*, Australian Scholarly Publishing, Melbourne.

Kevin Fewster (ed.), 1990, *Gallipoli Correspondent: The Frontline Diary of C. E. W. Bean*, Allen & Unwin, Sydney.

L. F. Fitzhardinge, 1979, *William Morris Hughes*, Vol. 2, Angus&Robertson, Sydney.

Bill Gammage, 1980, *The Broken Years: Australian Soldiers in the Great War*, Penguin, Melbourne.

John Robertson, 1990, *Anzac and Empire*, Hamlyn, Melbourne.

Geoffrey Serle, 1982, *John Monash: A Biography*, Melbourne University Press, Melbourne.

Peter Spartalis, 1983, *The Diplomatic Battles of Billy Hughes*, Hale & Iremonger, Sydney.

Alistair Thomson, 1994, *Anzac Memories*, Oxford University Press, Melbourne.

14

'ON THE

THRESHOLD

OF

ACHIEVEMENT'

Australians had confirmed their virility as a nation on the battlefields of Gallipoli, Palestine and the Western Front, expunging the prewar doubts that had called into question their ability to continue holding the continent for themselves. But the war had also brought the Japanese that much closer to Australia, occupying the former German island colonies from the north Pacific to the equator. Under Hughes, Australia's postwar purpose was to occupy the continent, every part of it. The prewar idea of Australia having a 'dead heart', that much of the arid interior was useless for farming even with the use of underground water, was overturned as the nation enthusiastically embraced the concept of 'Australia Unlimited'. It became an article of political faith that no area of the continent was unsuitable for farming and that Australia was capable of becoming the 'richest and most powerful ... nation of the world'.

Prime Minister Billy Hughes returned in triumph from the Versailles peace conference of 1919. He had been anxious to prevent the burst of postwar liberal internationalism, sponsored by the American president Woodrow Wilson, from calling into question the claim by Australians to the continent. The Japanese had wanted to insert into the covenant of the newly established League of Nations a racial equality clause which Hughes saw as a threat to white Australia. He feared it could be used to force Australia to pull down its colour-based barrier to the entry of non-Europeans. He was equally anxious that the mandate from the League which gave Australia control over former German New Guinea should not prevent Australia from monopolising that colony's trade and deciding who could enter there. If Japanese or Chinese traders were permitted entry into New Guinea, as the Germans had allowed, Hughes feared that the future European occupation of the Australian continent would be imperilled.

When his trenchant defence of these perceived Australian interests was questioned by President Wilson, Hughes riposted that he spoke for 60 000 dead. Which he did. In the event, Hughes achieved both his aims, at the cost of causing further offence to the Japanese. On his return to Australia, Hughes proclaimed to the federal parliament in Melbourne that his greatest achievement at Versailles had been his defence of white Australia. He told the assembled representatives that Australians, who were 'more British than the people of Great Britain', now had the 'capacity to achieve our great destiny, which is to hold this vast continent in trust for those of our race who come after us ... The White Australia is yours. You may do with it what you please ...' One of their first acts was to deport many of the Germans and other aliens interned during the war and also to combat the anti-imperialism and growing nationalism of the partly Irish Catholic working class. Imperial visitors were imported to stir the crowds into protestations of loyalty to a distant Crown, while any so-called disloyal elements who could not prove their status as Australian nationals were deported.

Although an ex-Labor man, and now the leader of the conservative Nationalist Party, the Welsh-born Hughes was an unabashed British imperialist. Like many Australians of the time, his notion of the British Empire was one based upon ideas of a British race and civilisation spanning the globe, rather than upon narrow definitions of British nationality and possession confined to the British Isles. In other words, the empire belonged to the British people rather than to Britain, and to all the British people whether they lived in Canberra, Cape Town, Vancouver or London. Although the war was supposed to have seen the birth of an Australian nation on the battlefield of Gallipoli, the returned soldiers were swept into a movement for the glorification of empire – the Returned Soldiers' and Sailors' Imperial League of Australia (RSL) – which had recruited 150 000 members by 1919. And Australia was effectively tied into the apparatus of empire by its continuing reliance on the waning strength of the British navy to protect the sparsely populated continent.

While Canada and South Africa pressed for their status as semi-independent British dominions to be spelt out in some sort of declaration by Britain, Australia baulked at the idea of committing the imperial relationship to precise legal form, fearing that it would hasten the empire's dissolution. But the Australians could not block the changes. One change they approved was the creation by Britain in 1925 of a separate Dominions Office, which was hived off from the Colonial Office. As the Dominions secretary Leo

Amery observed, it would mean that 'Colonial Office officials [would no longer be] writing to a nigger one minute and then turning round and writing in the same strain to Dominion Prime Ministers'. Britain went even further the following year when the Balfour report acknowledged that the dominions and Britain were autonomous communities, equal in status and united under the king as members of the British Commonwealth. It was further confirmation of the status they had won in wartime and it was enshrined in law in 1931 by the Statute of Westminster. Australia remained wary that it might encourage the breakup of the empire and declined to ratify the statute, despite various practical advantages for doing so, until 1942.

To cement Australia into a system of imperial defence, Britain's Admiral Jellicoe toured the Far East to report on the postwar defence of the far-flung empire. He recommended that the key to the empire's defence in that part of the world be a naval base to be built with dominion contributions at Singapore. Its strategic position was meant to prevent any Japanese attack on Australia, since any invasion force from Japan would be threatened by the existence of a base along its lines of communication. Some may have wondered whether a naval base at Sydney would not have been an even better defence for Australia. But few put their doubts into words. And there were reasons for their relatively complacent attitude.

The Washington Naval Conference of 1921–22 saw the world's naval powers agree to restrict the size of their navies in the hope of averting a renewal of the prewar race for naval supremacy between Britain and Germany. Under the agreement, Britain restricted the size of her navy and acknowledged Japanese naval supremacy in the western Pacific. Under American pressure, London renounced the Anglo-Japanese alliance, thereby effectively throwing in her lot with the Americans in any future Pacific war. It was an acknowledgment by London that American assistance in any future European war was more important than the alliance with Japan. Australia, which had taken some comfort from the Anglo-Japanese alliance, now found itself exposed to the renewed possibility of a future Japanese challenge, albeit distant at the time. The immediate effect of the conference was effectively to divide the Pacific between America and Japan, while Britain committed itself to build the naval base at Singapore as a barrier to Japanese expansion into the Indian Ocean. Despite the distant possibility of a Japanese threat, there was considerable confidence throughout the war-weary world that a conflict could be averted by the ongoing process of disarmament, backed up by the new League of Nations.

Because the war had emphasised the isolation of Australia from its European suppliers, and its vulnerability to a blockade of its trade routes, the postwar period witnessed a determined push for the industrialisation of its economy behind an ever-higher protective tariff wall which sheltered local producers from overseas competition. Although the tariff gave a preferential rate to British imports over foreign imports, there was still a positive incentive for British manufacturers to establish factories in Australia, which many of them did. Australian consumers were exhorted to buy Australian and, if that was not possible, to buy British. A 'great white train' was organised by the Australian-made preference league to tour New South Wales' country towns in 1925 promoting Australian manufactures. It was claimed that the time had come for manufacturers to take the initiative from importers, that the 'path to self-reliance is along the track of secondary industries' which would provide 'the shortest cut to national wealth and security'.

Despite the bluff self-confidence encapsulated in the concept of 'Australia Unlimited', popularised in a book of the same name by E. J. Brady, there was still a sense of Australia being a nation under threat from alien influences. An influenza epidemic that had gathered strength in war-ravaged Europe descended upon Australia as the army of returned servicemen, who had seen so much death at close quarters, now visited death upon their homes. Quarantine measures were ineffective in keeping out the deadly virus. First appearing in Australia in January 1919, within three months 700 victims had died in Victoria and 95 in New South Wales. Theatres and cinemas were closed and state borders were patrolled to prevent infected people spreading the disease. Even Anzac Day was cancelled. By the time it had run its course, 12 000 Australians had died from it.

The government also sought to quarantine Australians from alien ideas. The harsh provisions of the *War Precautions Act* were kept in place until 1920 and were buttressed by the *Customs Act*, with the Customs minister determined to 'defend and preserve Australia for the Empire'. In 1925, the government tried unsuccessfully to deport as illegal immigrants two trade union leaders who had been involved in a shipping strike. 'Australia was not their native land', argued an employer's newspaper, 'and they love it so little they are hell-bent on converting it from a Paradise into a desolation.' It likened the men to 'victims of mental diseases that are both infectious and devastating'. One of the men had been in Australia for 32 years and the other for 15 years. They were more Australian than Hughes' imperial-minded replacement as prime minister, the pukka, Cambridge-educated Stanley Melbourne Bruce who had spent many of his formative years in England and who would end them as a Viscount in the British House of Lords.

A ban on the importation of radical literature was easier to enforce. The propaganda of the Australian Communist Party, which had been formed in 1920, was likened to an epidemic capable of infecting the minds of susceptible individuals. The government caught within its customs net everything from Russian newspapers and works of the British Communist Party to Irish nationalist songs and tracts of the Indian nationalist, Mahatma Gandhi. They were all seized and torn to pieces. Popular films were also targeted, particularly American ones which were blamed for disturbing social changes that saw mixed bathing, women smoking and an apparent increase in urban crime. Censors banned films suggesting 'sexual passion'; those that undermined marriage; those that were 'subversive of morality or virtue'; those that encouraged crime; and those offensive to religion. The moves had wide public support, with one woman calling for all bedroom scenes to be banned so as to preserve 'the sacred intimacies of the mother mystery'.

Even Australian-made films came under the censorious gaze of the timid British Australians. When plans were announced in 1926 for an American company to film the classic convict novel *For the Term of His Natural Life*, there were widespread calls for its export from Australia to be banned, thereby destroying its economic viability. A Tasmanian bishop warned of the film's effect on 'British prestige', while others worried at the effect on migration and foreign investment. It was suggested that current scenes of Australian development should be inserted at the end of the film. The film went ahead under these strictures and was a hit with Australians when it was released. The Hobart *Mercury* was pleased that 'genuine long-faced, English-looking people had been chosen for the cast'.

The furore over the film had revealed the lingering fears in Australian minds about their ability to populate and develop the continent. These fears prompted them to turn against the geographer Griffith Taylor when he had the audacity to argue the essential impossibility of the grandiose assumptions underlying 'Australia Unlimited'. Popular predictions of Australia's population potential varied from an astronomical 200 to 500 million. In contrast, Taylor pointed to the rainfall statistics over much of the continent to support his argument against such a lush vision ever being achieved. Rather than a population of hundreds of millions, which would put the question of Australia's proprietorship beyond question, Taylor suggested that Australia could expect to have just 20 million by the end of the century. This was something Australians could simply not accept. For his insights, Taylor was effectively hounded from the country as Australia embarked on projects to achieve the potential that was proclaimed for it and to populate its wide expanses.

More efforts were made to increase the birthrate. The existing ban on the import of contraceptive devices was buttressed by banning the export of locally produced devices, thereby making them that much more expensive to sell in the limited Australian market. As a result, abortion was a common resort for women anxious to limit their fertility. Although Customs officers remained on guard against contraceptive devices, being warned in 1928 about some from Paris that were designated as being toothbrush holders, the birthrate remained stubbornly low. Even though the population passed six million in 1926, the birthrate was less than in 1911. And only 40 000 immigrants arrived to add their numbers to the existing population. Australia, observed the *Sydney Morning Herald*, could only retain 'white Australia' if it abandoned 'empty Australia'. To try and boost the numbers,

New South Wales introduced child endowment payments of five shillings a week for each child in 1927, while the federal government followed suit 14 years later.

In an effort to continue the conquering of the continent's interior spaces, returned soldiers were despatched into the bush to serve as small farmers on yet more schemes of closer settlement. The schemes were sold to the taxpayers as a way of paying the 'debt of honour' that the nation owed to its surviving servicemen, while some political leaders embraced the schemes as a means of removing men experienced in the ways of war from cities where unemployment might drive them into the arms of the new Communist Party. Some 37 000 ex-soldiers answered the call, but many were undercapitalised or inexperienced in the ways of rural life. The hardships of the bush and bankruptcies drove about half of them back to the cities. Others managed to hang on to their properties and, in many cases, even to do well. They drove into town on roads constructed or improved by revenue raised from a new duty on petrol that was designed to make accessible 'large areas of undeveloped country'.

In order to ensure that Australia realised the full potential that its boosters held out for it, the new Australian prime minister, Stanley Melbourne Bruce, looked to Britain for assistance. What Australia wanted, proclaimed Bruce, was men, money and markets. The men were British men to help continue the occupation of the continent; the money was British capital to provide the infrastructure to support such an occupation; and the markets were British markets for the produce these men would grow on the land they subdued. At the 1923 Imperial Conference in London, Bruce announced that Australia's aim was to 'populate her country' so that she was no longer 'a very small people occupying a very vast territory'. The federal government, which had assumed control of immigration schemes from the states in 1920, borrowed British money to finance the emigration of British men to cultivate the Australian wilderness, growing produce for the British market. Group settlement schemes brought Britons to Australia to clear land on a communal basis which was then divided into small farms. A large, forested area of south-west Western Australia was developed using this scheme at great cost and with little immediate benefit.

While Canada recruited migrants from throughout eastern Europe to fill its 'empty spaces', Australia concentrated on recruiting from Britain alone. Ethnicity became as important as race in determining entry to Australia's pristine shores. Restrictions were introduced on southern Europeans as thousands diverted to Australia after the doors to the United States slammed shut. Whereas 87 per cent of Australia's arrivals in 1923 were described as being 'British white', only 81 per cent were so described in 1924. With around ten per cent unemployment, trade unions led the protests against the newcomers. The government was sensitive to any allegations that it was watering down the sacrosanct level of Australia being 98 per cent British and quickly imposed a range of restrictions directed at southern Europeans. The restrictions were tightened even further in January 1925 when Italians were required to have £40 before being permitted to land and all other southern Europeans were restricted to just 400 new arrivals per month. It did not stop the protests.

A meeting in Mildura of some 450 protesters in February 1925, described as being white Australians and British-born, banned working with any of the newcomers. As with the earlier support for 'white Australia', the protests were not just about jobs but had a real racial undercurrent. The RSL branch in the Melbourne suburb of Essendon protested against Australia being a 'dumping ground for the scum of the Mediterranean ports', while Melbourne branch representatives of the RSL met to protest against 'decadent alien races' transforming Australia into a 'polyglot nation', as if it and every other European nation could not be described as polyglot already.

Many Italians headed for the sugar fields of north Queensland where, in the 1890s, several hundred of their compatriots had been imported in a vain attempt to end the industry's dependence on the indentured labour of Pacific Islanders. In a visit to Townsville, a Baptist minister reported that Italians were making north Queensland 'hot-beds of low morals', it being 'not uncommon to walk around and not hear a word of English'. It was time for another royal commission, this time into the social and economic effects of aliens in north Queensland. As it happened, the commission reported that Italians were good workers, good unionists and lived according to acceptable Australian standards. Nevertheless, it urged that unemployed Italians be transferred to other areas and that Italian clubs be discouraged. The federal government's aliens registration law, a hangover from the wartime regulations, was used to track the settlement patterns of non-British migrants and to stop large numbers congregating in any one place. Meanwhile, government restrictions on the entry of southern Europeans was taking effect as Bruce promised to maintain Australia's 'racial purity'. He was supported by Ambrose Pratt of the Industries Protection League who claimed that Australians were the 'purest' people in the world and the 'only white race in the world exclusively to own a continent'.

British Australians were divided about the value of the Italian and other southern European immigrants. Some worried about the threat to their jobs from Italian competition; some worried about the threat to Australia's Protestant majority by the entry of Catholic Italians; some worried about the increasing Italian ownership of farming land; and some were worried by the different language and customs of the Italians which they feared would not easily assimilate into British Australia. The defenders of the Italians argued they were assets to Australia as law-abiding, land-developing and nation-building citizens. As Brisbane's Roman Catholic Archbishop Duhig pointed out in 1925, Italians 'do not hang about towns, but go straight to the land' where they work until becoming farmers and raising large families. Duhig warned, 'If we do not allow into this country those that will fill up the vacant spaces instead of crowding into cities, then we may expect trouble in the future and trouble too, from people who may be much more alien to us than Italians or Germans.' Duhig, who had spent pleasant years in Rome and proved a stalwart defender of his Italian parishioners, did not find many supporters for his views in a postwar era when ideas of British ethnicity held sway.

The rising Labor MP, Dr H. V. Evatt, defended Australia's restrictive immigration at the International Labour Migration Congress in London in 1926. Evatt deflected moves against white Australia by advising that the Australian labour movement was 'bitterly opposed to southern European immigration, especially Italian', because of the numbers in which they were arriving and racist attitudes towards southern Italians. He was backed at home by Labor leader Matt Charlton, who asserted the party's determination 'to cultivate a purely Australian sentiment and maintain the virility of the race by restricting it to white people'. According to their tortured definitions, it seemed that southern Europeans were now outside their definition of 'white people'.

Such a classification of Europeans was supported in the works of eugenicists such as J. H. Curle who argued forcefully for the scientific breeding of the human race. In his widely-read eugenicist tract, *To-day and To-morrow*, Curle warned Australians in 1926 against the admission of too many southern Europeans:

> *You are getting scared about your emptiness; in order to fill up with whites, you are taking any whites—the dregs of Europe. They won't do your strain any good. The Greeks for example! You are letting in too many Greeks ... Go slowly on the South Europeans; your ideal should be quality, quantity means nothing at all.*

By sticking rigidly to its exclusionist immigration policy, Curle predicted that Australians 'could become perhaps the finest white peoples in the world'.

Definitely outside the pale were black immigrants, although some were admitted on temporary permits as entertainers in the popular dance halls of Sydney and Melbourne. They were there to entertain, not to intermingle with white Australians, as one troupe of black Americans discovered in 1928 when they incurred the wrath of Victorian police officers. The police had raided their flat late one night after seeing through the window three white women being 'pulled about'. The jitterbugging women were arrested for vagrancy and a thousand Australian men turned up to silently witness the sight of white women who would willingly consort with black men. The women, who were all allowed to use assumed names for their court appearance, were acquitted since they were all gainfully employed. But the dancers were run out of Australia, catching the first train to Sydney to connect with a US-bound vessel. Arriving at Sydney, they were followed around the city by a hostile crowd as they sought unsuccessfully to secure accommodation. Future visits by black American entertainers and boxers were banned 'in the interests of "white Australia" and moral decency'. Billy Hughes, deposed as prime minister, seized on the case to attack his own government's immigration policy. 'This bit of the world belongs to Australians', proclaimed this former British migrant made good, 'and must be preserved from the entry of undesirables' which, in Hughes's view, ranged from black Americans to Italians and Greeks.

Although the immigration schemes never realised the grandiose hopes of the government, the land under cultivation increased markedly during the 1920s. Land under wheat increased by a third, while there was considerable expansion of sugar, dairying and fruit growing. Often the farms were too small and uneconomical without the payment of government subsidies and the provision of protected markets. Fortunately, the money borrowed to finance their passages from Britain and their establishment on the land was underpinned by the income from wool and wheat prices which remained comfortably high for most of the 1920s. Australia was repeating its experience of the 1880s, expanding onto marginal land and sometimes breaking up extensive and efficient sheep farms into small and inefficient dairy and wheat farms.

The conquering of the outback was assisted by new technology that saw aircraft break the relative isolation of distant pastoral properties, allowing for regular mail services and even the provision of medical services by means of a 'flying doctor' who could be contacted by the new pedal wireless sets installed in many station homesteads. The regular wet season that cut off contact across the tropical north for months at a time was effectively at an end. The first commercial air service was not between Melbourne and Sydney but between the towns of Geraldton and Broome in the far north-west of Western Australia at the start of the 1921 wet season. As an Australian booster observed in 1924, the coming of aircraft would mean that the 'far bush must lose much of its sense of isolation, especially for women accustomed to urban life'. On the ground, the stagecoaches, bullock drays and camel trains that provided transport to those parts of the outback beyond the reach of the railways faced increasing competition from the new motor trucks that provided the sinews of a quicker and more reliable transport service. Whereas a bullock dray might cart a wagon-load of wool 15 miles in a day, a truck could cover ten times that distance. And the advantages of motor transport improved even more as the Commonwealth began in 1923 to finance the construction of new 'developmental roads' together with the improvement of existing arterial roads.

The isolation of the bush was further cut by the establishment in 1923 of a commercial radio station in Sydney. As further stations were set up to cover the continent, farmers were able to receive daily weather forecasts and updated reports from local and foreign markets. Ideas were even floated of establishing a ring of meteorological stations around the Antarctic continent, linked by wireless, to provide long-range weather forecasts for the Southern Hemisphere. Such a chain of bases would also help to buttress Australian, New Zealand and British claims to large parts of Antarctica, claims they attempted to assert with the despatch of an Australian-led exploring and scientific expedition in 1929–30 under Sir Douglas Mawson.

The extension of wireless services in Australia would help the gramophone to civilise the bush, allowing women and children to join their menfolk in the outback knowing that they could ameliorate the often unbearable loneliness with some of the city amenities. In extolling the new service, the acting prime minister Earle Page acknowledged that 'the "Lonely Bush" has long been a phrase that Australians have not liked' and that it could now be expunged from Australian conversation since the civilising entertainment beamed into the bush from the cities would mean that the 'word "lonely" will be eliminated from Australian life'. It would also ensure 'continuous connection with other parts of the Empire' and encourage migration. The new technology would take some time to make its impact and loneliness would continue to be synonymous with bush life, as the journalist Ernestine Hill confirmed with *The Great Australian Loneliness*, a book published in 1937 which recorded her meanderings across the interior.

The federal government accelerated its attempts to develop the Northern Territory, although never fulfilling its deal with South Australia in 1911 to construct a railway from Adelaide to Darwin. In a short-lived experiment in 1926, the government divided the Territory into North and Central Australia. Bruce was explicit about the purpose. With only 3400 white people compared to some 25 000 Aborigines, the Northern Territory posed a danger to the preservation of white Australia. He claimed that Australians needed to show the teeming populations of Asia that they were using the land or else face having it taken from them. By so doing, argued Bruce, Australia would 'consolidate our claim to that area'. He suggested that Western Australia cede its tropical parts to the federal government so that they could be administered and developed as a unit. Instead of populating the north-west with white people, the white population was actually decreasing, with the work of the pastoral properties being done by poorly-paid Aborigines. In 1920, the Western Australian government had established a North-West department, based in Broome, which was mainly directed towards the encouragement of agriculture in place of pastoralism. Cotton and bananas were two of the products tried, but with little success, and the department was abolished in 1926. Despite this, and their own development efforts coming to nothing, the federal proposal was rejected by the Western Australians.

Once they were successful in effectively occupying the north, white Australians would acquire a claim of moral proprietorship which they could flourish in the face of any country that disputed their right to it. However, they had to overcome the widespread conviction that the tropics were unsuitable for occupation by white people. As J. H. Curle argued in *To-day and To-morrow*,

> It has been proved over and over again that British stock will not thrive in the tropics. Grown people may go there and thrive; but their children, if born and reared there, will deteriorate, and the second generation will begin running to seed. I do not think tropical Australia will prove the exception.

Not that it mattered, according to Curle, since the Australian tropics were 'mostly poorish, unwatered country' that would not solve the population problems of countries like Japan. Despite this mixed assessment, Australians were determined that their tropics be occupied by a population that was white and overwhelmingly British. Although the main population group in the Northern Territory was Aboriginal, they were no longer seen as a potent threat to the European possession of their lands. Acts of resistance by Aborigines were dealt with, as they always had been, by punitive expeditions unleashing massive retaliation upon any Aborigines coming within their sights.

In 1926, there were allegations that more than 30 Aborigines had been killed by a police party and their bodies burned in the Kimberley in retaliation for a white man having been killed. Complaints from a missionary led to a royal commission, the report of which caused two police constables to be charged with murder, only to be subsequently acquitted by a magistrate for lack of evidence. Indeed, as has recently been argued by Rod Moran, the massacre may have been invented by the mentally disturbed missionary. Other killings certainly did occur. But they did so against a background of increasing sympathy by urban Australians for the plight of the Aborigines. The Adelaide *Advertiser* claimed that the alleged massacre in the Kimberley had 'shocked all humane people in the Commonwealth, and created an irresistible demand for public action to save the remnant of the black population from extinction'. However, as Marjorie Barnard and Flora Eldershaw later asked, was their anxiety to 'save the dark people ... only in the same spirit that they want to save the koala from extinction?' Anyway, the public anxiety was slow to be addressed by governments. The administration of Aboriginal affairs was divided between the states and the federal government and no common approach proved possible. Instead, the killing went on for a time. Even when the guns fell silent, Aborigines continued to be killed in great numbers through the wilful neglect of their health and welfare. For his part, Curle confidently predicted that the Aborigines would 'hardly last out this century' and no attempt should be made to avert their passing:

*Evolution rejected these peoples, and knows best; our sadness, as we
see them pass, need be no more than sentimental. Evolution has
spared us. Is not that the supreme consideration?*

There was certainly little attempt in the Northern Territory to stem the
continuing demise of the Aborigines.

The federally administered Northern Territory was the scene of
countless massacres and individual killings. The pastoralists could not survive
without cheap Aboriginal labour on their cattle stations. However, they
complained about the Aborigines being unreliable as workers, while others.
took livestock for food or as a means of retaliating against the invaders. The
whites went armed to guard against retaliatory attack from Aborigines held in
check by the system of terror. In 1927, one station boss referred to the
Aborigines as 'the Territory's biggest problem. They are a menace in many
ways. They are gradually dying out. They might be better away, but at present
they cannot be done without.' In 1928, the killing of a white man by
Aborigines north-west of Alice Springs prompted another punitive
expedition, this time under the control of mounted constable William
Murray, who conceded that 31 Aborigines were killed. Missionaries estimated
that as many as 100 had been killed. Again, Murray was exonerated by a
subsequent inquiry. And his deeds were later written up as acts of heroism in
Sydney's *Sunday Sun* by Ernestine Hill, who portrayed the murderous Murray
as the 'Man Whose Gun Keeps White Men Safe in the Wilds'.

When human rights were being ignored so blatantly, it is not
surprising that the question of land rights was not even on the agenda. In its
scathing editorial, the *Advertiser* had referred to the Aborigines as 'the
original *occupants* of this continent' rather than the original *owners*. There
was no question in European minds of Aborigines being conceded their land
rights in compensation for their past dispossession, particularly when more
basic rights were being ignored. Aborigines were being beaten, raped and
often killed with hardly a white hand being raised to prevent it. Aborigines
were denied education and health care, while in Western Australia they were
not allowed into Perth without a permit. Although there was an Australian
Inland Mission hospital at Alice Springs, it refused to treat Aborigines who
consequently went blind with treatable trachoma or died from diseases such
as yaws.

Estimates of the Aboriginal population suggested that the 'full-bloods'
still seemed set to die out over time, despite attempts to protect the remnants
as a curiosity of Australia's past. While the 'full-bloods' were declining in
numbers, the numbers of part-Aborigines were increasing faster than the
increase in white Australians. To deal with what was perceived as a problem,
children of mixed heritage were taken from their parents and placed in
rudimentary 'homes' in Alice Springs and Darwin from where they were

expected to graduate into jobs in the pastoral industry or, for the girls, into domestic service. It was intended that they should sever their links with their Aboriginal mothers and the customs of their people and be absorbed into the white community. Some were sent south to Adelaide and Melbourne for this purpose. As Prime Minister Stanley Melbourne Bruce observed in 1927 when requesting that South Australia accept young 'quadroons' and 'octoroons':

> *If these babies were removed, at their present early age, from their present environment to homes in South Australia, they would not know in later life that they had aboriginal blood and would probably be absorbed into the white population and become useful citizens.*

But the South Australian premier rejected the proposal, claiming that it would be 'greatly to the disadvantage of South Australia' since 'persons with aboriginal blood almost invariably mate with the lowest class of whites'.

In 1927, a new parliament house, painted stark white, was opened in the nation's new capital of Canberra, marking a further step in the continuing process of constructing a nation capable of occupying the continent. It was a planned city set well away from the sometimes plague-ridden and debilitating coastal cities and would, hoped the Hobart *Mercury*, mark the 'beginning of a general exodus from the overgrown towns to the vacant country'. Public servants accustomed to the civilised surroundings of Melbourne and destined to be shifted to the bush capital were assured that it was not 'alive with venomous snakes', as many of them apparently feared.

A 'raggedly picturesque' elder of the local Aboriginal tribe which had been dispossessed of their land by the squatters, and were now about to be dispossessed again by this act of nation building, turned up to observe the proceedings. The officious police tried to turn him away but were dissuaded by the crowd which took the side of the Aborigine, with a sympathetic clergyman protesting that 'the native had a better right than any man present to a place on the steps of the House of Parliament'. The crowd then listened to the moderator of the Presbyterian church thank God 'for having given us this fair land as an inheritance' while Prime Minister Bruce confidently predicted that Australia was 'on the threshold of achievement' which would see 'millions of the British race ... people this land'. 'Who can foretell', he asked rhetorically, 'how great may be the part our nation will play in the years to come?' Two years later, the nation's hopes were dashed when the Wall Street Crash sent the world economy spiralling into depression.

Recommended Reading

Geoffrey Bolton, 1992, *Spoils and Spoilers*, Allen & Unwin, Sydney.

E. J. Brady, 1918, *Australia Unlimited*, George Robertson, Melbourne.

F. K. Crowley, 1970, *Australia's Western Third*, Heinemann, Melbourne.

F. K. Crowley, 1973, *Modern Australia in Documents*, Vol. 1, Wren Publishing, Melbourne.

J. H. Curle, 1926, *To-day and Tomorrow*, Methuen, London.

David Day, 1996, *Contraband and Controversy*, Australian Government Publishing Service Press, Canberra.

M. Barnard Eldershaw, 1939, *My Australia*, Jarrolds, London.

Heather Goodall, 1996, *Invasion to Embassy: Land in Aboriginal Politics in New South Wales 1770–1972*, Allen & Unwin, Sydney.

L. St. Clare Grondona, 1924, *The Kangaroo Keeps on Talking or the All-British Continent: A Description of Australian Life and Industries*, Victoria Publishing House, London.

W. J. Hudson and Jane North (eds), 1980, *My Dear P.M.: R.G. Casey's Letters to S.M. Bruce 1924–1929*, Australian Government Publishing Service Press, Canberra.

Marilyn Lake, 1987, *The Limits of Hope: Soldier Settlement in Victoria, 1951–38*, Oxford University Press, Melbourne.

Stuart Macintyre, 1986, *Oxford History of Australia*, Vol. 4, Oxford University Press, Melbourne.

Andrew Markus, 1990, *Governing Savages*, Allen & Unwin, Sydney.

Rod Moran, 1999, *Massacre Myth*, Access Press, Perth.

J. M. Powell, 1988, *An Historical Geography of Modern Australia*, Cambridge University Press, Cambridge.

Deborah Bird Rose, 1991, *Hidden Histories*, Aboriginal Studies Press, Canberra.

Richard White, 1981, *Inventing Australia*, George Allen & Unwin, Sydney.

15

'OUR CLAIM TO BE ALLOWED TO REMAIN A WHITE AUSTRALIA'

At the opening of the new federal parliament building in Canberra in 1927, Prime Minister Stanley Melbourne Bruce had predicted that Australia was on 'the threshold of achievement'. Instead, it was on the threshold of the worst depression it had ever experienced. From a decade when hope was in the ascendant, Australia slid into a decade of fear and hopelessness as armies of the unemployed trudged the outback looking for work. Instead of 'Australia Unlimited', with all the growth that vision implied, the overriding concern became one of simply holding onto what Australians had already achieved. By 1929, Canberra had just 7000 inhabitants and there was talk of closing it down.

During the 1920s, Australia had borrowed money from London to promote British migration and the intensive settlement of the continent. It had financed small farms and provided the infrastructure necessary to make them viable, such as railways, schools and marketing schemes. Borrowed capital also went into promoting the industrialisation of the economy. The increasing debt was incurred in the confidence that Australia's great future would allow it to keep up the repayments. Such was the confidence in Australia's future that the Wall Street Crash in October 1929 was seen initially as advantageous for Australia. Even a month later, as its effects began to lengthen Australian dole queues, the new Labor government of James Scullin predicted a return to prosperity in the new year.

Contrary to Scullin's prediction, the depression was disastrous for Australia. It had been floating on a sea of British loans and been buoyed up by high wool and wheat prices. When wool and wheat prices fell in the wake of the depression, the flow of loan funds from London dried to a trickle. The government cut its budget to suit its reduced circumstances, which spread despondency even further. Unemployment climbed to 30 per cent of registered trade union members in 1932 after rarely reaching ten per cent during the 1920s. A more graphic indicator was provided by the per capita beer consumption, which shrank from 11 gallons per annum in 1928 to seven gallons in 1933. The Labor government fell apart over whether the wage earners of Australia or the bondholders of Britain would have to tighten their belts to see the nation through the troubles. Scullin found himself hemmed in by the conservative banks and business interests, by the head of his own Commonwealth Bank and by the visiting British banker Sir Otto Niemeyer who advised further financial stringency. Niemeyer noted in his diary that, despite the depression, members of the Melbourne Stock Exchange were still 'obsessed with the exploded doctrine of the enormous potentialities of Australia'.

Scullin succumbed to pressure from the bankers. Pensions and wages were cut while import duties were raised, and the Australian pound was cut loose from gold and devalued against sterling. This made Australian exports of primary produce more competitive on the world market. The plan was to restore Australia as a producer of primary produce and extinguish plans for secondary industry. Despite a glutted world market, Scullin exhorted the nation's wheat growers to grow even more wheat. In a radio broadcast to wheat farmers in March 1930, Scullin claimed optimistically that their 'misfortunes are blessings in disguise'. By shifting from sheep to wheat, more of the continent's virgin soil could be tilled:

> *There are large areas of land producing only wool that could produce both wheat and wool. Intensive cultivation will go far towards the salvation of Australia. The wheatfarmers have a golden opportunity to give the lead.*

When they did so, they found that the price slumped even further.

The soldier settlers of Victoria's Mallee region had tilled its dry soils during the 1920s with some success. But now they battled against both the falling prices and the counterattack of nature as drought exacerbated their predicament and they watched their soil blown away in dust storms. A newspaper article in 1934 portrayed their plight in terms of war, with the farmer

...out in No Man's Land, which is no longer No Man's Land, but is conquered territory. Despite his lack of the sinews of war, despite the inclemency of seasons and the depression of the market, despite his inability to send his children to school beyond the little Mallee township five miles away, despite the widespread ruin about him ..., he has not given back his square mile of sand to Nature who endowed it so capriciously.

But many were forced to abandon the struggle or shifted back into pastoralism as wool prices recovered. Others turned to glib political panaceas as the solution to their problems.

As elsewhere in the world, Australians reacted to the apparently intractable economic problems, which seemed beyond the ability of the normal democratic process to solve, by supporting a range of popular movements expressing disenchantment with politicians in general and the Labor governments in particular, both Scullin's federal government and the New South Wales' government of the populist demagogue, Jack Lang. Political parties were seen as being sectional, looking after the narrow interests of particular groups in the community while, during this time of national crisis, no-one seemed to be looking out for the interests of the country as a whole. Hundreds of thousands flocked to the banner of the All for Australia League which was supposedly above political parties. Others met secretly in various quasi-military groupings to discuss seizing power from governments they believed to be dangerously communist and therefore to have lost their legitimacy. Yet others in the countryside sought to split off from the centres of power, whether it be Sydney or Canberra, and chart their own course out of the depression. In Western Australia, the inhabitants voted to tear the federation asunder and leave Australia altogether. However, the British government, not wishing to become embroiled in Australia's political upheavals, saved the day by refusing to entertain their demand.

There were also groups like the Melbourne-based Empire Honour League which believed that 'the whole Satanic Force of the Evil Spirit World' was behind the threat to socialise the country. It feared a natural majority of industrial workers, old age pensioners and farmers would give Labor a majority at the 1934 election and planned to fight it by placing a million bibles in the pockets of a million Australian boys and girls. All its patrons were prominent Protestants. Apart from bibles, it was intended that people defined as 'disloyalists' should not be permitted to stand for parliament, to vote for parliament or to occupy public office, especially in teaching. It appealed for support from 'every right thinking Britisher'.

Such groups on both the left and right were hampered by their divided loyalties. The fascist-leaning New Guard broke up a communist meeting in Wollongong in December 1931, burning seized communist literature in the manner of the Nazis but then gathering around the righteous flames to sing, not a Nazi anthem, but 'God Save the King'. It and other right-wing movements concentrated more on defending the established order than on seeking to replace it. And their objectives were largely achieved by the established institutions. In May 1932, the New South Wales' governor dismissed the Labor premier, Jack Lang, after Lang tried to repudiate interest payments on British loans, arguing that the bondholders of Britain should also share the pain of the depression. Lang went quietly, stood for re-election and lost. Similarly, Scullin was sent to the polls by parliament and lost when his popular acting treasurer, 'Honest Joe' Lyons, crossed to the conservative side. For their part, communists waved red flags which confirmed their alien inspiration and prevented them from cloaking themselves in the garb of Australian nationalism.

Once Scullin was tossed from office in 1931, the conservative political ascendancy returned to what seemed to be its natural place in the seats of power. Occupying some of the front seats were men with close attachments to Britain and its empire. Men such as former prime minister Stanley Melbourne Bruce who was despatched to London as Australian High Commissioner and stayed to become Viscount Bruce. His acolyte Richard Casey, who represented Bruce in London in the 1920s, and who was now seen as a prospective Australian leader. Casey later served as a member of the British war cabinet, then British governor of Bengal before returning to his career in Australian politics, finally becoming Australian governor general and being elevated to a British baronetcy. And there was Robert Menzies, who would become Australia's longest serving prime minister before being awarded the order of the garter and being made Lord Warden of Britain's Cinque Ports.

Given his background, Menzies was the most surprising of the three in the strength of his affections for Britain. He had been brought up in the small Victorian country town of Jeparit where his father, a storekeeper of Scottish origin, serviced the struggling wheat farmers of the Wimmera district. Menzies won scholarships to public schools and Melbourne University where he took a first class honours degree in law. He only went to Britain for the first time in 1935, after rising through the Victorian and Commonwealth parliamentary ranks to become attorney general. As Menzies caught his first sight of England, he scribbled in his diary:

> At last we are in England. Our journey to Mecca has ended and our minds abandoned to reflections which can so strangely (unless you remember our traditions and upbringing) move the sense of those who go 'home' to a land they have never seen.

Under leaders such as this, it was not surprising that Australia held tight to Britain as the international situation steadily deteriorated during the 1930s in both Europe and the Pacific.

Australia was committed to the system of imperial defence under which each dominion was responsible for its own local defence and they and Britain would all unite to defend the empire wherever a threat developed. Central to the imperial defence system in the Indian and Pacific oceans was the Singapore naval base, which remained uncompleted and bereft of a fleet. Instead of the fleet that Admiral Jellicoe had envisaged for it when proposing the base in 1919, it was decided that Singapore would become a base that could withstand attack for several months until a fleet could be sent from Britain. It was a mark of Britain's relative decline as a naval power. The only seas she continued to rule with any confidence were the ones that washed the shores of her own island. The problem which few wanted to confront was the question of a two-front war. If Britain was simultaneously threatened in Europe and the Pacific, how would a fleet be found for Singapore in time to prevent its capture? Like the dutiful dominion that it was, Australia continued to accept repeated British assurances that a fleet could be sent in such circumstances. It could take some confidence from the other European powers with interests in the Pacific. The Dutch and French had colonies and navies to defend them in the seas between Australia and Japan. And the United States had forces on the Philippines. Moreover, Japan was occupied with its ongoing war in China and was also restrained by the possible threat from Russia. All these factors helped to allay Australian concerns about the value of the British defence guarantee, allowing it to economise on its home defence while concentrating its resources on promoting economic recovery and the further development of the continent. Australia's reliance on Britain for its defence was mirrored in its economic dependence upon Britain.

Under an agreement reached at Ottawa in 1932 with British representatives, Australia allowed British manufacturers greater access to its market by raising the tariff on non-British goods in return for Australian primary products receiving greater access to the British market. The effect was to encourage more British manufacturers to establish factories in Australia where they could save on transport costs to the Australian market and avoid the tariff, albeit a preferential one, against British imports. The primary produce provided with preferential markets in Britain came mainly from the closer settlement schemes, such as fruit, wine and butter. While trade within the empire increased as a result of this agreement, it did so at the expense of foreign countries which objected to being shut out of imperial markets. Japan and the United States, the two Pacific powers of most importance to Australia, were particularly critical of the British move from free trade to imperial autarky. Despite the Ottawa Agreement, there was some recognition in Canberra that the British Empire could not alone solve Australia's economic conundrum, that markets would have to be found outside the empire. The conservative foreign minister, John Latham, took a goodwill mission to Japan and other Asian countries in 1934, which led to trade commissioners being stationed in Batavia, Shanghai and Tokyo. But Australia's early Asian push sputtered out when Latham resigned from parliament soon after his return. And it was completely reversed in 1936 when the government deliberately snubbed the Japanese partly in order to please British manufacturers.

Trade with Japan had been increasing during the 1930s as Japan bought more wool to clothe its troops in China and for possible use in Siberia against Russia. In return, it was selling more cotton piece goods to Australia at the expense of British manufacturers. At the same time, American car manufacturers were making valuable inroads into the Australian market at the expense of British models. The government reacted in 1936 with a so-called trade diversion policy which cut back Japanese and American (including Canadian) imports into Australia and diverted them to British manufacturers, at the same time hoping to boost Australia's secondary industry, particularly the production of cars. Australia had seriously miscalculated in the mistaken belief that Japan would not retaliate. But Japan did so, seriously reducing its purchases of wool. Australia had succeeded in offending the two Pacific powers it most needed to retain friendly relations with, while placating Britain.

Although this mad policy seemed to be predicated on the historic understanding that Australia would exchange its primary produce for Britain's secondary products, its principal impulse was really to boost secondary industries in Australia. As the rising conservative politician Robert Menzies informed the Royal Empire Society in June 1936, the old economic compact between Australia and Britain was no longer viable. During the 1920s, Australia had tried to physically occupy the continent's broad expanses by aspiring to settle a million men on its untilled vastness and by opening up Australia's tropical north to European occupation. The collapse of primary produce prices in the early 1930s, and the inability of Britain to absorb all that Australia was capable of growing, saw Australia acknowledge the economic impossibility of making the continent's distant and relatively infertile parts fruitful through intensive cultivation. The government increasingly looked to the development of secondary industries as the main means to support a great population and thereby assert and secure its proprietorship over the entire continent. As Menzies informed his London audience, it was the development of manufacturing that would ensure 'a thickly populated Australia 50 years hence'. It would be factory workers as much as farmers who would fend off the feared Asian hordes.

The evaporation of this vision threatened the 150-year-old drive to claim the moral proprietorship of the continent by occupying its vast interior and tilling its soil. By provoking a Japanese ban on the purchase of Australian wool, the trade diversion policy made this vision seem even more ephemeral. As the agitated secretary of the Quambatook Agricultural Society reminded Prime Minister Lyons in 1936, who was doing his personal best to populate the country by having 11 children, the policy of trade diversion would hamper 'the successful occupation of the land, which must form the basis of our claim to be allowed to remain a White Australia and integral part of the British Empire'. Trade diversion had tried to satisfy both traditional British Australians and those backing industrialisation. It failed miserably and the government was forced to back down in the face of the Japanese retaliation and the protests of the wool growers.

Asserting a claim of effective proprietorship over the continent required Australia to have a sufficient population to occupy its many parts. However, the 1930s saw renewed concern about the faltering birthrate as Australians delayed their marriages or turned to the contraceptive advice that was increasingly on offer. Engaged women were sent unsolicited material on contraceptives, despite Billy Hughes railing against it in parliament as being 'opposed to the vital interests of the community'. Some imported books on birth control that would have been denied admission in the 1920s were now allowed through customs. However, the ban on imported contraceptives stayed in place, although it was slightly eased to allow in contraceptives provided they did not include instructions. Similarly, an American film showing the birth of a baby was banned by the censor in case it turned young married women 'against motherhood and the inconvenience and suffering entailed'. Restrictions on birth control remained sufficiently strict to force many women to resort either to the Racial Hygiene Association, with its aim of improving the Australian race through selective breeding, or to endure the dangers of an illegal abortion. Despite these official impediments, sufficient women were able to control their fertility such that the birthrate again plumbed the alarming depths seen in the early 1900s, while predictions were heard of the population soon reaching a point at which it would begin to inexorably decline, much like the Aborigines.

Instead of books about 'Australia Unlimited', there were books on Australia's national decline, based to a large extent on the decline of the birthrate and its implications for Australia's earlier hopes of future greatness. As in the early 1900s, women were held responsible for endangering the nation's future by seeking roles in society outside of the traditional one of home and hearth. Women wanted to control more than just their fertility. There were demands for 'equality with men', with role models such as the aviator Amy Johnson showing by her feat in flying from London to Darwin in 1930 that women could emulate men in the most taxing of tasks. Popular new periodicals such as the *Women's Weekly*, begun in 1933, encouraged women to look beyond their assigned role as 'man's plaything' despite warnings from the Catholic Archbishop of Brisbane that the 'modern girl' intent on 'breaking down the barriers behind which her sex found honour in the past is contributing in no small measure to the killing of true romance'. Unemployed men railed against a system that left them without work, and their families without an adequate income, while single women were working on low wages. Women, claimed journalist Warren

Denning, were in 'ruthless and relentless competition with men'. In this worrying era of economic and political uncertainty, it raised fresh doubts about the virility of Australian manhood.

Despite the failure of the birthrate to respond to official restrictions and public exhortations, and the failure of British migrants to arrive in the required numbers, there was continuing opposition to making up the population deficit with southern Europeans. Although limits imposed in the 1920s had reduced the numbers of southern Europeans gaining entry to Australia, there was still anxiety about Australia's Britishness being diluted. With unemployment so high, Scullin had increased the restrictions imposed by his conservative predecessor against Italian immigrants by halving the numbers allowed admittance. Ironically, the numbers of British wanting to emigrate to such a depressed economy decreased even faster so there was a rise in Italians as a percentage of total new arrivals. At the same time, they were outnumbered by disillusioned Italians departing from Australia. These statistics did not stop Scullin from cracking down on several shiploads of Italian men *en route* from or about to leave Italy. Sixty-six of them were prevented from landing when their vessel arrived in Sydney in December 1930.

The Italians appealed to Mussolini, while the Italian press argued that Australians, with their empty continent, had 'a moral duty to admit a certain regular percentage of migrants'. This was not what Australians wanted to hear, reminding them as it did of their failure to achieve a claim of moral proprietorship over the continent by effectively occupying its empty spaces. Soon after, 101 Italians were prevented from landing at Fremantle, despite some of them being naturalised Australians, causing further tensions in Australian–Italian relations. Scullin, who happened to be in Rome at the time on his way to London, explained to the Italian press and to Mussolini that Australia was not an empty continent and that most of it was unsuitable for intensive development. This did not prevent an Italian official arriving in Sydney in February 1932 to press for a liberalisation of Australia's restrictions, pointing to Italy's population pressures and Australia's relative emptiness. Meanwhile, 14 of the Italians detained on board their ship escaped ashore in Sydney, where they were soon arrested, gaoled and subsequently deported.

The deported Italians joined a growing outflow of disgruntled British migrants who failed to find opportunities in the depressed economy. Customs officers trained to look for illegal stowaways seeking to enter Australia now found themselves stumbling across stowaways seeking a way out of Australia. Between 1930 and 1936, there was a net exodus of 30000 Britons from Australia. When this was set against the inflow of some 150000 non-Britons, mainly southern Europeans, who arrived in the four decades after federation, it was found by 1936 that the previously sacrosanct figure of Australia's population being composed of 98 per cent British stock no longer applied. To the anger of MPs and the shock of the press, the figure had dropped to just 97 per cent.

While assisted passage schemes for British immigrants were resumed in the late 1930s, they failed to evoke much interest in Britain, prompting Australia to consider turning to sources in northern Europe for their immigrants. As a government minister argued in 1937, while trying to placate public concern, 'we can hardly slam the door on the rest of the world'. To allay public concern about the influx of non-Britons, authorities used the *Aliens Act* to track their movements and residences in order to stop them creating 'alien blocs'. The implication was clear: six million Australians did not have the moral right to exclude non-British immigrants from the continent's 'empty spaces' if they were not willing or able to develop those lands themselves.

The sugar industry of north Queensland was a particular concern of some Australians who were alarmed at the growing concentration of Italians during the 1920s, arousing historic fears of the continent's northern parts, in the relative absence of British Australians, being occupied by aliens. A North Queensland British Preference League was formed in 1930 to defend 'British Australia' by seeking to ban Italian ownership of farms, to ensure the predominance of British workers on the cane fields and to boycott Italian-owned businesses. The president of the Innisfail chapter of the league sought support in the state parliament, claiming that

> ... *the trend of affairs in this Far North constitutes a definite menace to Australian ideals. In a population of about 100 000 there are 7000 of one foreign race [Italians], and double that number of other races — black, yellow and 'piebald'.*

Its appeal met with some success. Cane growers agreed to increase their employment of British cane cutters so that 85 per cent overall would be British and 90 per cent in the sugar areas south of Townsville. The populist, Sydney-based *Smith's Weekly* ran rabid headlines in 1930 describing Innisfail as the 'Town of Dreadful Dagoes' where 'Foreign Scum Oozes from its Highways'. Across the continent in the gold town of Kalgoorlie, a two-day riot in 1934 saw Italians, Greeks and Yugoslavs become the target of rampaging British Australians angered by the killing in a brawl of one of their number and concerned to expel what they regarded as the alien, competing element from their midst. Two more men were killed before the tumult died away.

The Italians defended themselves as best they could. In north Queensland, their numerical strength in some areas helped to provide protection against the attacks, while a long-standing treaty between Italy and Britain provided partial protection against official attacks. At the same time, Italian Australians tried to assuage suspicions about their intentions. A poem in an Italian–Australian magazine answered the more common complaints made against them by anxious British Australians. Entitled *The Italian Farmer*, it claimed that Italians would help 'To keep Australia white' while subduing the bush through unsubsidised hard work rather than crowding the cities and competing for scarce jobs. They would also defend Australia in the event of war. As one verse argued:

> *The soil has speech that I understand,*
> *There's a song in the furrow sweet;*
> *Then show the way to your idle land*
> *That is far from your noisy street;*
> *And my song shall ring to the sunny sky*
> *Where the vines their fulness yield;*
> *For there's nowhere a happier man than I*
> *In the pride of his home and field.*

The federal government also tried to allay public concern about the Italian minority in the tropics. A government pamphlet in 1935 conceded that around ten per cent of sugar workers were classified as 'foreign', but claimed that they were helping to populate the 'fertile coastal lands of the Far North', thereby securing otherwise 'unused areas' that were 'highly suitable for human occupation' and 'particularly vulnerable, being on the direct trade route between Asia and the Commonwealth'. It implied that if Italians were not introduced to help occupy the north on behalf of British Australians who preferred to remain in cooler southern climes, the Asians would soon seek to do it instead. As one senator reminded his colleagues in May 1936, northern Queensland had 'room for at least 10 000 000 people' and 'no other part of Australia is so inviting to an aggressor'. The Italians may have posed the lesser evil but, in the minds of many, they still *were* an evil. A Labor senator claimed in 1937 that three per cent of Queensland's population was comprised of such 'aliens', compared with one per cent in New South Wales; another MP claimed that 'the Nordic population of Australia' was being 'pushed out of primary production by aliens'. Pressure was applied to buy back farms from owners of Italian origin, even if they were naturalised, and to restrict future farm sales solely to British buyers. As one agitated Britisher complained, because of the Italian presence, 'there is no town band, flower shows or horse racing' while another berated the Italians for allegedly eating 'snakes, koalas, crows and anything else on which they could lay their hands'.

Aboriginal activists in Melbourne joined in the outcry against the Italians, suggesting that it was 'British Australian aborigines' rather than Italians who should be used to develop the north. In February 1938, William Cooper of the Australian Aborigines' League informed Interior Minister John McEwen:

> *Aborigines, not southern Europeans, are those who should develop the outback. We can do it, under white guidance, better than any others for the climate has no terrors for those who have never known a more favorable one.*

According to Cooper, an Aboriginal elder from Echuca in Victoria who had embraced the Christian religion, 'the peopling of Australia's unsettled areas with civilised Aborigines' was 'the best way to close Australia's back door'. Cooper had spent much of his long life seeking to improve the lot of his fellow Aborigines.

Prior to federation, Cooper had sought unsuccessfully for a grant of land for his people on which they could farm, arguing that it was but a 'small portion of a vast territory which is ours by Divine Right'. After moving to Melbourne in 1933, Cooper began organising a petition to the King 'asking him on our behalf to do his utmost in taking suitable steps in preventing the extinction of the Aborigines race' and seeking the election by Aborigines of a member of federal parliament. Clearly aware of white Australian fears and anxious to assuage them, Cooper wrote to Interior Minister Paterson in June 1937 appealing for Aborigines to be uplifted to 'culture and civilisation' and arguing that Aborigines were

> ... capable of producing a yeomanry that can open up and develop the outback better than anyone else. We are acclimatised, and as our primitive people become civilized, they lose the aboriginal culture and outlook taking on the psychology of the white man.

Proclaiming the loyalty of Aborigines to the British Crown, Cooper argued that the 'development of Australia by civilized Aborigines' would provide a 'bulwark for the defence of your land and ours'.

Cooper was encouraged by the response he received from Canberra where the government of Joseph Lyons expressed concern for the Aboriginal plight. Cooper believed that a federal takeover from the states of responsibility for Aboriginal administration would soon lead Aborigines into the light of civilisation and away from the darkness of extinction. The federal administration of the Northern Territory should have given Cooper little cause for confidence. So-called protectors of Aborigines, who doubled as police, allied themselves with pastoralists and organised the massacres of Aborigines who contested the pastoral presence. As the chief protector of Aborigines in central Australia and sergeant of police observed in justification of the 1928 massacre, 'If this country is to be settled with a healthy white population, we must give the pioneers every protection both for themselves and their stock.' The chief protector for the Northern Territory during the 1930s, Dr Cecil Cook, agreed, claiming in 1938 that 'the native actually has become an intruder in a white man's country. Politically, the Northern Territory must always be governed as a white man's country, by the white man for the white man.' Most white Australians, if they thought about it at all, would have agreed with the sentiments of Cook. They would certainly not have conceded Cooper's contention that the ownership of the continent had been unjustly taken from the Aborigines and should now be shared. They preferred to take solace in the prevailing view, propagated by Daisy

Bates, an Anglo-Irishwoman from Tipperary who had devoted much of her life to living among the Aborigines in a vain attempt to soothe their passing, that the Aborigines were destined for inexorable extinction.

The 'full-blood' Aborigines certainly seemed to be dying out, but it was through wilful neglect by those charged with their support and care. On the cattle stations of the Northern Territory, Aborigines who had been forced to abandon their traditional lifestyles and provide labour for the cattle industry were provided with little or no wages and rations that were barely sufficient to keep them alive. Rations issued by the government were little better. According to a report by anthropologist W. E. H. Stanner in 1938, most of the Aborigines in Australia who were no longer pursuing their traditional lifestyles were 'badly under-nourished' on a 'wretchedly inferior diet', leading to a desperately high infant mortality rate. Stanner cited the experience on one cattle station over four years in the late 1920s when only ten children survived out of 51 babies born. Another leading anthropologist, Norman Tindale, pointed to the typical Aboriginal diet provided by their white protectors or employers which was restricted to 'small amounts of tea, flour, and sugar or treacle sufficient to keep the recipient alive. One result is that such folk show little of the joy of living, never, in fact, being properly alive.'

The care of Aborigines on reserves was left in the hands of missionaries who largely taught them of a God that would bring joy in another life. For certainly few would find joy in their present lives. While so-called full blood Aborigines were declining in numbers, concerned officials noticed that there were a greater number of so-called half-caste Aborigines. A meeting of state and federal officials in 1937 heard that the mixed race Aborigines had increased more than twofold in number since the Great War. According to Dr Cook, this alarming explosion in numbers, as the white population of the Territory declined, posed a menace to the 'purity of race in tropical Australia' which could see it 'doomed to disaster'. The officials agreed that 'the destiny of the natives of aboriginal origin, but not of the full blood, lies in their ultimate absorption by the people of the Commonwealth' and called on the Commonwealth to help finance 'a considerably extended programme of development and education' so that these people of mixed heritage could be 'uplifted' to a higher level of civilization preparatory to their absorption. Then the 'Aboriginal question' would be solved. 'White Australia' would be secured, and the problem of wresting the moral proprietorship of the Australian continent from its Aboriginal peoples would disappear forever.

Many of these mixed race children, particularly the girls, had long been taken forcibly from their Aboriginal mothers to be detained in rudimentary hostels where they were trained to perform servile domestic positions for white society while the boys were trained to service the pastoral industry. This policy was now extended and formalised. Over time, after marriage into the lower rungs of white society, it was confidently expected that their Aboriginality and their colour would be bleached from them and their descendants. They would become Europeans, while their 'full-blood' mothers would continue on their inexorable path to extinction. As Cook had informed Ernestine Hill in 1933, the 'problem of our half-castes will quickly be eliminated by the complete disappearance of the black race, and the swift submergence of their progeny in the white'. But the plan faced opposition from inhabitants of the southern cities to which these mixed race girls were intended to be sent. A proposal to send 20 of them to Melbourne encountered opposition from various women's groups who protested against what they described as 'this insidious attempt to mingle with the community women of illegitimate birth, tainted with aboriginal blood, the offspring of men of the lowest human type'. As Andrew Markus has pointed out, it also faced opposition from state protectors of Aborigines who had little faith in Aborigines being able to assimilate themselves.

In 1938, New South Wales celebrated 150 years of European occupation. The invasion tableau of Governor Phillip landing ashore was re-created along with the formal act of asserting legal proprietorship. Native plants and about 20 Aborigines were brought to Sydney to decorate the scene, the Aborigines standing spearless in shorts while white Australians dressed as Phillip and his unarmed officers once more took possession of the Aborigines' land. There were no convicts in evidence. Later, one million locals watched a pageant wind through Sydney streets honouring pioneers who had led 'Australia's March to Nationhood'. Just as the Aborigines were spearless and Phillip and his officers unarmed, there was no sign whatever that the subsequent occupation of the continent had been won to a large extent by the labour of the convicts and only after a sporadic but long-running war on the frontier. The pageant was also almost devoid of any representation of Australia's part in the First World War. The diggers, the convicts and the Aborigines were sent to the back of the Australian historical stage, while Australians pretended that their history was marked by peaceful occupation and development.

While some Aborigines played a docile part in the proclamation pageant, others like William Cooper met to protest against the government policies of protection which they argued were akin to extermination under a different guise. While the Commonwealth government was sometimes sympathetic to their plight, it was the states that controlled the lives of most Aborigines down to the most intimate detail. Among many other things, government officials determined where they could work, if at all, where they must live, who they could marry and whether their children would be taken from them. With Aboriginal resistance largely broken, they were left to appeal to the fair-mindedness of white Australians. During the sesquicentenary, they reminded white Australians that 150 years of white people's progress had been 150 years of 'misery and degradation' for the Aborigines. They demanded equal rights and 'new laws for the education and care of Aborigines' so that they could raise themselves to the level of the whites and not die from treatable diseases as so many of them were doing.

The racial thinking of the time dictated that the 'weaker' black race had to be separated from the 'stronger' white race in order to preserve the former. Many thought that such preservation was doomed to failure. In the year of the sesquicentenary, Daisy Bates published a book evocatively entitled *The Passing of the Aborigines*. She argued for a 'King's High Commissioner' to be appointed to supervise 'the wonderful easing of their inevitable passing'. The book was written with the assistance of journalist Ernestine Hill who had earlier glorified the murdering practices of mounted constable Murray in the Northern Territory.

While the apparent dying out of the 'full blood' Aborigines seemed to see off this lingering threat to their possession of the continent, a much more potent one was forming in the northern Pacific, with Australia facing renewed fears about Britain's ability to defend them against it. Long before their aircraft carriers appeared off Australia's northern shores, Japanese pearling luggers working the offshore pearling beds were prompting concern. An MP warned in 1931 that Europeans were being forced out of the Western Australian pearling port of Broome where 600 Europeans were outnumbered by 800 Asiatics. He darkly predicted that it would 'be the first port taken in this country by foreigners'. Others were more concerned with the attractions that north Queensland or the Northern Territory held out to prospective invaders, while the governor general, Lord Gowrie, warned move generally that 'greedy eyes are turned on this great undeveloped country of Australia'. He was stating what most Australian had long believed.

The continuing, and so far futile, attempts by white Australians to securely occupy northern Australia and develop its resources took a curious turn in the late 1930s when a proposal was put forward for a Jewish organisation to purchase a huge pastoral property of seven million acres in north-west Australia and transform it into irrigated land capable of supporting 50 000 Jewish refugees from Europe. It was a measure of the white Australians' frustration in not being able to populate the north themselves, and also an indication of their deepening fears of a Japanese invasion, that the proposal received support from both federal and state governments. The former prime minister, S. M. Bruce, now Australian High Commissioner in London, suggested that it should be supported on 'strategic and other grounds'. For its part, the *West Australian* argued in July 1939 that 'Australians would not be justified in denying persecuted Jews access to a territory which they have demonstrated their own incapacity to handle'. Having secured their claim of over the tropics, Australians could not justifiably exclude people who might be able to do so on their behalf. A reader agreed, arguing that it would 'help us defend the empty north against invaders', while a Western Australian MP was more blunt: 'In my opinion the proposition can be boiled down to one question, "Are we going to have Jews or Japs?" I say, let us have the Jews.'

The Western Australian government gave its backing to the plan and a group of prominent churchmen, business leaders and academics in Perth urged the Commonwealth government to approve it, arguing that the Jewish refugees would 'make a new home in this country, which they would help to develop to their advantage and ours'. The pro-immigrationist *Sydney Morning Herald* also lent its support, reminding its readers that 'Only by developing and populating this great continent can we justify our right to hold it in a land-hungry world'. But the Second World War had already begun and more urgent calls were being made on the federal purse. Moreover, the plan was opposed by Jewish Australians who were mainly of British background and had assimilated into Australian society. The influential Australian Jewish Welfare Society opposed what it described as 'large black settlements inhabited by large numbers of foreign settlers incapable of absorbing Australian habits or even of learning the English language'. It was also opposed by the anthropologist A. P. Elkin who warned that it would lead to the demise of the remaining Aborigines in the north-west who had 'been "refugees"', apparently doomed to extinction from the day we took and occupied their country'. It was not finally rejected until 1944 when Prime Minister John Curtin announced that his government could not support 'group settlement of the exclusive type contemplated'.

Jewish refugees still came to Australia, but in limited numbers and under the auspices of the Australian Jewish Welfare Society and in the face of bureaucratic obstruction by officials who feared that 'Australia will be flooded with them'. Such fears were given currency by the president of the Victorian Legislative Council who described Jewish refugees in Melbourne as 'slinking rat-faced men under five feet in height with a chest development of about twenty inches' and warned they would 'breed a race within a race'. In recognition of this anti-Semitism, the Society advised refugees on arrival:

> *Do not speak German in the streets and in the trams. Modulate your voices. Do not make yourself conspicuous anywhere by walking with a group of persons all of who are loudly speaking in a foreign language ... Remember that the welfare of the old-established Jewish community in Australia, as well as of every migrant depends on your personal behaviour.*

The outbreak of the Second World War saw this small stream of refugees dry to a trickle while many poignant appeals from Jewish refugees in Germany and Poland were left to gather dust in government filing cabinets.

While the argument over the prospective Jewish settlement in the Kimberley continued in the months before the outbreak of war, the government responded to repeated scare stories of the unguarded northern approaches by establishing a patrol service of the continent's northern coastline. Using a couple of small patrol boats, the service arrested several Japanese luggers which were found near Aboriginal reserves, careening their hulls of algae and other growths. It was feared that any cohabitation between the Japanese and the 'protected' Aborigines might produce an invigorated race capable of reversing the Aborigines' apparent decline. For his part, William Cooper had appealed in February 1937 for an 'adequate patrol' of the northern coast to prevent Aboriginal girls becoming 'vehicles of Asiatic lust'. A new aluminium patrol boat was introduced with a small cannon fitted to its bows. But it was limited to firing blank shells. It would be all noise and no substance. As such, it epitomised the Australian defence effort at the very time that a most determined effort was about to be made by Japan to contest the Australian claim over the continent.

Recommended Reading

Paul R. Bartrop, 1994, *Australia and the Holocaust, 1933–45*, Australian Scholarly Publishing, Melbourne.

Rosemary Campbell, 1989, *Heroes and Lovers: A Question of National Identity*, Allen & Unwin, Sydney.

Michael Cathcart, 1988, *Defending the National Tuckshop*, McPhee Gribble, Melbourne.

David Day, 1996, *Contraband and Controversy*, Australian Government Publishing Service Press, Canberra.

William A. Douglass, 1995, *From Italy to Ingham: Italians in North Queensland*, University of Queensland Press, Brisbane.

Leon Gettler, 1993, *An Unpromised Land*, Fremantle Arts Centre Press, Fremantle.

John Gunn, 1985, *The Defeat of Distance*, University of Queensland Press, Brisbane.

Frank Huelin, 1983, *Keep Moving*, Penguin, Melbourne.

Janet McCalman, 1984, *Struggletown*, Melbourne University Press, Melbourne.

John McCarthy, 1976, *Australia and Imperial Defence 1918–1939*, University of Queensland Press, Brisbane.

Andrew Markus, 1988, *Blood from a Stone: William Cooper and the Australian Aborigines' League*, Allen & Unwin, Sydney.

Andrew Markus, 1990, *Governing Savages*, Allen & Unwin, Sydney.

Bede Nairn, 1986, *The 'Big Fella': Jack Lang and the Australian Labor Party 1891–1949*, Melbourne University Press, Melbourne.

Henry Reynolds, 1986, *Dispossession: Black Australians and White Invaders*, Allen & Unwin, Sydney.

16

'A CITADEL FOR THE BRITISH-SPEAKING RACE'

The Second World War saw Australians come face to face for the first time with their deepest fear, the prospect of an alien invasion that might dispossess them of the island continent as surely as they were continuing to dispossess the remaining Aborigines. The war would test the defences of the decaying British Empire as never before and determine whether 'white Australia' would receive another breathing space in which to secure its proprietorship over the land.

Just as Andrew Fisher had been speaking at a public meeting in Colac in 1914 when he made his memorable comment about Australia standing beside Britain to the 'last man and last shilling', Prime Minister Robert Menzies was also in Colac when Germany sparked its second world war this century by invading Poland on 1 September 1939. Although an orator of some mark, Menzies could not summon up a memorable phrase fit for the terrible occasion. After the horrors of the Western Front, it was difficult to re-create the enthusiasm of 1914. Instead, lawyer that he was, Menzies simply reiterated the tired conservative dogma that 'If Great Britain was at war, Australia was a belligerent country'. At the same time he called the conflict 'lunacy' and hoped that the chances for peaceful negotiation were not yet over. In fact, Menzies had suggested to Chamberlain just a few days previously that the Poles be pressured to be reasonable to the German demands. Their differences, said Menzies, were not worth a war.

The war erupted regardless and Australia, as part of the 'British world', was in it. So when news of Britain declaring war was announced over the BBC short wave radio service, Menzies, after consulting with his cabinet colleagues, announced to the Australian people that it was his 'melancholy duty' to declare that, as a result, Australia was also at war. There was no question of Australia standing aside, as Eire decided to do, or even of delaying a decision until the parliament had met to provide its imprimatur to the decision, as Canada and South Africa did. As Bill Graham, a wheat farmer from Gulgong, recalled: 'To my generation it was truly the mother country. They had developed Australia, they had helped to populate Australia, and so we were just one of the family of the British Empire.' As such, there was little question in the minds of most Australians that they would support their fellow Britons across the sea. But there was some attempt this time, albeit short-lived, to set limits to the Australian commitment, just as South Africa decided to confine its forces to the African continent. Unlike the last war, Australia could not be assured of the support, or even benign neutrality, of Japan, which instead seemed set to swoop on the largely undefended outposts of the various European empires.

With Germany still concentrating on its defeat of Poland, the 'British world' had an opportunity to consider its options in a way that was not possible in the previous war. This breathing space allowed Menzies to hold back on committing a second expeditionary force until the security of the Pacific could be assured. This assurance was necessary to secure the support of those who believed that the first call on the nation's forces should be the defence of its own continent rather than its participation in a distant war. Such arguments had been high on the agenda in the 1937 federal election, with the Labor Party pushing for the primacy of local defence, based on a strengthened air force and army, while the conservatives defended their traditional allegiance to imperial defence, based on a strong navy, as providing the best security for Australia. The fact was that there was no simple answer to the defence conundrum faced by the people of such a lightly populated continent.

The conservatives claimed rightly that Australians could not hope to defend the continent alone and had to depend upon the assistance of the mother country. The Labor Party, along with elements of the army and defence-minded commentators, argued that the mother country was unlikely to defend Australia, since a threat to Australia was only likely to arise at a time when Britain was preoccupied with the situation in Europe. In such circumstances, British resources would necessarily be retained in the European theatre despite pre-existing promises to Australia. As such, Australia had to do as best it could in defending itself. Of necessity, neither argument could be proven before the eruption of the awful circumstances against which they were designed to meet. And then it could be too late.

Unlike the First World War, the Labor Party retained its equivocal attitude to this second European war. Its leader, John Curtin, the reformed alcoholic and anti-conscriptionist who had been gaoled for his beliefs in the First World War, stressed the necessity to make the defence of Australia paramount in government calculations. In a radio broadcast to the Australian people on 10 September 1939, Curtin warned of the opposition that would be mounted to any attempt by Menzies to denude the defences of Australia for the sake of the war in Europe. Without naming Japan, Curtin held out the prospect of 'Australian soil' being attacked by nations that were presently neutral. Australians would have been in no doubt as to which nation he had most in mind. At the same time, Curtin allayed any concern about Labor's essential loyalty by proclaiming his party's commitment to 'the maintenance of Australia as an integral part of the British Commonwealth of Nations'.

In order to assuage the concerns of his Labor opponents, Menzies sent his supply minister, Richard Casey, to London to seek an assurance from Britain that it would send the promised fleet to Singapore in the event of Japan entering the war. As First Lord of the Admiralty, Winston Churchill was happy to give such an assurance, confident that it would never be called upon and realising that it was the only way to get the Australian troops committed to Britain's cause in the European theatre. Churchill promised to send a fleet if Japan invaded Australia in force. Of course, it would be too late by then. Because of its long-time commitment to imperial defence, Australia did not have the forces or supplies to hold out against a serious Japanese invasion while Britain took the months required to assemble and despatch a powerful fleet to the Far East. To dispel any lingering Australian doubts, Casey assured Menzies that Britain would place the security of Australia above her interests in the Mediterranean and that a squadron of battleships would be sent 'from the moment that danger to either Singapore or Australia developed in a manner which made their protection a real and practical war need'. Privately, Churchill confided to the British War Cabinet that this assurance was 'more elastic' than the assurances Britain had given Australia in 1937.

Despite the relatively unsatisfactory British assurance, Menzies announced the despatch of another expeditionary force to fight in a European war. He made this commitment of troops to the Middle East due to the mounting popular pressure for such a commitment to be made and because New Zealand had pre-empted the Australians by announcing their own expeditionary force. Menzies also used the uncertainty he created concerning an Australian expeditionary force to pressure Britain into buying the Australian wheat harvest. Britain later undertook to purchase for the duration of the war the Australian production of wool, meat, wheat, butter, cheese, dried and canned fruits, and eggs. At the same time, Menzies continued to hold the United States at arm's length, refusing to allow Pan American Airways to steal a march on the British by establishing a direct air link across the Pacific to Australia, despite New Zealand allowing such a link.

Given his background as a boy born in the bush, Menzies' deep and abiding attachment to Britain was a rather curious feature of his outlook. And it became more curious as it endured in the face of fundamental shifts in world politics. In her book *Robert Menzies' Forgotten People*, Judith Brett has pointed to Menzies' ambivalence towards the land and landscape of his birth. He was far from alone in this. Menzies had been born in 1896 to a Scottish storekeeping couple in the recently established town of Jeparit in the Mallee region of north-west Victoria. A flat, semi-arid expanse bisected by the Wimmera River and a series of lakes, the Mallee was one of the last areas in Victoria to be invaded by Europeans and have its original inhabitants dispossessed. As a boy, Menzies was a witness to the final chapters in this lamentable tale, with the remnants of the Wotjoballuk people still living as curiosities on the margins of Jeparit society. While Aboriginal words were used to name the town and its river, the remaining Aboriginal people were mostly moved by the 1920s to a reserve in Gippsland. With this episode of dispossession being acted out in the background of his boyhood experience, it is not surprising, as Judith Brett has observed, that Menzies was infected with the casual racist assumptions of the time and betrayed 'a certain discomfort' about recalling the presence of the Aborigines who were hardly more than shadows in his childhood memories.

Similarly, the bush of his boyhood, the Mallee scrub and largely level landscape seemed to arouse no affection in Menzies. As he recalled it, the Mallee was a place of hurricane-force winds, devastating droughts and dust storms, from where Menzies mentally escaped by reading of other times and places, largely the soft landscapes of England and Scotland, and from where he physically escaped by dint of hard work, winning scholarships that would take him to public school in Ballarat, then to Wesley College in Melbourne and later to Melbourne University. Jeparit seemed to have left no mark on a young man whose personal Mecca by the time of his graduation was in London. Although raised on a literary diet of imperial derring-do, Menzies did not rush into the trenches of the First World War despite having a commission in the Melbourne University Rifles. Family pressure, after his two brothers had enlisted, kept him out. Undeterred by his own anomalous position on the sidelines, this gung-ho jingoist joined in the loyal chorus that pushed others into the trenches. Now, after shoving his way through the ranks of state and federal politicians, the stout figure of Prime Minister Menzies could lead the local choir as it sang in more muted tones of the continuing duties owed to mother Britain and the glories to be had on the battlefield.

Menzies was far from alone in his ambivalence towards the bush and of being Australian rather than British. Australians were still seeking to come to terms with the rhythms of the land, its silences, its testing vastness that they feared could yet leave them vanquished. The poet Harold Stewart, who later left Australia for good, openly acknowledged that Australia was 'a country that repels me. I find it very alien and hostile. As a small child of five or six, I was taken to see the bush and I burst into tears of inconsolable grief and had to be taken home.' Tens of thousands of Australians abandoned the continent in the 1930s, many of them after failing to find the opportunities it supposedly offered. The attempts to physically pacify the bush through the closer settlement schemes of the 1920s had been, at best, a mixed success. The great majority of Australians still huddled in a few coastal cities, their backs to the bush and their eyes on the rising Japanese empire across the water.

From their city redoubts, Australians continued their attempts at mentally pacifying the bush. Bushwalking clubs became popular in the 1920s, promoting short, safe forays into the remaining patches of bush that still blotched the edges of the bloated cities, while *Walkabout* magazine was established in 1934 to pacify the bush through photojournalism, much as the Heidelberg School had done through their paintings. Australian films, plays and novels of the time remained centred on the bush rather than the city. The Jindywoborak literary movement of the late 1930s tried to overstep these cautious attempts to Australianise their culture by degrees, jumping instead straight to an indigenous Australian culture that would turn its back on its English past and enmesh with the landscape and tap into the secrets of the dying Aborigines. Its founder, the Adelaide poet Rex Ingamells, lambasted his fellow Australians for living the 'hollowest of shams', occupying an 'Unknown Land' that was not understood while trying to re-create in it the forms and values of distant Europe. Like many an inland river, the movement soon disappeared with little trace of its passing.

Apart from the sentimental attachment that Menzies and most of his ministers had for Britain and the interests of its empire, the government was largely hostage to its lack of defence planning in the 1930s. By the time it began to boost its defence budget in the late 1930s, it found that the order books of most defence manufacturers in Britain and the United States were already full to overflowing with British and American orders. To cover the consequent inadequacies in its defences, the Australian government was a staunch supporter of Britain's appeasement policy, hoping to buy peace in Europe to ensure its security in the Pacific. Now that those hopes had collapsed, and with little scope for its defences being augmented in the short term, there appeared to be no alternative other than to place the future of white Australia in the hands of imperial defence planners in the hope that Britain's successive promises to protect Australia from invasion would be fulfilled.

Nearly four decades after federation, Australia still had no standing army, no tanks and an inadequate stockpile of munitions. Its land force relied upon some 80 000 part-time and inadequately equipped militiamen. It had no modern fighter planes, making do with an American trainer aircraft instead, and it had no bombers. The main strength of its small navy was concentrated in six cruisers that were capable of protecting Australia's trade routes from isolated attacks but not of confronting a sizeable naval force intent on an invasion of the continent. It had neither battleships nor aircraft carriers. Once war was declared, it was intended that the Royal Australian Navy act as an echelon of the British navy. And the defence forces were commanded by British officers on secondment from London and often pursuing Britain's interests rather than Australia's.

At the urging of its high commissioner in London, Stanley Melbourne Bruce, Australia agreed to train thousands of airmen for Britain's use in Europe and the Middle East. Under the Empire Air Training Scheme, airmen would be given basic instruction in Australia on British-supplied training aircraft before going to Canada for advanced training and then to Britain where they would be incorporated within British units. Menzies promoted the scheme to the Australian public as providing Australia with a mighty air armada capable of securing its defence from Japan. Menzies suggested that the presence of these unarmed and underpowered training aircraft in Australia would either deter Japan from attacking Australia or, if the worst happened, be capable of repelling a Japanese invasion. In making this commitment of Australian manpower for the war in Europe, Menzies unashamedly implied that he was adopting the Labor Party's priority of local defence based on air power after the conservatives had strenuously opposed it in the election just two years before.

Now Menzies pointed to Australia's defence predicament as 'a relatively isolated country with a small and scattered population and an enormous and vulnerable coast line', with no possibility of the continent being defended adequately in the near future by either its naval or military forces. So, in words that could have been taken almost verbatim from the Labor Party's 1937 manifesto, Menzies extolled the 'great mobility and striking power' of aircraft in the defence of the continent, claiming that they would provide 'a powerful deterrent against the descent to our waters of vulnerable transports filled with invading troops'. If anyone doubted the efficacy of training aircraft in repelling a Japanese invasion, Menzies assured them that the planes would only have to cope 'with seaborne aircraft of limited power and carrying capacity'. Though the skies over Australian cities certainly became crowded with the clamour of these droning planes, they were clearly incapable of providing the defence that Menzies proclaimed for them. What was worse, the air force was transformed into a giant training organisation for a far-off war rather than preparing itself for the invasion that could soon beset its own shores. Still, it proved popular with Australian men who regarded the air force as the glamour service which would allow them to avoid a possible war in the trenches along the horrific lines of the previous war. As one recruit explained to his wife on enlistment, if he was killed, his death in the air force would be 'quick and clean'. He was killed soon after reaching England.

In January 1940, prior to embarking for the Middle East, 6000 men of the 6th Division, Second AIF marched through Sydney streets crowded with some half a million cheering onlookers. The prime concern of the *Sydney Morning Herald*, which reported their passage through the sea of confetti and excited flurry of Union Jacks, was to confirm for its readers that the physical attributes of this fresh offering of Australian manpower matched those of their predecessors in 1914. It claimed that these 'young, bronzed, clear-eyed' men of 'Australia's brave new army' were 'proud bearers of the standard bequeathed to them by the original Anzacs'. The paper described how 'they strode forward with youthful step, heads erect, eyes shining with the glow of health and the pride of achievement'. Sandy Rayward, a member of the 6th Division, recalled his motivation for enlisting:

> *I think it was high adventure: going to places we'd never seen before, the thought of the First World War and the high hopes and the great actions that were instilled in us in history, Gallipoli and the whole of France; and we couldn't get away quickly enough actually. It was just to get over there and let 'em know how good we were ...*

Aborigines were also concerned to prove themselves, while also hoping that service in the forces might improve their personal position and perhaps lift the lot of their people. In January 1939, Aboriginal activist William Cooper, who had lost a son in the First World War, had complained to the federal government of returning Aboriginal servicemen from that war being 'pushed back to the bush to resume the status of aboriginals'. Many were denied old age pensions because of their Aboriginality. Why should an Aborigine assist with the defence of Australia, asked Cooper, when they had 'no status, no rights, no land and ... nothing to fight for but the privilege of defending the land which was taken from him by the white race without compensation or even kindness'. Despite Cooper's threat to withhold cooperation with the coming war effort until they were given the rights of citizens, many Aborigines joined the forces regardless. Fifty were accepted into the militia in Darwin, while historian Robert Hall has identified 22 Aborigines and Torres Strait Islanders who had enlisted in the Second AIF by the end of 1939. Others were turned away from recruiting offices by officials who remained dubious about the desirability of having Aborigines in the ranks where they would be defending the racist tenets of white Australia. After the army advised in February 1940 that the enlistment of Aborigines would not be acceptable to the 'normal Australian' serviceman, regulations were introduced restricting enlistment to those 'substantially of European origin or descent'. After protests, these regulations were moderated in practice to allow the 'general suitability' of the recruit to be taken into account. This allowed 26 Aborigines, out of 43 eligible individuals, from the Lake Tyers reserve in Victoria to be accepted into the AIF in July 1940. However, most were discharged within a year.

The initial rush to enlist by white Australians had slackened off as the so-called phoney war period continued into 1940. The raising of a second division of the AIF was announced in February 1940 but recruitment was slow. It was not until the German onslaught against France and the rout of the British expeditionary force at Dunkirk that any sense of urgency was created in Australia. Menzies had not helped the situation with his advice for Australians to maintain an attitude of 'business as usual'. His advice had been meant to avoid any panic, but its effect was to instil a feeling of lethargy that proved difficult to lift. With Britain about to fight for its life, Menzies increased the tempo of Australia's war effort, now calling for an 'all-in' effort. To emphasise the point, on 22 May 1940, Menzies appointed Essington Lewis, managing director of the iron and steel conglomerate BHP, as a munitions supremo to boost local production of war supplies while at the same time announcing the formation of a third division for the AIF, the ill-fated 8th Division that would be captured in Singapore 18 months later.

On 5 June, in the wake of the Dunkirk evacuation, Menzies spoke at a 'win the war' meeting in Melbourne's Town Hall which concluded with 20 men of the First AIF, armed with rifles and bayonets fixed, symbolically passing a torch to 20 men of the Second AIF. Many of the men of the First AIF were still young enough to serve a second time. The daughter of a Mallee soldier-settler recalled how her father was caught up in the hysteria, leaving his wife and six children to manage their marginal wheat farm while he rejoined the AIF:

> He began to think that joining up maybe could help out with their finances, although Mum was against it. I also think he wanted to get away from the strain of the last few years with a young family and all the hardship of the Depression. I think he saw it as a type of adventure.

He never returned to his Mallee block, dying instead as a prisoner of the Japanese in Singapore's Changi gaol.

With Italy now in the war on the German side, many Italian Australians found themselves subject to the restrictive provisions of the *Aliens Act*, while public pressure called for all aliens to be detained. Several thousand Italian Australians were interned for the duration of the war, many of them having been identified as having fascist sympathies while others were innocent victims of a distant war. Those not interned had their movements and civil rights severely restricted. Many of the Italian internees were from the sugar growing areas of north Queensland and were railed south to camps in New South Wales or South Australia. Others were conscripted into civil construction corps.

Although the fall of France had possibly dire consequences for the defence of Australia, the loyal dominion made serious sacrifices during this period to avert a possible defeat of Britain. It allowed Britain to 'jump the queue' and take over a number of aircraft that Australia had ordered from the United States as well as ones that were being assembled in Australia. Rather than looking to its own defence, Australia despatched 50 million rounds of ammunition from its own insufficient stocks. With the loss of the French fleet from the Allied side, Australia was much less likely to see the promised British fleet in the Pacific. Rather than seeking American assistance to fill this naval vacuum, Australia appealed to Roosevelt to save Britain from imminent German invasion. It was not a mark of Australian confidence in its effective proprietorship over the continent, but the reverse. It was further confirmation that its proprietorship over the continent was so insecure that it would be washed away without the promised protection of the tattered imperial defence umbrella.

Australia's predicament was graphically displayed when Menzies met with defence chiefs and the newly appointed director of information, the newspaperman Keith Murdoch. They were informed by defence chiefs that it would be no use mobilising 200 000 men to secure the continent against a possible Japanese invasion since there was nothing with which to arm them. The part-time militia, depleted by the dispatch of the Second AIF to the Middle East, had not yet reached 75 000 men trained for four months. Moreover, the available arms and ammunition would only allow Australian forces to defend the continent for less than a month before they would have to capitulate to a Japanese invasion. As the director of information sagely observed, 'That is what you cannot tell the public.' When Murdoch later suggested that the public would love to know that the government was making tanks, Menzies seized upon the advice, ordering offhand that such a program be started at once. Over the following three years, it would consume the labour of thousands of workers before being finally abandoned without a single operational tank being produced.

In September 1940, one year into the war, Menzies went to the people at a general election, his government crippled by the tragic death of three of its senior members in a plane crash at Canberra the previous month. While being determined 'to do everything that we can to keep Australia safe from attack, invasion or conquest', Menzies also reminded Australians in his policy speech in the Camberwell Town Hall that they were 'not only politically, but morally, spiritually and materially, an integral part of the great British family of nations' and must 'make the highest possible contribution to the war effort of Britain, the vital centre of that family, wherever and whenever that contribution can be made'.

By 1941, Australia had committed three of its divisions to the Middle East and one to Singapore, leaving in Australia just the conscripted militia and the woefully inadequate air force for local defence. On 3 January 1941, the Australian troops saw their first significant action at Bardia in Libya, with Billy Hughes, now minister for the navy, expressing his relief that they had maintained the 'traditions set up by those of 1914–18'. In words reminiscent of Charles Bean, the journalist John Hetherington confirmed that these men of the Second AIF

> ... who, since childhood, had read and heard of the exploits in battle of the First A.I.F., who had enlisted and trained under the shadow of their fathers' reputation as soldiers, had come through their ordeal by fire and built a reputation of their own ... The Australians had tasted battle and they liked its harsh flavour.

Two weeks later, Menzies left for London ostensibly to consult with the British government about the coordination of imperial defence, particularly with regard to the situation at Singapore. Following the 1940 election, Menzies was a politically embattled prime minister dependent on the votes of two independent MPs for his survival. Despite appeals to Labor leader John Curtin, the Labor Party refused to join Menzies' United Australia Party in a national government along the lines of Britain. That left Menzies vulnerable to defeat at any time as criticism of his half-hearted war leadership mounted. It was largely to shore up his political position that Menzies embarked upon the trip to London.

En route to London, Menzies visited Singapore and saw for himself its pathetic preparations and its incompetent commanders. In the Middle East, he met with Australian troops before flying on to the blitzed imperial capital where he was accorded a triumphant welcome. The British press likened the corpulent colonial to a Greek god, although Menzies was more an aesthete than an athlete. The sustained praise proved to be too much for him, confirming what he already suspected, that he had a grander destiny than the cramped political stage in Canberra. In time, it would help to prompt him into a concerted attack on Churchill's war leadership with the ultimate aim of the scholarship boy from Jeparit, a political cleanskin in British eyes, being in a position to replace a discredited Churchill.

Almost immediately after his arrival in London, Menzies was prevailed upon by Churchill to commit Australian forces in the Middle East to an expedition to shore up Greece, which was stoutly defending itself against an Italian invasion but anticipating a German invasion. Churchill hoped, in a strategy redolent of the Gallipoli fiasco, to thereby create a solid Balkan bloc, based upon Greece and Yugoslavia, that would withstand the Germans and draw Turkey into the war on the British side. It was, as it soon proved to be, a hopeless cause. When British and Australian forces started landing in Greece, the Germans diverted forces that they had been massing for an attack against Russia and poured them into Greece. It was Gallipoli all over again. Instead of withdrawing his overwhelmed forces to the Middle East, Churchill sent them to the island of Crete where, after heavy fighting, a German parachute attack secured the airfields for an airborne invasion. Another and more costly withdrawal was forced upon the imperial troops.

Meanwhile, British forces in the Middle East had been weakened by the Greek diversion just as their Italian opponents in Libya were strengthened by the arrival of Germany's General Rommel and the first echelon of his future *Afrika Korps*. Rommel soon pushed the British back into Egypt, leaving behind a mixed force, including the 9th Australian Division, hemmed into the port of Tobruk. In the midst of this military turmoil, Churchill's political position was undermined while Menzies was encouraged to believe that he might eventually be able to replace Churchill as British prime minister. Whispers in his ear from meddling British newspaper magnates, from disaffected military leaders and even from Churchill's own colleagues, all combined to convince Menzies that the leadership of the empire might lay within his grasp. It was a heady ambition for anyone, but particularly for Menzies with Britain being the centre of his world.

Menzies was motivated not only by political ambition but also by a wish to save the empire, and thereby Australia, from the disaster to which it seemed to be heading under Churchill's direction. With France out of the war and the United States determined to stay on the sidelines, Menzies could only foresee a wasting war that would destroy his beloved Mecca and its wider empire. Although Germany would also be enfeebled by such a titanic slogging match, Menzies feared that the only victor would be the Russians, waiting and watching warily from the sidelines, and that the steady enfeeblement of Britain would entice the Japanese into the war.

With such a rich political prize in view, Menzies largely abandoned his campaign to secure defence equipment for Australia and Singapore in favour of securing his political advancement instead. He left London in May 1941 with a promise of some superseded aircraft that Britain did not want, and with no assurance regarding a British fleet for Singapore. On his way home to Australia, he toured the United States and Canada trying to garner support for his political ambition. While there, the Germans stormed into Russia, incidentally upsetting the momentum of Menzies' political campaign as the astute Churchill recovered much of his squandered political capital in Westminster.

When Menzies finally flew into Sydney in May 1941, after just over four months abroad, he scribbled in his diary, as the flying boat bucked and shuddered in the turbulent air, of the 'sick feeling of repugnance and apprehension' that overtook him as he contemplated the political struggles that awaited him before he could rejoin the main game in London. He spent the following two months trying to shore up his political position at home while simultaneously pressing for an imperial conference in London that he hoped would lead to his return as the imperial representative in the British War Cabinet. But the other dominions refused to play Menzies' game and he eventually resigned as prime minister in August 1941, still hoping that he might get to London in some other capacity. But his efforts over the next 18 months were blocked each time by Churchill. The episode had revealed the strong attachment to empire and to things British by a man born in the bush of Scottish parents and who, as Australian prime minister, was prepared to abandon the country of his birth during a time of war for the chance of taking the imperial helm. It revealed the tenuous nature of nationalism even among native-born Australians, many of whom still looked loyally to a London they had never seen.

The war did not wait for Menzies to play out his political game plan. Australian forces trapped by Rommel in Tobruk were managing to hold out against the Germans. Menzies feared the political effect of the besieged port being overwhelmed and its mainly Australian defenders being captured. He called for the Australian component of the Tobruk garrison to be evacuated. Such an operation would require a difficult and dangerous operation by small ships operating at night in seas over which German aircraft held command of the air. It would also imperil the British preparations in Egypt for an offensive to roll Rommel's spectacular advance back into Libya. For all these reasons, the evacuation call was resisted by Churchill, whose political future could well hinge on the security of Britain's bastion in the Middle East.

When Menzies' short-lived successor as prime minister, Arthur Fadden, reiterated the calls, Churchill again refused to budge. He was dismayed by the apparent political calculations that were driving the repeated Australian requests. When the Labor prime minister John Curtin took up Menzies' and Fadden's call in October 1941, Churchill claimed that it would endanger the planned British offensive that was designed to lift the siege. He beseeched Curtin, 'for the sake of Australia and history', not to press his call, warning that the 'effect on the prestige of the Australian troops would be very great when the full facts and the correspondence became known'. But Curtin was adamant and Churchill finally backed down. He had wrongly blamed the Australians for the fall of Greece, expecting that their lightly armed soldiers could have held the mountain passes against the German tanks and dive bombers in the manner of the Spartans at Thermopylae. He now blasted the Australians over Tobruk. The sorry episode sullied the reputation of Australians in official British eyes just as Australia was about to call for British assistance to ward off the Japanese.

Fortunately for Australian self-esteem, the British disgust over the Tobruk evacuation was kept hidden from public view. Even Churchill's postwar publication of the cables that flashed between London and Canberra over the issue did little to detract from the Australian view of their soldiers' undeniable bravery in holding out for so long against Rommel's enveloping forces. It was, after all, largely a decision of the politicians in Canberra and could not reflect unduly on the reputation of the garrison. In Australian eyes, the evacuation from Tobruk was likened to the earlier evacuation from Gallipoli. The Australian commander, Major General Morshead, claimed his troops 'went with our tails up', while the Melbourne *Age* reported that they had 'fought as gallantly and gloriously as their fathers on Gallipoli'. They would have more difficulty in fitting the behaviour of some of their troops at Singapore into the Gallipoli legend.

The British base at Singapore had been sold politically to the Australians as providing a naval barrier between Japan and Australia. It was no such thing. Primarily, it was a naval barrier against Japanese expansion into the Indian Ocean where the rich array of British colonies and dominions stretched in an arc from Malaya through Burma and India to Kenya and South Africa. Because of the tensions in Europe, no fleet was ever based at Singapore. Instead, it was intended that the base be able to withstand a siege from the sea for nine months, by which time it was anticipated that reinforcements would have arrived from Europe. But the island was poorly garrisoned with a mixed force of British, Indian and Australian troops and protected by superseded aircraft. Only at the last minute were meagre measures taken to protect the Malayan hinterland.

If Singapore was the weak linchpin of Australia's defence, the Philippines was the weak linchpin of Singapore's defence. Britain was relying on the United States to deter the Japanese from mounting a southerly thrust at the oil-rich islands of the Dutch East Indies and the rubber plantations of Indochina and Malaya. As the United States persisted in resisting British attempts to embroil it in the European war, the British increasingly looked upon a possible war in the Pacific that would involve America against Japan as a way of getting the Americans into the European war 'by the back door'. But they feared the possibility of provoking a war with Japan that would, as in the European war, leave the Americans on the sidelines. Such an outcome would spell disaster for Britain.

So Britain encouraged American efforts to tighten the economic embargo against Japan while at the same time building up their forces in the Far East. While the United States planned to base a force of new heavy bombers in the Philippines, in the mistaken impression that they could sink Japanese battleships, the British sent a squadron of heavy ships to Singapore with plans to build them up to fleet strength by March 1942. Both moves heightened Japan's sense of imminent encirclement, suggesting to its leaders that its window of opportunity, through which it might seize for itself an Asian empire from the embattled European powers, seemed to be closing.

The arrival of two British battleships, the *Prince of Wales* and the *Repulse*, in November 1941 had a double purpose for Churchill. If their well-publicised arrival at Singapore kept Japan out of the war, that would be well and good since it would not distract British attention and resources from the European war and would avoid the possibility of Britain finding itself fighting Japan alone. On the other hand, the despatch of the two powerful battleships could be seen in Tokyo as the first echelon of the promised Far East fleet and thereby provoke Japan to strike immediately while the American forces in the Philippines and the British at Singapore were still weak. This is what happened.

While Churchill was willing the Americans and Japanese into a Pacific conflict, the United States and Japan were already on a collision course. To ensure the collision eventuated, Britain helped to derail the final attempts at peace talks in Washington, although they were probably doomed anyway. By this time, Japan was already amassing a powerful fleet of battleships and aircraft carriers that would descend upon the American naval base at Pearl Harbor before turning to the south-west Pacific to attack, among other places, the British bastion of Singapore and Australia's northern gateway of Darwin.

Curtin reacted to the sudden, but not unexpected, Japanese attack on Pearl Harbor with a radio broadcast to the Australian people in which he defended their claim to the continent. Describing it as the 'gravest hour of our history', Curtin promised to 'hold this country, and keep it as a citadel for the British-speaking race, and as a place where civilisation will persist'. Captain Arthur Phillip in 1788, and many others after him, had justified the dispossession of the Aborigines in terms of the European civilisation that was planted in the virgin soil of the Australian continent. Curtin was now justifying their continuing occupation in terms of protecting that civilisation. In a speech to parliament on 16 December, Curtin reminded Australians that

> ... in more than 150 years no enemy has set foot in this country. In the months ahead that tradition will remain with us. Never shall an enemy set foot upon the soil of this country without having at once arrayed against it the whole of the manhood of this nation in such strength and quality as to show our determination that this country shall remain for ever the home of the descendants of those people who came here in peace in order to establish in the South Seas an outpost of the British race.

Although the Japanese descent on South-East Asia fulfilled the historic Australian fears of an Asian invasion, Curtin could take confidence that their attack on Pearl Harbor had drawn the United States unequivocally into the Pacific war. Few imagined the forfeits that would have to be paid in the Pacific before the power of the American and British forces finally set limits to Japanese expansion.

Although talking in terms of the 'British-speaking race', Curtin's words would have resonated in the minds of his listeners in the familiar racial terms of white Australia. In his speech to parliament, Curtin was quite clear and unabashed about what Australians were defending. It was their 'white Australia' policy. At the same time, he was anxious to rebut any suggestion that the provocative policy provided any justification for the Japanese declaration of war or for the possible dispossession of Australians from their continent:

> Our laws have proclaimed the principle of a White Australia. We did not intend that to be and it never was an affront to other races. It was devised for economic and sound humane reasons ... We intend to maintain that principle, because we know it to be desirable.

The *Sydney Morning Herald* was similarly concerned to establish the right of Australians to their occupation of the continent, pointing to the '150 years of peaceful development of our island heritage'. Wondering whether Australians had held their 'rich inheritance too lightly', the paper took comfort from their experience 'on many a foreign battle-field [where] the quality of Australians as a fighting race has been proved to the world'. This was no idle comment. As Gulgong farmer Bill Graham later observed, 'The invincibility of the Australian soldier was something that we really thought, and relied upon.' It helped to steady the Australian resolve as they prepared to face the Japanese foe, confident also that they could count on the long-promised British protection.

It would not have been part of Churchill's plan for the powerful naval ships, the *Prince of Wales* and the *Repulse*, to fall victim to the Japanese, as they did dramatically on 10 December 1941. He had intended, in the event of Japan's entry into the war, that the ships act as a 'vague menace' in the Far East, deterring the Japanese from over-extending their reach. But they were quickly sunk by Japanese torpedo bombers off the Malayan coast as a Japanese invasion force landed nearby. Despite some stiff fighting from the imperial defenders, the lightly-equipped Japanese troops fought their way down the peninsula until they looked across the narrow stretch of water that separated Malaya from the island of Singapore. The defending garrison found itself fighting to protect a bomb-ravaged city crowded with refugees and a naval base devoid of ships.

Australians looked on with horror as the long-time shibboleth for the security of their adjacent continent seemed set to fall to the advancing Japanese. Despite their earlier disparaging of Japanese military prowess, it now seemed as if the Japanese, rather than the Australians, were invincible as soldiers. Maurie Jones, then a schoolboy in Perth, recalled the 'general feel of real terror because they were just sweeping south so fast. We thought well, we're next. And we were fully expecting Western Australia to be invaded.' There was little to celebrate on Australia Day, 1942. As a mark of its concern, the government cancelled the traditional holiday, at least for war-related workers. Some, though, could see a benefit in Australia's position of extreme danger. If the Japanese managed to land on Australian shores, it would allow the Australians to buttress their partly secured claims of proprietorship over the continent by fighting for it and, hopefully, repelling an Asian invader. Thus, the Melbourne *Argus* observed, almost with relief, that Australia was 'at last ... directly engaged in a struggle for our own survival; and out of the sombre anxieties and grim resolutions of the hour the Australian nation is born'. While Gallipoli had given Australians much-needed confidence in their military valour and their consequent ability to ward off a hostile challenge to their occupation, it was not the same as actually repelling such a challenge on their own soil.

The promised British fleet that was intended to steam to the rescue of Singapore never came. Britain decided instead to retain its ships in the Mediterranean and sent 50 Hurricane aircraft, in crates, to beef up Singapore's air defences. At Australia's frantic insistence, Churchill also diverted a division of British troops that had been destined for Burma. It was too little too late. The capture of the British division soon after it landed at Singapore provided Churchill with another reason to berate the Australian government. Instead of trying to save Singapore, Churchill pushed for its evacuation, preferring to buttress Burma and prevent the Japanese from threatening India, the real jewel in the British crown. Australia resisted this, alleging that it would constitute an inexcusable betrayal. But the empty base was doomed, and most of its defenders were destined to endure a harrowing time as prisoners of the Japanese.

Although the Japanese attackers were hard-put to press home their attack against Singapore, and although they were outnumbered two to one by the defenders, the Japanese air superiority and command of the surrounding seas sealed the base's fate. On 8 February 1942, Japanese troops managed to land on the shore of the island at the point where the Australian 8th Division was defending. Securing their lodgment, the Japanese forced the British commander to capitulate on 15 February to end the useless slaughter of his soldiers and the unprotected civilians. In the subsequent mayhem, recently-landed Australian troops pushed civilians aside in their rush to escape capture by commandeering vessels in the ravaged harbour. Even the commander of the 8th Division, Major General Gordon Bennett, joined in the exodus from Singapore, leaving his men behind as he fled to the safety of Australia from where he criticised the British performance at Singapore. As reports of the disaster filtered back to London, Singapore was added to Tobruk, Crete and Greece in the litany of disasters for which Australia was blamed by British political leaders.

In a meeting of the British War Cabinet on 26 January, one minister was so frustrated with what he regarded as the carping Australians, who were trying to buttress their defence position at the expense of British interests elsewhere, that he scribbled angrily to a colleague that Australia was the 'most dangerous obstacle in the path' of the British government. There was little appreciation in London of the enormity of the psychological blow suffered by Australians as the Japanese swept through South-East Asia unimpeded by any significant British resistance. Farmer Bill Graham recalled how, following the fall of Singapore, 'it was a fairly cold sort of feeling to realise then that Britain was not able to do what we expected her to do—to back up and defend Australia. She was too busy of course defending herself, but it was a bit of a let-down when we found out that Britain couldn't do it.' More worrying, with the loss of Singapore, was that Australia was now wide open to attack. The end of 'white Australia' seemed imminent.

Recommended Reading

Judith Brett, 1992, *Robert Menzies' Forgotten People*, Macmillan, Sydney.

F. K. Crowley (ed.), 1973, *Modern Australia in Documents*, Vol. 2, Wren Publishing, Melbourne.

David Day, 1999, *John Curtin: A Life*, HarperCollins, Sydney.

David Day, 1986, *Menzies and Churchill at War*, Angus&Robertson, Sydney.

David Day, 1988, *The Great Betrayal*, Angus&Robertson, Sydney.

Betty Goldsmith and Beryl Sandford, 1990, *The Girls They Left Behind*, Penguin, Melbourne.

Robert Hall, 1989, *The Black Diggers*, Allen & Unwin, Sydney.

Laurie Hergenhan (ed.), 1988, *The Penguin New Literary History of Australia*, Penguin, Melbourne.

David Horner, 1992, *High Command: Australia and Allied Strategy 1939–1945*, Allen & Unwin, Sydney.

M. McKernan and M. Browne (eds), 1988, *Australia: Two Centuries of War and Peace*, Australian War Memorial, Canberra.

A. W. Martin, 1993, *Robert Menzies*, Vol. 1, Melbourne University Press, Melbourne.

Joanna Penglase and David Horner, 1992, *When the War Came to Australia*, Allen & Unwin, Sydney.

17

'THE

BATTLE

OF

AUSTRALIA'

For more than 150 years, the Australian hold on the continent had been underwritten by the power of the British navy. The dramatic fall of Singapore, and the loss of its empty British naval base, revealed the limitations of Australia's traditional insurance policy. The Japanese sweep southwards to Australia's northern shores also revealed the awful reality of the historic, but previously hypothetical, fears concerning the partial occupation by Australians of their 'empty continent'. Now, faced with their long-held fears, many Australians reacted like rabbits caught in a car's headlights. From their huddled coastal cities, there was nowhere to escape, except to the largely unfamiliar and often forbidding interior. Undaunted, some Australians fled to relatives in the bush; others prepared to hide in the mountains or planned even to commit suicide rather than fall into the hands of an Asian invader.

In order to try and galvanise Australians into action after nearly two and a half years of a largely distant war, Curtin dramatically proclaimed on 16 February 1942 that the 'fall of Singapore opens the Battle of Australia' and called for a total war effort by all its citizens. The following day, he reminded Australians that they were 'the sons and daughters of Britishers' and that, ever since 1788, 'this land has been governed by men and women of our race'. By alluding to the relative longevity of their occupation of the continent, Curtin was implicitly equipping them with the moral authority to repel the Japanese who sought to take it from them, while his allusion to their racial identity as 'Britishers' was an attempt to equip them with the confident sense of superiority over Asian races that had been instilled by decades of imperial propaganda. While trying to steel his fellow white citizens to resist the invaders, Curtin also demanded that Britain fulfil its oft-repeated promise to defend its distant dominion. Churchill, who was in Washington ensuring that there was no undue leakage of Allied forces to the Pacific, passed the responsibility for Australia's defence to the Americans, privately describing the Australians as coming from 'bad stock' while the British high commissioner in Canberra dismissed Australians as an 'inferior people'. Churchill thought that a taste of bombing would do the Australians good. The taste came soon enough.

On 19 February 1942, a devastating Japanese bombing attack on the north Australian capital of Darwin left nearly 250 people dead and hundreds injured. Australia was now confronted as never before by its historic fear of an Asian invasion. The ailing Curtin, who was in hospital when Darwin was bombed, now called on Australians to give 'everything to the nation', while official communiqués played down the damage and deaths so as to prevent panic among the populace down south. Panic happened anyway.

Many of the defenders of Darwin had been recently posted there from the south and were still, as the journalist Douglas Lockwood observed, 'strangers in a strange land'. One serviceman who had sailed into Darwin in December 1940 recalled his impressions of this isolated outpost that was seven days by ship, or two days by air, from Sydney: 'Some men couldn't believe that they were still in Australia, it seemed so different and exotic.' Making it more exotic than most other places in Australia was the community of Asian Australians and the large number of Aborigines providing labour in the town as the government tried to remedy its woeful defences. These pre-Pearl Harbor times were 'roaring days' for Darwin, as the government money attracted to the town 'Malays, Chinese, Filipinos, Japanese, Javanese, whites, browns, blacks, brindles, pure-bloods, halfcastes, quarter-castes and nondescripts of all shapes and sizes'. For their part, though, the troops drafted in from the south dismissed the Darwin area as a 'parched and mean land' or, as one soldier wrote, the 'arsehole of the whole world' with mosquitoes 'as large as blowflies' and the place 'lousy with malaria'. An Adelaide mechanic conscripted into the air force and performing night-time guard duty in the bush that ringed Darwin's RAAF base found it 'nerve-wracking' as 'all sorts of weird noises were heard'. When the Japanese seemed set to cut them off in Darwin preparatory to capturing the place, it was no wonder that many bolted for the bush and beyond.

The depleted civilian population of the town joined what one observer described as this 'great stampede':

People of all colours and creeds were fleeing and on all sorts of vehicles. Soldiers, sailors, airmen and civilians were simply 'going through'. They were walking, running, riding bikes, driving cars and some were even on horseback.

Even the town's sanitary truck was pressed into service. An employee at the Darwin post office, which lost many of its staff in a direct hit, recalled how 'the thought of *invasion* was in all our minds'. One civilian who did not wait for the Japanese to land claimed, tongue in cheek, that, once the bombing stopped, 'I got on my bike that quick I was in the Adelaide River before I realised the chain was broken.' Many followed his example, taking to the bush south of Darwin which now, ironically, was seen as a place of relative safety from the attentions of the Japanese. Others fled further south, some of them reaching Adelaide and Melbourne where panic-stricken citizens hourly expected an invasion. Newspaper reports minimised the losses, waiting nearly six weeks before the full toll was made known. Curtin tried to put a brave face on this first outside challenge to the European occupation of the continent, claiming that 'the armed forces and the civilians comported themselves with the gallantry that is traditional in the people of our stock'. If Australians were to face a Japanese invasion, it was important that they believe in their continuing prowess as a fighting people.

It did not stop them, though, from taking all manner of precautions to guard against the terrible possibilities that a Japanese invasion conjured up in their minds. Slit trenches became commonplace in many a suburban garden, even in the southern city of Melbourne. Others prepared for the worst, considering suicide and the killing of their children rather than face the prospect of falling into Japanese hands. In the event of invasion, a flying instructor in Brisbane was ready to fly his wife and child inland where his service pistol would end all their lives. Further south, a Swan Hill schoolgirl recalled overhearing her mother and a friend with children of a similar age deciding that 'if the Japanese got to Swan Hill, they would kill us rather than let the Japanese get us'. These drastic responses to a possible Japanese takeover were based on a common expectation, recalled by a Sydney machinist, of the next generation of Australians being

> *...half-caste Japanese, there is no question about that. After Singapore fell, no-one was under any illusions about that, that's exactly what was expected, and you can imagine how that traumatised the entire Australian population.*

In Perth, Dorothy Hewitt remembers 'posters showing the Japanese as less than human, as fanged animals really, who were sort of coming to rape your sister, your mother, your grandmother or anybody else about the place'. To guard against the unwanted consequences of such an eventuality, the good women of Gulgong in New South Wales were reassured by the local doctor that young girls and women would be issued with birth control devices, that were otherwise denied to them, if the Japanese invaded.

The Japanese sweep southwards was precisely the scenario that Australians had always anticipated would trigger a British response in defence of its dominion. As the British governor of New South Wales observed at the time, 'Deep in the Australian mind is embedded the belief that, come what may, Britain would look after Australia.' For years, Britain had retained Australia's allegiance to the system of imperial defence on the understanding that a British fleet would steam to Australia's defence in the event of a threat developing to its existence. However, in the wake of Pearl Harbor and the fall of Singapore, Britain was forced to reveal the real order of its priorities, in particular as between the Middle East and the Far East and, within the eastern theatre, between the Indian Ocean and the Pacific. To Australia's horror, the most distant theatre—the Pacific—was relegated last in the order of British priorities. This was in accordance with a pre-existing agreement between Britain and the United States by which each had agreed in early 1941, in the event of fighting a two-front war against both Japan and Germany, that they would concentrate their strength against Germany while fighting a 'holding war' in the Pacific. Only after Germany was defeated would they turn their attention to the defeat of Japan. Depending on how this strategy was interpreted at the time, this held out the prospect of Australian security being seriously imperilled.

In October 1939, Churchill had assured Australian minister Richard Casey that the defence of the Far East was a higher British priority than the defence of British interests in the Middle East and that Britain would, if necessary, abandon the Mediterranean to come to the assistance of Australia. It had been a promise that Churchill had been confident would never be put to the test. Now it was. And just at the time that Britain was facing a fresh challenge from Rommel's forces in the Middle East. There was no contest in Churchill's mind. Despite his earlier assurances to Australia, he instructed that only such reinforcements be sent from the Middle East to the Far East as would not threaten the British position in Egypt. This meant a division of British troops and a handful of aircraft. They were the first and last modern fighters to be sent to Singapore, and they were sent by ship in crates, arriving too late to affect the swift course of events. But the dispatch of these aircraft and the unfortunate sinking of the *Prince of Wales* and the *Repulse* allowed Britain, then and subsequently, to claim that it had faithfully fulfilled its defence obligations in the Pacific.

Similarly, the British decision to return two Australian divisions from the Middle East created the impression of an embattled Britain foregoing Australian assistance in order to help defend the dominion. The facts are more complicated. It was certainly Churchill rather than the Australians who first suggested their return, but Churchill never intended they be returned to defend their homeland. Instead, he wanted them to assist the futile defence of Singapore. When that became untenable, he wanted them to defend the Netherlands East Indies, and then, when that also became untenable, Burma. When Curtin insisted they be returned to Australia, Churchill unilaterally diverted them to Burma hoping the Australians would cave in. But Curtin didn't, at least as far as Burma was concerned. Despite incurring Churchill's ire over the issue, with Churchill blaming Curtin's refusal for the subsequent loss of Rangoon, Curtin insisted on their return to Australia. He justified his intransigence to Roosevelt, who had supported Churchill, on the basis that their return was necessary to safeguard Australia which only had 'a small population' and was 'the only white man's territory south of the equator'. However, he did cave in to British requests to have two Australian brigades from the Middle East stop over in Ceylon for several months to help defend that British colony against an expected Japanese invasion that never came.

In the face of the British failure to fulfil her defence guarantee, Australia was forced to rely on the United States for its defence. In a landmark newspaper article, published to mark New Year's Day 1942, Curtin announced that Australia 'looks to America, free of any pangs as to our traditional links or kinship with the United Kingdom'. The statement caused further dissension between Australia and Britain, with Churchill being particularly outraged by Australia's apparent lack of courage in the face of the Japanese. Roosevelt was also reportedly none too impressed, although he realised that he needed Australia as the best-positioned base from which ultimately to launch an offensive against Japan.

The Americans began sending assistance to Australia to ensure that it would not be defeated by the Japanese. Starting in January 1942 with a trickle of untested troops, an increasing stream of American troops, aircraft and submarines began to flow towards Australia. At first, Australia was adamant that only white Americans be sent to its rescue. On 12 January 1942, the all-party Advisory War Council warned of the 'probable repercussions of the use of coloured troops on the maintenance of the White Australia policy in the post-war settlement'. As a result, Australia refused point-blank the notion of being defended by black Americans, informing its minister in Washington, Richard Casey, that it was 'not prepared to agree to [a] proposal that [a] proportion of [the] United States troops to be despatched to Australia should be coloured', although it indicated that it had 'no objection to coloured troops calling at an Australian port en route to destinations outside Australia'. However, when a shipload of troops arrived in Melbourne shortly after, Customs officers refused permission for any black American soldiers to land on Australian soil.

With Australian security dependent on American assistance, the government belatedly acknowledged that its rigid colour bar would have to be relaxed for the duration of the conflict if it was not to offend its American saviours. So it backed down on the understanding that the Americans would be sensitive to Australian views on the matter. And they were, keeping the limited numbers of black American troops mainly in northern Australia where they were used as a construction corps. By May 1942, some 5000 black American servicemen were stationed in Australia, 2000 of them at Townsville where they were building an aerodrome. The local Trades and Labour Council urged the government to declare that their presence would not affect the working conditions of white Australians. Curtin refused, fearful that a public declaration would only draw attention to the presence of the black Americans who were otherwise largely out of sight of most Australians and kept by the Queensland censor from the pages of newspapers. Instead he gave a private assurance to the council. In Sydney, where some of these black Americans were also stationed, they were moved from their initial camp on a sports oval in a residential area to a more secluded industrial location. In Brisbane, black Americans were segregated to the working class area of south Brisbane where Aborigines also were largely confined. By April 1944, the number of black Americans had been reduced to just 1584, all of them being based either in Queensland or the Northern Territory, while a further 23 494 were stationed in New Guinea and the adjacent islands.

Despite considerable Aboriginal enthusiasm about joining the war effort, an attempt to enlist Aborigines of the Kimberley district into an auxiliary force was successfully resisted by the Western Australian commissioner of native affairs who was anxious to retain the Aborigines as a compliant labour force. Moreover, he argued that the Aborigines knew 'nothing about patriotism or loyalty to His Majesty the King and the British Empire as we whites understand the words'. The few hundred pastoralists in the region were also implacably opposed to any suggestion of the Aborigines being armed and organised. As a white proponent of the Aboriginal force argued in a letter to Prime Minister Curtin,

> The white men who have lived and worked with the natives for years have exploited them shamefully and are exploiting them shamefully now … They know … that if the natives were organised for war … they would also be organised automatically for the peace and would not be willing to suffer further exploitation after the war. They might even demand justice.

Although Curtin seemed sympathetic, stiff bureaucratic opposition killed the proposal. So the Kimberley Aborigines were restricted to scouting and other activities in support of white troops who would otherwise have been unable to find their way about the bush and live off its resources. Aborigines not involved with the defence forces were subjected to severe restrictions as to their movements and employment. In other places across the north, such as Arnhem Land and the Torres Strait Islands, the indigenous peoples were used in regular armed formations, and as coastwatchers, to warn of any invasion attempt and to repel any that occurred.

While using Aborigines in some situations, white Australians worried that the Aborigines in northern Australia, with their knowledge of the land, might join with the Japanese to fight against them. An Aborigine visiting Thursday Island prior to Pearl Harbor was told by an islander that 'there would be a war with Japan soon' but 'the Japs would be fighting just the whites, not the coloured people of Australia, and that we should be helping the Japs'. A correspondent to the *Sydney Morning Herald* in early 1942 described Aborigines as 'the most dangerous race in the north today', while an inhabitant of north Queensland claimed that Aborigines around Cooktown looked forward to a Japanese victory after being informed prior to Pearl Harbor by Japanese pearlers that 'the country belonged to the blacks, had been stolen from them by the whites and that "bye and bye" they (the Japs) would give it back to them (the blacks)'. Partly to guard against such an alliance, Aborigines around Darwin were moved far south where many were used as cheap labour to support the army, while Aborigines at a mission near Cooktown were moved more than 1000 kilometres south when concern was expressed about the loyalty of the German missionary in charge. Sixty of the 235 Aborigines moved to cooler climes had died within a year. While isolated pastoralists across the north were provided with rifles and machine-guns and organised to form a guerrilla force to resist any Japanese invasion, many regarded the Aborigines as a potent security risk liable to side with the Japanese. Some part-time pastoralist soldiers were prepared to shoot them, as they and their forebears had been doing for half a century or more, to forestall such a threat. Fortunately, it never came to such a pass.

While being concerned at the effect on white Australia posed by the presence of black American troops, Australians took great confidence from the arrival in Australia of American General Douglas MacArthur who had been ordered out of the Philippines by President Roosevelt, before they fell to the Japanese, and made supreme commander of Allied forces in the south-west Pacific. MacArthur landed in Darwin on 17 March before making his way south to Melbourne by train. In announcing MacArthur's dramatic arrival in Australia, Curtin claimed that there were already 'very substantial American forces in Australia', which there were not. Curtin was trying to boost the shattered morale while also deterring the anticipated Japanese invasion. At the same time, he felt impelled to assure Australians that this invading army of Americans that was beginning to descend on them was made up of people who 'speak like us, think like us, and fight like us'.

In the Australian mind, conditioned by countless matinee Westerns, MacArthur personified the US cavalry that rushed over the hill with bugle blowing and flag flying to the last-minute rescue from the Indians of so many embattled white 'settlers'. The *Bulletin* hailed him as an American 'national hero' and a sign of an American commitment to preserve Australia 'as a free white English speaking nation'. MacArthur played up to these expectations. In a speech at a welcoming parliament house dinner, MacArthur claimed there was a strong link between the two countries based on 'that indescribable consanguinity of race' and pledged the 'full resources of all the mighty power of my country and all the blood of my countrymen'. As journalist Brian Penton observed at the time,

> *Not even John Barrymore could have looked a more convincing hero than this handsome general, affirming in Shakespearian periods his personal pledge to fling the Japanese back ... The humblest of his privates was uniformed like an officer, and looked as though he had just stepped from under the Kleig lights. The negroes that came to do the menial jobs all talked like Stepan Fetchit. Australia just knew that from now on the story was sure to have a happy ending.*

Which it eventually did, but not before many anxious months and much hard fighting, most of it by Australian land forces.

In some ways, the American invasion of Australia was as unsettling as a Japanese invasion, upsetting relations between men and women that were already under strain from the experience of the depression and the appearance of the 'new woman' in the postwar decades. Australian men who had gone off to fight in the Middle East, and who returned in their unfashionable uniforms during 1942 and 1943, expected for their far-off feats to be greeted by grateful Australian women, but found instead that there were hundreds of thousands of American servicemen competing for the affections of those women. Between 1942 and 1945, it has been estimated that perhaps one million Americans passed through Australia, some staying in the country for prolonged periods, although there were never more than 200000 at any one time. The culture shock for Australian women was considerable. A Melbourne dress designer recalled wistfully that the 'first time I ever saw a man carrying a bunch of flowers was the Americans'.

Many women succumbed to the attention they were paid, although some rejected it on principle, or tried to. As one Brisbane girl recalled:

> *A lot of ill feeling arose because they could afford to take the girls out to expensive places. My friends and I thought it was disloyal to our boys to go out with Americans, and we went dancing at an all-Australian club on Friday nights. One evening I did meet an American. I thought he was joking when he proposed marriage that same night, and I treated it very lightly. Six weeks later he married a girlfriend of mine.*

While some of these Australian women found themselves either deserted or widowed by their smooth-talking husbands, some 12000 women left Australia for the United States as war brides, thereby raising the threatening image of fertile Australian women deserting the nation's shores. As well, married women with their husbands in the forces, or perhaps imprisoned by the Japanese, sometimes found the attentions of the Americans difficult to resist after perhaps years alone. The Japanese played on the situation by suggesting in their propaganda broadcasts to Australian troops that, in their absence overseas, the Americans were seducing their womenfolk. The consequent rivalry engendered between Australian and American servicemen often spilled over into street brawls, some of them, such as the 'Battle of Brisbane', leading to loss of life.

Even without the Americans, women coping alone in the absence of their husbands developed a sense of independence and drew on strengths that sometimes they were not aware they possessed. An Adelaide woman, Agnes Williams, who was married just prior to the war and whose husband joined the AIF, remembered the war years as a time

> ... during which, of necessity, women developed a self-confidence and independence previously foreign to their characters in most cases. We had to make decisions without consulting or considering husbands, and most of us I believe rose to the challenge. Thus, when the war ended we were not prepared to cast that hard-earned freedom back into those dear, dead days before 1939.

Sometimes, the effect could be catastrophic for all concerned. Betty Carter was nine years old when the war broke out. Her father, a Sydney factory worker, enlisted and was sent to Singapore where he was captured by the Japanese and later drowned when a ship taking him to Japan was torpedoed by the Americans. After his departure,

> Our life went on but it was different. My mother began to smoke cigarettes, and went out at night. My grandmother stopped visiting us. We never went to Sunday School any more.

Her mother took up with other men, went on the grog and the children were put in a children's home. While individually Australian men faced the fear of losing women they had come to regard as their own, Australians as a whole faced the fear of losing a continent they had come to regard as their own.

For several months after the fall of Singapore, white Australians faced their long-feared prospect of an Asian invasion. Such an invasion, they believed, would rob them forever of their partially secured claim to the proprietorship of the continent. Britain could contemplate the prospect of a possible German invasion of the British Isles in the knowledge that they might suffer a short-term occupation but that their long-term hold on the islands would not be contested. Churchill suggested that Australia should steel itself to face the possibility of such a temporary fate for herself.

But Australia could not share Churchill's bravado, despite Curtin conjuring up 'the spirit of Anzac' to embolden Australians in the dark days of April 1942 so that Australia would be forever 'the home of the Anzac people'. If an Asian invasion was successful, white Australians believed it would signal their permanent dispossession.

Such fundamental fears lay behind the increasingly frantic appeals that Australian representatives addressed to Britain and the United States during those first dramatic six months of 1942. At the end of March, Australia's external affairs minister, Dr H. V. Evatt, implored Churchill to be the 'saviour of Australia', warning that it 'may have only six weeks to live' before it suffered 'violation by yellow hordes'. Later that year, Prime Minister John Curtin echoed these sentiments when he told a meeting of the Commercial Travellers' Association that there was 'nothing worth having in this land ... which could survive a Japanese victory'. Such comments were predicated on the assumption that a Japanese conquest of Australia would mark the end of the Australian nation. Whereas Britain could count on rising again from the ashes of defeat, Australia could not. Once occupied by an Asian invader, it could never be reclaimed by Europeans.

At the same time, the successful repelling of an Asian invader by Australian forces would do much to reinforce their claim of proprietorship over the continent. As the Sydney journalist Brian Penton observed in 1943,

> There were some who believed that Australia would come to more good than harm if, in this war, she had to fight on her own soil in defence of that soil, if everyone of her citizens was forced to spill some blood and sweat in personal sacrifice against an invader.

Clem Christesen, editor of the literary magazine *Meanjin*, was one of those who saw a stout defence on Australian soil having a cathartic effect on his fellow Australians. In the March 1942 edition, Christesen forecast that:

> It may well be that before the year is out we shall hear a sound that has never before been heard in Australia—the roar and bark and thunder of Australian armed forces, their backs to the wall in this last asylum, defending their native country: their 'culturally sterile', 'economically limited', unloved country; defending it stubbornly, bitterly, courageously.

Such a defence, suggested the writer Vance Palmer, would determine 'not only whether we are to survive as a nation, but whether we deserve to survive'. Without such a climactic struggle for possession of the continent, Australians would remain with 'no monuments to speak of, no dreams in stone, no Guernicas, no sacred places. We could vanish almost without a trace.' The spilling of blood on their relatively new-won soil would secure their proprietorship in a way that had not previously been possible. But, apart from sporadic Japanese raids by aircraft or submarines, the great climactic battle for the Australian continent was never fought, at least not on Australian soil.

Instead, Australia was saved by the Japanese decision not to attempt an invasion. Although the Japanese navy was keen to attempt an invasion after their surprising success against both Singapore and Pearl Harbor, the Japanese army was wary of diverting too many divisions from its major effort in China and refused to make the invasion of Australia a short-term aim. Ironically, just as the Japanese navy had provided protective cover for white Australia during the First World War, now the stout fighting of the Chinese and the latent threat of the Russians effectively prevented a Japanese invasion of white Australia in the Second World War. Instead, the Japanese decided to try to isolate Australia by capturing a string of Pacific islands off its eastern coastline to cut it off from American assistance. Australian defence chiefs interpreted the Japanese moves as preparatory to a massive invasion of the Australian continent. Their view was shared among the Australian population. The deputy mayor of Townsville recalled the panic in that town by March 1942 when a Japanese invasion was expected any day: 'People were scared stiff ... People just flocked away: they couldn't get on trains out of Townsville quick enough.'

The American naval victories of the Coral Sea and Midway Island in May and June 1942 effectively killed the Japanese capacity to invade Australia. Although a Japanese landward advance against Port Moresby in August 1942, across the daunting heights of the Owen Stanley Range, caused a renewed invasion scare in Australia, that was also beaten off with the capture of Kokoda in November 1942, causing the *Canberra Times* to claim that it had added to the 'renown of Australians as fighters'. Also beaten off was the Japanese attempt to isolate Australia by capturing the offshore Pacific islands, which was defeated by the American victory on Guadalcanal. By the end of 1942, there was little possibility of Australia being invaded even had Japan the will to do so. But the awful spectre of such an invasion made Australians more determined than ever to ensure that they never had to face such a prospect again.

For a time, Australia aspired to extend its sub-empire in the south Pacific, hoping to reserve for itself and New Zealand a predominant interest in many of the now-conquered European colonies in the Pacific as a way of ensuring after the war that she would never again face the possibility of dispossession. As the prominent Australian businessman W. S. Robinson advised Evatt in 1943:

> We must not forget that the East, with all its cruelties, lies at our door ... Australia and New Zealand have a total population of about 9 000 000 whites. Their neighbours are 1 000 000 000 of the coloured races—only a few hours away by air ... Australia and New Zealand are in the uncomfortable position of having most to lose and the greatest chance of losing it.

He reminded Evatt of Australia's vulnerability to air power, arguing that Australia's security depended upon it controlling an arc of territory from northern Australia stretching some 2400 kilometres to encompass Singapore, the Netherlands East Indies, New Guinea and the adjacent islands. 'These are the areas', wrote Robinson, 'in which we cannot afford to permit those opposed to our ideals of life and to our ways of living to establish himself in the air.' Moreover, by combining with British and American capital to exploit the resources of these areas, Australia could generate sufficient prosperity 'to attract the millions of white people we so urgently require'.

This vision was given short-lived substance in the ANZAC Agreement which was reached at Canberra in January 1944 by the Australian and New Zealand governments. Without consulting Britain, the two Pacific dominions declared unilaterally a Monroe Doctrine for the Pacific, proclaiming that the sovereignty of Pacific territories should not be altered in any postwar settlement without their express agreement. Both dominions were offended by their exclusion from various Allied conferences discussing postwar boundaries and other issues. But the ambitious assertions of the ANZAC Agreement failed for the simple reason that Britain and the United States refused to recognise it. Moreover, the government was advised by its army chief, General Blamey, that its ambition of controlling an arc of territories was simply beyond Australia's means. Instead, British Australians would try and ensure their continued hold on the continent by other means.

During the 1943 federal election campaign, which saw the Labor Party returned with a resounding win, Curtin informed Australians that they had lived through their 'darkest hour' and were 'now confronting the dawn of a victorious and better day'. The dawn would be heralded, and the continent secured for white Australians, by an ambitious program of postwar reconstruction. Gone was the discredited notion of 'Australia Unlimited'. A parliamentary committee on social security had acknowledged in September 1941 that Australia could no longer 'sustain the claim that [it] is the social laboratory of the world'. The late 19th century vision of Australia emulating the United States had largely dissipated in the dust of the depression. As Brian Penton observed, the national soul-searching provoked by the depression 'turned more and more Australian eyes to the quiet, decent, prosperous, happy democracies of the Scandinavian peninsula' as 'a model for this continent's future development'.

Instead of 'Australia Unlimited', there was the more realistic notion of 'Australia Limited', which became the title of a book in 1942 by the Sydney zoologist A. J. Marshall who described Australia as a 'second-rate lump of parched earth' which would need 'all the brains, energy and guts at our disposal to make any sort of success of it at all'. The sober, prewar assessments of geographer Griffith Taylor had been largely accepted. By August 1945, Calwell could inform his parliamentary colleagues, without fear of attack from the boosters, that much of Australia was 'situated within a rain belt of less than 10 inches per annum and this area is, therefore, largely uninhabitable'.

Hundreds of thousands of Australian servicemen could confirm Calwell's prognosis after having seen at first hand the relative lack of development potential of Australia's arid interior. Many had never previously set foot outside their familiar urban environments and now found themselves in uniform and in the bush awaiting a possible Japanese invasion. Tens of thousands served in the Northern Territory, many of them travelling there by train and truck through a landscape that was often forbidding and seldom welcoming or familiar. Their arrival opened up areas of Australia that previously had been practically closed to Europeans. The rough bush track that snaked alongside the telegraph poles south from Darwin to Alice Springs was transformed into a tarmacked road, while another road was constructed from Tennant Creek across the Barkly Tableland east to Queensland. While built mainly by Australian labour, they used American machines that arrived en masse under the Lend-Lease scheme and stayed after the war to continue the conquering of the continent's spaces.

As Penton argued in 1943, Australians had long been driven by 'a sense of discontent in an inhospitable, unbeautiful, ungentle land':

> *The migrant Briton had not fitted himself into it, could not bear its continental immensity. Huddled with his fellows in the great cities he tried to keep his eyes away from its grey emptiness, burning plains, silent bush, oppressive monotony. Far from loving it— he hated it.*

Even that great spinner of bush yarns, Henry Lawson, had been moved to write, 'Death is about the only cheerful thing in the bush.' Now, the wartime presence of so many urban Australians in the interior hastened the process by which they were slowly coming to terms with their landscape, and even coming to love it. Although for many Australians, to know the bush was still not to love it, the war gave them confidence that they might at last secure it and subdue it.

The new army of bureaucrats in Canberra, emboldened by their successful handling of the wartime economy, now began to plan with confidence the social, economic and even physical reshaping of postwar Australia through government direction in ways that would finally establish an effective claim of proprietorship over the continent. In November 1942, Evatt held out the prospect of the government, as part of postwar reconstruction, promoting the

> *... regional development of industry in the less industrialised States and in rural areas, [and developing the] physical resources of Australia to help support a larger and more prosperous population,*

e.g. by road development, water conservation and irrigation, soil protection and improvement, and productive public works of all kinds ...

Once again, there would be a renewed attempt to promote 'the growth and settlement of population' in the bush, ostensibly 'to avoid the evils of congested and overcrowded cities'. A department of postwar reconstruction had been established in late 1942 and, after Labor won the 1943 election, it was placed under the ministerial control of the treasurer Ben Chifley. He faced a seemingly impossible task even to achieve the scaled-down vision of 'Australia Limited'. And his task was made more difficult when a referendum in 1944, which would have given the government greater powers to centrally plan the economy along wartime lines, was lost to the justifiable conservatism of the traditionally cautious Australian electorate.

In 1943, Brian Penton had outlined in the pages of his book *Advance Australia Where?* a gloomy prognosis for Australia. According to the latest depression-battered figures, the growth of Australia's population seemed set to peak at 7.5 million in 1973, after which it was estimated that it would begin to decline. It was an alarming prospect, that the much-vaunted Australian race would be saved from the Japanese only to be subdued gradually by its own apparent unwillingness to procreate and its inability to attract sufficient immigrants. The Menzies government had tried to reverse the trend when it introduced child endowment of five shillings a week for each white child under 16 years of age after the first child. While not expecting to have 'any spectacular effect on the birth rate', it was expected to increase it somewhat, while also causing 'some reduction in mortality among children and an improvement in their health and quality'. They were all issues of great moment to a society that was fighting for its survival. Child endowment also answered to some extent the desire for an improved society to emerge from the war.

Customs officers continued to do what they could to keep their fellow Australians ignorant of contraception. Imported books on sex education or contraception were scrutinised closely and banned if they were too detailed and, presumably, useful to their potential readers. In April 1940, *The Right Use of Sex* was banned because it was 'of such an intimate nature as to make its indiscriminate distribution unwise'. The demands of war forced the government to soften its stand against contraception in one respect. It was no good withholding condoms from troops who would otherwise be liable to suffer from venereal diseases. So contraceptives were distributed to the troops despite complaints by the *Catholic Weekly* that the government was thereby subsidising sin. To appease such critics, the Labor government used national security regulations in September 1942 to ban the advertising of contraceptives as 'a first step to meet the great national danger involved in the fall of the birth-rate'. As well, the local production of contraceptive caps was banned, ostensibly to conserve the scarce supplies of rubber, while the information minister, Arthur Calwell, called upon Australians to practise 'self-control instead of birth control'.

In order to give Australians the confidence to procreate, a range of social welfare measures, including maternity benefit, was announced in February 1943. In explaining the move, Curtin sang the familiar refrain, arguing that 'our post-war aim must be the physical development of our country, linked up with expanded production and an increase of population'. Instead of Penton's predicted population of 7.5 million, Curtin announced in December 1943 that the government was aiming to have a population of 20 million. Several months later, he raised the projected population to 30 million. And this sought-for population was to be both white and predominantly British. Australia was determined that the war would not force it to abandon its cherished 'white Australia' policy. So the colour bar stayed firmly in place. Although agreeing to accept prisoners of war from Britain, it stipulated that none should be black. Jewish refugees fleeing from Hitler's genocide, including 300 French children, were refused admission to Australia's pristine shores. Chinese indentured labourers on the island of Nauru, where they had been mining phosphate to fertilise Australian farms, found themselves being evacuated to Australia only to be sent into the centre of the continent to work in segregated conditions in a tungsten mine. When they protested at their treatment, they were handed over to the American forces for use outside of Australia provided that they would not be returned to Australia at the end of the war.

Chinese crewmen on ships fleeing to Australia in the face of the Japanese found themselves still subject to the rigours of the 'white Australia' policy. Although the Australian authorities could hardly send them back, many of them were sent off to a military detention camp before being drafted into an army labour corps. The war also saw Asian Australians interned for the duration of the war. Many Italian Australians from north Queensland were also interned after the entry of Italy into the war. Italians had been brought to Australia in the 1890s to try and replace the dependence of the sugar industry on the labour of Pacific Islanders. Many had prospered to the extent of owning their own farms. This had led to calls after the First World War for such farms to be turned over to returning British Australian servicemen. These calls were repeated during the Second World War when the north Queensland branch of the RSL demanded that coastal land owned by 'aliens' should be given to ex-servicemen so that northern Australia could again be controlled by British Australians. To ensure that Italians could not recover their prominence in this region that was so vulnerable to invasion, an RSL conference in June 1943 demanded internment for all enemy aliens and a 20-year ban on postwar immigration. The government had other plans.

In December 1943, Curtin announced his government's plans for a massive postwar immigration program designed to defend the security of 'white Australia'. Addressing a Labor Party conference, Curtin assured delegates that the program would not look to Asia to make up its numbers. The labour movement had long resisted the notion of importing non-European indentured labourers to develop the continent. Australia could not have Asians, said Curtin, because of their 'antagonism to the white man'. At the same time, warned Curtin, Australian manufacturers would face the problem of selling their products to Asian countries while 'strenuously refusing them access to an empty Australia'. Hence the need, Curtin argued, for the labour movement to abandon its traditional opposition to a mass immigration program, based upon fear of them flooding the labour market and threatening hard-won working conditions, and to support the entry of sufficient white immigrants to fill up those persistent 'empty spaces'. Such talk set off alarm bells in some Labor circles, with a meeting of Labor women in Sydney in March 1944 expressing alarm at the possibility of the 'white Australia' policy being reviewed as part of postwar reconstruction and called on Curtin to 'give an outspoken and emphatic assurance' that it would remain inviolate.

The information minister Arthur Calwell, who was appointed as immigration minister, was a convert to Curtin's cause, explaining to the House of Representatives in August 1945 that the one lesson of the war was that 'we cannot continue to hold our island continent for ourselves and our descendants unless we greatly increase our numbers'. He predicted that there would be another challenge within 25 years 'to our right to hold this land' and announced moves to boost the population. Although the government had signed an agreement with Britain to provide assisted passages for British migrants from 1947, when shipping was expected to become available, Calwell was careful not to alarm his colleagues in the labour movement. The assisted passage scheme would only proceed if Australia was enjoying conditions of relatively full employment so that the migrants would not depress wages and working conditions. Moreover, Calwell maintained that the 'most important phase of population building' was 'natural increase'. As before, the preferred new Australians were the babies born to existing Australians. So plans were made to increase the birthrate and lower the infant mortality rate. Calwell suggested that Labor's protective social welfare programs and policy of full employment would produce conditions of economic security that would induce 'young Australian families to have larger families'.

This overwhelming impulse to secure itself against future challenges saw Australia reaffirm its prewar commitment to imperial defence, despite Penton warning against the 'temptation to bury our heads in imperial self-enclosure'. The lesson of the war, argued Penton, was that the 'Empire can no longer guarantee [Australia's] safety in a global war'. Although the fall of Singapore should have revealed the bankruptcy of imperial defence, and the Australian defence of New Guinea should have given the nation confidence in its ability to defend itself, Australians preferred to believe that their security had been secured solely by the fighting of the US navy at Midway and in the Coral Sea. As the secretary of the defence department, Frederick Shedden, observed, the war 'should have convinced all Australians that their future will hinge on the maintenance of the goodwill of our powerful friends'. Or, as Curtin echoed, Australia must remain 'harnessed to other nations' because of the 'teeming millions of coloured races to the north of Australia'. With the United States unwilling to assume the burden of defending postwar Australia, the dominion looked back to Britain for its security. When visiting London in May 1944, Curtin had tried to reawaken British sympathy for Australia by portraying the dominion as 'a British community in the South Seas' which corresponded 'in purpose and in outlook and in race to the Motherland itself'. If this British community was to secure its effective and moral proprietorship over the continent before it faced a further challenge to its occupation, it would have to dramatically increase its population numbers and develop the resources of the continent.

Australians took some confidence from their wartime experience when the perceived valour of their troops seemed to follow in the traditions set at Gallipoli. While their withdrawal from Tobruk was seen by British observers as a sign of national cowardice, it was likened by Australians to the successful evacuation from Gallipoli. While the defeats in Greece, Crete and Singapore caused British political and military leaders to question the bravery of Australian soldiers, these same defeats were held up for Australians as further examples of Anzac courage. When announcing the end of the Pacific war to his radio audience, Curtin's pipe-smoking successor as prime minister, Ben Chifley, claimed that Australian soldiers had 'battle honours thick upon them from every theatre of war' and that they had played crucial parts in the ultimate victory: 'Australians stopped the Japanese in their drive south, just as they helped start the first march towards ultimate victory in North Africa.' The Gallipoli legend had to be maintained, for it had become central to the Australian self-image and was required in the continuing battle to subdue those extensive parts of the continent that were capable of development. The men returning with their battle honours were now required, announced Chifley, to 'join together in the march of our nation to future greatness'.

Recommended Reading

Frank Alcorta, 1991, *Australia's Frontline: The Northern Territory's War*, Allen & Unwin, Sydney.

Rosemary Campbell, 1989, *Heroes and Lovers: A Question of National Identity*, Allen & Unwin, Sydney.

F. K. Crowley (ed.), 1973, *Modern Australia in Documents*, Vol. 2, Wren Publishing, Melbourne.

David Day, 1999, *John Curtin: A Life*, HarperCollins, Sydney.

David Day, 1992, *Reluctant Nation*, Oxford University Press, Melbourne.

Robert Hall, 1989, *The Black Diggers*, Allen & Unwin, Sydney.

Michael Heyward, 1993, *The Ern Malley Affair*, University of Queensland Press, Brisbane.

Douglas Lockwood, 1992, *Australia's Pearl Harbor: Darwin 1942*, Penguin, Melbourne.

Noel McLachlan, 1989, *Waiting for the Revolution: A History of Australian Nationalism*, Penguin, Melbourne.

Ross McMullin, 1992, *The Light on the Hill: The Australian Labor Party 1891–1991*, Oxford University Press, Melbourne.

Brian Penton, 1943, *Advance Australia Where?*, Cassell, London.

E. Daniel Potts and Annette Potts, 1985, *Yanks Down Under 1941–45*, Oxford University Press, Melbourne.

18

'THE FLAG

OF WHITE AUSTRALIA

WILL NOT

BE LOWERED'

Although the Second World War had nearly realised Australia's historic fears of an alien invasion, it had also given white Australians considerable self-confidence. It was the first time that the bulk of its forces had been largely deployed in the direct defence of the Australian continent. Although they had not had to fight a climactic battle on Australian soil, their presence in large numbers on the streets of Australian cities provided an exaggerated impression of the nation's potential strength and capabilities. This view was enhanced by the spectacular development of secondary industries which saw four-engined bombers being produced by a country that previously had been unable to make a motor car. Whereas the First World War had restored faith in the virility of Australian manhood, the Second World War inspired faith in the ability of centrally planned, scientific organisation to solve the ongoing problem of securing the effective occupation of the continent. But the self-confidence was tempered by the widespread fear that Australians remained vulnerable to a further challenge to that occupation.

To ward off such a challenge, Australians adopted an immigration program designed to attract an unprecedented flow of new 'settlers', and not just from Britain. At the same time, the ongoing efforts to develop the continent's resources and occupy its habitable expanses became almost frenzied. They also sought the continued protection of a great power ally so that Australia could concentrate its energies on this development without having to be distracted unduly by the need to defend itself from external attack. Previously, their proprietorship of the continent had always been backed by the worldwide power of the British navy. Ever since federation in 1901, Australians had skimped on their defences, relying on imperial defence for their security as they channelled resources into the development of the continent. As the events of 1942 revealed, Australia had tied itself to an empire that was sinking beneath the weight of its global responsibilities. Nevertheless, at the end of the war, Australians clambered back aboard this wallowing empire. There seemed to be nowhere else to go.

While embracing American assistance when it arrived during the desperate days of 1942, the Labor government soon became suspicious of American territorial and economic ambitions in the Pacific and sought to restrict their postwar expansion to the north Pacific. For their part, Australian men resented the competition from their brash American 'cousins' for the attention of Australian women. Despite the events of 1942, Australians believed that Britain remained as its most reliable ally in the event of another conflict, that links of race, sentiment and self-interest would ensure British support in future conflicts in ways that had not proved possible in the previous world war. Although the external affairs minister, Dr H. V. Evatt, did try to obtain a postwar defence pact with the United States to supplement its links with Britain, Washington was not interested in a formal pact or even an informal declaration of responsibility for the defence of Australia and New Zealand. In a last-ditch attempt to reach a deal with the Americans, Evatt proposed the joint use of Australian and American bases in the Pacific as a way of 'showing to the world that the countries concerned ... would be almost certain to be working together in time of war'. But this was also refused because of the conditions that Evatt wished to attach to the agreement. America was not yet ready to assume the role of world policeman.

To try and reinforce the frayed British defence ties, Australia allowed Britain in 1946 to establish a guided missile range in the interior of South Australia. Named Woomera after the Aboriginal throwing stick, the range was established on arid expanses of land far to the north of Adelaide where Aborigines still pursued their traditional lifestyles largely untouched by two centuries of European occupation. Any hesitancy in federal parliament about establishing the base on Aboriginal land was overcome with the assurance that the 'probability of a missile falling on them is remote', while the presence of the joint facility would 'increase the capacity of Australia to defend itself with the latest weapons' which was 'important in view of our small man-power and large territory'. If white Australians could not occupy the 'dead heart' of their continent, at least they could now use it to research new ways of defending the continent.

Although the Allies had successfully repelled Japan's wartime lunge towards Australia, the end of the war did not lay to rest Australia's abiding fear of Asia. Only isolated voices argued for Australia to engage in meaningful dialogue with Asia and develop trade relations as the surest way of averting a future threat. Journalist Brian Penton had argued in 1943 for Australians 'to build ourselves into the Asiatic economy' which would allow Australians to 'reconcile two ends which seem at the moment to conflict hopelessly—our desire for a higher standard of living and our desire for security on the fringe of Asia, the world's most populous and under-privileged hemisphere.' Although Goulburn's Bishop Burgmann had echoed this call in 1946, arguing that Australians should acknowledge their future as an oriental nation, few were prepared to listen. The war had seemed to confirm to Australians the threat posed by Asia and they emerged from the conflict more intent than ever on holding Asia at arm's length, other than as a possible market for Australian goods. They were also determined that the 'white Australia' policy be kept firmly in place.

While Hitler's attempted genocide of European Jews had helped to discredit the racial theories that partly underpinned the 'white Australia' policy, public support in Australia for a non-discriminatory immigration policy was slow to appear. 'White Australia' was so entrenched as an article of political faith that politicians feared to question it. It was left to religious figures such as Bishop Burgmann, and sections of the press, to count the cost to Australia in its relations with newly independent Asian countries and to call for the watering down of its restrictive provisions. When some 1000 Anglo-Indian ex-servicemen and their families sought entry to Australia in January 1948 following the bloody partition of British India, they were screened for colour before their ship left Bombay, prompting a furore in India and leading to a reassessment of white Australia. 'The problem of where to draw the colour line is delicate and difficult', observed the *Sydney Morning Herald* sagely, but 'in the special circumstances which have arisen in India, the White Australia policy should be applied with humanity and flexibility.'

The newspaper was supported by the Australian section of the World Council of Churches which called for a quota system that would 'cease to give offence to coloured peoples, and which will be in closer touch with the realities of the present world situation'. Reflecting the popular fears, the council warned that Australia 'cannot afford to antagonise adjacent peoples with populations exceeding ours fiftyfold and with enormous potentialities for development'. A correspondent to the *Sydney Morning Herald* backed the churches, noting that the Indian troops who had fought alongside Australians during the war were barred from 'this open-spaced continent' while preference was 'given to former enemies, like Italians'. Most of the Indians were 'no darker than a Bondi life-saver' and should be admitted to 'help develop our rural areas'. Another correspondent attacked the 'apparently fear-complexed policy' which was pushing Australia towards 'race suicide'.

Such arguments were swept aside by a government whose Customs officers remained armed with the infamous dictation test and which was even then forcibly repatriating those among the non-Europeans who had fled from the Japanese to find short-lived sanctuary in Australia and who wished to remain there. The continuing effort to 'purify' the Australian race would proceed unabated, with white Australians being fortified in their lingering racism by the advice of such visiting 'experts' as the Dutch geneticist Dr Arend Hagedoorn, who warned Australians in May 1949 against intermarriage which would lead to 'colour blindness and feeble mindedness'. Although the distinguished military historian C. E. W. Bean dismissed such talk as being 'very like the kind of trash that Hitler spoke', the government was careful to maintain their strict colour bar. Rather than being based on discredited racial theories, the government justified their continuing ban on the entry of non-Europeans as being based upon considerations of assimilation, arguing that such people would not be able to be absorbed into Australian society.

An Englishman whose Chinese wife and stepdaughter were deported to Malaya was astounded: 'I knew this sort of thing could happen in Nazi Germany and Russia', he said, 'but did not expect that it would in a British Dominion.' Although Malayan authorities retaliated by deporting two Australian women with Chinese husbands, Calwell was adamant about protecting the supposed sanctity of 'white Australia'. If these few hundred were allowed to remain, he argued, 'the Australia we know will soon cease to exist'. One of the few who managed to slip past the racial barrier was a 12-year-old orphan boy from Dutch Timor who stowed away in the wheel bay of an RAAF aircraft in 1946 on a flight to Darwin. Despite being mangled by the retracting wheel and burnt by the exhaust, he somehow survived the perilous journey only to be informed by immigration officials that he faced deportation to Timor after several months' recuperation in hospital. Strong protests from the Darwin community saw Calwell relent. It was an isolated incident.

The government suffered a setback to its plans when the High Court disallowed its attempt to deport the Indonesian widow and eight children of a man who had died while serving as a commando with Australian forces. The family had been living in Australia for seven years and the woman had since married an Australian man. Despite the court ruling and a chorus of protest from neighbouring countries, Calwell remained unrepentant, proclaiming to the annual conference of the Australian Natives Association in the Victorian rural town of Bendigo that 'so long as the Labor Party remains in power there will be no watering down of the White Australia Policy'. However violent the criticism, continued Calwell, he was 'determined that the flag of White Australia will not be lowered'.

With the troubled Labor government facing an imminent election, Calwell stood firm, closing the legislative loophole that the High Court had exposed and continuing with the government's expulsions. According to Calwell, it was a matter of survival for white Australia:

> We have to hand down this country to our children and our children's children in the same manner as we received it from our fathers and as they received it from their fathers ... We can have a white Australia, we can have a black Australia, but a mongrel Australia is impossible, and I shall not take the first steps to establish the precedents which will allow the flood gates to be opened.

Menzies's conservative opposition sat mute during the debate, apparently fearful of being portrayed as opposed to 'white Australia'. It was left to the *Sydney Morning Herald* to provide a prescient note of warning to Calwell's blinkered politics, predicting that Australia

> ... will one day be challenged for its exclusion of Asiatics. It is then that we shall see, in its full measure, the harm done to our name and to our cause by Mr. Calwell's flamboyant defiance of simple humanity.

Such warnings had little effect. Australians were anxious to secure their hold on the continent before the feared Asian challenge to their occupation. They would hardly be willing to allow these self-same Asians to immigrate legally and take the continent slowly by subterfuge

Non-white Australians who could not be deported suffered for their colour. As an anonymous non-white correspondent complained to the *Sydney Morning Herald* in January 1948, despite his education at good Sydney schools, despite being a second-generation Australian and despite having served in Australian forces, he still could not get a job during a time of full employment. 'I always wear my ex-Serviceman's badge', he wrote, 'but they generally look at my face instead of my badge.' Immigration officers deployed in Britain and Europe ensured that Australians would be saved the embarrassment of practising racial discrimination against newcomers by rigorously screening them on the basis of their colour. Those Europeans of a swarthy appearance who might attract glances or worse on Australian streets, were required to strip for a medical officer to determine whether it was the sun or their racial origins that had caused their colour.

Behind the government's strict application of the 'white Australia' policy, a fundamental redefinition of Australian identity was occurring. While not including Asians within the definition, it did widen sufficiently after the war to include immigrants from Europe. The first tentative moves in this direction had been made prior to the war when British immigrants had failed to come in the required numbers and small numbers of southern Europeans had been admitted. It was clear from this experience that Australia would have difficulty meeting its postwar immigration targets from Britain alone. Brian Penton had predicted as much in 1943, arguing that Australians would have to overcome their historic prejudices and accept large numbers of southern Europeans in their midst. By 1949, such immigrants were being openly sought, and in large numbers.

An official report in 1945 had warned that even an influx of 40 000 immigrants a year would only cause Australia's population to grow to nine million, far fewer than the 20–30 million that the continent was now believed able to sustain and which were needed to ward off a possible future Asian invasion. A more massive influx than 40 000 a year was clearly required and the memory of 1942 impelled Australia to achieve this population quickly. 'Populate or perish', a phrase coined prior to the war, became the Australian watchwords for the postwar world. The discarding by the Labor Party of its traditional opposition to sponsored immigration schemes was made easier by the surprising situation of relatively full employment that Australia enjoyed during the postwar period. The government aimed for an annual population increase of two per cent, half from immigration and half from natural increase. This meant an influx of 70 000 migrants a year. Double that number would be arriving by 1949.

To assuage public concern about non-British immigrants being included within the large-scale influx, the government had initially emphasised that immigrants would be drawn overwhelmingly from Britain and Ireland. In November 1946, the immigration minister, Arthur Calwell, announced that, while the government would allow entry to displaced refugees from Europe, he hoped that there would be ten British migrants for every one foreign migrant. He reminded Australians critical of this policy that 'without adequate numbers this wide brown land may not be held in another clash of arms'. He called on them to 'give their maximum assistance to every effort to expand its economy and assimilate more and more people who will come from overseas to link their fate with our destiny'. The following year, after it had become clear that British immigrants would not come in the numbers the government required, Calwell toured the camps of displaced persons in northern Europe, personally selecting a shipload of largely blue-eyed immigrants between the ages of 15 and 35. When their ship arrived in Melbourne, Calwell was on hand for the perfect 'photo opportunity':

> The men were handsome and the women beautiful. It was not hard to sell immigration to the Australian people once the press published photographs of that group.

It was the first of many ships that would bring by 1952 tens of thousands of displaced persons, known disparagingly as 'reffos' or 'Balts'.

Calwell's support for an immigration program composed overwhelmingly of British migrants, and his rigid upholding of 'white Australia', was a propaganda smokescreen designed to hide this reality from an Australian public still anxious about European immigrants. Despite the inexorable trend of the statistics which slipped steadily towards southern Europe, the conservative opposition still dreamed of Australia drawing its population overwhelmingly from Britain. Richard Casey, who had returned to Australian politics after wartime service for Britain, first as British minister for the Middle East and then as governor of Bengal, had more experience of Asia, although not necessarily empathy with it, than most Australians and was acutely conscious of Australia's state of underpopulation. In his book *Double or Quit*, Casey called in 1949 for a 'centrifugal movement from Britain to the outer reaches of the Commonwealth and Empire, of people, industries and capital', suggesting that 'a considerable part of the future of the British race will lie in Australia'. The support for immigration by the Liberal Party leader, Robert Menzies, was based upon similar considerations. Like Casey, Menzies saw it as shifting the centre of empire from Britain to Australia. *En route* by ship to Britain in 1948, Menzies wrote an unpublished paper calling for the redistribution of population from Britain to the dominions, arguing that a British migrant 'is not lost to Britain, he merely serves the true interest of Britain in another part of the British Empire'. Such sentiments represented a last, longing look at a fast-fading dream. As Calwell well knew, and as Menzies would find for himself during the 1950s, there was no alternative to non-British immigration if Australia was to solve its labour shortage and fulfil its postwar dream of developing the continent.

Although Australia was prepared to look further afield for its immigrants, British migrants were given preferential assistance. Australia signed an immigration agreement with Britain in 1947 which provided for the free passage to Australia of British ex-servicemen and their families. Other British immigrants would pay a subsidised rate of just £10. The shortage of shipping at the end of the war caused Australia to lose its opportunity of attracting mainly war-battered Britons. Hundreds of thousands of British people who enquired about migrating lost interest when it took two years to establish the assisted passage scheme and up to another two years before people were interviewed for acceptance into the scheme. As shipping became available, the number of assisted immigrants increased from 6303 in 1947 to 28 943 in 1948 and 118 840 in 1949. Many of these immigrants were non-British, drawn from the camps of displaced persons in western and northern Europe. In March 1948, as New South Wales experienced an estimated shortage of 100 000 workers in the coal, steel, textile and transport industries, the assisted passages scheme was extended to cover ex-service personnel from western and northern Europe. Between 1948 and 1951, around 180 000 displaced Europeans were brought to Australia, helping to cause the annual percentage of British immigrants to drop from 66 per cent in 1948 to just 41 per cent in 1949, although the government was ostensibly planning to bring 90 000 Britons and just 60 000 Europeans that year.

Apart from war refugees, who were mainly from northern and central Europe, an increasing proportion of European immigrants were unassisted immigrants from Italy, Greece and Yugoslavia, sources of immigration that Australia had largely disdained in the past. Their arrival now was not without opposition. Following Italy's wartime alliance with Germany, Queensland had introduced a wartime ban on non-Britons buying land in that tropical state. At the same time, thousands of Italian prisoners of war, sent to Australia for the duration of the conflict, were returned to Italy at the end of the war despite the desire of some to stay in Australia. But the pressing postwar need for labour on the cane fields caused the discrimination against Italians to be reviewed. Initially, Australia looked to refugees from northern Europe, and British and Irish sources, as labour for the cane fields. However, the labour shortfall in the sugar industry was such that, by 1948, it was acknowledged that Italians would provide the best long-term solution. Calwell backed a plan for importing Italians to provide the millions needed for the occupation of northern Australia. He had the enthusiastic backing of the Queensland Labor government which encouraged migrants to that state to 'go on the land instead of cluttering up the labour market'. As a result, the cosmopolitan nature of other Australian cities would not be replicated to the same extent in Brisbane.

In 1948, it was announced that 500 northern Italians, who would be of lighter complexion than their southern counterparts, were to be admitted as cane cutters. The *Sydney Morning Herald* reassured any readers concerned about this influx of former enemy aliens that northern Italians had 'made good settlers before the war' and a 'due quota' could be safely mixed into the 'inflowing stream' of migrants as Australians came to realise that 'room must be made for newcomers from Europe if Australia is to be held as a white man's country'. As Prime Minister Ben Chifley made clear in May 1949, Australia's eight million people needed to be supplemented with 'virile people from other countries' so as to fully develop the economic potential of the continent and to thereby 'justify before the world our retention of such a great country'. To doubters within the Labor ranks, Chifley pointed to the possible threat from Asian nations which would otherwise 'be looking at us' and pressuring Australia to provide 'an outlet for their populations'. If it was a choice between Italians and Chinese, there was no doubt where white Australian preferences lay, however grudgingly.

If British Australians could no longer ensure their overwhelming predominance through the operation of the 'white Australia' policy, it was essential that some other way be found to ensure that non-British Australians did not effectively dispossess British Australians by stealth. The answer was to assimilate them upon arrival into the wider society. The wartime registration of aliens continued to try and prevent the concentration of particular nationalities in any one area. The *Aliens Act* in 1947 created an Aliens Assimilation Division to register, control and assimilate all non-British members of the community. It was designed to prevent their concentration in particular areas or industries and generally to 'promote the speedy and trouble free absorption of all migrants into the Australian community'. On another level, so-called aliens would be expected to leave their language and their culture behind when stepping ashore on Australian soil and to embrace the language and culture of the existing society. Migrants previously known as 'white aliens' were officially referred to as 'New Australians', although on the streets of Australian cities they were still referred to disparagingly as 'wogs' and 'dagoes'. The unifying factor for this increasingly disparate society was changed from being British to adopting the largely undefined Australian way of life.

Apart from immigration, the government intended to increase the number of its citizens by boosting the stubbornly subdued birthrate which had fallen so low during the depression and subsequent war that British Australians were no longer replacing themselves. Child endowment, which had been introduced by the federal government in 1941, was increased after the war in a way designed to encourage larger families. No money would be paid until the second child had been born. Women who had been drawn into the work force during the war were sent back into the spreading suburbia of brick veneered homes to save their society by procreating. Although the birthrate responded to such official encouragement, rising from a rate of 17 per thousand in the 1930s to 24 per thousand by 1947, their increased living standards prompted couples paradoxically to restrict the number of their children to an average of two or three. By 1949–50, the population was increasing at 3.5 per cent a year rather than the planned-for two per cent a year. Both the rate of natural increase and the level of immigration had exceeded the most optimistic wartime projections.

The steady accretion of a larger Australian population through immigration and natural increase, with all its members meant to be assimilating into this ill-defined Australian way of life, went some way towards allaying the wartime fears of British Australians being dispossessed in their turn. However, population was insufficient in itself. It was not enough to fill the 'empty spaces' of Australia. They also had to be developed, not only to ensure that their effective occupation would be secured, but also to ward off any challenges to their claim of moral proprietorship over the continent. Journalist Brian Penton had asked in 1943

> ... *whether Australians are going to begin living in their country as permanent abiders rather than as temporary exploiters* ...

> *They may yet decide that the job is too big, that the adjustments which Asia demands of them are too painful, and up like a cloud of locusts, leaving the remnants of Australia Felix to the crows, and rabbits, and drifting sand.*

His question was predicated on the fearful assumption that the end of the war might see a return to depressed economic conditions as world markets for Australian exports dried up once they were no longer driven by the demands of the war. However, the unexpected postwar prosperity and conditions of full employment allowed Penton's question to be answered in the affirmative. Moreover, great strides had been made during the war in opening up the interior.

The roar of powerful American-supplied machinery, often operated by black American construction units, had cut through the tropical outback, carving roads where rough tracks had once meandered, laying out airfields in an ordered array across the north, and constructing ports on beaches where crocodiles still heaved themselves ashore. Darwin, which had been a garrison town for the duration of the war, was destined to become the planned capital of the north as Canberra was of the inland. Or so they hoped. While Darwin's development was held back by bureaucratic hands, much of the heavy equipment brought to Australia by the Americans was left behind to continue with the process of opening up the distant bush. As with the First World War, returned servicemen were again sent into the bush to battle with the elements, although on a smaller scale than the sometimes disastrous schemes of the 1920s. Only 3200 had taken up farms in Queensland by 1950.

This careful approach to soldier settlement was cast aside in the British-promoted Peak Downs scheme in central Queensland under which half a million acres was to be developed for agriculture and the raising of pigs for the British breakfast table. The Queensland government gave its enthusiastic backing, along with half a million pounds. According to Labor premier, Ned Hanlon, 'Australia's empty spaces must be developed and what better avenue exists than rural agriculture?' The initial losses, claimed Hanlon, were 'very much less than the cost of a battleship'. There was a direct link in his mind between national defence and the development of such schemes. He would also have been conscious that the Queensland Labor Party was controlled by the rural-based Australian Workers Union which naturally advocated agriculture before industry. Despite Hanlon's claims of ultimate success, the vagaries of the climate and the market for pigs combined to kill the scheme by 1953, although it left an enduring legacy when the land was broken up into 60 smaller farms, growing sorghum on which cattle were grazed.

The soldier settlers were joined in the bush by many of the immigrants brought to Australia under the displaced persons scheme, together with those brought under assisted passages, who were sent into the bush to become 'true

Australians' and adopt the 'Australian way of life'. The conditions of their passage entailed them working for two years wherever the government decided. Many were directed into 'timber-getting, sawmilling and forestry', subduing the bush with their axes and saws and producing in 1950 alone an estimated 120 million super feet of timber. Others were sent north to work on the cane fields of northern Queensland. However, as the demographer A. J. Rose pointed out in 1958, any 'immigrants displaying marked proclivities for the open spaces are acting strongly against the true Australian tradition of huddling in the towns and cities'. Despite the encouragement given to rural settlement, there was a continuing drift of population from the countryside into the cities as mechanisation of farms allowed greater production with less manpower. By 1947, the number of Australians employed in secondary industries was far greater than those employed in primary industries. While 28 per cent of the work force were in factories, only 18 per cent were on farms. And much of the labour force for the factories was provided by immigration. Of nearly a million new workers added to the labour force between 1947 and 1957, more than 70 per cent were immigrants. Most of them were absorbed by factories, perhaps after a year or two working in the bush in accordance with government direction as many saved to bring out their wives and families.

Many of these new factories were established in buildings that had been used to produce munitions during the war and were now transformed to peacetime use. An aircraft factory in Melbourne was fitted out with a car production line from which rolled off in 1948 the first locally produced motor cars. It was the culmination of many years' work by successive governments that finally reached fruition with crucial financial support from Ben Chifley's Labor government. Instead of a British manufacturer, as Menzies had sought in 1941, or a local Australian firm, it was the giant American firm, General Motors, that was given the nod to provide cars for the Australian market. It was welcomed by the Melbourne *Age* for having, along with other new industries, added 'materially to the ability of Australia to defend its soil and its people in time of war'.

Just as Australians had been obsessed during the 1920s with the notion that they could usefully occupy their entire island continent, from its well-watered eastern coastline to its arid interior, so now they became obsessed with the apparent potential held out by the almost magical power locked within the atom. The unlocking of that awesome power as witnessed by the destruction of Hiroshima and Nagasaki had brought relief for Australians at the end of the Pacific war. As Alice Cawte has shown in her book *Atomic Australia*, their destruction had also awoken thoughts within the minds of Australians that they might also unlock that power to secure their claim on the continent. Australia was better endowed than most countries to draw on atomic power. While it was then believed to be poorly endowed with reserves of coal, oil and gas, and with only limited potential for hydro-electric power, it had some of the biggest reserves of uranium in the world at a time when uranium reserves were believed to be strictly limited. The Melbourne *Age* was so excited by the potential of the atom that it predicted the development of atomic power based on Australian uranium would make the coal, electricity and gas industries 'obsolete'. If atomic power could be developed, it could solve the problem of providing electricity in the bush and allow the government to achieve its vision of decentralising industry into inland centres.

The excitement over the potential for atomic power was compounded by Australia having scientists who had been involved in the Allied atomic weapons project and who were anxious to use their knowledge to prove its peaceful possibilities. Australia's leading atomic scientist, Mark Oliphant, was so moved by the possibilities inherent in the atom, although peaceful atomic power was as yet untested, that he proclaimed his confidence in Australia being

> now at the stage which America reached around the beginning of
> this century—on the verge of enormous development—and I
> believe that industrial atomic power is coming in time to take part
> in this development.

The Labor government expressed its confidence in such pronouncements by establishing a research school of nuclear physics, with Oliphant as its head, as the centrepiece of the new Australian National University established in Canberra in 1946. The minister for postwar reconstruction hoped that it would 'allow us to become the masters, not the servants, of our physical environment'.

According to the overly optimistic external affairs minister, Dr H. V. Evatt, the peaceful development of atomic energy would end forever 'the old economic conflicts, the struggle for living room [and], the jealously guarded economic rights in power resources', and thereby remove at a stroke the main causes of war. It would bring a cornucopia of wealth for the world, thereby removing the incentive for the 'teeming millions' of Asia to covet the 'empty' continent. Atomic power also held out the possibility of Australia having increased influence in the world. While the United States had the bomb, Australia was one of the few countries that had the uranium that was essential for producing bombs. But it was Britain and the United States that had a closely guarded monopoly on the secrets of atomic science.

While the United States kept a tight grip on its atomic secrets, Australia sought to use its imperial affiliation to obtain access to the secrets from Britain. So keen was Australia to obtain the benefits of atomic power that it proposed that Britain establish an experimental atomic pile in Australia rather than in Britain. It suggested that the pile, which was designed to test the feasibility of atomic power, should be built in Australia, where 'open spaces are plentiful', because of the possibility that it might explode 'scattering its contents into the atmosphere and into the countryside'. Moreover, Australia needed the power that such atomic piles were expected to provide if it was to achieve its aim of decentralising industry and population into the interior. Of course, those open spaces were still occupied in large measure by Aborigines, some of them even managing to live their traditional lifestyles.

In several ways, the war had been a liberating experience for Aboriginal Australians. Across the north, many Aborigines were brought into the money economy, being paid wages by the armed forces for their labour instead of being paid in food and tobacco as they had been by pastoralists. By 1944, perhaps a fifth of the Aborigines in the Northern Territory were employed by the army. Although they were often kept under strict control in fenced-off labour camps and were not paid regulation amounts, one Aborigine recalled the great contrast with their previous treatment by the pastoralists: the army 'treated us like people, not just blackfellas'. It also, of course, allowed urban Australians to see and relate to Aborigines, many for the first time in their lives, and to reflect on the dispossession and oppression of the Aborigines. Aborigines began performing jobs previously restricted to white Australians. They handled machinery, drove trucks and even flew planes. Several became officers in the armed forces with white people under their control. Others, who fought alongside white troops, found that racism disappeared on the battlefield. Aboriginal Harold Stewart, who joined the Second AIF artillery, recalled how, 'the closer we were to danger, [the] closer we were to one another. The fellows put away all their prejudices and we were one, really one.' Hospital facilities in the Northern Territory, which were formerly barred to Aborigines, were now open to them without discrimination.

After the war, though, Aborigines found themselves back within the confining restrictions of government paternalism and largely at the mercy of the pastoralists. Some 6000 Aborigines who had fought to defend Australia from the Japanese, or who had provided labour for the services, again found themselves barred from pubs, subject to racist taunts and returned to more menial employment. Leonard Waters, a Queensland Aborigine, had worked as a shearer before joining the RAAF where he rose to become a fighter pilot. After seeing action in Borneo he was repatriated to Australia where he returned to shearing. Reg Saunders, a Victorian Aborigine, had worked in a timber mill before enlisting in the Second AIF and serving in New Guinea as a platoon sergeant, where his brother was killed fighting on the Kokoda Trail. Saunders was so outstanding in his leadership qualities that he managed to overcome army prejudice and be promoted to the rank of lieutenant. Although hailed in the press at the time, Saunders was reduced after the war to working as a tram conductor.

Many white ex-service personnel enrolled in university courses as a way of improving their prewar position. Those at Melbourne University were able to hear Manning Clark present in 1946 the first regular course on Australian history. This was a sign of the growing Australian nationalism that allowed the study of Australian history to be regarded as a respectable field of study for its own sake. Previously, the history of Australia had been taught largely as an episode in British history. While the Oxford-educated Clark had elevated the study of Australian history, it remained the history of white Australia with the Aborigines largely absent from the story. Australians were still largely refusing to reflect on their past other than as a triumph of European civilisation in the wilderness. This was partly what A. A. Phillips later called the 'cultural cringe', but it was also partly a sublimated fear of what Australians might find if they looked too closely at their past. They might overlook most of the massacres that lingered on in white folklore and Aboriginal oral histories, but they could not overlook the central fact of Aboriginal dispossession and the steady disappearance of the race. As has been noted, Clark implicitly suggested in the first volume of his subsequent history of Australia that the Aboriginal dispossession was justified by the coming of European civilisation in its place. There was still massive ignorance about the nature of Aboriginal society and the complexities of their culture. In 1947, educationist K. S. Cunningham wondered at the thousands of Australians who had 'studied the language and culture of ancient Greece or Rome' while 'next to none have been trained to study and record the life of the Australian aboriginal whose ancient culture was passing away forever'.

While traditional Aboriginal cultures were certainly being eroded, there was no longer any doubt that Aborigines were no longer doomed to extinction as had been assumed for so long. Rather than being a dying race, Aborigines were increasing in numbers and demanding with greater force the rights that had long been denied them. There would be more opportunities in the postwar period for achieving these rights, particularly in the context of decolonisation and the United Nations' declaration on human rights. It is a sad reality of Australian history that white Australians have often responded to Aboriginal protests only after international pressure has been threatened or brought to bear. During the 19th century, groups like the London Missionary Society and other anti-slavery groups exerted pressure from London, through the British government, to try and ameliorate the official treatment of Aborigines. During the early 20th century, the attention of British newspapers to the continuing killings and mistreatment of the Aborigines was a concern to Australian governments anxious to ensure that the flow of British capital was not imperilled by such adverse publicity. Now there was the prospect of even greater pressure being brought to bear through the United Nations, and in the context of a postwar world where racial discrimination would face mounting resistance. Accordingly, federal government spending on Aborigines doubled after the war, albeit from a very low base. Despite the spending, the direction of official policy remained the same, with the government continuing with its immediate prewar policy of assimilation, directed particularly at Aborigines of part-European background. Like the non-British migrants, they would be absorbed into the wider society of British Australians, leaving little trace of their former selves. At least, that was the plan.

At the same time, the rights of citizenship were being gradually extended to indigenous Australians. In March 1949, Chifley's Labor government extended the franchise to those Aborigines who had served during the war and those considered to have 'sufficiently developed the attributes of civilisation as to be deemed capable of exercising the right to vote'. Those qualified to receive the federal franchise were those Aborigines eligible to vote in state elections or those in the defence forces or who were former members of the defence forces. However, Aborigines were not entitled to vote in Queensland and were therefore denied the federal franchise while in Western Australia strict regulations allowed to vote only those who could satisfy a magistrate that they were suitable. Such suitability largely depended upon them having abandoned their tribal associations. Upon such a judgment being made, they would no longer be considered as Aborigines and be released from the strict guardianship of the government and considered as British subjects. Under the policy of assimilation, Aboriginal Australians were expected to merge, voluntarily or forcefully, into the wider white community, adopting their customs and beliefs and discarding their tribal associations and their links with the land. They were meant to become white Australians with black skins, with the black skins being expected to fade over several generations of contact with white Australians.

While some adult Aborigines managed to escape the authoritarian hand of government by being licensed as honorary 'whites', juveniles of part-Aboriginal background were snatched from their mothers as part of a long-standing program of racial bleaching. In December 1949, as white Australians were voting Bob Menzies into power, a patrol officer flew into isolated Wave Hill station in the Northern Territory to snatch five half-caste children from their Aboriginal mothers so that they might disappear into white Australian society. The practice of snatching so-called half-castes went back to the beginnings of European occupation. Now it was organised with the power of the modern state and its modern technology, but not without increasing misgivings by those charged with carrying it out. In this case, the patrol officer reported that:

> The removal of the children from Wave Hill ... was accompanied by distressing scenes the like of which I wish never to experience again. The engines of the plane are not stopped at Wave Hill and the noise combined with the strangeness of the aircraft only accentuated the grief and fear of the children, resulting in near-hysteria in two of them.

The officer gave sweets to try and calm the children, while the mothers were pacified later with a photograph of their child and a length of dress material. In future, he suggested, children should be taken away by car, preferably by a white woman and preferably when they were either 12 months of age or older than six years of age. His objections had little effect on a program that continued into the 1970s.

These outrages occurred far from the sight of most Australians who were mostly unaware of what was being done in their name. Those who knew of it could rest content that the program was done ostensibly for the benefit of the children concerned. They could also take comfort from other changes in the treatment of Aborigines, with social services such as child endowment being made available to Aborigines living in the white community. This had the effect of encouraging them off Aboriginal reserves to become dwellers on the fringes of white society, dark shadows in the bush around country towns.

While the policy-makers in Canberra and the state capitals could pontificate on the desirability of having inclusive policies towards Aborigines, many ordinary Australians were determined through discriminatory social practices to keep Aborigines at bay. In country towns, Aborigines were often segregated into separate sections of cinemas, or not allowed in at all. They were not permitted to see films involving interracial conflict or ones where the activities of the characters brought the white races into disrepute. Aborigines were often denied entry to municipal swimming pools, due to ill-informed fears about it leading to unintentional miscegenation. Despite all this, like the migrants, Aborigines were meant to adopt the Australian way of life, a heady mixture of beer and barbecues, leisure and lawnmowers, only to find that it was kept beyond their reach.

Under the *Nationality and Citizenship Act* of 1948, British Australians were conferred for the first time with the status of Australian citizens while still retaining, in common with all subjects of the King, the status of British nationality. In a poll taken at the time, most respondents indicated that they would prefer to be considered as British subjects rather than Australian citizens. It was a sign of their sentimental allegiance and the continued uneasiness by many Australians with their predicament of living in a sparsely settled continent so distant from the fount of their national affection. Despite this lingering sense of dual allegiance, there were a declining number of Australians who saw their ultimate destiny as being back in the British Isles. They would fulfil Penton's wartime hopes and become 'permanent abiders' along with the hundreds of thousands of refugees fleeing from a Europe to which most had no wish to return. They would tie their destiny to that of the Australian continent and establish links to the alien and unforgiving landscape that would gradually overwhelm their former links to other places and other times.

If Australians were going to establish enduring links to the landscape, they would have to modify their rapacious approach to its development.

Prior to the war, there was increasing appreciation of the environmental damage caused by European farming methods. In 1938, Francis Ratcliffe's *Flying Fox and Drifting Sand* tried to combat the notion of the Australian landscape merely waiting for the farmer's plough to turn it from an unproductive wasteland into an oasis. Rather than a young virgin soil, Ratcliffe emphasised the fragile nature of the Australian landscape and its susceptibility to periodic droughts. This concern was reflected in the work of governments and geographers investigating the causes and extent of the soil erosion that was eating away at the thin Australian soils. Even the poet A. D. Hope was moved to observe in 1943 how

> *They call her a young country, but they lie:*
> *She is the last of lands, the emptiest,*
> *A woman beyond her change of life, a breast*
> *Still tender but within the womb is dry.*

After the war, Elyne Mitchell's *Soil and Civilisation* (1946) blended mysticism, religion and ecology to plea for a less rapacious exploitation of the continent's fragile landscape. She claimed that 'a century and a half of settled life on this continent' had seen 'comparatively little of the real spreading of the roots that is necessary to give strength for fine achievement'. She enjoined Australians 'profoundly to belong to the land' and 'not forget that its history, before we came, was one in which the individuals of a few tribes travelled through their lives profoundly joined to the land that fed them and gave them some part of their dreams'. She called for a 'university of the soil' that would teach its students 'to become aware of and to interpret the essential Australia' and to 'fuse into wholeness this country and our English and European culture'. This notion, of somehow combining their European background with the Australian landscape to create links to the land akin to those enjoyed by the Aborigines, was a constant undercurrent in Australian thinking from colonial times to the present day. It is something that all supplanting societies seek to establish, from Israel to Ireland, and East Timor to Argentina.

Mitchell's words were swept away by the onrushing tide of the development ethos, as Australians tried with renewed vigour to exercise dominion over the natural landscape that they had usurped from the Aborigines. To their horror, it seemed that they would not have Calwell's predicted hiatus of 25 years before another challenge appeared on the horizon to their half-completed claim on the continent. The communist victory in China in 1949 raised a more terrible spectre of possible dispossession, fusing Australians' historic fear of Asian hordes with their new Cold War fear of international communism. While Australians concentrated their energies on populating and developing the continent, they sought to keep these potent threats at bay by sheltering as they had always done beneath the defence umbrella of a 'great and powerful friend'.

Recommended Reading

❦

Judith Brett, 1992, *Robert Menzies' Forgotten People*, Macmillan, Sydney.

Alice Cawte, 1992, *Atomic Australia*, New South Wales University Press, Sydney.

David Day, 1996, *Contraband and Controversy*, Australian Government Publishing Service Press, Canberra.

Ross Fitzgerald, 1982, *A History of Queensland: From 1915 to the 1980s*, University of Queensland Press, Brisbane.

Harry Gordon, 1988, *An Eyewitness History of Australia*, Penguin, Melbourne.

Patricia Grimshaw, Marilyn Lake, Ann McGrath and Marian Quartly, 1994, *Creating a Nation, 1788–1990*, McPhee Gribble, Melbourne.

Robert Hall, 1989, *The Black Diggers*, Allen & Unwin, Sydney.

James Jupp, 1995, *Immigration*, Oxford University Press, Melbourne.

Harry Martin, 1989, *Angels and Arrogant Gods: Migration Officers and Migrants Reminisce 1945–85*, Australian Government Publishing Service Press, Canberra.

Brian Murphy, 1993, *The Other Australia: Experiences of Migration*, Cambridge University Press, Melbourne.

J. M. Powell, 1988, *An Historical Geography of Modern Australia*, Cambridge University Press, Cambridge.

Geoffrey Serle, 1987, *The Creative Spirit in Australia*, revised edn., Heinemann, Melbourne.

19

'THRUSTING THEIR RED SPEAR-POINTS TOWARDS AUSTRALIA'

obert Menzies returned to power in 1949 just as Australia's world was being changed beyond recognition. The Dutch were expelled from nearby Indonesia, the communists came to power in China, and the Russians ended the American atomic monopoly by exploding their own bomb. These events occurred in the wake of the British withdrawal from India and Burma. There was the spectre of Asian communists expanding, according to Menzies, in a 'south-easterly direction' and becoming a 'grave threat to Australia'. It was more imperative than ever that the continent be peopled, developed and defended.

The renewed Australian fear of an Asian invasion had elements of geographic determinism with the Malayan peninsula pointing south and dagger-like at the largely undefended and unoccupied north of Australia. The Country Party leader, Arthur Fadden, had warned during the 1949 election of the Chinese 'thrusting their Red spear-points towards Australia' while the 'advance guards of Communist forces' were 'extremely active' in Burma, Siam, Malaya and Indonesia. Fadden promised to beef up the defence of north Australia so that 'our military strategists know the course of every creek and the contours of every hill so that if we are challenged we will know the terrain as clearly as we can trace the lines on the palms of our hands'. As Fadden implied, despite the Australian defence effort across the northern parts of the continent during the Second World War, Australian defenders would still be as flummoxed as any invader by the unfamiliar climate and terrain of tropical Australia.

While Fadden could speak in the context of a fear-driven election campaign about the prospect of repelling an invasion, it was difficult to sustain such a spectre in the face of Asian realities. As even Menzies conceded in March 1951, no Asian power was capable of invading Australia since none of them had the naval or air power to do so. However, that did not mean that Australia was secure, not in the context of the Cold War. It just meant that it would have to fight far from its shores to combat 'Communist imperialism' wherever it raised its head in the world. It caused Australia, by 1951, to dispatch forces simultaneously to opposite ends of Asia—to Malaya and Korea—where they fought alongside British and American forces, and to base two fighter squadrons in Malta in 1952 while Britain was negotiating her departure from Egypt. The Australian commitment to Korea, which was announced prior to Britain's commitment, was a sign of Australia's growing attachment to the United States, the renewed security relationship matching the increasingly important economic relationship.

While Menzies was at best ambivalent about the notion of a formal defence pact with the United States, which might erode cherished imperial links, it became the determined aim of his external affairs minister, Percy Spender, to achieve one as a means of averting a future threat from China or a resurgent Japan. Initially, he hoped for a pact linking the British Commonwealth with the United States and capable of holding Asia at bay. At the same time, he sought through the Colombo Plan to engage with Asia in projects of peaceful development that would undercut the appeal of communism and avert a threat arising to Australia. 'No nation can escape its geography', intoned Spender, suggesting that it was 'an axiom which should be written deep into the mind of every Australian'. When Britain was reluctant to join his proposed joint defence pact, Spender pressed ahead with proposals for a pact just with the United States, pointing out as justification to the American president, Harry S. Truman 'the isolation and vulnerability of Australia'.

America's former reluctance to conclude such a pact now dissipated in the face of their need to obtain Australian agreement to the proposed 'soft' peace treaty with Japan. Spender assured the Americans that the Australian public would not countenance such a treaty unless they could be assured at the same time that the Americans would guarantee Australian security. Spender expressed a fear that a resurgent Japan might join with communist China as part of an expansionist Asian phalanx. Although the United States wanted both the Philippines and Japan to be part of such a pact, Australia and New Zealand successfully pressed for it to be just 'a white man's club'. Although the provisions of the resulting ANZUS treaty hardly amounted to a certain guarantee of American assistance in the face of an attack on Australia, the treaty was largely read as such by the Australian public and also, hoped Spender, by the countries of Asia. Over time, the ANZUS treaty would replace the discredited system of imperial defence as the ultimate guarantee of the claim by British Australians of effective proprietorship over the continent.

British objections to the pact were brushed aside, even by confirmed Anglophiles such as Richard Casey, who replaced Spender as external affairs minister in 1951. As Casey confided in his diary, '[T]he Americans are the only people who can in fact help us in South-East Asia or the Pacific.' While ANZUS was originally intended as a foil to ward off a resurgent Japan, it quickly became seen instead as a bludgeon with which to deter 'Communist imperialism based on the mainland of China'. As Menzies argued when announcing an increased commitment to Malaya in 1955, 'With our vast territory and our small population we cannot survive a surging Communist challenge from abroad except by the co-operation of powerful friends, including in particular the United Kingdom and the United States.' Privately, Casey urged that Australia should support 'the idea of an American base being established on Australian soil' as a physical expression of the ANZUS treaty that might avert a future challenge. Australian defence strategy was directed to the same end, being based upon the concept of 'forward defence', meeting such a challenge 'as far north of Australia as possible'. This would eventually see, in the 1960s, Australian proprietorship of the continent being defended in the paddy fields of Vietnam.

Despite this fearful talk of expanding communist imperialism, Australian defence expenditure fell sharply during the 1950s to less than three per cent of its gross national product. After the fall of the French garrison at Dien Bien Phu to the Vietnamese forces of Ho Chi Minh in 1954, Australia, New Zealand, the United States, Britain and France formed the South-East Asia Treaty Organisation (SEATO) to underwrite the security of the Philippines, Thailand and Pakistan and, upon request, to defend the former French territories of Indochina. In order to further shore up the prestige and power of the crumbling British Commonwealth, Australia allowed the British to explode atomic bombs on its territory, first on an island off its north-west coast in 1952 and later on the mainland itself. Despite confident weather predictions, the fallout from these tests, which were undertaken on Aboriginal land in central Australia, spread in a band across settled Australia. In tests of trigger devices, highly radioactive plutonium was scattered across a wide area of central Australia. In 1956, as the tests continued, Menzies was used as a dupe by the British to negotiate with Egypt's President Nasser prior to the disastrous Anglo-French-Israeli campaign to capture the Suez Canal. The incident shattered any remaining Australian commitment to the Suez Canal as the front line of Australia's defence and confirmed the growing doubts about Britain's world power status. In the wake of Suez, Australia fell further in the shadow of the United States, with its forces purchasing mainly American equipment rather than British.

Despite the threatening horizon, Australians enjoyed unparalleled prosperity during the 1950s as full employment and easy credit allowed for the purchase of consumer and other goods. Car ownership tripled during the 1950s as savings accumulated during the war, as well as from the prosperous postwar years, were spent on locally produced Holden cars. The cars connected the city centres with the far-flung suburbs, which spread too quickly for public transport to keep pace. Between 1947 and 1961, the population of Australian cities increased by 50 per cent. Individual homes set on quarter-acre blocks were the norm in this quiet celebration of Australian space which allowed for an ample vegetable garden and fruit trees and perhaps some fowls, all to supplement a diet that remained largely British-bland. By digging the soil of their suburban allotments, Australians made some connection with their fenced-off parts of the continent while, on Sundays, they drove into the nearby bush for picnics and made further comfortable connections, albeit often cursory, with the wider landscape. However, their ambivalence about the landscape lingered as they planted mainly European flowers and shrubs around their owner-occupied homes, transforming each allotment that had been hacked from the bush into a transplanted English garden in which transplanted Britons might feel at home.

The novelist Martin Boyd, who had returned to Australia in 1948 after many years in Europe, captured it well in 1953 when he pointed out that white Australians

> ...have not yet completely absorbed the influences of our new terrain. The spiritual and the natural worlds do not correspond. Our outer things are not yet fully in accord with those which are within. They did not grow through long centuries of life on Australian soil...

Australians were not 'white Aboriginals' but transplanted Europeans still groping to accommodate themselves to their surroundings. For Boyd, that meant Australians having, 'from time to time, to be brought into contact with the land where we formed our spiritual secretions'—Britain. The link with Britain, argued Boyd, was 'a far deeper and stronger one' than the link with the United States, being based on 'a common blood and a common loyalty'. As such, an Australian travelling to Britain goes 'on a pilgrimage which everyone of his countrymen hopes to make before he dies'. Boyd himself had already abandoned Australia once again, leaving for London in 1951 before later establishing himself in Rome.

The same year that Boyd returned to Australia, albeit briefly, the writer Patrick White abandoned his sojourn in London to return to his New South Wales origins. Ambivalent about returning to Australia after 14 years overseas, most of it in London, White found that his restless wanderings had not expunged his youthful links to the Australian landscape which comfortably enveloped him upon his return. As he informed an English penfriend, 'I had not realised how Australian I am underneath until I came back and saw it and smelled it again'. Despite dissatisfaction with the sputtering cultural life of Sydney, White stayed on determinedly, writing his intense novels of the Australian bush—*The Tree of Man* and *Voss*— which set universal themes of mankind's quest for understanding against an unforgiving Australian background devoid of any gentle Heidelberg brushstrokes. White hoped that his work 'may be helping to people a barely inhabited country with a race possessed of understanding'. But his complex novels were more widely read outside of Australia than within it.

White's return to Australia, and the international acclaim that his work generated—culminating in the Nobel Prize in 1973—were signs of an important change in Australian cultural life. It was no longer essential to go overseas to achieve fame or to tackle the important issues of life. The writer Alan Moorehead had observed of the inter-war years that:

> To go abroad—that was the thing. That was the way to make your name. To stay at home was to condemn yourself to nonentity. Success depended upon an important imprimatur from London, and it did not matter whether you were a surgeon, a writer, a banker, or a politician; to be really someone in Australian eyes you first had to make your mark or win your degree on the other side of the world.

Although this did not end with the war, and still remains true to some extent today, White's experience indicated that Australia could provide a sufficient canvas on which artists of whatever medium could explore the human condition. Much of their exploration in these postwar years related to the development of a culture that was essentially Australian.

In their book *My Australia*, which provided a largely celebratory exploration of Australia's past and present, Marjorie Barnard and Flora Eldershaw had claimed that only the Aborigines 'had a culture that was essentially Australian'. They accepted the common assumption that the Aborigines were dying out and pointed to the implication for white Australians:

> With them is dying their close and unique knowledge of the Australian earth. They knew its secrets, but they could not transmit them to us. We have had to learn all over again for ourselves and raise up images in our own idiom.

But how could Australians do so when they were carrying so much cultural baggage from their European origins? In the 1930s, Rex Ingamells had suggested in vain that they drop their European baggage and pick up the idioms of the Aborigines. In the 1950s, writers tried different ways to establish the legitimacy of the white Australian presence. In her novel *Keep Him My Country* (1955), Mary Durack followed the line of Katharine Susannah Prichard's classic novel, *Coonardoo* (1929), portraying a white station owner who developed a spiritual relationship to the land by means of a sexual relationship with an Aboriginal woman, suggesting that white Australians might after all be able to tap into the secrets of the Aborigines and develop a relationship to the continent that was more spiritual than rapacious. Durack was well placed to write about such matters, having been descended from pastoralists who had driven cattle across the 'top end' from Queensland to the Kimberley where they had dispossessed its Aboriginal people. Also from the Kimberley came the prize-winning novel by Randolph Stow, *To the Islands*, which was published in 1958. The book's main character, a white missionary approaching death on an Aboriginal reserve, abandons his Western mental baggage in the bush, comes to an accommodation with the land and adopts the beliefs of its Aboriginal people as the landscape slowly saps his life. As for Stow, he left for England in 1966 where he remained.

The predicament posed by Barnard and Eldershaw would not admit of an easy solution. Despite the insightful efforts of those like Stow, there was no great Australian novel waiting to be written that would tell it all and allow white Australians to claim at last an intimate association with the land that might rival that of the Aborigines. Rather, it would take time and the work of many writers and artists to chip away at the disdainful continent before it took on an appearance of familiarity greater than that evoked by the green fields of England. While writers wrestled with the problem in their novels, painters such as Russell Drysdale and Sidney Nolan began to paint the landscape in tones of uncompromising starkness. The garish central Australian watercolours of the Aboriginal artist Albert Namatjira were also snapped up by urban Australians hoping, perhaps in the manner of their former patronage of the Heidelberg artists, to connect with the continent more closely through Namatjira's Aboriginal eyes. These cultural strivings had to survive in a Cold War atmosphere where radical writers were denied official patronage and modern art was widely regarded as a decadent distraction from the nation's development agenda. While the artists and writers tried to bring the continent within their mental compass, governments and companies continued to try and physically conquer the continent.

The 1950s saw Australia embark upon a prolonged economic boom during which there seemed to be no limit to what might be achieved. Whether under the Labor or conservative party, both state and federal governments took a leading role in sponsoring 'development'. As Fadden announced in 1950, 'Governments and all their connected authorities are pushing on with large programmes of works to provide power, fuel, water, transport, housing, hospitals and schools for a larger population and a more highly developed economy.' He spoke of the 'faith, held almost universally in Australia and by many people abroad, that this country is capable of immense progress in the coming years'. The official confidence was matched in the private sector as companies expanded to cater for the needs of the growing population with its insatiable appetite for housing, domestic appliances to clutter up their homes and motor cars to connect the scattered suburbs. Much of the frenzied expenditure in the 1950s was financed by so-called easy payment plans.

While government concessions and tariff protection sponsored most of the new factories, the marvels of hydro-electricity provided part of the power for the production line. The greatest engineering feat that Australia had ever accomplished, the Snowy Mountains Scheme, was inaugurated in 1949. The example of similar schemes, from the Tennessee Valley Authority in the United States to various examples in Stalinist Russia, had shown planners what could be achieved by using the authority of the State to harness the labour of a compliant work force. In the case of the Snowy Mountains Scheme, much of the labour was provided by immigrants directed to work in the primitive and harsh conditions as a condition of their assisted passages. The scheme was designed to divert water from the Snowy River, which otherwise flowed uselessly into the sea off eastern Victoria, so that it flowed instead through the mountains of the Great Dividing Range to join the rivers of the Murray–Darling system. As it passed through the tunnels and a series of dams, the diverted water was harnessed to power a hydro-electric scheme before being used to irrigate the Riverina region of New South Wales, allowing irrigated agriculture to take the place of pastoralism. The whole scheme was designed to promote the more intensive settlement and cultivation of inland Australia while also doing much to promote the further industrialisation of the seaboard cities by adding to their resources of electric power.

The Snowy Mountains Authority was established by the federal Labor government using its defence powers, and completed by Menzies' Liberal government. It was promoted as being capable of providing 'great assistance ... to the industrial effort' in time of war. Not only would it supply cheap and abundant electricity to Melbourne and Sydney, but it was also expected that it would allow the development of 'great inland cities, which can feed out their secondary production to the coastal capitals of Australia'. Such inland cities would allow Australians to populate the interior with factories, since farms had largely failed to settle sufficient numbers in the bush, with the percentage of population residing in rural areas falling from 20.31 per cent in 1954 to 17.86 per cent in 1961. Governments made repeated efforts to avert this trend.

There were a number of proposals for harnessing the tropical floodwaters of the wet season that otherwise coursed uselessly into the sea or spread across the interior before disappearing into the inland deserts. One scheme that was not proceeded with involved the diversion of water from north Queensland rivers through the mountains of the Great Dividing Range to provide a constant flow for the otherwise intermittent Cooper's Creek which, when it flowed, watered the far outback all the way to Lake Eyre. They were visionary schemes conjured out of Australia's postwar self-confidence and the overwhelming drive to secure its proprietorship over the continent. Such schemes could not only help to secure the continent against threats from outside forces, but also conquer those forces of nature which had stubbornly resisted the efforts of British Australians to settle its harsh interior. The Snowy Mountains Scheme was a dramatic attempt by this new class of central planners to mould the natural world to suit the purposes of the supplanting society. The war had promoted such bureaucratic planners into seats of power and influence. And the neglected inland city of Canberra, which would now be fed power from the Snowy Mountains, was their capital. Managed development of the continent was their aim, and few of them considered the possible environmental costs of their plans. Among the wilder suggestions floated before a credulous public were proposals to modify the climate by using atomic bombs to create mountain ranges or using atomic power for the large-scale desalination of water as a means of making the recurring and ruinous droughts a distant national memory. It was not all empty talk.

Previously uninhabitable swathes of the interior were able to be occupied profitably by scientific developments that saw trace elements added to the soil of the Ninety Mile Desert in western Victoria and the brute force of bulldozers flatten millions of hectares of brigalow scrub country of western Queensland for cattle grazing. Such developments were driven by the injunctions of those anxious to establish beyond doubt their occupation of the continent. As the economist Colin Clarke warned in 1950, Australians had to 'quickly settle all the available land in Queensland to its fullest capacity, [or] somebody will come and do it for us'. With this end in mind, suitable land closer in to the cities was distributed by governments to returning servicemen and immigrants for more intensive development and settlement than pastoralism could provide. Much of it was devoted to dairying, with Australian taxpayers and consumers subsidising uneconomic herds producing butter for the British market.

Successive mineral discoveries scattered across northern Australia shifted the official focus away from such schemes for a time. In 1953, the first oil reserves had been discovered some 1130 kilometres north of Perth. Although not of economic size, it opened the possibility that other reserves were there to be discovered. And they were, although it was not until 1960 that the first commercial oilfield was discovered at Moonie in Queensland. Five years later, enormously valuable gas and oil fields were discovered in Bass Strait, close enough for the gas to be piped to power the cities of Sydney and

Melbourne while the oil went far to make Australia almost self-sufficient. Mineral discoveries were given a powerful boost in December 1960 when the government lifted its prewar embargo on the export of iron ore. Within a year came news of massive finds of iron ore in Western Australia, while geologists found all manner of other minerals once they started looking for them.

A conference in Canberra on northern development in 1954 concluded that the discovery of these mineral resources 'made it more than ever necessary to have a population to defend the North'. Moreover, Australia could only achieve a claim of moral proprietorship over the continent's tropical north if it 'exploited to the full its mineral resources and its capacity for food production'. As the governor general, Sir William Slim, pointed out, 'twelve hundred million pairs of eyes looking hungrily for land' would question the right of Australians to control the continent's north if they 'see to the south of them a million square miles occupied by only 100 000 Australians'. For a time during the 1950s and 1960s, Australians hoped that the answer to their ongoing quest to secure the occupation of the continent might be found locked within the atom.

The allure of abundant atomic power, or even limitless nuclear power, together with the strategic imperatives of the Cold War, prompted the conservative government of Robert Menzies to sponsor a uranium rush across northern Australia in the early 1950s. Prospectors, lured by a lucrative government reward of £25 000, discovered many small reserves of uranium in Western Australia and the Northern Territory, while the massive Mary Kathleen reserve was found near Mount Isa in 1954. Following the earlier exhaustion of its gold deposits, Australia at last had something of value in the tropics sufficient to draw Europeans into the northern parts of the continent. The government sponsored the development of a uranium deposit at Rum Jungle, less than 100 kilometres from Darwin, where the town of Batchelor was built in 1956 to house the 600 workers for the nearby mine. It was the first of many such modern mining towns to appear across the north during the following decades. Surveying the scene at Rum Jungle, the crusading chief of the Atomic Energy Commission, Phillip Baxter, proclaimed it as proof that 'white labour can operate successfully a venture of this kind in the tropics'. For his part, Prime Minister Menzies thought Rum Jungle was the 'most exciting thing I have seen in my life', combining as it did 'capitalist enterprise', 'Government Agency' and 'the simple Australian trade unionist and his wife'. This mixture of forces, proclaimed Menzies, 'superbly illustrates and justifies—the Australian way of life'.

In extolling the benefits of atomic power, and thereby ensuring support for his organisation, Baxter played upon the historic fears of Australians and held out the prospect of such power enabling them to secure their hold on the continent. 'There is no doubt', he argued in 1955, 'that the production of cheap power from uranium will be a major contribution to the problem of developing this last large land mass which is available to the white races.' However, even as he was speaking, new reserves of coal and oil were being discovered in Australia which would reduce the attractiveness of atomic energy. By the time the practical feasibility and economic viability of atomic, and then nuclear power, was proven, Australia had found itself to be so well-endowed with conventional fossil fuels that much of the imperative driving the atomic juggernaut had been dissipated. When Australia's only nuclear reactor was opened at Lucas Heights near Sydney in 1960, the prospect for nuclear power providing electricity for industries in the south-eastern capitals was grim, given the new-found availability of cheaper coal reserves. However, it was hoped that its research might lead to the development of small nuclear reactors 'particularly adapted to the needs of the inland'. With such cheap and reliable power sources scattered across the interior, Australians might yet be enticed into settling there in large numbers. With this same end in view, the MP for Victoria's Mallee district suggested in 1962 that nuclear bombs be exploded to make dams along the Murray where 'land was cheap and no one lived'.

The Australian development mania was accorded the royal seal of approval during the 1954 visit of the recently crowned Queen Elizabeth. At a time of Cold War turbulence, the 1954 Royal Tour provided a sense of certainty and continuity in a fast-changing world. In a burst of loyal fervour, the Queen was greeted by some one million Australians when she stepped ashore at Farm Cove in Sydney. Over the next eight weeks, she went on to visit every other capital city except Darwin, as well as 70 towns. Perhaps as many as seven million Australians paid homage to the first reigning British monarch to visit Australia. Such was the excitement that 100000 people rushed to Sydney's Palm Beach after wrongly hearing that the Queen was visiting there. While providing Australians with her reassuring presence, she was used by Australians to focus world attention on the development of the continent. Novelist Martin Boyd hoped that it would 'turn the eyes of the people of Britain to Australia, to awaken a fresh interest in our country, and to give them a better idea of its reality'. The Queen was taken on an aerial tour of northern Australia, touching down at mining and other developments, while the Duke of Edinburgh was presented by the South Australian premier with a rock of uranium in a mulga wood box. At a dinner in Canberra's parliament house, Menzies assured his Queen: 'You may count on us. We are yours.' However, as a sign of the new regional realities, the Queen unveiled a memorial in Canberra to the American role in the Pacific war.

Despite attempts at decentralisation, it was to existing cities that most of the growth was directed, with suburbs spreading across the former 'green belt' of the urban hinterland. As in the 1900s, city dwellers were attracted by the social facilities and the more lucrative employment that was to be found in the growing number of urban factories that prospered behind the protective tariff wall. The growing car industry stimulated the steel industry which relied on the army of immigrants for its workers. Displaced persons were directed to man the foundries, with more than 1000 working at the Newcastle and Port Kembla steelworks by 1950. When a new steel mill was opened at Port Kembla in 1955, Prime Minister Menzies was moved to proclaim it as evidence of Australia having 'a greater potentiality than any country of the world'. With such large-scale investment in capital equipment, Australia's steel production doubled during the 1950s, largely obviating the need for imports and allowing steel to be exported alongside the traditional exports of wool and wheat.

Housing was high on the agenda of postwar governments, first to settle the returning service personnel and later the army of immigrants. With homes of their own, so it was thought, Australians would have the material confidence to procreate. As the government proclaimed in 1964 when introducing special assistance to encourage home ownership: 'Without proper housing, the process of marriage and family formation which are the very essence of Australia's future must be seriously impaired.' To provide further encouragement, Menzies extended the existing system of child endowment in 1950 to cover the first child as well. It was part of a conservative focus on the family 'as the cornerstone of Australian life and the key to our national progress'. The extension of child endowment was expected to ensure better nutrition for the nation's children and thereby build 'a better and stronger nation'. Catholic chemists urged the government to take the next step in this nation-building exercise by banning contraceptives now that families had no economic excuse for restricting the size of their families. With such a ban in place, Australian couples would have 'a normal family' and the nation would have a sufficient population to defend itself against a future invasion.

Although there had certainly been a postwar 'baby boom' brought on by the return to normality and the confidence to procreate that prosperity inspired, the surge in births had begun gradually to decline in the late 1950s as Australians increasingly opted for a washing machine or a motor car rather than incur the expense of additional children. As John Murphy has shown, the economic incentive to have additional children, in terms of child endowment and tax rebates, was also gradually reduced from the heights of 1950. Decisions to limit family sizes were made easier to achieve by the ending of wartime controls which allowed locally produced contraceptives to become available again, although imported types were still prohibited until 1959. The arrival of the contraceptive pill in 1961 allowed even greater control by couples over their procreative powers. With immigrants continuing to flow into Australia in great numbers, the government was relatively relaxed about the reduction in the birthrate.

Unlike the early 1900s, when Australians had worried about their declining birthrate being an indication of a declining racial vitality, such fears were much more muted in the 1950s. Just as the fighting of their young men on the battlefield of Gallipoli in 1915 had expunged such fears, so their victories on the sport fields during the 1950s helped to allay fears of Australians being sapped in their vitality by what Max Harris called the 'sedated quiescence' of suburban living. Australian sporting prominence, particularly in running, cycling, tennis and swimming, swelled the sense of national pride while providing confidence in the future of the Australian race. In 1950, the Australian team topped the medal tally at the Empire Games in Auckland, while its Davis Cup tennis team beat the Americans in New York. It was at the Melbourne Olympic Games in 1956 that the range of Australia's athletic prowess was displayed to the world. The Melbourne *Age* took great comfort from the strong showing of the Australian team, when it came third in the gold medal tally after the Soviet Union and the United States. In reports that had echoes of Ashmead-Bartlett at Gallipoli, the *Age* claimed that Australia's 'youth [had been] blooded in [the] Olympics', that its athletes had 'earned immortality' by their feats while the swimmers had 'proved themselves the strongest in the world'.

The 1950s also saw the lifesaver firmly enshrined in the pantheon of Australian masculinity, joining the resourceful bushman and the undisciplined but courageous digger. Bronzed, uniformed lifesavers had begun patrolling the shores of the continent as early as 1906, when Bondi's surf lifesaving club was formed, but it was in the prosperous and hedonistic postwar years that they took on a new significance. In the absence of large-scale wars, their quintessentially Australian and reassuring presence on urban beaches each summer provided additional physical confirmation of the continuing vitality of the Australian race in the face of the continuing influx of European migrants.

Under Menzies, Australia scoured further afield in Europe for the great numbers that it sought. Australians were assured by successive governments that their moral proprietorship over the continent depended upon them accepting into their midst a growing proportion of non-British migrants. In 1950, Menzies addressed a citizenship convention on the assimilation of so-called new Australians at which he argued that Australians had a duty

> ... to present to the world the spectacle of a rich country with a great people, with an adequate population—with a population which may justly say to the rest of the world: 'We are here; we propose to maintain our integrity as a nation; and our warrant for that is that we are using the resources which God has given into our hands.'

Only by continuing to support a mass immigration program, including continental Europeans, could Australia assert its moral claim in the face of possible Asian challenges to the contrary. By accepting Italians and Yugoslavs, Menzies implied, Australia might be saved from having Chinese or Japanese thrust upon them.

In 1951 the immigration minister, Harold Holt, signed an agreement with Italy providing for the assisted immigration of 75 000 Italians over the next five years. Despite this, the entry of Italians, particularly from southern Italy, faced considerable popular opposition and official stalling. Protestants feared that an influx of Catholic migrants from Italy and elsewhere would threaten their supremacy in Australia. Others continued to look upon Italians as not being really white. As late as 1964, less than half of respondents in an opinion poll regarded Italy as an acceptable source for migrants. While the more swarthy and less skilled or educated southern Italians were regarded in 1950 by the immigration department as being 'not the most desirable types from an Australian view-point', those from central and northern Italy were regarded as 'very suitable', including 'rural workers' and 'skilled men' who 'would be particularly useful for employment in tunnelling and constructional work in Australia, such as the Snowy Mountains Hydro-Electric Scheme'.

However, with unemployment increasing in 1952, government officials considered using the dictation test to dam the flow of Italians that were starting to flood into Australia, with nearly 20 000 stepping ashore in just six months. Mostly single men, they were confined without work in inland camps. Protests by the inmates of the Bonegilla camp near Albury led to soldiers from the nearby army camp being called out to quell them. Other demonstrations took place in Sydney and Queensland. The assisted passage scheme with Italy was put in abeyance for a time while Australia concentrated on assisting the more acceptable British, Dutch and German immigrants.

Immigration agreements had been made with seven European countries by 1952 which saw a babel of wide-eyed arrivals stepping ashore in Australian ports, although from 1951 the Menzies government redressed the balance somewhat in favour of British migrants. The government did what it could to defend British Australia by ensuring that the bulk of assisted passages went to British migrants and by launching a campaign in 1957 to encourage Australians to 'Bring out a Briton', a campaign that was warmly supported by the Protestant churches. It also in 1952 shifted the emphasis from unmarried and unskilled male workers to 'a true population-building aspect of introducing families who will contribute to the long-term development of Australia'. By 1963, two million postwar immigrants had added their numbers to the Australian population.

It was a program that enjoyed wide support during a period of almost uninterrupted economic prosperity. The Melbourne *Herald* reassured any doubters that a mass immigration program was 'essential to our development', and thereby to their continued prosperity. With the program extended to attract families and their dependants, there would be a 'steady growth in the numbers of customers over the counter, purchasers of things of all sorts— things which must be produced and which must have workers to produce them'. While the case for mass migration was irresistible, they were still to be white immigrants.

In November 1950, immigration officers were informed that 'Eurasians do not, on the whole, prove a very desirable type of migrant' and conditions regarding their admission to Australia were tightened up. Henceforth, they would have to show that they were 'approximately 75 per cent or more of European descent', that they were 'fully European in upbringing and outlook' and tended to be 'European rather than non European in appearance'. Prospective immigrants were required to produce documentary evidence of their origins, including sometimes photographs of their grandparents. If three out of four of them were white, then the person would be admitted. In doubtful cases, particularly when the facial complexion of the applicant suggested a non-European background, the immigration officer would resort to a rough rule of thumb by imagining how they would fit into the street scene of an Australian city.

Following the Hungarian Uprising of 1956, the immigration minister, A. G. Townley, had assured parliament that Australia's 'normal selection procedures may be modified' for these 'unfortunate victims of aggression'. While the age of these refugees was negotiable, their race was not. An immigration officer rationalised his rejection of a Hungarian applicant at a refugee camp in Austria. The refugee, he recalled, 'was a very well built, handsome, very dark fellow', who stayed around the doorway of the immigration office for days after his rejection:

> *I could see him all the time and he would look at me sort of pleadingly. But this fellow really was a very dark gypsy with crinkly black hair, and although I was sympathetic towards him, I visualised him walking down Martin Place and as such he would have been a 'stare object' ...for his sake as well as Australia's, I rejected him.*

The protection of white Australia by such officials was working. Whereas Asian Australians comprised around one per cent of the population at federation, they were only 0.28 per cent of the population by 1954. The *Bulletin*, which had ossified into a reactionary publication, still had 'Australia for the White Man' emblazoned across its cover.

Applications for permanent residency in Australia formerly depended mainly upon the racial origins of the applicant. Non-Europeans were almost invariably refused permission for such status, which was the first step to gaining Australian nationality. From 1940 to 1960, less than 2000 Asians were granted permanent residence status in Australia. However, during the 1950s it became more difficult politically to base bureaucratic decisions on racial criteria. Applicants for permanent resident status had to show instead that they had adopted the Australian way of life. Immigration officers had to assess whether applicants mixed with white Australians at work, lived among white Australians, and belonged to clubs and associations that involved white

Australians. Those judged to be taking a 'full part in normal Australian life' or a 'reasonable part in all of the circumstances' would usually be granted the desired status. In administering these rules, officials often allowed some relaxation in recognition that non-Europeans were excluded, either formally or informally, from most European clubs and activities. By 1961, officers were advised not to set their criteria too high and thereby expose the department to charges of unreasonable discrimination. They were to approve any applicant considered to be 'a respected member of the community' and to have had 'reasonable association with Australians'.

It was some sign that Australia was jettisoning the ideology of white Australia as its growing population (now increased from seven million in 1945 to more than 10.5 million in 1961) was becoming more comfortable in its occupation of the continent. The infamous dictation test had been abandoned in 1958 in favour of a system of entry permits which performed the same function in a less blatantly offensive form. From 1952, Japanese divers were readmitted to the pearl fishery along the continent's northern shores. The 1950s had also seen thousands of Asian students being educated in Australian universities under the Australian-initiated Colombo Plan, which was meant to undercut the appeal of communism to the impoverished Asian masses by promoting the development of their countries and thereby helping to ensure that they did not look to Australia's relatively empty continent for their economic salvation. Their presence in Australia helped to gradually overcome the Australian prejudice against Asians, although the so-called 'Asian' flu epidemic in 1957 still created panic in Australia with its connotations of alien invasion. In the event, only a handful of Australians died from the disease, compared with the 12000 who died from the Spanish flu in 1919. During the 1950s, opinion polls revealed that support for the admission of a token number of Asian immigrants increased from around 30 per cent of respondents to more than 50 per cent by 1959. That same year, in a reversal of accepted Australian racial dogma, the leading Australian medical researcher, Sir Macfarlane Burnet, argued that interracial marriages should be encouraged as they resulted in the best characteristics of each parent being inherited by their children. Unless they were Aborigines, many of whom were back where they had begun before the war, having their children snatched from them in an organised effort at forcible assimilation and cultural annihilation.

During the 1930s, Aboriginal activists such as William Cooper had written without success to politicians in an effort to better their lot. Their experience during the war had allowed some Aborigines to enjoy for the first time lives relatively untouched by racial discrimination. After the war, their own determination, combined with greater support for their plight among white Australians, ensured a gradual lifting of the onerous restrictions that were reimposed. In 1949, Aboriginal stockmen in the Northern Territory were given a basic wage for the first time, albeit at a lower rate than whites. In a sign of their new consciousness, 200 Aborigines in Darwin went on strike in 1951 to have the new rate doubled and to be given 'equal rights'. Aboriginal voices began to be heard on the international stage when tenor Harold Blair visited New York in 1949. He informed New York's *Herald Tribune* of Australian racism, pointing out that there were 'only 80 000 Aborigines left in Australia out of more than 700 000' and suggesting that 'That speaks for itself, doesn't it?' International attention continued to be focused on the treatment of Aborigines when Albert Namatjira, after being presented to the Queen in 1954 and having had his watercolours bought by white city dwellers and art galleries, was denied permission in 1955 to build a house in Alice Springs where he would have been living alongside white people. Not being an Australian citizen, he was restricted to living on a reserve outside the town limits. After being given such status in 1956, which allowed him for the first time to buy alcohol, he was gaoled for six months in 1958 after passing alcohol to a relative who was not a citizen. The case caused a massive furore, prompting the government to allow Namatjira to serve a reduced sentence on his reserve rather than in gaol. He died the following year of a heart attack.

The increasing sympathy by white Australians for the Aborigines and a willingness to rethink the 'white Australia' policy were reflections of the confidence of the greatly augmented Australian population in their ability to secure their claim upon the continent. Numbers were only part of the reason for this new-found confidence. Australians had emerged from the war conscious that they must 'populate and develop their vast continent or accept the probability of having it taken from them'. Their efforts to develop the resources of the continent had met with considerable success during the 1950s, with modern factories spreading across industrial areas of Australian cities, providing employment for the army of postwar migrants, both men and women, and consumer goods for the fast-growing population. Similarly, across the interior, irrigation and hydro-electric schemes, road building and the application of science to farming, together with mineral discoveries across the north, all combined to encourage an intensified settlement of the land. Even Darwin had grown in size, reaching 12 000 people by 1959 and being given the status of a city. However, their new-found confidence in their collective future was put at risk when their island of bountiful wealth was increasingly overshadowed by ominous developments in Asia which seemed to threaten once more their hold on the continent.

Recommended Reading

John Arnold, Peter Spearritt and David Walker (eds), 1993, *Out of Empire: The British Dominion of Australia*, Mandarin, Melbourne.

Geoffrey Bolton, 1990, *The Oxford History of Australia*, Vol. 5, Oxford University Press, Melbourne.

Richard Bosworth, 'Conspiracy of the Consuls? Official Italy and the Bonegilla Riot of 1952', *Australian Historical Studies*, October 1987.

Nicholas Brown, 1995, *Governing Prosperity*, Cambridge University Press, Cambridge.

Jane Connors, 'The 1954 Royal Tour of Australia', *Australian Historical Studies*, April 1993.

F. K. Crowley (ed.), 1973, *Modern Australia in Documents*, Vol. 2, Wren Publishing, Melbourne.

Peter Edwards, 1992, *Crises and Commitments*, Allen & Unwin, Sydney.

Ross Fitzgerald, 1985, *A History of Queensland: From 1915 to the 1980s*, University of Queensland Press, Brisbane.

Laurie Hergenhan (ed.), 1988, *The Penguin New Literary History of Australia*, Penguin, Melbourne.

W. J. Hudson, 1986, *Casey*, Oxford University Press, Melbourne.

Siobhan McHugh, 1995, *The Snowy: The People Behind the Power*, Angus&Robertson, Sydney.

David Lowe, 1999, *Menzies and the 'Great World Struggle': Australia's Cold War 1948–1954*, UNSW Press, Sydney.

David Marr, 1994, *Patrick White: Letters*, Random House, Sydney.

Alan Martin, 1999, *Robert Menzies*, Vol. 2., Melbourne University Press, Melbourne.

Harry Martin, 1989, *Angels and Arrogant Gods: Migration Officers and Migrants Reminisce 1945–85*, Australian Government Publishing Service Press, Canberra.

Brian Murphy, 1993, *The Other Australia: Experiences of Migration*, Cambridge University Press, Melbourne.

John Murphy, 2000, *Imagining the Fifties: Private Sentiment and Political Culture in Menzies' Australia*, UNSW Press, Sydney.

John Murphy, 'Shaping the Cold War Family: Politics, Domesticity and Policy Interventions in the 1950s', *Australian Historical Studies*, October 1995.

Lachlan M. Strahan, 'An Oriental Scourge: Australia and the Asian Flu Epidemic of 1957', *Australian Historical Studies*, October 1994.

Richard White, 1981, *Inventing Australia*, Allen & Unwin, Sydney.

20

'THERE IS

A CONTINENT

AWAITING OUR

CONQUEST'

The prosperity of the 1950s had encouraged Australians to answer Brian Penton's call in 1943 for them to become permanent abiders in the continent and not drift away as so many of them had during the 1930s. Not only that, but millions of Britons and Europeans answered the Australian need for population, albeit crowding into existing cities rather than filling up the persistently 'empty spaces' in the interior. No matter. There were jobs for all who wanted them, an expanding range of chrome-plated consumer goods in the shops and easy credit with which to buy them. Moreover, the Cold War world of Robert Menzies had seen Australia buttress its traditional imperial relationship with new defence links with the United States. Although Patrick White could bemoan Australia in 1964 as being 'a hateful country, and I think if I were 15 years younger I would go away and stay away for good', most Australians were well satisfied with their lot in life after enduring, as so many had, the privations of the depression and the agonies of the Second World War. And there seemed no end in sight to the material offerings that the continent had long kept hidden.

The rush of mineral discoveries in the 1950s became a stampede in the 1960s, as individual prospectors and foreign mining companies searched the furthest reaches of the continent for payable deposits. And they found them aplenty, everything from bauxite to iron ore, copper to lead, and even the gold and silver that had obsessed early seafarers in their fruitless search for the great south land. Some of the minerals were processed locally and contributed to the further industrialisation of the economy, with bauxite from the massive deposit on Aboriginal land at Weipa on Cape York Peninsula being shipped to the Bell Bay aluminium smelter in Tasmania. Much more, though, was shipped overseas in its raw state, contributing to the rapid postwar recovery of the Japanese economy. In either case, the effect was to spread prosperity unevenly across an Australian society that was increasingly taking such prosperity for granted. Unemployment became a fear of the distant prewar past, while increasingly grandiose visions of Australia's future greatness began once more to be expressed by the nation's boosters.

In October 1960, while opening the massive Warragamba Dam to secure water for Sydney, the New South Wales premier, R. J. Heffron, proposed calling his capital 'Sydney Unlimited' because 'there appears no limit to the scope and range of developments in prospect.' He predicted its population would more than double to five million by the year 2000. The boosters were once more in the ascendant and the cities were again being seen as signs of civilisation rather than as sores that sapped the national vitality. An opera house was built at great expense to a distinctive and difficult design on Bennelong Point on the shore of Sydney Cove. Paid for by a lucrative public lottery, the building became, not a white elephant as its detractors predicted, but a modern wonder of the world that would come to rival Ayers Rock as a representative symbol of Australia. Its belated opening in 1973 by Queen Elizabeth signalled a further sign of permanent occupation by the supplanting society, continuing the process begun by Arthur Phillip nearly two centuries before of establishing European civilisation in the Australian wilderness, while the flypast by nine F111 aircraft showed a determination to defend their occupation.

Neither was the forlorn figure of Bennelong forgotten in the celebrations. An Aboriginal actor atop one of the opera house 'shells' took on the role, informing the assembled thousands, and the millions watching television, that: 'Two hundred years ago fires burned on this point. The fires of my people and into the light of the flames from the shadows all about, our warriors danced.' This established a sense of continuity in the use of the land for cultural activity and, to some extent, between the pre-existing Aboriginal society and the British supplanters. In this way, the opera house could be portrayed as a natural development from previous Aboriginal activities that had occurred on Bennelong Point, and the Aboriginal actor's participation as a token of Aboriginal acceptance of their dispossession. Previously, it had been traditional in successive celebrations of the coming of European civilisation to have Aborigines restricted to non-speaking parts, acting as silent, non-violent witnesses to the British arrival and certainly not as active opponents to it. On one level the opening of the opera house followed in this tradition, but on another level it was a dramatic departure from it, acknowledging the existence of Aboriginal cultures and now, in the manner of the Jindyworabaks, seeking to incorporate aspects of the Aboriginal culture into the supplanting European culture.

The construction of the Sydney Opera House was an affirmation by white Australians of their determination to remain as permanent abiders in the continent. So too was the decision in 1959 by the Menzies government to proceed with the development of Canberra as the bush capital, after a virtual hiatus of 30 years. Menzies moved more of the public service there, excavated artificial lakes and constructed monumental edifices fit for the capital of the newly confident nation. From a virtual country town of just 20 000 people in 1945, Canberra grew to become a multicultural city of some 200 000 by 1970. This burst of building would continue for nearly 40 years as the grand vision of its long dead American architect, Walter Burley Griffin, took shape on the dry grasslands of the Molonglo plain. Further belated nation-building investments were seen in the opening in 1962 of a standard gauge railway line connecting Melbourne and Sydney without the need to change trains in Albury. A similar line stretched across the continent, connecting Sydney to Perth in 1970. All these cities began to throw up standard-style American skyscrapers that celebrated the postwar prosperity and the influx of massive American capital investment. American cars, albeit built in Australia, now dominated the peak-hour traffic snarls before shoving their way onto a growing system of American-style freeways. The first one was opened in 1958, funnelling traffic from the Sydney Harbour Bridge to the eastern suburbs across a raised 'expressway' that avoided the narrow city streets. It was celebrated as a 'striking symbol of Sydney's growth and maturity'.

These confident constructions in the cities were matched by further measures to proceed with the occupation of the continent. A bipartisan zeal was expressed by politicians backing this popular national mission. As opposition Labor leader Arthur Calwell exulted in 1963:

> To no other nation in the world has the opportunity been granted for the sole possession and development of a sea-girt land mass by a single people. To no other nation has it been given to unite their will and destiny upon an empty land of such vast extent ... Fortunately for us, there is a continent awaiting our conquest, and its name is Australia.

Calwell competed unsuccessfully with his Liberal and Country party opponents to identify the Labor Party with this development ethos. The Australian electorate lapped it up, supporting politicians who promised to pursue the development grail and thereby underpin their continued prosperity. Menzies appointed a minister for national development while, in Queensland, such was the development fervour that three state government ministers were responsible for promoting 'development'.

Western Australia was similarly obsessed with developing its state, with a minister, Charles Court, responsible for promoting development of its largely unpopulated northern parts. Court, an accountant turned politician who went on to become premier, took to it with a will, trumpeting in 1968 about his state being 'only at the beginning'. The beginning of what, was left to the imagination of his audience. Echoing Calwell, Court repeated the Australian mantra to an electorate that continued to be bedazzled by development:

> We are a handful of people privileged to develop a great continent ... In our north west and Kimberley we have half a million square miles—an area as big as the whole of the Republic of South Africa.

Western Australians had taken confidence from their hosting of the 1962 Commonwealth Games, that Perth, 'the capital of a pioneering State of only 750 000 people spread over 1 000 000 square miles', had been able to provide the required facilities for such an international sporting event. The *West Australian* linked the games to the overriding development effort, suggesting that the success of the games had 'put a seal on the dramatic developments taking place from one end of Western Australia to the other'. When the Queen returned to Australia in 1963, she toured development projects that had been on the drawing board during her visit in 1954.

As always in the Australian context, development meant more than just promoting prosperity and providing jobs. It was intimately involved with occupying the 'empty spaces' of the continent, with subduing the 'wilderness' and defending against a possible invader. As some critics of the prevailing development ethos pointed out at the time, it would have been more appropriate to direct development to the existing centres of population, the places where workers and consumers already lived, rather than to try and direct them to isolated situations where most people would rather not live but which they nevertheless would like to see 'developed'. But these voices were largely overwhelmed, as geographer Griffith Taylor had been in the 1920s, by the bleating army of boosters.

One of the most dramatic developments to be pushed by the boosters was centred on the Ord River in the Kimberley district. As early as 1945, research was conducted into ways that the waters of the Ord River could be harnessed for the irrigation of tropical crops, such as cotton and sugar. The army had set up several farms in the Northern Territory during the war where it had successfully grown vegetables for the troops stationed across the north, thereby overturning doubts about the possibilities of tropical agriculture. But the success was small-scale and only made possible by the expanded local market for the produce provided by the wartime garrison. More ambitious schemes, like that proposed for the Ord River, to convert indifferent cattle country into closely settled, agricultural communities, would take decades of experience with the tropical environment and massive infusions of government money before they could become viable. However, the vision for the Ord made all that effort and expenditure seem worthwhile. According to one of its main proponents, the scheme would combine irrigation-based agriculture, hydro-electricity and tropical industries to which it was boldly predicted some half a million people would be attracted by the 1980s.

Experiments at the Ord River during the 1950s convinced the development-minded government in Perth to construct a diversion dam on the river as a precursor to a massive irrigation scheme. This scheme received the go-ahead from the federal government in 1967, along with a similar scheme near Bundaberg in central Queensland, at a time when the government was about to face a senate election. The government's backing for the schemes allowed it to claim that it was developing the north. Initially, the Ord River scheme was intended to settle 500 families on 200 000 acres to grow mainly cotton. It appealed to the popular imagination as a means of populating the north in a way that mechanised mining was incapable of doing. While mining towns grew like mushrooms across the north, they disappeared just as quickly once the mineral deposits had been exploited, leaving no permanent population to effect the occupation of the tropics. There was a continuing ambivalence about mining developments which were necessarily transitory and failed to provide a long-term answer to the problem of securing Australia's occupation. As Perth's *West Australian* newspaper argued in supporting the Ord River development:

> *Only when the northern river valleys are supporting prosperous agricultural and pastoral communities will Australia be able to claim that it is firmly on the road to redressing the balance between the north and the south.*

Only then, would white Australians be able to proclaim to the world that they were making beneficial use of the continent's 'empty north' and claim the moral right to retain possession of it.

The Bundaberg scheme, which was not completed until 1975, was designed to provide water for nearly 1500 additional sugar growers as part of a large-scale expansion of the sugar industry. Like many schemes to populate the north, the expansion of the sugar industry did not make economic sense since it was based upon relatively small farms growing a product that was heavily protected by the tariff on the domestic market and effectively subsidised on the world market by the Australian consumers, as it had been since federation. The social and political benefits of occupying the north with a white population on small farms, that would in turn ensure the viability of the nearby coastal towns, outweighed the economic considerations.

There were also doubters, people prepared to stand up against the prevailing flow of confident developmentalism and question its rationale or where it was heading. In May 1963, the rising Liberal MP Peter Howson, who had spent most of his life in England, wondered quietly whether 'the constant pressure for "rapid economic growth and development" is necessary'. But he kept his reservations to himself while publicly lining up in his party's development brigade. It was left to the economist Bruce Davison to play the part that the geographer Griffith Taylor had played to his cost in the 1920s. In his book *The Northern Myth*, Davison raised serious questions about the economic viability of major projects such as the Ord River scheme, suggesting that it made more sense to direct development money to the existing centres of population. Like Taylor, Davison's warnings were brushed aside by politicians eager to earn votes by rooting around in the development trough on behalf of their northern electorates. Other writers took a wider swing at the deadening materialism of Australian society.

Alan Seymour's play *One Day of the Year* was barred from the Adelaide Festival in 1960 for portraying a jaded commemoration of Anzac Day against a background of empty, materialistic suburbia. When it did get a run in Sydney, one self-appointed critic blasted it for lacking 'the nobility of theme and thought that is the true expression of a proud young nation'. Australians had sought muscular immigrants to help subdue the continent and were slow to embrace those who dared to question the myths that brought order and confidence to their existence. As this critic claimed:

> *The Australians who really matter are not always highly intelligent,*
> *cultured warriors. But in war they fight like tigers, and in peace*
> *they drive onward with admirable confidence.*

That same year saw the publication of architect Robin Boyd's *The Australian Ugliness*, which poked aesthetic holes in the Australian dream homes that had been strewn across the spreading wasteland of suburbia.

As the prosperity of the 1960s lunged along, the *Bulletin* editor, Donald Horne, fired a misdirected broadside hoping to deflect it onto new paths. In his bestselling *The Lucky Country* (1964) Horne described Australia as 'a lucky country run mainly by second-rate people'. The question mark that was originally intended to complete the title was left off. This proved to be a fatal error, although not for its sales. In the context of the 1960s' mineral boom, the book's title was embraced as expressing an essential truth—that Australia really was a lucky country and Australians a fortunate people. Countless Australians took advantage of a boom in air travel and a lowering of fares to travel overseas in the 1960s on a level that had not been seen outside of wartime. Most returned with a firm conviction, freely expressed to friends and relations as they nodded through their holiday slide shows, that 'we don't know how lucky we are'. Australia really was a lucky country, just like Donald Horne said it was. Even Peter Howson, despite his earlier reservations about the development binge, reacted defensively to Horne's book:

In spite of critics like Horne in The Lucky Country, *this is a fortunate period of Australia's history ...; we will be grateful in the years to come for this fortune, in which we have been able to build a nation at peace.*

Nevertheless, the critical works of writers such as Seymour and Horne gave heart to other intellectuals as the expanding and multi-ethnic population created an enlarging and more diverse intelligentsia. In a letter to his American publisher in 1962, Patrick White, while conceding that Australians '*are* a boring race, and the constant realisation of it makes me desperate', took some solace from being able to discern a 'change [that] is taking place, only very, very slowly; there is so much dead wood keeping the live growth back'.

Much of the 'dead wood' was held in place by a continuing fear of Asia, and the various development schemes across the north were launched against a background of officially inspired hysteria about a communist thrust from South-East Asia lunging from China through Vietnam and, eventually, to Australia itself. Conservative governments did not have to work hard to convince Australians about the seriousness of the threat to their occupation of the continent. They looked upon Asia as an overcrowded continent and feared that the people of Asia looked avariciously upon Australia as an empty and undeveloped continent. Their continuing efforts to populate and develop the 'empty north', and their escalating military commitment to Vietnam, were parts of the same defensive policy that was rooted in their historic insecurity as a supplanting society.

The development binge of the 1950s had been made possible by the supposed security provided by the ANZUS and SEATO treaties which allowed Australia to run down its defence forces. To ensure continued British and American support, it committed token forces to Malaya and encouraged American involvement in Vietnam. It was then that the limits of the ANZUS treaty were revealed during the Indonesian takeover of West New Guinea. Despite strong protests from Australia, which feared the prospect of sharing a border with Indonesia in New Guinea and the possibility of Indonesia extending its illegitimate claim to the whole island, the lack of US support forced the Dutch to capitulate. A possible threat to Australian security had arisen and ANZUS had been found wanting. Labor leader Arthur Calwell warned that Indonesia might extend its imperial ambitions to grasp 'at Timor, then at Papua-New Guinea and finally ... at Northern Australia'. But Australia's scope for independent action was severely circumscribed by its feeling of vulnerability, with Menzies being left to limply remind the Indonesians of Australia's 'great and powerful friends'. The episode had made clear that treaties were not sufficient to guarantee Australian defence. The government intensified its efforts to encourage both Britain and the United States to remain engaged on the ground in Asia, a policy that would culminate in the American commitment to Vietnam.

As well, following the Indonesian takeover, Australia agreed to allow the United States to establish a naval communications base at North West Cape in Western Australia. The base allowed communication with American submarines operating in the Indian Ocean from where they could potentially launch a nuclear strike against the Soviet Union and perhaps thereby draw Australia into a nuclear war. More importantly, from Australia's point of view, it was hoped that the base would increase the American commitment to Australia under the ANZUS agreement and, along with other US bases established around northern Australia, provide a powerful deterrent against Indonesia challenging the proprietorship of the continent's relatively empty north. It would also allow Australia to continue skimping on its defence spending so that it could concentrate on developing the continent. As the external affairs minister, Sir Garfield Barwick, informed parliament in May 1963, Australian hosting of the base was in accordance with its obligations under the ANZUS treaty and was 'of critical significance to the security of this country [and] to the possibility of its continued growth'.

With the confidence provided by this base, Australia committed its meagre forces to the defence from Indonesian attack of the new Malaysian federation, thereby helping to retain Britain's defence commitment to the region. Menzies remained blithely confident that Britain retained the will and the power to defend Australia and justified the Australian involvement in Malaysia in terms of it creating a reciprocal obligation on the part of Britain to defend Australia. Although there was no formal treaty between Australia and Britain, Menzies claimed that 'we know and she knows that in this part of the world we look to her, and she looks to us. We each apply in a spirit of mutual confidence a golden rule of mutual obligation.'

At the same time, to hedge their bets, Australia sent 30 army instructors to Vietnam in May 1962 to help retain America's growing commitment to the region. The gesture helped to clothe the increasing American involvement, numbering some 11 000 personnel, with the politically acceptable colours of a multinational force akin to the earlier commitment to Korea. The instructors, and the thousands of Australian service personnel who later joined them, would risk their lives and some would shed their blood in far-off Vietnam in a misguided attempt to secure their claim of effective proprietorship over the Australian continent. The commitment was justified to the Australian people as an insurance policy to ensure a sympathetic American response in the event of Australia being threatened. Just as the string of bases across northern Australia and American capital investment in the Australian economy gave the United States a direct interest in the defence of Australia, so the Australian contribution to Vietnam would create a moral commitment by the United States to respond if a threat developed to Australia. It would also involve the United States on the ground in Asia where it could act as a counterweight to the feared Asian axis that seemed set to link China, North Korea and Indonesia.

When the United States requested a greater effort from Australia, its ambassador in Washington urged Canberra to be 'as positive and as prompt as possible', arguing that Australia should try to achieve 'such an habitual closeness of relations with the United States and sense of mutual alliance that in our time of need ... the United States would have little option but to respond as we would want'. In June 1964, 30 more military advisers and six transport planes were sent to Vietnam. That same day, the first Australian in Vietnam was killed, supposedly defending his country at a distance. Meanwhile, Australian defence spending slumped to just 2.65 per cent of gross national product.

The external affairs minister, Paul Hasluck, claimed Australia was in South Vietnam 'to halt the southward move of Mainland China' and to demonstrate 'that aggression will fail'. It was not for some idle principle that Australia made its commitment, but 'to ensure the defence and the survival of our country'. It hoped to do this, as it had hoped to do in Korea, by establishing a world 'where territorial integrity is respected'. Such respect, argued Hasluck, was 'vital to our own existence'. If the populous nations of Asia could be made to acknowledge the territorial integrity of their neighbours, including Australia, then the claim of British Australians to the continent would be more secure.

As 1964 drew to a close, Australia faced the awful prospect of having its forces committed to separate conflicts stretching from New Guinea to Vietnam. Its forces were engaged in an undeclared war in Borneo as Indonesian 'irregulars' resisted the formation of the new federation of Malaysia; other forces were stationed in Singapore and on the Malayan peninsula; and instructors were based in Vietnam. At the same time, it feared that Indonesia would extend its claim to West New Guinea to cover the eastern half controlled by Australia. In October of that year, China had exploded its first atomic bomb and Indonesia was talking openly of an Asian axis with China and North Korea.

In November 1964, Menzies announced a dramatic increase in defence spending, raising it from just 2.6 per cent of gross national product to 4.6 per cent in three years. With the help of conscription, the army was to be almost doubled from 22 000 personnel to 37 000. Without the support of America and Britain, observed Menzies, 'Australia's task in defending so vast a territory with so few people would be a fearful one'. The government was trying belatedly to close the yawning gap in Australia's defences caused by two decades of economies while the nation had concentrated on development. Although the increase in defence spending was considerable, it was still hardly commensurate with the threat that Australia was meant to be facing. Neither did it indicate any retreat from the national obsession with development. As the future prime minister John Gorton assured his senate colleagues that same month:

There is no need, and it would be quite wrong, for this country ever to try to hold a large standing army in being. We have too much else to do. We have too much scope for development, too many other requirements, and too many economic needs.

The American commitment to Vietnam effectively plugged the gap for Australia, with the security of the American presence in South-East Asia compensating for the weaknesses in the Australian armoury. As the urbane air minister, Peter Howson, acknowledged in his diary in February 1965:

While there is a crisis to our north, we have the protection of UK and USA. But if the crisis is solved, then we could find ourselves defensively naked until our new preparations are complete in 1968–69.

The Vietnam War allowed Australia to count on the support of the United States and thereby continue to economise on its local defence relative to the possible threats that it was facing in its region.

The cost began to mount when Menzies announced in April 1965 the despatch of an army battalion to Vietnam, claiming that 'the take-over of South Vietnam would be a direct military threat to Australia and all the countries of South and South East Asia' and was 'part of a thrust by Communist China between the Indian and Pacific Oceans'. According to Howson, the commitment to Vietnam was worth it even if the war was ultimately lost. It allowed Australia to 'honour our obligations in ANZUS and SEATO' and to expect in return 'our allies to help us if the Australian mainland is attacked'. The government agreed that service personnel killed in the conflict would be flown home to be buried in Australian soil. For a commitment of 1500 personnel, at a time when the Americans were planning a commitment of 600 000, Australia was still managing to buy the appearance of a defence guarantee on the cheap. This allowed Australia to delay adopting a policy of 'fortress Australia', which would, according to Howson, 'slow down our rate of growth if it happens'. The fighting in Vietnam was not so much defending Australia against the imagined communist thrust as defending the development thrust in Australia by economising on defence.

Australia's initial commitment to Vietnam was necessarily limited when it still faced the prospect of possible conflict on two fronts with Indonesia. Following the right-wing coup in Jakarta and the subsequent pogrom against the Indonesian Communist Party and its mainly Chinese supporters, that threat was lifted and an increased Australian commitment to Vietnam made possible. The government waited until Menzies' retirement as prime minister in January 1966 before his successor, Harold Holt, offered to boost the Australian forces to 4500 personnel, including conscripts for the first time. Later that year, Hasluck talked of how China 'overhangs the region with a population of 1000 million under a regime which ... represents all that is most illiberal and backward-looking and violent in Communist thought'. With its relatively tiny commitment, Australia was helping to ensure that American forces interposed themselves between its 'empty continent' and those overhanging Chinese.

Although voices in the Labor Party predicted an expensive debacle for the Australian and American forces, the government was confident of an American victory and even of the British remaining in the region for at least another decade, either in Singapore or on the Australian mainland itself. After a visit to Vietnam in May 1966, Holt exulted to a colleague that Australia would 'get protection in the South Pacific for a very small insurance premium'. The following month, after Britain decided to begin a phased withdrawal from the Far East, Holt left for Washington to assure President Lyndon Baines Johnson that Australia would go 'all the way with LBJ'. When Johnson reciprocated by visiting Australia in October 1966, emphasising to the American public that the United States was not alone in Vietnam, Howson thought the visit had confirmed at last that 'Australia has an umbrella—or a shield'.

Johnson's reception by the Australian public was unprecedented for a foreign politician, providing a graphic demonstration that the United States had gone far towards replacing Britain in the affections of the Australian public while Johnson's presence, the first by a serving American president, gave Australians confidence in the strength of the American alliance. Not since the Queen's visit in 1954 had Australians shown such public fervour, although there were anti-Vietnam demonstrations, mainly by students who might soon be forced to fight there. Just as the Queen's 1954 visit had boosted Menzies' electoral stocks, so Johnson's visit helped to ensure Holt's hold on office when he held an election straight afterwards, winning a resounding victory largely on the issue of Vietnam. After the election, Holt increased the commitment to 6300 troops and later to more than 8000. The 'very small insurance premium' amounted to 504 service personnel killed in Vietnam and a society divided as deeply as the conscription debates had done during the First World War. And their lives were wasted.

Australia had gone to Vietnam as a means of getting the Americans to make good their supposed defence guarantee under the ANZUS treaty by committing ground forces on the Asian mainland. For similar reasons, it had sent token forces to Malaya in support of the British, hoping thereby to prolong the commitment of British forces to the Far East. The policy backfired in both cases. The British announced in 1967 their withdrawal from east of Suez despite Australia reminding Britain of its historic defence obligation to defend Australia in return for Australian contributions in past wars. It even urged that British forces be based in Australia from where they had been withdrawn nearly a century before. But Britain declined, conceding that it was no longer a world power. Two years later, America's President Nixon effectively conceded defeat in Vietnam, announcing at Guam that America would gradually withdraw and no longer be involved in Asian land wars. As America began its staged withdrawal from Vietnam, so too did Australia, with all except its advisers leaving by the end of 1971.

Australia's support for the United States in Vietnam had backfired, helping instead to drive its greatest friend out of South-East Asia and to call into question the basis of the ANZUS treaty. It was a very different Australia that faced the prospect of American withdrawal from Vietnam and the British withdrawal from east of Suez. British Australians had used the 25 years after the Second World War to secure their claim of proprietorship over the continent by populating and developing it under the aegis of their 'great and powerful friends'. In the process, the ethnic composition of the society was inadvertently transformed from its former, predominantly British stock, while the development of the continent, particularly in the north, helped to strengthen Aboriginal demands for land rights. Now it faced the problem of a declining birthrate and an increasing reliance upon migration for its continuing population growth upon which further development and prosperity were believed to depend.

The introduction of the contraceptive pill had led to people delaying childbirth and having fewer children. Two, rather than four, children per family became the norm. The birthrate slumped from 24 per thousand in 1947 to 19 per thousand by 1967 and just 15.7 per thousand by 1978. Even though the population had passed the psychologically important ten million mark in 1959, there was still a perception that Australia needed 'a rapid increase in its population'. As the Catholic activist B. A. Santamaria reminded Australians in 1966:

> The basic facts about the continent are that it is geographically isolated at the feet of South-East Asia, that our population is only 11.5 million and that over the past four years its rapidly declining birth-rate has become a major problem.

Santamaria opposed both the pill and the greater participation of women in the work force which would limit their ability to produce children. He called for 'heavy and progressive increases in child endowment' to encourage women to remain at home and to have larger families. To solve any labour shortage created by the absence of these women from the work force, he proposed that Australia turn to the Philippines for immigrants. This suggestion, which was not adopted, was a further sign of Australia's increasing rejection of its 'white Australia' past.

It was ironic that, as Australians were fighting in Vietnam to prevent a supposed Asian thrust towards Australia, the government was progressively dismantling the formerly hallowed 'white Australia' policy to allow the admission of non-Europeans. Changes to the *Immigration Act* in 1957 had allowed non-Europeans to become permanent residents after 15 years, while the sham of the dictation 'test' had been dropped in 1958 to appease critical international opinion. The former move allowed some long-time residents of Asian background to secure their position in Australia at a time when the society had almost succeeded in the task that it began at federation of 'bleaching' its society white. The arrival of more than a million European migrants after the war ended forever talk of keeping Australians British. The resistance to Asian migration was also weakened despite attempts by Menzies and other old-time conservatives to hold the line. In 1961, as pressure mounted for a token admission of Asian migrants, Sir John Latham, former chief justice of the High Court and conservative politician, warned against any relaxation of the 'white Australia' policy which he claimed could create 'another festering sore of racial hatred'.

Although the official use of the term 'white Australia' was allowed to lapse out of deference to the growing number of independent African and Asian nations, the racial barrier stayed in place, resulting in further ludicrous situations that caused Australia international embarrassment. In one case in 1964, a British man in Australia applied for his twin brother in England to join him. While the man in Australia was of European appearance, the other twin was found on interview to be 'very swarthy and dark' and was consequently rejected. They were the sons of a British father and an Indian mother. At a time when Japan had become, by 1963, Australia's most important export market after Britain, and Australia was making strenuous efforts to develop new markets in Asia to replace its traditional European markets that seemed set to close with the prospect of British entry into the Common Market, the 'white Australia' policy had clearly become an economic liability. Instead of helping to secure their unchallenged hold on the continent, it was raising questions around the world as to the right of white Australians to keep their continent.

Australia faced the prospect of becoming an international pariah along with South Africa, and later Rhodesia, which were the target of international criticism and economic boycotts in the 1960s because of their racist policies. With its treatment of the Aborigines, its colonial policy in New Guinea and the 'white Australia' policy, there was much for Australia to be defensive about. In June 1965, Justice John Kerr warned that:

> *Whilst the Labour [sic] Party, and indeed the Government parties, insist upon keeping the White Australia policy as a fundamental matter in Australian politics, we are going to have a bad time in international debates. The real question is not whether we are going, in the long run, to be forced to retreat from this policy, but rather how far we are going to retreat?*

That same month, the Labor Party dropped support for 'white Australia' from its platform, although initially it was a rather cosmetic change. As its immigration spokesman Fred Daly explained, the new Labor policy 'maintains the principle of Australia's established immigration policy which has been endorsed by all governments since Federation' while recognising 'the need for administrative action, tolerance and understanding to meet changing circumstances and to avoid ill-founded criticisms'. In other words, any embarrassing incidents that revealed the racial basis of the immigration policy would be handled more sensitively by a Labor government, although the underlying policy would remain in place. Australia would stay white.

Shortly before he retired in January 1966, Menzies had told a late night meeting of his ministers over drinks that he hoped they would 'never alter the White Australia Policy'. However, while Menzies could hold back the tide of change during his 17 years in power, once he was gone his more liberal successor as prime minister, Harold Holt, signalled a relaxation of the 'white Australia' policy. Holt had been instrumental as immigration minister in the 1950s in promoting the entry of southern Europeans against the Anglophile inclinations of Menzies. Now his government announced that non-Europeans could gain permanent resident status after just five years in Australia rather than the 15 years required earlier. This reduced, but did not entirely eliminate, the racial discrimination against them. Non-Europeans possessing skills required by Australia would also be allowed admission with their families, although 'the basic aim of preserving a homogeneous population will be maintained'. The new policy would admit 'selected non-Europeans capable of becoming Australians and joining in our national development'. As a result, the number of Chinese in Australia increased to an estimated 23 000 by 1969, bringing it close to the pre-federation figure in absolute terms although much less in percentage terms. The government was not leading public opinion any more but struggling to catch up with a people who had become increasingly relaxed about the prospect of a token Asian presence in Australia. A Chinese Australian was elected president of the Northern Territory Assembly in 1965 and the following year made mayor of Darwin.

The new-found equanimity by Australians about admitting a trickle of Asians to their annual flood of European immigrants was partly due to their confidence in all these immigrants sloughing off their ethnic heritage and adopting the Australian 'way of life'. As the immigration minister, Bill Snedden, proclaimed in the late 1960s, he was 'quite determined we should have a monoculture, with everyone living in the same way, understanding each other, and sharing the same aspirations'. With such a large proportion of European migrants, Australians could no longer centre their identity upon being British. Moreover, in a fast-changing world where racism was attracting international opprobrium, it was no longer possible to centre their identity upon being 'white'. So, in floundering for an alternative, they fixed upon a hazy sense of being 'Australian' in which an attachment to traditional Australian values of mateship, social equality and 'a fair go' gradually replaced race as the core identity. By 1971, Prime Minister John Gorton was able to assure an audience in Singapore that Australia would soon display a 'complete lack of consciousness of difference between the races'. This began to be reflected in the immigration policy where, by 1972 and prior to the official abolition of the 'white Australia' policy, Australia was already admitting around 10000 non or part-Europeans a year. However, as an immigration officer recalled, the administration of the policy was not changed overnight. There still remained within the immigration department two sections, one dealing with white applicants where 'you were out to approve anyone who popped their hand up and said they wanted to come to Australia' and a section dealing with non-whites where 'it was a question of trying to keep as many from getting in as possible'.

Gorton was distinctive in his prime ministership for fostering a greater sense of nationalism, proclaiming himself as being 'Australian to the bootheels' and suggesting that Australians now had 'a burgeoning faith in ourselves as Australians first'. An outpouring of history books had helped to underpin this new-found faith. Russel Ward's *The Australian Legend* in 1958, the first volume of Manning Clark's *A History of Australia* in 1962 and Humphrey McQueen's *New Britannia* in 1970 were just some of the major works that prompted a major and ongoing process of reinterpreting Australian history. No longer would it be possible to write Australian history as an uninterrupted story of material progress, or as a sideshow of the British Empire. Advertisers latched on to the new mood by propagating in their images and jingles a worrying return to breast-beating nationalism. Patrick White was scathing in his denunciation of this development when writing to a South African friend in 1968:

> *We are a smug, piddling country, blowing our own trumpet for all*
> *we are worth, while our achievements are few and mostly material.*
> *I stay here only because Australia is my blood, but at heart I realise*
> *after a long time I am Anglo-European.*

Perhaps the breast-beating was a reaction to the Australian defeat in Vietnam, when the Gallipoli legend had been tested anew and found wanting, or even unwanted. The most enduring image from the war was of Australian soldiers using water torture on a Vietnamese woman. The breast-beating on television, often associated with sporting events, helped to instil a martial confidence in a people who seemed to have lost the ability to fight on the battlefield. Although Australian soldiers in Vietnam still boasted to their American counterparts that one Australian digger was worth ten Americans, few at home would have agreed. The Vietnam War was, as Calwell had warned it would be, a dirty unwinnable war that had brought discredit upon Australia and shame and embarrassment to the men who fought in it. As Robin Gerster observed in his study of Australian war writing, the Vietnam experience caused 'a lapse in Australia's characteristic reverence for its fighting men'. The reverence was refracted instead onto its cricketers and other international sportspeople. Two of the sportspeople who shot to fame in the 1960s were Aborigines.

In 1968, 20-year-old boxer Lionel Rose won the world bantamweight title in a bout in Tokyo against Japan's Masahiko 'Fighting' Harada. Coming just 23 years after the end of the Second World War, the fight was not without its symbolic undertones and some Australians would doubtless have preferred the victory to have been won by a white Australian. But Lionel Rose was fêted nonetheless, being named Australian of the year. Meanwhile, tennis fans were witnessing the remorseless rise of another Aborigine in the person of Evonne Goolagong who collected a string of Australian titles before winning the Wimbledon title in 1971 at the age of 19. Their successes would have helped to increase sympathy for the Aboriginal cause, although Aboriginal demands were focusing more on the fundamental question of land rights rather than requesting, as before, a helping hand onto the bottom rungs of white society. The Aboriginal footballer turned pastor, Doug Nicholls, had led a protest in 1963 against an attempt by the Victorian government to close the Aboriginal settlement at Lake Tyers in Gippsland. He went on to be knighted in 1972, using the occasion to focus attention on land rights, and was made governor of South Australia in 1976.

The 1960s saw the extension of some basic human rights to Aborigines. From 1962, they were allowed to vote but, unlike white Australians, were not required to register. In 1966, South Australia became the first state to ban discrimination in the provision of services on the basis of a person's colour. That same year, the federal arbitration commission gave Aboriginal workers in the Northern Terrritory pastoral industry equal pay with their white counterparts but introduced it over three years and allowed lower wages to be paid for workers classed as slow. Although the case was an important legal victory, it led to a loss of jobs for Aborigines in the pastoral industry. Over the longer term, though, it sparked Aboriginal protests which would eventually lead to the granting of land rights.

In August 1966, in the wake of the case and its delayed implementation of equal pay, the Gurindji people on Wave Hill cattle station in central Australia went on strike for higher pay and were promptly sacked by the exploitative British meat company, Vesteys. Davis Daniels, the secretary of the Northern Territory Council for Aboriginal Rights, appealed to the United Nations, turning the international spotlight on Australia's treatment of its indigenous people. While concentrating on their poor living conditions, Daniels also raised the question of land rights, calling for 'a say in controlling and working the land' which had been 'taken from us and handed over to big pastoral companies, often foreign controlled, and to wealthy mining companies'. He complained that legal equality was useless 'until we have equal pay for equal work, proper housing, education and training and some control at least over our sacred tribal areas'.

In March 1967, the Gurindji people took their destiny into their own hands by occupying part of their traditional lands on Wave Hill, earning the support of several trade unions and student groups from southern cities. Although the Australian people empowered the federal government that same year to legislate on behalf of Aborigines, allowing it to override the states, there was no overnight improvement in the condition and treatment of Aboriginal people. The Gurindji people would have to wait until the 1970s before being handed back part of their land. Meanwhile, some ten per cent of infant deaths continued to be suffered by Aborigines despite them comprising only about two per cent of the population. These infant mortality rates, and the incidence of preventable diseases among Aborigines, such as trachoma, were on Third World levels. Although these conditions would take decades to ameliorate, the 1960s saw Aborigines finding a more determined voice for their grievances and meeting with a more receptive audience, particularly in the south-eastern cities.

White Australians were confronted for the first time by the history of their callous mistreatment and murder of the Aborigines. In a major three-volume work published in 1970, the anthropologist C. D. Rowley charted the destruction of Aboriginal society. The work of Rowley and others gradually changed the perception of traditional Aboriginal society from being a doomed Stone Age people living in a state of wandering barbarism to a society with a complex culture living fruitful, organised lives. Archaeologists also helped the process by discovering the ancient remains of Aborigines which greatly extended the time frame of Aboriginal occupation of the continent while also greatly enhancing the understanding of the relative sophistication of that ancient society. Aboriginal resistance to the European takeover was also being written about. In his book *The Chant of Jimmie Blacksmith*, published in 1972, novelist Tom Keneally painted a tragic portrait based upon real events of an Aborigine in New South Wales who attempted to play the white man's game only to find himself battered by racism and provoked into futile and bloody resistance.

While white Australians were prepared to look with greater sympathy upon Aborigines, they were not yet prepared to concede land rights to them, at least not on the scale that some Aborigines were beginning to demand, particularly when it involved mining developments on Aboriginal reserves. In a landmark court case in 1971, the Aborigines on Gove Peninsula in the Northern Territory failed in an attempt to stop the mining of their land for bauxite. The court upheld the doctrine of *terra nullius*, that Australia was a land with no owners when it was claimed by the British in 1788. When Prime Minister Billy McMahon used an Australia Day address in 1972 to rule out the possibility of the government conceding land rights, Aborigines resorted to a dramatic action that symbolised to the world their plight as outsiders in their own continent, establishing a 'tent embassy' on the lawn opposite parliament house in Canberra. McMahon dithered for months before sending in the federal police to remove the Aborigines.

The Aboriginal tent embassy represented a direct challenge to the legitimacy of nearly two centuries of British occupation of the continent. Although the main focus was on land rights, the more fundamental question of sovereignty was also raised by the very pitching of the self-styled embassy. Australians were as divided over the question of Aboriginal land rights as they were over their participation in the Vietnam War. Some Australians saw the demand for land rights as posing a potent threat to their proprietorship of the continent, while others sensed that an accommodation with the Aborigines would make their proprietorship more, rather than less, secure. Just as the Labor Party had opposed the Vietnam War, now too did its leader, the Sydney lawyer Gough Whitlam, pledge his party's support for the Aboriginal cause. Before the year was out, he would have a chance to make good on his pledge.

Recommended Reading

Don Aitkin, 1984, *The Life of Politics: The Howson Diaries*, Viking, Melbourne.

Glen Barclay, 1988, *A Very Small Insurance Policy*, University of Queensland Press, Brisbane.

F. K. Crowley (ed.), 1973, *Modern Australia in Documents*, Vol. 2, Wren Publishing, Melbourne.

Peter Edwards, 1992, *Crises and Commitments*, Allen & Unwin, Sydney.

Ross Fitzgerald, 1985, *A History of Queensland: From 1915 to the 1980s*, University of Queensland Press, Brisbane.

Robin Gerster, 1987, *Big-Noting: The Heroic Theme in Australian War Writing*, Melbourne University Press, Melbourne.

Harry Gordon, 1988, *An Eyewitness History of Australia*, Penguin, Melbourne.

Donald Horne, 1964, *The Lucky Country*, Penguin, Melbourne.

Lenore Layman, 'Development ideology in Western Australia 1933–1965', *Historical Studies*, October 1982.

William Lines, 1991, *Taming the Great South Land*, Allen & Unwin, Sydney.

Harry Martin, 1989, *Angels and Arrogant Gods: Migration Officers and Migrants Reminisce 1945–85*, Australian Government Publishing Service Press, Canberra.

Gregory Pemberton, 1987, *All The Way: Australia's Road To Vietnam*, Allen & Unwin, Sydney.

John Rickard, 1988, *Australia: A Cultural History*, Longman, London.

C. D. Rowley, 1970, *The Destruction of Aboriginal Society*, Australian National University Press, Canberra.

Alan Trengrove, 1969, *John Grey Gorton: An Informal Biography*, Cassell, Melbourne.

Nancy Viviani (ed.), 1992, *The Abolition of the White Australia Policy: The Immigration Reform Movement Revisited*, Griffith University, Brisbane.

A. T. Yarwood, 1968, *Attitudes to Non-European Immigration*, Cassell, Melbourne.

21

'THE NATURAL
AND DESIRABLE
FUTURE'

For 30 years, ever since repelling the Japanese from their shores in 1942, white Australians had sought to secure their claim over the continent by populating it with people of their own race, developing it with the help of international capital and defending it with the help of powerful friends. All these policies came under attack from the late 1960s onwards. Not only was the 'white Australia' policy discredited and discarded by 1973, but the bipartisan support for a mass immigration program began to be eroded under the pressure of mounting unemployment. Moreover, the program had inadvertently changed the nature of Australian society by undermining its former Anglo-Celtic predominance. The postwar development binge had certainly brought prosperity, but it was unevenly distributed and the disparities of wealth were worsening over time. The development had been financed with overseas capital, which had left the Australian economy at the mercy of international financial markets. Moreover, much of the capital had been directed to the mining sector which threatened to turn Australia into a fast depleting quarry. Australians wondered what would happen when the minerals were exhausted. And they wondered too about the security they could expect from an American ally that had been bloodied and defeated in Vietnam.

The ongoing process of securing their proprietorship over the continent would continue but in radically different directions made possible by changes in the wider world. The prospect of another challenge that Calwell had feared so much in 1945 had receded. The Japanese were certainly rejuvenated from the war but were tied firmly into a military alliance with the United States and an economic alliance with Australia, exchanging their manufactured goods, particularly cars, for Australian raw materials, much as Britain had done before. As for the feared Chinese, their supposed thrust through Vietnam had come to nothing despite the American defeat in Vietnam; and neighbouring Indonesia had lost its former threatening aspect with the downfall of Sukarno in 1965. The Americans were bloodied by Vietnam but retained their superpower status in a world made more secure by the ongoing process of *détente* between the United States and the Soviet Union. American bases still cast their protective, futuristic shadows across the Australian outback between Indonesia and the settled south-east of the continent.

Just as their historic sense of an external threat was diminishing, Australians were becoming more comfortable with their effective occupation of the continent, and with their geographic situation in South-East Asia, now that their numbers were approaching Curtin's wartime aim of 20 million. The advent of the contraceptive pill, and the work of the women's movement, combined to send the birthrate plummeting, but there were no royal commissions, draconian bans on contraceptives or drastic measures to reverse the trend. In 1970, South Australia became the first state to legalise abortion despite critics of the legislation worrying about 'the long-term effects on the State's population'. Other states followed suit. There was also increasing public acceptance of homosexuality by a society that had previously flaunted its masculinity. And there was a radical easing of the censorship regulations that had kept Australians cosseted for so long. The fear of outside influences was abating.

Australians were no longer finding it so necessary to go 'home' to England to prove themselves, although tens of thousands still went each year, many for working holidays or to trace their family roots. Any special place that Australians believed they might have had in the affections of Britain were revealed on arrival at Heathrow, where they now found themselves lumped into the 'other' queue with African and Indian arrivals and forced to endure grilling by suspicious immigration officers about their reasons for visiting Britain. The rites of passage, the ritual of 'going home', now became the rites of rejection, gradually convincing Australian travellers that their own affections should no longer be divided. Discarding their former 'cultural cringe', they now embraced anything Australian, whether in the arts, education or business, sometimes regardless of its real worth.

With their new-found confidence, Australians were counting the costs of their fears, which had sent their troops to Vietnam and produced cities bloated with recent arrivals. While Canberra expanded along orderly, planned lines financed by federal government money, the infrastructure of other Australian cities was unable to keep up with the demands being placed upon it. With 20 per cent of Sydney being unsewered, the *Medical Journal of Australia* was not far wrong in suggesting in March 1970 that Australian cities were 'creaking and suffocating in their own excreta'. Urban roads had failed to keep pace with the demands being made upon them as car ownership increased at great speed, while public transport systems stagnated or, as in the case of Sydney's trams, were removed altogether. In their rush to promote private development, governments had sacrificed public infrastructure.

The historic victory of the Labor government of Gough Whitlam in 1972 was swept in on a rising tide of dissatisfaction with the familiar Australian mantra of development and with the election-winning Cold War rhetoric of the conservatives. It was 40 years since the depths of the depression, and many of the young Australians who voted in the Labor government had no direct experience of unemployment. Growing up in a time of perpetual prosperity, they had seen suburbs sprawl beyond the reach of such basic services as sewerage and public transport. Some had also been pressed into service to fight a feared Chinese foe only to watch Australian wheat farmers sell their harvests in Beijing and their American ally establish relations with China in 1972 without consulting or informing Australia.

When Whitlam asked Australians to choose 'between the habits and the fears of the past, and the demands and opportunities of the future', most opted to explore the hazy opportunities that he held out for them. With the economy starting to stutter under the gnomic control of Billy McMahon, sufficient Australians were prepared to place their trust in Whitlam's promise to restore them

> . . . to their rightful place in their own country—as participants and partners in government, as the owners and keepers of the national estate and the nation's resources, as fair and equal sharers in the wealth and opportunities that this nation should offer in abundance to all its people.

As Whitlam's promise suggested, his election did not mark the end of the development binge. Instead, like Chifley's postwar government, it began a binge directed by public servants rather than private entrepreneurs. Government planners would minimise the social costs of development by providing the public infrastructure and support services. The colourful immigration minister, Al Grassby, called on some 250 000 expatriate Australians in 1973 to return to Australia 'to build their nation and take part in the new developments now planned'.

The historic attempts to encourage closer settlement of the land were largely abandoned, although some voices continued to call for new immigrants to be located outside of the existing capital cities. The difference now was that such calls were motivated by the need to alleviate perceived overcrowding and the consequent environmental stresses evident in cities such as Sydney, rather than by any impulse to till the soil. A succession of droughts and the evidence of land degradation, together with declining returns from the traditional staples of wheat and wool, led Australians to abandon their former idyllic notions of securing their possession of the continent by tilling its often thin and fragile soils. Instead, the Whitlam government sought to decentralise urban growth by inflating strategically located towns across the interior into inland cities.

Just as previous governments had harboured hopes of decentralising population through the exploitation of hydro-electric and even atomic power, so the Labor government pushed forward with plans for decentralising population from the 'creaking' cities into the bush. There were even plans mooted at one stage to use Arab oil money to finance a scheme to tow icebergs from Antarctica to provide water for the 'greening' of inland Australia. The historic dream shared by so many explorers of stumbling across the mythical inland sea could become a reality. But it came to nothing. As for the several attempts at decentralising urban growth, only Albury-Wodonga enjoyed any measure of success, and that proved short-lived. Of the 14.5 million Australians in 1981, some six million lived in just two cities, Sydney and Melbourne.

While Australians were less concerned with being physically dispossessed of the continent, they were increasingly concerned that they were being economically dispossessed by the massive influx of mainly American capital that had seen important sections of Australian secondary industry and mining being controlled by American countries. Large swathes of the inland were also bought by American companies to raise cattle that would eventually find their way into American hamburgers. Australians had largely secured their effective control over the continent, while control of the economy had shifted from London to New York. Anti-American feeling inspired by the Vietnam War flowed over into opposition to American investment. Even the conservatives under Gorton had proposed ways to 'buy back the farm', as they put it, with its metaphorical overtones of land and tilling the soil. It was not farms but factories and mines that were central to the Australian concern about foreign control. Whitlam's election slogan, 'Buy back Australia', answered this concern by being directed more towards asserting greater control over Australian mineral resources which would be used to underpin industrial development in Australia rather than being exported in a raw or semi-processed state. These mineral resources, often extracted from Aboriginal land, were largely controlled by American companies selling Australian resources cheaply to Japanese companies and leaving Australians concerned that they were missing out on the fruits of the continent's munificence.

When huge reserves of natural gas were discovered off the north-west coast of Western Australia, ambitious schemes were drawn up by the Labor government to pipe the natural gas clear across the continent to power industries in the eastern seaboard cities. Instead of trying to shift population to the site of these new reserves of energy, government planners would shift the energy to the existing population centres while also allowing its decentralised inland cities to tap into the pipelines as they passed. When it used questionable methods to try and raise the massive amounts of money necessary for such a scheme, the government became locked in a bitter wrangle with the conservative opposition that eventually saw it tossed from power by the governor general, Sir John Kerr, in November 1975. Persistent stories of the involvement in Whitlam's dismissal by the American Central Intelligence Agency (CIA) have never been satisfactorily explained away.

The CIA need not have been concerned. Despite its rhetoric, the Whitlam government was retreating from its former economic nationalism and admitting the need for continued foreign investment to underpin Australia's faltering prosperity. Like most developed economies in the wake of the 1970s' oil crisis, the Australian economy was beset by the simultaneous occurrence of both unemployment and inflation. Australians became concerned for their living standards which depended, as they always had done, on the rapacious exploitation of the continent's resources. The election that was called following the peremptory dismissal of the Whitlam government confirmed Labor's fall from public grace. With the subsequent lifting of many of Labor's restrictive controls on mineral developments, there was a renewed resources boom in the late 1970s as foreign money was shovelled into the development of iron ore, coal, oil and bauxite deposits.

Australians had taken confidence during the 1960s and 1970s from the indications all around them that their continent was capable of bountiful development. The ironic intention of Donald Horne's *The Lucky Country* was ignored by Australians keen to seize upon the sentiment of its title. Horne continued to profit by their wilful ignorance, producing a series of books that played on the title of the original. By the early 1970s, the term 'lucky country' had become synonymous with Australia. With his ambitious plans for public development, Whitlam had been as captive as anyone to this national image. Hence the widespread dismay and disillusionment when inflation and unemployment ravaged Australia during the 1970s. Earlier visions of Australia Unlimited, of Australia emulating the United States, now seemed laughable while the lucky country was looking distinctly tarnished.

While the initial years of the Whitlam government had given Australians some confidence of being able to achieve a prosperous and independent future, the collapse of the economy and the dismissal of his government saw a surge in vacuous nationalism that was drummed into Australians in the form of advertising jingles thumping out from their television sets. The jingles celebrated an ignorant 'ocker' image that was directly descended from the troops that had stormed the cliffs at Gallipoli. It was a time for doers rather than thinkers, with vague images of a future Australian greatness, built on a cooperative partnership of private capital and willing workers, being held out to Australian audiences. In 1977, a campaign entitled 'Project Australia' brought business, government and trade unions together to harness this brash Australian nationalism to a renewed, but diffuse, development crusade, enjoining their fellow citizens:

Let's pull together with all our weight,
if we're going to make Australia great.
'Cause if we don't, it'll be too late.

As the jingle suggested, fear and hope continued to vie for supremacy in the national psyche. Manning Clark thought that the noisy nationalism indicated that Australians 'deep down . . . still do not know the answer to the simple question: Where do we belong?'.

The initial years of the Whitlam government had given Australians some confidence in them being able to achieve an independent future but left them confused as to what that future might be. Whereas Horne had helped to pave the way for Whitlam's social engineering, encouraging Australians to believe that it might be capable of achievement, Whitlam's conservative successor, Malcolm Fraser, scotched their dreams and promised only a scaled-down vision of Australia's possible future greatness. As a wealthy pastoralist from the lush grasslands of Victoria's Western District, Fraser was imbued with a sense of the seasonality of life, that people have to work hard during the good times in order to be able to sustain themselves during the hard times. Like Australians prior to the First World War, Fraser was concerned that decades of affluence had left Australians flabby. The former army minister called for the creation of 'a rugged society' that would encourage, among other things, 'individual strength and initiative'. In a sentence that came to typify his government, particularly in the minds of his detractors, Fraser lectured Australians that 'life is not meant to be easy'.

But how could Australians prove their credentials as a 'rugged society' in the absence of a war? The Vietnam experience had left them with little to celebrate in terms of their masculinity, and military values were widely disdained in the wake of that conflict. Whereas Australians had welcomed conscription in 1964 as being able to 'make men' of their increasingly long-haired youths, conscription was not a viable political option in the 1970s. From their comfortable couches, Australians were left to take solace in the televised feats of their sportspeople. However, even this seemed to bear out Fraser's concern about Australia being flabby when Australian representatives at the Montreal Olympics in 1976 returned with no gold medals among their tally, compared with eight won at the previous games. Overall, the Australian performance at Montreal was its worst since 1936.

It prompted a period of intense reflection on Australians' physical prowess in terms reminiscent of the early 1900s. As political scientist Don Aitkin observed,

*We are in for a period of national breast-beating about our decline
as a sporting 'power' . . . Australians ran, rowed, swam, sailed,
cycled and rode better than anyone else or, if you want to be more
accurate, disproportionately well, and that said something about
the kind of country we lived in . . . What has happened to us?
Is this the beginning of the end?*

To arrest the apparent decline, and get Australians off their collective couches
to engage in physical activity, the 'Life. Be in it' campaign was promoted
nationally, while an Australian Institute of Sport was established in 1980 in
Canberra to develop professionalism and excellence in the next generation of
sportspeople. Sporting facilities were constructed or upgraded across
Australia, with the sporting prowess of their youngsters doing for modern
Australians what the gallant physical prowess of the diggers had done for early
Australians on the battlefield of Gallipoli. Playing the game was not enough.
Australians had to win.

Although there was little sense of an imminent military threat to
Australia in the 1970s, the confidence that this produced was eroded
somewhat by the ignominious defeat of their American ally in Vietnam which
prompted Australians to re-examine their historic reliance upon great and
powerful friends. America's determination under Nixon not to become
involved in another land war in Asia, and its call for its Pacific allies to be
more self-reliant in their defences, raised doubts about the value of the
ANZUS treaty. Australia seemed more alone than ever in its region and was
forced to accelerate its efforts to build diplomatic bridges to Asian nations
that it had formerly held at bay. In 1973, Whitlam declared his determination
to destroy the spectre of the 'yellow peril' that had haunted Australians for so
long, encouraging them instead 'to shed the old stultifying fears and
animosities which have encumbered the national spirit for generations and
dominated, often for domestic partisan purposes, the foreign policy of this
nation'. The government of China was recognised and a range of other
diplomatic moves made to signal to the world that Australia was no longer
either a British or an American dependency.

It was a mark of Australia's new-found maturity based on its discovery
that it could stand alone in its region in the relatively non-threatening context
of the *détente* era. It was a sign also of Australians becoming comfortable with
their geographic situation. In a speech to the national press club in Washington
in July 1973, Whitlam conceded that Australians had previously harboured a
'vague and generalised fear of our own environment, the feeling of being alien
in our own continent and our own region'. He argued that the election of his
government marked a 'new nationalism' in Australia reflecting 'the realisation
that we are there to stay as a people'. There was less toadying to the American
ally. Instead, Whitlam blasted the bombing of Hanoi as 'murderous', ended

Australia's participation in SEATO military exercises and renegotiated the agreement for the US communications base at North West Cape in Western Australia to provide for greater Australian participation in its operation. In moves reminiscent of the 1944 ANZAC Agreement with New Zealand, the Australian government now sought to keep its region clear of great power rivalries and to look upon its neighbours as having 'a common interest . . . in consolidating the security and stability of this region as a whole'.

With the withdrawal of the United States from Vietnam, Fraser's government was faced with the prospect of having to develop a more self-reliant defence policy. Fraser tried to retain America's commitment to the region by warning darkly of Russian naval moves in the Indian Ocean and of the danger to Australia of a Russian naval base in postwar Vietnam. This failed to evoke much response from Washington and did little to reassure Australians that the Americans had any real commitment to the defence of Australia. He also sought allies in Asia to contain this apparent Russian expansion. After pontificating during the Vietnam War about the threat from China, Fraser now looked to Beijing to provide a bulwark against Russia, even to the point of supporting the Chinese invasion of Vietnam. With this return to conservative scaremongering, the sense of threat increased in the minds of the Australian public. In 1976, following the fall of Saigon, 51 per cent expected Australia to be threatened within 15 years. However, they were almost equally divided over the main source of the threat as between Russia and China. Despite Fraser's warnings of Russian designs, a small margin considered China to be the greater threat. But the fears were greatly muted compared to earlier decades. When a Chinese archaeological exhibition toured Australian cities in 1977, around ten per cent of Melbourne's population queued to see it.

Fraser's first trip overseas in June 1976 took him to Japan and China, reflecting the changing focus of Australian defence and diplomacy. In an ironic twist, the populous nations of Asia were now seen as possible guarantors of white Australians' proprietorship over their continent. Nevertheless, just as they had clung to Britain after Singapore, the basis of Australian defence remained their alliance with the United States. After all, despite its experience in Vietnam and fears of its relative decline as a world power, the United States remained the most powerful nation in the world, with its various communications bases across Australia continuing to emulate in Australian minds the Singapore naval base in the 1930s. Unlike the 1930s, Australians could rest secure in the 1970s that they faced no immediate threat to their hold on the continent. The credibility of alien invasion fears was dented by the failure of Asian communism, after the fall of Saigon in 1975, to rush on to the Australian continent as conservative politicians had freely predicted in the 1950s and 1960s. By April 1979, the chief of the defence forces conceded that an invasion was 'very unlikely'.

The most likely source of conflict was with neighbouring Indonesia.

The earlier tension over Malaysia had been settled but there remained the question of New Guinea where, since 1962, Australia had shared a land border with Indonesia following the forced withdrawal of the Dutch from West New Guinea, now Irian Jaya. In order to minimise the likelihood of a future conflict, and to avert the increasingly critical gaze of the United Nations, Australia increased the pace of its preparations for eventual withdrawal from Papua New Guinea. In an almost indecent rush to be gone, Whitlam conferred self-government on New Guinea in 1973 and then independence in 1975. Henceforth, Australia and Indonesia would no longer share a land border across which rebels from Irian Jaya were fighting for their own independence from the Javanese empire that had devoured them. Whitlam called it 'a day of liberation for Australia as much as for Papua New Guinea', disassociating Australia in the eyes of world opinion from the stink of imperialism and reducing the possible sources of friction with Indonesia. As his predecessor, Arthur Calwell, had warned, a dispute with Indonesia in New Guinea could lead to Indonesian demands on the Australian mainland.

So anxious was Australia to reduce the risk of any Indonesian challenge to its possession of the continent, that it condoned an extension of Javanese control to the former Portuguese colony of East Timor. Because of its fear of an independent East Timor becoming a destabilising influence in the region, and thereby causing Australia to divert more resources to defence, the government gave a green light to an Indonesian invasion of East Timor in 1975. Whitlam rejected Portuguese appeals for Australian assistance in separating the Timorese combatants, suggesting instead that it was 'part of the Indonesian world'. In 1978, the Fraser government overrode widespread public disquiet to recognise the Indonesian legal claim over the whole island. As Frank Crowley observed, Australian support for East Timorese independence was sacrificed for the sake of its 'long term relations with Indonesia, its closest potential enemy'. While Australia condoned the Indonesian takeover partly to ensure the continued stability of the Javanese empire, the government found that its claims of effective and moral proprietorship over Timor were impossible to secure. Rather than stabilising the region through its approval of the takeover, Australia has found to its cost that the takeover has destabilised its closest and most important neighbour and led to both it and Australia being criticised in world forums.

Although there were no looming, alien threats to Australia's hedonistic existence, their historic fears of dispossession were still invoked to some effect. It was now Australia's ample resources of minerals and energy, rather than its 'empty spaces', that were seen as providing an incentive for a possible invasion. When public and union pressure restricted the development of uranium mines, the former chairman of Australia's Atomic Energy Commission, Sir Phillip Baxter, claimed in 1976 that Japanese officials had threatened that 'Japan would take uranium by force if Australia refused to sell it'. And he suggested they would have a moral right to do so. Opposition to uranium mining involved fears of nuclear proliferation, despoiling of the environment in Australia and overseas, and interference with Aboriginal sacred sites. Whether it was fear of the Japanese or the lure of the rising uranium prices, the Fraser government relaxed the controls on its export. In March 1977 the foreign minister, Andrew Peacock, warned Australia that it remained 'a sparsely-populated, and richly-endowed country in a world which is going to be increasingly over-crowded, short of food, energy and other essentials, and seized of the importance of how the world's resources are distributed and utilised'. In an energy and resource-hungry world, it was argued that the strength of Australia's claim of moral proprietorship over the continent depended on it being willing to extract and sell its rich reserves of raw materials just as in earlier times its claim had depended on it pursuing efforts to populate its 'empty spaces' and till its indifferent soils.

The changing complexion of the Australian population under the impact of the postwar immigration scheme also helped to deflect hostile comment about the Australian occupation of the continent. With nearly 15 million inhabitants by 1980, and the massive development of its mining industry, it was not so easy to portray Australia as occupying an 'empty continent'. Moreover, earlier resentment in Asia about the 'white Australia' policy had become more difficult to sustain with the official ditching of that term and the gradual dismantling of its offensive regulations, culminating in 1973 with Whitlam's announcement of a racially blind immigration policy. With the world's second-highest proportion of migrants among its population, Australia also abandoned talk of assimilation and confidently embraced a policy of multiculturalism.

With Australia being largely cut loose by the United States, there was no mileage in being perceived as a European outpost in an economically advanced and politically assertive Asia. It was far better for their continuing possession of the continent to project Australia as a society open to all races. Although the comparisons were not that close, Australians could not ignore the South African experience which demonstrated the problems of surviving as an isolated supplanting society, holding an alien continent at bay with discriminatory policies. Moreover, the former policy of assimilation had been predicated on a desire to preserve the existing Anglo-Celtic nature of the host society in the face of the large-scale infusion of migrants. The official adoption of multiculturalism was a belated acknowledgment that the host society had been transformed. It could not help but be changed by the massive and largely peaceful influx of migrants. To take just one group, some 275 000 Italians had arrived in Australia between 1947 and 1981. They had been absorbed without violent reactions, whereas the entry of a few thousand Italians in the 1920s had provoked uproar across Australia. There were also domestic political advantages to be gained from embracing multiculturalism. The abandonment of assimilation might also make Australia more attractive to the increasing proportion of migrants, up to

20 per cent by the 1970s, who left Australia after finding it not to their liking, although some later returned when their memories of their countries of origin were also found not to measure up. Their return was an acknowledgment, however grudging, that Australia had come to represent 'home'.

Whitlam's accession to power was partly the result of this so-called ethnic vote to which he had made a special appeal. Under Whitlam, radio stations were set up to cater for ethnic audiences with programs in their own languages. By the time that Whitlam was pushed from power in 1975, multiculturalism was entrenched as a bipartisan policy, with Whitlam's conservative successor, Malcolm Fraser, promising ethnic television stations to provide news and entertainment in a variety of languages. Although the former governor general, Paul Hasluck, expressed concern in 1976 at the consequent fragmentation of society, observing that 'We have homogenised the milk but not the people', a government inquiry in 1978 backed the new policy, urging that the 'ethnic identity' of the various migrant groups should be 'interwoven into the fabric of our nationhood'. The Fraser government's acceptance of the inquiry's recommendations was partly a political response to an electorate that could no longer be ignored, and partly a response to migrants who were abandoning Australia in greater numbers. Among other things, the ethnic television programs were meant to encourage ethnic groups to 'maintain their language and develop their cultures' so as to 'contribute to a greater sense of self-esteem and confidence' while also providing information and advice that would 'assist non-English speaking migrants to settle'.

It was an acknowledgment that assimilation was no longer effective when dealing with migrants who were neither economic nor political refugees and who retained a real option of returning to their countries of origin. In 1975, for the first time since the war, more people left Australia than arrived. If Australia was to be secured and the society bound together, it would have to make official allowance for the cultural diversity that was so apparent on its city streets. British Australia was long dead, other than in the nostalgic imagination of the elderly and in some pockets of rural and suburban Australia. Its replacement, the 'Australian way of life', was redefined to become more eclectic. There was a positive embracing of minority cultures by the dominant culture. Migrants who had been through the assimilation process in the 1950s and 1960s were now bemused to find themselves encouraged to proclaim languages and cultures that many of them had discarded. Australia's international image, which had been defined for so long by the offensive and exclusive provisions of the 'white Australia' policy, was gradually transformed into the image of an inclusive society.

Although the Labor government had adopted an avowedly non-racist immigration policy in 1973, the immigration figures remained dominated by Europeans. By 1974, just 14 per cent of immigrants were from an Asian background. The Whitlam government was as concerned as its predecessors that the majority of its migrants be drawn from a European background. Moreover, the economic recession led to a drastic reduction in the overall numbers of immigrants, with the annual target being cut from 140 000 in 1972–73 to 50 000 in 1975–76. With the ex-shearer Clyde Cameron installed as immigration minister in 1974, there was a return to a positive preference for British and northern European migrants, although they did not prove easy to entice. With unemployment among unskilled workers relatively high, and skilled Europeans being increasingly harder to recruit, the immigration department turned to South America, rather than to Asia, to make up the numbers. Fraser's government continued this effort. As an immigration officer sent to Chile in 1976 recalled, 'The inhabitants of South America were seen as being something between those in Europe and Asia, largely European.' That changed as thousands of refugees from the Vietnam War were allowed into Australia after Whitlam's fall in 1975.

The surge in Asian immigration, part of it by refugees fleeing from Indochina to Australia in small boats, caused echoes of 'white Australia' to be heard. Their unregulated arrival on the still sparsely populated northern coastline raised the long-feared spectre of the 'yellow peril' spilling its teeming millions into Australia's 'empty north'. One Canberra bureaucrat, who had 'always debunked the Yellow Peril theory' of an Asian invasion, was now worried as to what Australia could do if 'hordes descend on us peacefully'. At the same time, a newspaper editor compared Australia to a lifeboat and wondered, 'in a world of vastly increased population', how Australia should react 'when they try to climb on board'. Hysterical warnings about Australia becoming 'a cesspit for coloured refugees' and of an 'Asian take-over' helped to spark some popular opposition to their entry. The right-wing National Alliance warned of Australia being 'absorbed into Asia. If we don't say no now, it will be too late.' Although Whitlam resisted the entry of Vietnamese, fearing that they would provide a natural electorate for the conservatives and complicate Australia's relations with Vietnam, the conservative government of Malcolm Fraser was more accommodating.

With the acceptance of multiculturalism, it was difficult to refuse entry to Asian immigrants. Fraser could take comfort that most of them were refugees from Asian communism and therefore would doubtless become doughty defenders of the Australian nation and dutiful supporters of the conservative cause just as many of the displaced persons had proved to be in the 1940s and 1950s. A Vietnamese migrant who arrived in Sydney in 1978 after fleeing Vietnam pointed out that his fellow Vietnamese Australians were 'willing to build the country with other Australians' while holding onto their Vietnamese identity:

> I was born and grew up in Vietnam. Nobody has the right to ask
> me to forget the country. But as an Australian citizen I have to

serve the country. So I can't say 'I'm a Vietnamese living in Australia'. I'm an Australian person from Vietnam.

It was estimated that people of Asian background made up around two per cent of the Australian population by 1978, while three years later it was calculated that 200 000 Australians had been born in Asia while another 70 000 were born in Australia of Asian parents. From 1976 to 1980, immigrants from an Asian background comprised more than a third of all immigrants.

Over time, this would lead the way for multicultural Australia to be increasingly redefined as Asian Australia, as the only way finally to secure proprietorship over the continent. They would weave their Asian identity into the predominantly European tapestry of Australia, presenting a more complex and hopefully acceptable image to the countries of Asia. By 1981, only 79.4 per cent of the population was born in Australia compared with 90.1 per cent in 1947 and 82 per cent in 1901. The changing complexion of Australian society might allow it to become a kind of chameleon in the south-west Pacific, adopting the new-found guise of 'Asian Australia' as a means of warding off the possible predatory attentions of its neighbours. Asian immigrants might also provide the continuing population growth required by Australia that its existing citizens were disinclined to provide.

During the 1970s, the annual population growth had slowed to just 1.4 per cent, while in 1975, more people left Australia than arrived, as the immigration program was cut back under Whitlam and dissatisfied migrants fled from Australia's depressed economic conditions. The birthrate continued its slow decline, reaching just 15 per thousand in 1979, the lowest rate experienced since 1788. Despite this, there was no attempt, as in the past, to limit the use of birth control methods. In fact, the Whitlam Labor government reduced the sales tax on the contraceptive pill to make it more readily available, while the restrictions on abortion were also largely lifted during the 1970s. After being encouraged into the home during the 1940s and 1950s, women fortified by feminist ideology were now encouraged to take up paid employment where they enjoyed equal pay with men and were assisted by government-funded childcare centres. With its population reaching 15 million by early 1982, Australia was becoming more comfortable with its claim over the continent, particularly as this period also saw a substantial shift of population north to Queensland and the Northern Territory and across to Western Australia, which passed the one million mark in 1971, even though most of it was concentrated in Perth.

When Darwin was devastated by a cyclone on Christmas Eve, 1974, most of the population of 48 000 were evacuated in a massive airlift. The fury of the storm renewed questions about the suitability of the tropics for white occupation. However, despite several voices suggesting that the northern capital be abandoned to the wilful elements, a reconstruction commission was established which successfully resurrected the isolated outpost. Ironically, part of the northward shift in population was due to a tourist boom in Queensland, where white Australians now welcomed thousands of Japanese and other Asian tourists, and where Asian investment, particularly in real estate development, increasingly underpinned the state's prosperity. Most of this shifting population still headed for urban areas. Despite persistent attempts to do so, Australia was largely unsuccessful in shifting population from the south-eastern coastal cities. Mining developments required little manpower, while the continuing mechanisation of farming, and the amalgamation of smaller farms into more economic units, released people from rural pursuits faster than they could be attracted by closer settlement schemes. Drifting into the cities, they joined the continuing influx of immigrants, most of whom never went further than the city in which they landed before settling down. While urban Australians made forays into the bush, it was usually by car or four-wheel-drive vehicle rather than by bushwalking. There remained a continuing ambivalence about the bush that was expressed in the slang term—'bush bashing'—for going into the bush in a four-wheel-drive vehicle.

The bush, or nature, was capable of fighting back as it always had done, dealing out storms, floods, droughts and even earthquakes to test the resolve of Australians to remain in occupation of the unforgiving continent. Fifteen people died in bushfires in Victoria in 1969, six of them after being caught in their cars on the four-lane highway connecting Melbourne and Geelong. Eighty fires raged across Victoria that day, battled by 130000 largely volunteer firefighters. Worse was to come in 1983 when massive bushfires across Victoria and South Australia killed 72 people and burnt out more than three million hectares and more than 2000 homes. Ironically, the new-found predilection for so-called native gardens, with their highly flammable eucalypt trees, made even the outer suburbs of Australian cities susceptible to the flames. Rain, or the prolonged lack of it during a drought, could also test the resolve of Australians. Torrential rainfall across much of eastern Australia in January 1974 saw widespread flooding submerge thousands of houses in Brisbane and the Gold Coast and drown 14 people, while prolonged droughts still brought despair to farmers, forcing some to retreat to the cities.

Some of the farmers abandoning their farms had taken up land on irrigation schemes in the Murray–Darling basin in the 1950s, ringbarked the eucalypt trees and planted crops or created lush orchards growing fruit for the British market. Britain's entry into the Common Market had cut into their incomes. But worse was to come as the saline water table gradually rose in the absence of the thirsty eucalypts. Plants withered and died from the salt, while the rivers carried the salt downstream. The area affected was estimated in 1975 to be more than 9000 square kilometres. As geographer J. M. Powell notes, 'A creeping death was moving inexorably over Victoria's northern plains.' It was not only in the 'garden state' of Victoria. In Western Australia, the main diversion dam of the Ord River scheme had been opened with much fanfare by Prime Minister Billy McMahon in 1972 and 300 farmers settled on their small allotments of some 250 hectares to grow cotton. With their plants beset by boll weevils, so much DDT was applied in a vain attempt to stop their depredations that the costs of pesticide eroded any profit they might have been able to make. Cotton was abandoned as the surviving farmers, subsidised to stay on, cast around for alternative crops.

The disappointment of the Ord River scheme was just one example of the deflated confidence by Australians in their ability to conquer nature. Early settlers had introduced alien plants and animals that had proceeded to despoil the fragile ecology of the continent and even threaten the European hold on the interior. The spread of prickly pear across Queensland had rendered millions of hectares useless for pastoralism or cropping, while the recurrent plagues of rabbits devastated pastures. The scientific eradication of prickly pear and the control of rabbits by the myxomatosis virus during the 1950s had given confidence to those who thought nature might yet be conquered, that white Australians could continue to shape the landscape to suit their balance sheets.

The ongoing need to occupy the continent and subdue the wilderness increasingly conflicted with the growing awareness of the Australian ecology that was widely depicted as fragile. When the Victorian government attempted in the late 1960s to develop the Little Desert area of north-west Victoria, one of the last pristine areas of the state, it faced stiff opposition from a growing lobby of environmentally conscious people. While the government argued predictably that 'the country could not afford not to develop land', it was forced to back down by the mainly urban environmentalists who questioned the underlying rationale for the desert's despoilation, that it was necessary to 'justify possession'. As environmental views became increasingly accepted around the world, Australians would increasingly argue that their possession was justified by their lack of rapacious development of environmentally sensitive areas, that they were holding the continent in trust for the world and for future generations. With the environmental effects of development being increasingly apparent, white Australians made uncomfortable comparisons between the effects of their use of the land over 200 years and the Aboriginal use over many millennia.

Academic study of Aboriginal society, its history and its archaeology, blossomed in the 1970s with more than 100 books being published on the impact of European invasion upon Australia's indigenous people. The increased knowledge about the longevity of Aboriginal occupation, which now was believed to span some 40 000 years, and the understanding about the complexity of their culture caused unsettling conclusions to be drawn by white Australians. Historian Lyndall Ryan observed how Aborigines did not

> *. . . view their past in European terms. Aborigines are not concerned to know when they arrived in Australia because they know that their cultural existence began here. They have no cultural roots in another part of the world. This is a concept that few white Australians, whose cultural roots lie outside Australia, can understand.*

They could more readily understand the extent of the war on the Australian frontier which was played out for them across the pages of countless history books. 'The great Australian silence', that anthropologist W. E. H. Stanner had complained of in 1968, had been broken. By the time that Bernard Smith delivered his Boyer Lectures on ABC Radio in 1980, pointing to the 'locked cupboard' of Australian history, it had already been broken open and its disturbing contents displayed by historians to a generation of students. Aboriginal voices were also being heard, both in ongoing campaigns for land rights and in a growing body of literature, with novels, poems and plays by Aboriginal writers opening windows for white Australians into their indigenous worlds.

Under pressure from southern sympathisers, and in accord with his electoral mandate, the Whitlam government accepted the recommendations of a royal commission in 1974 that all missions and reserves in the Northern Territory, where most of the Territory's Aboriginal people lived, should be passed to the control of Aboriginal land councils and that other traditional lands be purchased by a government land fund, with the land being held in trust in perpetuity on behalf of Aboriginal communities. The legislation was not passed until 1976 when the Fraser government continued the Whitlam initiative. Under the Northern Territory legislation, the Gurindji people finally received title to some of their land at Wattie Creek, although most of the best land in the Territory still remained firmly under the control of white pastoralists with their leasehold titles.

While public sympathy for the Aboriginal cause increased, the official reaction remained mixed. Although land rights were extended to many Aborigines under federal jurisdiction, the great majority of Aboriginal Australians lived in the states. South Australia followed the federal government, ceding some ten per cent of its land in 1981, all of it distant desert country in the far north-west of the state, to its traditional owners, the Pitjantjatjara people. However, in Queensland and Western Australia, states where the development ethos still held sway and Aboriginal demands posed a threat to their dreams of easy wealth, the discredited policy of assimilation was still in force. Queensland's populist premier, Joh Bjelke-Peterson, who had been involved as a contractor in the bulldozing of Queensland's extensive brigalow country, spoke with almost a religious fervour of mining and tourist developments that were transforming his extensive state and told Aborigines who wanted the development bulldozer to be kept from their settlements: 'I want you to be a Queenslander like me.' He warned officials in his lands department against bureaucrats from Canberra buying up pastoral leases with the intention of having the land 'slipped to the blacks'. Although the federal *Racial Discrimination Act* of 1975 was passed under the external affairs power of the constitution, allowing the federal government to override the states, both Labor and Liberal governments usually shrank from the possible political costs that could be incurred in confronting a determined state premier.

Bjelke-Peterson was supported by pastoralists and mining companies concerned at the possible implications for their balance sheets of Aboriginal land rights, while farmers, and even some urban Australians, worried where the Aboriginal claims might end. They disputed whether Aborigines should be accorded a greater moral claim to land from which they had been dispossessed and which had then been developed and farmed by successive generations of white Australians. The fact was that, after 200 years of occupation, white Australians had developed intimate links with land that sometimes had been in their family's possession for perhaps four or five generations. Some could look out onto homestead graveyards where great-grandparents rested after the back-breaking work of transforming the landscape for European purposes. As Frank Crowley observed in his survey of the 1970s, *Tough Times*, there was a growing perception that

> ... *white Australian farmers with their ancestral claim to the land did not have as many rights as Aborigines, even though their forefathers had hewn their properties out of the bush over a hundred years previously, and their descendants had cultivated, nurtured and improved them.*

White Australians in southern cities could be satisfied that they had assuaged their consciences by ceding control of distant Crown lands but were unsettled to discover Aborigines in their midst making claims on their urban landscape.

Even in Tasmania, where all Aborigines were thought to have disappeared with the death of Trucanini, the 1981 census recorded 2688 people proclaiming their Aboriginal heritage. Many were the descendants of Tasmanian Aboriginal women who had lived on Bass Strait islands with sealers. Overall, the number of Australians proclaiming their Aboriginality had increased during the 1970s from 106000 to 160000. It was not because of a surge in the Aboriginal birthrate, but because of people now feeling able to declare their background without fear of discrimination. As well, official programs to encourage the education of Aboriginal people and otherwise provide for their welfare made it advantageous for people to declare their Aboriginal origins. With Aboriginal groups mounting serious challenges to the legality of their dispossession and shining an international spotlight on widespread instances of continued mistreatment, the implications were serious for the claim of moral proprietorship of the continent by non-indigenous Australians just at the time when their claim of effective proprietorship was more secure than ever. Their attempts to resolve this dilemma would preoccupy Australians for the rest of the century.

Recommended Reading

Stephen Alomes and Catherine Jones (eds), 1991, *Australian Nationalism: A Documentary History*, Angus&Robertson, Sydney.

E. M. Andrews, 1985, *Australia and China: The Ambiguous Relationship*, Melbourne University Press, Melbourne.

F. K. Crowley, 1986, *Tough Times: Australia in the Seventies*, Heinemann, Melbourne.

F. K. Crowley, 1973, *Modern Australia in Documents*, Vol. 2, Wren Publishing, Melbourne.

Ross Fitzgerald, 1985, *A History of Queensland: From 1915 to the 1980s*, University of Queensland Press, Brisbane.

Robin Gerster, 1987, *Big-Noting: The Heroic Theme in Australian War Writing*, Melbourne University Press, Melbourne.

W. J. Hudson (ed.), 1980, *Australia in World Affairs 1971–1975*, George Allen & Unwin, Sydney.

Mark Lopez, 2000, *The Origins of Multiculturalism in Australian Politics*, Melbourne University Press, Melbourne.

Noel McLachlan, 1989, *Waiting for the Revolution*, Penguin, Melbourne.

David Marr (ed.), 1994, *Patrick White: Letters*, Random House, Sydney.

Harry Martin, 1989, *Angels and Arrogant Gods: Migration Officers and Migrants Reminisce 1945–85*, Australian Government Publishing Service Press, Canberra.

Brian Murphy, 1993, *The Other Australia: Experiences of Migration*, Cambridge University Press, Melbourne.

J. M. Powell, 1988, *An Historical Geography of Modern Australia: The Restive Fringe*, Cambridge University Press, Cambridge.

Review by Lyndall Ryan in *Historical Studies*, October 1982.

Gough Whitlam, 1985, *The Whitlam Government*, Viking, Melbourne.

22

'THE END
OF THE
GREAT
LIE'

In January 1988, 11 sailing ships slipped through the heads of Sydney Harbour to mark the bicentenary of European settlement. Previously, such occasions had been celebrations of European progress in the Antipodes and had been marked by re-enactments of Captain Phillip's landing at Sydney Cove, with Aborigines perhaps making a token resistance to the peaceful landing or no resistance at all. This time, Aborigines from around Australia converged on Sydney to protest at two centuries of European occupation while the official theme for the Bicentenary—'living together'— attempted to assuage their anger. In an explicit rejection of that original supplanting of their sovereignty over the continent, more than 20 000 Aboriginal people and their supporters marched behind a flag of their own, designed in the elemental Australian colours of black, red and gold. As in 1938, they argued that the anniversary of their dispossession was not a cause for celebration but a cause for sorrow. Nobel Prize-winning novelist Patrick White refused to have anything to do with the celebrations as there was 'too much to be ashamed about'. Other Australians agreed but most partied nonetheless.

The Sydney Opera House, cultural symbol of European civilisation, was a major focus for the celebrations, providing an implicit moral justification for the British occupation. Governor Phillip's 'gift' of European civilisation could now be seen as having been established in the former 'wilderness'. While this reassured many Australians, the Bicentenary prompted many others to reassess the moral basis of their presence in a continent when it was being vigorously challenged by the descendants of the original occupiers. The question of whether Phillip's landing constituted an act of invasion or merely of settlement became a matter of considerable historical and political debate. Some dismissed the distinction, and any resulting guilt, by arguing that the Aboriginal occupation of the continent was doomed and suggesting that the Aborigines were fortunate that it was the British, rather than some other European power, which had done the dispossessing. As conservative commentator Padraic McGuinness argued in the *Australian* in June 1994, 'Given the alternatives of the times, the Aborigines were extremely lucky that it was the relatively gentle British ... who got here first.' It was an argument the descendants of the decimated Aborigines found difficult to accept. Despite the many historians examining the 'war on the frontier', many Australians remained ignorant of its horrors and continued, like their colonial forebears, to regard the drawn-out process of dispossession as being imbued with a sense of sad inevitability.

To mark the Bicentenary, a new parliament house costing more than $1 billion was constructed in Canberra to replace the 'temporary' and outmoded edifice that had served that role for 60 years. The new building required the removal of a hill overlooking the capital. The parliament was then constructed and some of the hill placed back on top to partly cover it. So the parliament burrows into the ancient soil, making an emphatic and unmistakable statement of possession. If the lesson is lost on anyone, a huge aluminium flagpole, the tallest aluminium structure in the world, towers over the parliament flying an enormous Australian flag, albeit with a British Union Jack still incorporated in its design. The alien nature of the construction was mitigated by incorporating links to the pre-existing Aboriginal society, dotting the walls with Aboriginal art and setting Aboriginal-designed patterns into the pathways outside. It was a means of obtaining belated Aboriginal concurrence in the British occupation of the continent while still proceeding painfully towards some acknowledgment of Aboriginal land rights.

The other major part of the official Bicentenary spending went to extend roads into the interior and, most symbolically, to tar the highway that skirts its way around most of the continent's coastline. It allowed modern Australians to mimic on land what Flinders had done from the sea nearly 200 years before. It was not uncommon to see Australians, particularly upon retirement, take up the challenge of charting the continent's circumference from the comfort of a campervan, thereby symbolically making their own individual claim of belonging before perhaps retiring, as an increasing proportion of them did, to a hobby farm in the bush. Canberra, with its array of grand public buildings, from its war memorials to its art galleries, also became increasingly a place of pilgrimage for modern Australians. The Union

Jack that these visitors observed on the parliamentary flagpole was a reflection of past certainties rather than contemporary realities. Australia had been transformed from the hesitant federation that had originally adopted that symbol of dependence.

In 1788, Captain Arthur Phillip had claimed legal proprietorship over New South Wales in the name of England's King George. The following year, the French had raised the radical banner of republicanism over Europe. Its shadow rarely fell across Australia. Although republicanism appeared in the demands of the gold-diggers of the 1850s and the arguments of the *Bulletin* in the 1880s and 1890s, its appeal was always limited among a people whose loyalties to empire often overrode their loyalties to nation. For more than 200 years, Australia's relatively egalitarian society has retained its allegiance to King George and his successors. This has been due partly to the fresh infusions of loyal Britons who have continually diluted Australian nationalism. But it was also due to the implications of republicanism in an Australian setting. It is not just a different form of government but entails cutting the bonds of empire and asserting a measure of independence that Australians have not yet been prepared to do. There are also considerable practical difficulties in achieving a republic under the provisions of the constitution which requires approval of a majority of electors and a majority of states before changes can be made to it. A republic is such a fundamental change, with uncertain practical benefits, that it would be impossible for it to be achieved without clear bipartisan support. Until recently, this was not possible.

Nevertheless, the support for a republic was increasing in step with the growing sense of Australian nationalism. In 1964, the nation saw its first national newspaper, the *Australian*, at the same time as the Australian film industry was beginning its renaissance. In acknowledgment of the trend, advertisers increasingly played on nationalism to sell their products. Whereas the wartime prime minister, John Curtin, could not conceive of any national anthem but 'God Save the King', his Labor successor in 1972, Gough Whitlam, made 'Advance Australia Fair' the national song. Although Malcolm Fraser reinstated God Save the Queen in 1976, Australians voted for Whitlam's choice when they were asked at a referendum in 1977, choosing it in preference to both the British anthem and 'Waltzing Matilda'. The influx of non-British immigrants has seen a gradual erosion in the support for the British monarchy ruling in Australia. However, the link between nationalism and republicanism was not a direct one. Even Whitlam's sacking by the Queen's representative, Governor General Sir John Kerr, in 1975 gave only short-lived impetus to the republican movement before it died away again. Since the Queen had not been complicit in Kerr's action, the British monarchy's position in Australia largely escaped unscathed. Although Bob Hawke might have deprecated the need for a republic, the growing public support for such a move provided a further sign that Australians were becoming increasingly comfortable with their proprietorship over the continent and thereby increasingly comfortable with the notion of standing alone in the Asian region without the soothing reminders of empire. The removal of the last constitutional connection to Britain, and perhaps the simultaneous disappearance of the Union Jack from the Australian flag, would also help Australia to adopt a chameleon-like pose in Asia by removing reminders of its past as a European outpost. At the 1993 federal election, Hawke's successor as Labor leader, Paul Keating, had the republic firmly on his program and, with his re-election, could claim a mandate for pushing on with moves to introduce it. In a more controversial move, he also proposed removing the Union Jack from the Australian flag, something from which he later retreated. One of his main arguments for Australia becoming a republic has been to change the way the country is perceived in Asia. As he told an audience in Singapore in January 1996, the republic was necessary for Australia's 'long term national cohesion', arguing that it would

> . . . help describe us to ourselves and to others. It will help define our complex identity, help articulate our ambitions and values, help fuse the links between the old Australia and the new.

There were also party political advantages in adopting a measure that had the potential to divide his conservative opponents. Although the constitutional problems of achieving a republic by the proposed date of 2001 were considerable, the barrier to change was gradually breaking down as conservative politicians began to propose the sort of republic they would favour rather than blindly resisting the inevitable. As a sign of how far Australia had moved, there was considerable support for appointing a prominent Aborigine as the founding president. Queensland academic Richard Nile pointed to the 'very strong psychical and emotional link between Aboriginality and the republican debate', suggesting that a proposal for an Aboriginal president would ensure public acceptance of the republic.

For more than 200 years, and despite occasional good intentions, British Australians had played the part of invaders, sweeping the Aborigines off their land and into the dustbin of history. They claimed the legal proprietorship of the continent by engaging in the legal fiction of *terra nullius* which claimed that Australia was a land without owners when claimed for the British king by Captain Phillip. As such the Aborigines could have no rights to the land they had occupied for perhaps 120 000 years. Despite the public commitment to land rights by prime ministers Whitlam and Fraser, the provision of land rights remained patchy during the 1970s. Where it was conceded, it was presented more as an act of charity than a recognition of an inherent right. The federal government remained reluctant to impose a national system on the states. Indeed, when the newly elected Labor prime minister, Bob Hawke, proposed extending the land rights system of the Northern Territory to Western Australia after his accession to power in 1983, he was forced to back down in the face of opposition from the mining companies which played on the fears of Western Australians that Aborigines were taking over the state. The Australian Mining Industry Council had argued in 1981 that land rights, and the possible curbs on mining development that they would entail, would undermine Australia's 'special reponsibility to make its resources available to the world community on equitable terms'. One of their leading spokesmen, Hugh Morgan of the Western Mining Corporation, went somewhat further in 1984, suggesting that the granting of land rights would represent 'a symbolic step back to the world of paganism, superstition, fears and darkness', implying that it would endanger the basis of Australian prosperity and infringe the rights of property-owning suburbanites. Exactly a century before, a Northern Territory pastoralist had compared Aborigines to Siberian wolves who must give way to the 'tide of civilization' or be crushed like 'the venomous serpent' for resisting 'progress'. There was a clear connection across the century between these sentiments and those of Morgan and other miners. But this time there were many more voices raised in support of Aboriginal rights.

In 1985, there was a symbolic handover of Ayers Rock, the largest monolith in the world, to its traditional Aboriginal owners who restored its Aboriginal name—Uluru—and then allowed the National Parks Service to administer it. Other geographical features around Australia have also been renamed with their original Aboriginal names. While explorers were not averse to adopting Aboriginal names for mountains and rivers that they 'discovered', it was done as part of the claiming process in a way that incorporated the Aboriginal names, along with the landscape they described, as possessions of the supplanting society. In contrast, the renaming of features that were given European names, which has been done largely at the behest of the Aboriginal people, effectively expunges from the modern mental landscape the historic traces of the European act of dispossession and reasserts the Aboriginal right to be recognised as the prior occupiers of the continent. As such, it has proved as unsettling to some present-day Australians as the original renaming would have been to Aborigines. At the same time, some acts of renaming have been done by white Australians anxious to connect their present to the Aboriginal past. Despite its renaming, Uluru remained a prime tourist destination, not only for overseas visitors but for white Australians who had their own sense of the rock's sacredness. The white person's dreaming track wound to the summit of its red heights from where, close enough to the centre of the continent, they could unknowingly trample the susceptibilities of the rock's Aboriginal keepers, who preferred that the rock not be climbed, and symbolically assert their own individual claims of proprietorship over the continent whose red soil spreads out in all directions.

The restoration of Uluru and other territories into the hands of their traditional owners helped to create the impression in the minds of many white Australians that Aboriginal people were receiving more than their due and even beginning to undermine the claim of white Australians on the continent. However, Aboriginal people knew they were still being excluded from large areas of Australia that were controlled by pastoral leasehold, while the land that had been restored to their control was largely land for which no economic use had been found. Where mineral reserves were discovered on Aboriginal land, they had limited say in deciding whether they would be developed. In order to establish a lasting *modus vivendi* between indigenous and non-indigenous Australians, and perhaps circumscribe the Aboriginal claims, a committee of prominent Australians was established in 1979 under the chairmanship of the former Reserve Bank chairman and head of the Council for Aboriginal Affairs, H. C. Coombs, to push for a formal treaty between the two societies that would allow them to share the continent. It was unable to make headway with its proposal, although the idea was taken up by the Pope during his visit to Alice Springs in 1986 when he called for a 'just and proper settlement'.

Prior to the Bicentenary, with Aborigines threatening to disrupt the national celebrations, Hawke resuscitated the idea of a peace treaty or compact with the Aborigines which could include some acknowledgment in the Australian constitution of the prior Aboriginal occupation of the continent. But no agreement was reached on what such a treaty should contain. Aborigines remained suspicious of its purpose, while conservative politicians worried about its implications. In June 1988, the future Liberal Prime Minister, John Howard, argued that a treaty would constitute a 'form of apartheid', suggesting instead that Australia 'get back to the notion, whether in immigration or Aboriginal affairs, that we are one nation, one people, with one future'. Considering the abysmal health and other living conditions which cause Aboriginal people to enjoy a life expectancy some 20 years shorter than other Australians, it was not surprising that Aborigines wondered how they could share in the common future to which Howard had alluded. There was, however, some attempt to address their plight that same year with the establishment of an Aboriginal and Torres Strait Islander Commission which extended much more control over their lives to Aboriginal people. Most importantly, the Act setting up the commission acknowledged in its preamble that the Aborigines and Torres Strait Islanders were 'the prior occupiers and original owners of this land', although it still implied that the legal ownership of the continent had somehow passed from Aboriginal hands.

Meanwhile, non-Aboriginal Australians were continuing to come to terms with the continent and with its original inhabitants in ways that increased the support among Europeans for the Aboriginal cause and which, in turn, helped to further secure the non-Aboriginal claim over the continent. Native trees and bushes were introduced into Australian gardens, bringing native birds back into the cities that had been home for decades to introduced sparrows, pigeons and starlings. Popular television programs, and four-wheel-drive vehicles, took urban Australians safely into the bush in the same way as the *Bulletin* had brought stories of the bush safely into the cities for the amusement of their grandparents. Books on 'bush tucker' and bush medicines, produced for the coffee tables of urban Australians rather than for practical use, informed them of the physical secrets of the bush, the plants that had allowed Aborigines to live for so long and so well, those that were safe to eat and how to prepare them. At the same time, the growth of the environmental movement raised the consciousness of all Australians about the damage done to the environment in just two centuries of European settlement compared with the Aboriginal use of the land over millennia. Scientists who had formerly sought to conquer nature in Australia now increasingly sought to adapt their methods to the rhythms of the land. As the anthropologist Norman Tindale had observed, Aborigines traditionally based their claims of proprietorship over their territories partly 'by reason of knowledge'—that is, through their understanding of the annual cycle of nature's bounty. By acquainting themselves with the physical secrets of the bush, white Australians sought to share in the claim of moral proprietorship enjoyed by the Aborigines.

The children of white Australians were tucked up in bed with the spiritual secrets of the bush, absorbing the Dreamtime stories of the Aborigines as they read of the rainbow serpent rather than of Enid Blyton's Noddy. During the 1980s, Aboriginal art began to take the place of the Heidelberg artists on the living room walls of 'middle Australia' and to be reproduced on coffee mugs and T-shirts, imparting its secrets of the Aborigines' relationship to the landscape and its creatures. Much of the art represented Dreamtime stories confirming Aboriginal ownership of particular parts of the continent, but it was usually not seen as such by its non-indigenous purchasers. Instead, it was embraced as providing closer and distinctively Australian connections to the landscape. When a new Qantas service was being initiated to Japan, the jumbo jet of Australia's national airline replaced its familiar red kangaroo on the plane's tail with an all-over Aboriginal design of kangaroos painted according to their ancient motif. Qantas claimed that it constituted 'the world's largest piece of modern art' which would be 'carrying the ancient dreamtime journeys of Australia's Aboriginal people further than ever before'. By doing so, an Aboriginal motif was presented to the world as being quintessentially Australian. It was a declaration to the world that the continent's Aboriginal past had been subsumed by the supplanting society of Europeans. Similarly, a wine from 'south-eastern Australia' was marketed in Britain in 1995 under the name 'Tarrawingee', declaring itself to have been grown in a region 'steeped in Aboriginal history'. How this was meant to affect the quality of the wine was not explained, although the description of the wine as 'a fine, stylish blend giving a full sunny flavour with a hint of exotic fruit' might have been used as a description of the Australian people, or at least of how modern Australians would like others to see them. Drinkers could presumably imbibe the wine's Aboriginal heritage.

By sharing in parts of the Aboriginal knowledge, however inadequately, white Australians were hoping to share in the intimate Aboriginal connection to the landscape. In 1943, Marjorie Barnard and Flora Eldershaw had lamented in *My Australia*, with its possessive title, that the expected demise of the Aborigines would also see the demise of

> ...*their close and unique knowledge of the Australian earth. They knew its secrets, but they could not transmit them to us. We have had to learn all over again for ourselves and raise up images in our own idiom. We shall never know the earth as they know it, we brought too much with us.*

Now that the Aborigines were not dying out, white Australians could again attempt to incorporate the Aborigines' spiritual links to the land into their own psychic life, and establish a claim of moral proprietorship that connects to the longevity of the Aboriginal occupation.

Just as many postwar Australians celebrated the convict background that their parents and grandparents had been anxious to disavow, so now there were a growing number of people of mixed descent celebrating the Aboriginality that, in some cases, their parents and grandparents had been anxious to conceal. Perhaps the most well known was Sally Morgan whose new-found Aboriginality was proclaimed in her bestselling book, *My Place*, the title of which provided an implicit rejoinder to Barnard Eldershaw's earlier work by being both a belated celebration of Morgan's new-found Aboriginality and an assertion of Aboriginal land rights and sovereignty. In its wake, and with Aborigines continuing to seek recognition of their land rights in the courts, the struggle over both these issues came to dominate the political agenda. Some non-indigenous Australians feared that the end-point of Aboriginal demands might mean their own dispossession, although Aborigines usually reassured them that they were simply wanting to share the continent on a new basis of equality and respect for the rights of both communities. As Hobbles Danayarri of the Yarralin community in central Australia assured historian Deborah Bird Rose in 1980,

> *I'm speaking about now. We're friends together because we own Australia, every one of us no matter who—white and black. We [can] come together, join in ... That will be all right. That will make it better from that big trouble. You know before, Captain Cook made a lot of cruel, you know. Now these days, these days we'll be friendly, we'll be love each other, we'll be mates.*

The chance truly to be mates finally came in 1992 when the notion of *terra nullius* was finally swept away in a historic decision by the High Court.

The court was hearing a case brought by Eddie Mabo and several other people from the Murray Islands in the Torres Strait, almost within sight of the island where Captain Cook had claimed New South Wales for England. Mabo died before he could hear the court throw out the notion of *terra nullius* and declare that the Murray Islanders had always enjoyed a form of traditional native title over their island which had never been superseded by European occupation. The implications were considerable for Aborigines in similar positions on the mainland. Fearmongers talked of the decision threatening the houses of every white Australian. To his enduring credit, Prime Minister Keating managed to allay such fears and to convert this legal decision into a political compromise acceptable to the Aborigines, the mining companies and many, but not all, white Australians. On 21 December 1993, after months of difficult and sometimes heated negotiation with the states and other interested bodies, Keating successfully enshrined this form of native title in legislation, establishing a tribunal to assess land claims and a fund to compensate those Aborigines whose land had been alienated. It also confirmed the freehold and leasehold titles of other Australians. The passage of the Act, proclaimed Keating, marked 'the end of the great lie of *terra nullius* and the beginning of a new deal ... a turning point for all Australians'. It might now be possible for Aboriginal and other Australians to concede that both groups have rightful claims of moral proprietorship over the continent and to agree to share it.

While Aborigines busily gathered evidence for future native title cases, Keating encouraged non-Aboriginal Australians to assimilate the heritage of Aboriginal people, including their all-important links to the land, into the wider Australian nation and thereby finally make secure their claim over the continent. Keating argued that indigenous art would allow non-Aboriginal Australians to 'learn about who we are, and how we fit into the story of the continent' and claimed that 'the heritage of indigenous Australians' was part of

> ...our nation's heritage. It is an element of what sets us apart from
> all other nations. It informs our understanding of the land, and
> our sense of belonging.

Although such sentiments were dismissed by National Party leader Tim Fischer, who claimed to be 'as Australian as any Aborigine', they found favour with many Australians, who responded supportively when the successful Aboriginal athlete Cathy Freeman completed a lap of honour at the 1994 Commonwealth Games in Canada carrying the Aboriginal and Australian flags. The Aboriginal flag was subsequently recognised as an official Australian flag. When Keating travelled to Singapore in early 1996, he was careful to incorporate the continent's Aboriginal past into the new image of the Australian nation that he projected for his Asian audience. Disclaiming any attempt to portray Australians as Asians, Keating argued instead that:

> *We can only be Australian and can only relate to our neighbours as Australians. Our history, including the 40 000 year history of our indigenous people and the histories of the 150 different cultures from which Australians derive, make us unique in the world.*

By wrapping themselves in their continent's Aboriginal past, and overlaying the British past with the multicultural present, nonindigenous Australians sought legitimacy for their own occupation of the continent and for their presence in the Asian region.

Despite the introduction of the *Native Title Act*, many other issues remained unresolved. For instance, what official status should be given to traditional Aboriginal law? Can Aborigines claim trial under Aboriginal law rather than European law? Moreover, while the issue of land rights seemed to have been largely resolved, the more fundamental question of sovereignty remained. If Aborigines had title to their lands in 1788, surely they also enjoyed sovereignty over the continent and its islands. Starting with the 'tent embassy' in 1972 some Aborigines have already raised this question, demanding that they be regarded as a nation within a nation. A provisional Aboriginal government was established, with Tasmanian Michael Mansell as its secretary, explicitly challenging European sovereignty over the continent. Most Aborigines, though, were content to explore ways of sharing the country. A council for Aboriginal reconciliation was established in 1991 with support from both major political parties and with the stated aim of finding 'a way for indigenous and other Australians to share this country as equals'. The rationale for the process was set out by the outgoing prime minister, Bob Hawke, in December 1991:

> *If you're really serious in this country as you come to the end of this century, the first century of our existence as a nation, and you want proudly to take Australia into the 21st century, there is no chance that you're going to be able to do that unless you do have a reconciliation.*

As journalist Cameron Forbes observed in the *Weekend Australian* in August 1994, the successful conclusion to the reconciliation process would represent 'a gift from the Aboriginal people' that would finally 'give Australia moral legitimacy'.

For more than 200 years, white Australians had sought to claim the effective and moral proprietorship of the continent by populating its 'empty wastes' and developing its resources, particularly by replacing pastoralism with schemes of closer settlement that would allow for tilling of the soil. With the spread of environmental awareness, Australians now sought to claim the moral proprietorship of the interior by not developing all of its resources, by not encouraging immigration, by taking a leading role in international forums for promoting environmental protection and by respecting indigenous peoples. Areas of Australia from the Great Barrier Reef to the wilderness of south-west Tasmania have been declared world heritage areas from which developers are excluded. It effectively absolved Australians from the need to occupy all the distant and difficult corners of the continent, satisfying by other means the familiar need to establish their claim of moral proprietorship over the continent. There were still voices calling on Australians to 'populate the north', but they were meeting with much less resonance than in the more anxious postwar times.

When Northern Territory politician Marshall Perron called in September 1993 for greater Asian immigration into the Territory so that its still small population could increase to as much as 17 million, a correspondent to the *Australian* disputed that the continent was underpopulated and warned that there were 'any number of environmental problems that indicate our present population may not be sustainable over the long term and may have to be reduced'. Such sentiments were widely shared and represented a dramatic retreat from the historic push to populate the north that Perron was still advocating. Sustainable development became a buzz-word of the 1990s as Australians sought to reconcile their urge to develop the continent with their concern for the environment. Some looked to the Aborigines for guidance. The president of the National Farmers Federation, Rick Farley, suggested in July 1994 that their shared 'concern for sustainable use of the country' could 'help bind together Aboriginal and non-Aboriginal people in rural Australia'. There was some realisation that both groups shared roots to the continent and to the wider and ecologically fragile planet. As such, a sharing of knowledge was required, with farmers looking to traditional Aboriginal methods for guidance in their modern land management, particularly of arid areas, while Aboriginal councils drew upon scientific expertise to assist them in managing lands for non-traditional uses.

The more measured development and populating of the continent was a sign, not only of an increasing environmental awareness, but also of an increasing sense of ease with their geographic situation in Asia. Although the foreign minister, Bill Hayden, had urged in 1984 that Australia develop the capacity to make nuclear bombs as a deterrent to Indonesia, his advice was rejected by a government more anxious to build bridges to its neighbours than to build walls against them. The Hawke government accepted the more sanguine view of defence analyst Paul Dibb who declared in 1986 that Australia faced no immediate, major threat and that it would have 'at least ten years' warning of a substantial military threat'. It was clear from a calculation of regional military capabilities, argued Dibb, that 'an attempt to lodge and sustain substantial forces in Australia' was simply not possible in the foreseeable future and Australia would have plenty of warning of it becoming possible. Australia's historic fear of an Asian invasion that had underpinned its defence and foreign policies for so long was laid to rest. As Dibb concluded, there was 'no conceivable prospect of any power contemplating invasion of our continent and subjugation of our population'.

Dibb's confidence was also predicated on the relatively novel observation that Australia was 'one of the most secure countries in the world', being distant from likely centres of global military conflict and 'surrounded by large expanses of water which make it difficult to attack'. He also dismissed Australia's historic fears concerning the vulnerability of its sea lanes and the possibility of it being held to hostage by a naval blockade. Dibb pointed out that no island nation has ever been successfully blockaded and that 'evasive routing' of its shipping could defeat such a blockade. The length of Australia's coastline would prove as much a problem for an enemy as for the defenders. This observation marked a fundamental reappraisal of Australia's defence predicament. Dibb ended any lingering expeditionary force mentality among the services and called for a major realignment of Australian forces, shifting the weight of the Australian defence forces from its comfortable southern locales around Sydney and Melbourne. Dibb suggested that the most likely threat that Australia would have to face would be 'low-level harrassment and raids' and that the defence forces should be concentrated on dealing with such possibilities. His views were widely shared. An opinion poll in 1987 found that only 54 per cent of respondents were able to identify a foreign threat and the most likely one was distant Libya. Only 16 per cent suggested Indonesia, while six per cent nominated either Japan or China. This was less than the eight per cent of Australians who thought the United States posed the most likely threat.

Australia was projecting itself as a peaceful and worthwhile neighbour rather than as an outpost of the British Empire, or as a stalking horse for the Americans, in the hope that this would provide a more secure defence of its still lightly populated continent. In the absence of the great powers, there really was little alternative. Determined attempts were made to strengthen diplomatic, military and economic links with Asian countries that Australia formerly perceived as possible threats. In 1990, Australia signed a landmark treaty with Indonesia which divided the continental shelf between Australia and Timor and allowed for the exploitation of the considerable resources that are believed to lie beneath it. This removed a potential source of great conflict since their seabed boundaries overlapped. As Prime Minister Paul Keating informed an audience in Singapore in January 1996, Australia now sought to assure its security 'in Asia rather than from Asia', while a defence agreement with Indonesia was based on the newly developed understanding that 'neither Australia nor Indonesia threatens the other and that we have common interests in the stability and security of the region around us'. There was even some notion of finding a 'great and powerful friend' among the nations of Asia as an eventual replacement for the United States. Perhaps with this in view, Australia encouraged Japan to take a greater international role by sending peacekeeping troops to Cambodia and backing Japan for a permanent seat on the UN Security Council. While no credible Asian invasion was in prospect, Australian fears became concentrated instead on the rising tide of Asian immigration that flowed towards Australia after the Vietnam War.

In the decade to 1986, some 100 000 Asian refugees were allowed into Australia. Their arrival at a time of relatively high unemployment sparked considerable opposition. Historian Geoffrey Blainey called in 1984 for the Labor government to stop the 'slow Asian takeover of Australia' which would see them become 'the inevitable possessors of this land'. Blainey warned that the rate of Asian immigration to Australia was too great for them to be absorbed without tension and that they were creating ghettoes in Australian cities. But the Hawke government rejected his call to reintroduce a discriminatory immigration policy at the same time as it was intent on encouraging Australia to 'enmesh' with the fast-developing countries of Asia. Instead, the immigration minister Stewart West claimed that the 'increasing Asianization of Australia was inevitable'. It was the growing economic power of these Asian countries, and Australia's growing dependence upon them, that was motivating the dramatic change in Australia's direction. In words that harkened back to previous parliamentary debates down the decades, Hawke reminded Australians that they were 'a country of just over 15 million people ... in a region of billions of people' and that any hint of 'prejudice against that region would be not only immoral but also manifestly against the present and future best interests of the people of this country'.

Nevertheless, and perhaps as a concession to the racist undercurrents, Australia was unnecessarily brutal in its treatment of the few hundred Asian refugees who reached Australia by boat in the late 1980s. Rather than acknowledging the refugee status of these people—who came mainly from war-wracked Cambodia—the government labelled them 'boat people', which thereby neutralised any appeal they might make to the sympathies of the electorate. And then it kept many of them incarcerated for years at a time in a camp at Port Hedland in the far north-west of Western Australia where they were isolated from sympathisers. Some of the refugees resorted to jumping from the roof of their building to try and draw attention to their prolonged incarceration. Others gained some success through the courts. Many were forcibly repatriated to Cambodia despite the inherent dangers to life in that troubled nation. The treatment of the refugees contrasted with Australia's embrace of Asia and was reminiscent of the worst excesses of the 'white Australia' policy. Behind the treatment lurked the lingering fears of Australia being swamped by an invasion of such alien refugees. Despite these hangovers from white Australia, the positive changes in the Australian outlook reflected an implicit assertion by Australians that they have largely secured the effective proprietorship of the continent, even if part of this security comes from the population adopting an increasingly Asian aspect.

One of the rationales for establishing a British colony in New South Wales had been to provide a replenishment port for ships trading with China and other places in the Orient. While such trade was important in the early years of settlement, the dominance of pastoralism in Australia effectively tied the colonial economies to the British woollen mills. The blinkered racism and rampant imperialism of the late 19th century limited the trade opportunities that might have developed between the Australian colonies and their near neighbours. Two hundred years on, Australia refocused on the economic opportunities in its region. Its geographic proximity to the 'teeming millions' of Asia was regarded as an opportunity rather than a threat, with bipartisan agreement that Australia's future lies in Asia. A report to the foreign affairs minister, Andrew Peacock, in 1978 had described Australia as being 'Western with a difference', with its geography providing Australia with a vantage point from which to develop closer relations with the fast-developing nations of Asia. Australia came to realise that it was being surpassed in its rate of economic growth, although not in the size of its economy, by an increasing number of its South-East Asian neighbours.

In 1987, Labor treasurer Paul Keating warned Australia that it would become a 'banana republic' unless it sloughed off its sense of national complacency and met head-on the economic challenge posed by its Asian neighbours. Keating's comment caused a panic on international financial markets and a major acceleration by Australia of its efforts to 'enmesh' itself with its neighbours in ways that would have been unthinkable to the fathers of federation. This is as much a security concern as an economic concern. As the former foreign minister, Gareth Evans, argued, 'extensive economic linkages create mutual interests which can work to restrain any resort to military conflict'. By 1996, more than half of Australia's trade was with the countries of east Asia.

In order to secure this future, the highly protected Australian economy was opened up during the late 1980s, with the exchange rate of the Australian dollar being largely left to the mercy of the international financial community and the protective tariff wall being largely dismantled. The move helped to destroy many of the low-skill, labour-intensive industries, such as cheap clothing and footwear, that had provided so much urban employment in the past. At the same time, technological developments were forcing hundreds of thousands of white-collar workers out of employment in industries such as banking. In their place, Australia planned to place greater reliance upon a more highly educated work force producing elaborately transformed manufactures, such as computers and communications equipment, while also expanding its service industries, particularly tourism and education.

Tens of thousands of Asian students began to attend Australian universities. In turn, young Australians travelling overseas no longer necessarily headed for London, as they did in the 1950s and 1960s, or to the United States as increasing numbers did in the 1970s. A popular destination became one of the countries of Asia, whether to soak up the sun on a Bali beach, to trek through Vietnam or to work in Japan. Writers such as Christopher Koch, with his books, *Across the Sea Wall* (1965) and *The Year of Living Dangerously* (1978), had been taking Australian readers into Asia for some years. Now Australian tourists followed these literary trails that wound through the cities and countryside of an Asian continent that had long been disparaged and feared by Australians in equal measure. In 1982, 53 000 Australians visited China. Back home, their children increasingly learnt Asian rather than European languages at school, with plans for 60 per cent of primary students to be learning one of four Asian languages by 2006. The Australian airline, Qantas, was transformed into an Asian airline with more of its passengers flying from one Asian country to another rather than flying Australians, as previously, on their spiritual treks to London. Around 40 per cent of Australia's immigrants were Asian, such that the composition of Australia's population was predicted to be about 15 per cent of Asian origin by 2030. Mosques and Buddhist temples became common sights in the major cities. While assuming an increasingly Asian complexion, Australians still looked to the seeming certainties of their military past to help them confront the uncertainties of the future.

The Australian ambivalence towards military displays that had been fostered by their experience in Vietnam was gradually laid to rest. In 1985, the former commander of the Australian 'advisers' in Vietnam, Ted Sarong, complained about the hostile reception accorded to the Vietnam veterans by the Australian public, suggesting that:

> *Something has happened to our breed. We are not the people with the spirit and standards of 1914 and 1939. We are a people who send their soldiers to war, and spit on them when they come back.*

As Robin Gerster has observed, the reputation of the veterans was resuscitated by a succession of books that appeared in the 1980s drawing connections between the gallantry at Gallipoli and the fighting in Vietnam. In the words of one Vietnam novel, the Australians in Vietnam, despite being an insignificant part of the American war, 'were secure in the knowledge [derived from Gallipoli] that the Australian is superior to the man of every other nation'. Several histories centred on the battle of Long Tan when a severely outnumbered Australian force managed to hold off a force of North Vietnamese regular troops, killing 245 of them for the loss of 17 Australians. One of the books on the battle was subtitled 'The Legend of Anzac Upheld', while one of the military volumes in the official history of Australia's participation in the war was titled, *To Long Tan*. It was part of the process of absorbing the Vietnam experience into the national consciousness while forgetting those aspects that left Australians uncomfortable about themselves and their ability to defend their continent in a future conflict.

This process continued in the 1990s as Australians increasingly celebrated their supposed military prowess. Ex-servicemen from the Vietnam War were welcomed again through city streets in a move to heal old divisions, while a memorial to their dead was dedicated in Canberra on the avenue approaching the Australian War Memorial that had been erected for the dead of the First World War. That memorial now accepted for belated burial the remains of an unknown Australian soldier disinterred from a grave in France on the 75th anniversary of the war's ending, while publishers reprinted the official histories of the First World War along with more recent treatments. In a celebrated incident, Prime Minister Paul Keating kissed the earth at Kokoda where Australian troops had fought and died in defence of their continent in 1942. There were suggestions that the victory of the Kokoda Trail could provide a more appropriate day for a national celebration than either the anniversary of Captain Phillip's landing or the landing at Gallipoli. But nothing came of it. Instead, Anzac Day was elevated back into the affections of many Australians, with attendances at marches showing a large increase, while the Victorian premier, Jeff Kennett, pushed for schools to re-establish their cadet corps. An officially sponsored program of commemoration in 1995, timed for the 80th anniversary of Gallipoli and the 50th anniversary of the end of the Second World War, saw a multitude of community activities paying homage to past sacrifices and reassuring Australians of their status as a martial race.

The resurgence of public support for Anzac Day, and the glorification of past military feats and failures, suggested that some Australians still preferred the old certainties of a country that no longer existed. It was also seen in the fear-mongering about Asian immigration by historian Geoffrey Blainey and Liberal leader John Howard from the mid-1980s onwards. The decades-old bipartisan support for a large-scale immigration program could no longer be sustained. There was also a backlash against Aborigines in the wake of the Mabo win in the High Court and the Labor government's measures to lift their living standards and accord them rights that white Australians had long taken for granted. In opposing an extension of Aboriginal land rights and warning against Asian immigration, Blainey and Howard were playing to an audience made insecure by the effects of globalisation on the Australian economy and hostile to the new, more inclusive Australian identity that had been fashioned by the urban intelligentsia with the approval of the Labor government. They were farmers and rural poor who felt threatened by the relative rise of Aboriginal power and influence; they were workers whose jobs were threatened by cheap imports; they were Anglo-Celtic Australians who felt threatened by a multicultural Australia in which they seemed to have no place and who resented Keating's embrace of republicanism and his efforts to have them regard Australia as part of Asia. All these fears and resentments bubbled to the surface during the 1996 election.

Recommended Reading

J. Beaumont (ed.), 1993, *Where to Now? Australia's Identity in the Nineties*, Federation Press, Sydney.

Frank Brennan, 1995, *One Land, One Nation*, University of Queensland Press, Brisbane.

Peter Butt and Robert Eagleson, 1993, *Mabo: What the High Court Said*, Federation Press, Sydney.

Council for Aboriginal Reconciliation, 1993, *Making Things Right: Reconciliation after the High Court's Decision on Native Title*, Canberra.

Donald Denoon, 1983, *Settler Capitalism*, Oxford University Press, Oxford.

Paul Dibb, 1986, *Review of Australia's Defence Capabilities*, Australian Government Publishing Service Press, Canberra.

Gareth Evans and Bruce Grant, 1991, *Australia's Foreign Relations: In the World of the 1990s*, Melbourne University Press, Melbourne.

Tim Flannery, 1994, *The Future Eaters*, Reed Books, Melbourne.

Robin Gerster, *1987, Big-Noting: The Heroic Theme in Australian War Writing*, Melbourne University Press, Melbourne.

Bruce Grant, 1983, *The Australian Dilemma: A New Kind of Western Society*, Macdonald Futura, Sydney.

Wayne Hudson and David Carter (eds), 1993, *The Republicanism Debate*, New South Wales University Press, Sydney.

Paul Kelly, 1992, *The End of Certainty*, Allen & Unwin, Sydney.

William Lines, 1991, *Taming the Great South Land*, Allen & Unwin, Sydney.

Hugh Mackay, 1993, *Reinventing Australia*, Angus&Robertson, Sydney.

Richard Nile (ed.), 1994, *Australian Civilisation*, Oxford University Press, Melbourne.

J. M. Powell, 1988, *An Historical Geography of Modern Australia: The Restive Fringe*, Cambridge University Press, Cambridge.

John Rickard, 1988, *Australia: A Cultural History*, Longman, London.

Deborah Bird Rose, 1991, *Hidden Stories*, Aboriginal Studies Press, Canberra.

23

'AUSTRALIA CAN DO ANYTHING'

By the mid-1990s, many Australians were rejoicing in the newfound maturity of their nation. The country seemed finally to be confronting the spectre of its past and laying it to rest. The question of Aboriginal land rights, although not of sovereignty, had been conceded as valid by the High Court and enacted into legislation, sweeping away two centuries of official denial. The question of an Australian republic, first raised in the mid-nineteenth century, had been placed back on the political agenda and seemed set to be achieved by the end of the twentieth century. And the historic fear of an Asian invasion seemed to have been assuaged as Australia embraced its Indonesian neighbour and emphasised the primacy of its relations with Asia over its traditional relations with Britain and the United States. Just over two centuries after the British flag was raised on the shores of Sydney Cove, Australians were close to completing the prolonged process of laying claim to the continent, being comfortable with their occupation of it, and reconciling with its indigenous inhabitants. Or so it seemed.

As prime minister, Paul Keating had been instrumental in bringing these issues to the forefront of national consciousness. He had taken the High Court's Mabo decision and brokered a difficult legislative compromise between Aboriginal groups, pastoralists and mining companies. He had placed the republic on the political agenda and promoted public discussion of it. And he had made relations with Asia paramount and dismantled barriers to the free flow of trade and capital. But he had not been rewarded by an electorate made uneasy by the fast pace of economic change and the overturning of old certainties. There was disquiet among white Australians about the government's embracing of Asia and welcoming of Asian immigrants; there was dismay among traditionalists at the mooted cutting of constitutional ties with Britain; there was hostility from pastoralists and others about the perceived preferences accorded to indigenous Australians; and there was anger among displaced regional and rural dwellers who were concerned that the promised fruits of globalisation were enjoyed mainly by wealthy urbanites. There also was a sense of general insecurity as working conditions worsened, unemployment hovered around 10 per cent of the workforce, and income disparities widened. The middle classes were hurt, along with the usual victims, unskilled workers and their families, and the vaunted egalitarianism of the 'lucky country' was increasingly hard to find on city streets where homelessness had become rife, even among the young.

Although economic conditions were improving by the time of the 1996 federal election, Keating had, to many minds, moved too fast and too far beyond the everyday concerns of the average Australian. He had tried to sketch out a new national story that could allow Australians to be confident about their future in the Asia-Pacific region, to confront the crimes and tragedies of their past, as well as celebrate the triumphs, and to promote reconciliation between its indigenous inhabitants and the more recent arrivals and their descendants. He was punished at the polls for doing so. People who were being hurt by the economic forces of globalisation were inclined to blame easily recognisable targets that were close at hand and to seek simple solutions for their plight. Pauline Hanson, a red-headed proprietor of an Ipswich fish and chip shop, on the outskirts of Brisbane, stood for the Liberal Party at the 1996 election and articulated popular concerns about Asian immigration, multiculturalism and what she called 'the Aboriginal industry'. Although John Howard had talked in similar terms himself, Hanson was quickly dumped from the Liberal Party when media attention caused her candidacy to become a political liability in other parts of Australia. Her prompt removal from the Liberal slate helped to ensure Howard's decisive victory over Keating. Undeterred by her dumping, Hanson was elected as an independent with a sizeable majority by people who saw her as an 'anti-politician', as someone who could voice their concerns in Canberra. Which she did.

Hanson used her maiden speech in the House of Representatives in September 1996 to repeat her divisive comments about racial minorities. She warned that Australia was about to 'swamped by Asians', that Aborigines were benefiting unfairly from policies of positive discrimination and were pushing, with government and UN backing, for policies of separatism, and that supporters of multiculturalism were intent on dividing Australia. It was a familiar rant, its sentiments of fear and hate able to be traced back to the worried federationists of the 1890s and even further still to the gold diggers of the 1850s. Although her speech was illogical, even incoherent at times, it was a powerful and populist message that struck a chord with the many aggrieved people who had been made insecure by rapid economic and social changes and who felt alienated from a political process that they believed to be dominated by urban elites and interest groups. They were seeking scapegoats and Hanson provided them. Her springtime blossom of red hair and her eye-catching clothes, her tremulous but grating, even whining voice, her lonely position as an independent in a mostly male and largely hostile parliamentary chamber, all combined to create an image that was both vulnerable and, at the same time, defiant and strong. While the newspaper editorials deplored her racist views, many people in regional Queensland and New South Wales flocked to her banner.

With the assistance of activists from various shadowy right-wing groups, Hanson launched a political party which she called One Nation, a term that had been used in the past by Howard and also, in a different context, by Keating. Hanson and Howard used the term to hark back to the supposed 'golden age' of the 1950s, when the White Australia policy was still in place and immigrants and Aborigines were forced to deny their culture and assimilate into the dominant Anglo-Celtic culture. Hanson's views caused headlines in newspapers around the world, but particularly in Asia. Indeed, her name became more well-known abroad than that of prime minister Howard. The attention that she got was all the greater when Howard declined to rebut her views and instead defended her freedom to speak out. To many people, it seemed that he was endorsing her views and egging her on. Even former Labor leader and retired Governor General, Bill Hayden, attacked the 'intellectual bullies' who described Hanson's views as racist.

Hanson's views, and Howard's tacit encouragement of them, were seen by international observers as signs that Australia was slipping back into the old mindset of 'white Australia', popularly held in the 1950s when Howard was growing to maturity. They were views that he had articulated himself in various forms during the 1980s and they were views that were still widely aired on popular talkback radio shows. So it was not surprising that he ignored the uproar at home and abroad and gave 'Hansonism' his implicit blessing. There was also a political calculation involved — Howard was anxious not to upset the Hanson supporters, some of whom were what Howard termed 'Aussie battlers', and drive them back towards the Labor Party from where many of them had come. For his part, Labor leader Kim Beazley was also cautious in his denunciation of Hanson. It was left to Victoria's Liberal Premier, Jeff Kennett, to voice the loudest denunciation of Hanson and to place her beyond the political pale. As a result, and also because of the ethnic mix in Victoria, One Nation found that Victoria was the hardest state in which to establish a following.

The so-called 'Hanson phenomena' had the advantage for Howard of allowing him to capture the electoral preferences of the politically disaffected 'battlers' and also to wind back the Aboriginal land rights victories that had been conceded by the High Court in the Mabo and Wik cases and to cut back dramatically on the immigration program and government support for multiculturalism. Only when One Nation attracted serious support during the Queensland state election in June 1998 did Howard mount a serious attack on its policies and its leader, describing Hanson as 'deranged'. After according her political credibility for so long, and defending her right to make racially divisive comments, Howard's belated attack made no discernible impact on the election. It may even have added to her party's support, with eleven One Nation candidates being elected and the party attracting 23 per cent of the state vote. The election proved to be the high point of her support. Howard and the Coalition finally moved to diminish One Nation's political clout by putting it last on their how-to-vote cards during the subsequent 1998 federal election. As a result, Hanson lost her seat and the party managed to win only one Senate seat. The party of disaffected battlers and right-wing activists then became disenchanted with each other and even with Hanson herself. By 2000, national opinion polls were recording support for One Nation at just one or two per cent, although higher percentages were recorded in rural Queensland and rural New South Wales. Nevertheless, its supporters still had the potential of deciding the outcome of elections and Howard continued to play unashamedly to their prejudices.

In 2000, a portrait of Howard was unveiled by the National Portrait Gallery in Canberra. It showed Howard and his wife Janette in the garden of Kirribilli House on the shores of Sydney Harbour. He had achieved the ambition of every Sydneysider: to get a harbour view. The painting had no disturbing signs of the Aborigines or any other claimant who might disturb the tranquillity of Howard's occupation. It showed Howard as he liked to portray himself — as an 'average Australian' who spoke for what he called 'the mainstream'. He claimed proudly that he was more attuned to the values and opinions of suburban Australia than any other politician. Unfortunately, he proved to be right. Just when Australia needed a leader who was a cut above average, it was saddled with a politician who made a virtue of his ordinariness. Howard, whose second name is Winston, shared his namesake's dogged determination to attain power and his wily ability to hold on to it against political challengers. He also shared Churchill's nostalgia for a world that was past and could not be re-created. Whereas Churchill's childhood had been played out against the background of the British Empire's heyday, Howard's childhood in Sydney was played out against the unsettling effects of the Second World War, when an uncle was killed at the hands of the Japanese, and by the postwar influx of European immigrants that challenged the Anglo-Australian way of life.

Howard came to maturity during the assimilationist years of the 1950s, when his father, who died when Howard was just sixteen, was a small business proprietor in a part of suburban Sydney that was then mostly untouched by the postwar immigration intake. Despite the profound changes that took place in Australian society in subsequent years, Howard remained firmly wedded to the ideas that were popular under Menzies in the 1950s. He yearned for a monocultural Australia in which Aborigines would be blended into the dominant Anglo-Celtic society; he wanted race to be a factor in deciding an immigrant's fitness to enter Australia; he wanted women to be at home raising children; he wanted immigrants to abandon their cultures and adopt the Anglo-Australian culture as their own. Of course, he had to be careful propounding these views. For months after his election in 1996, Howard refused to use the word 'multiculturalism' in his speeches or to describe Australian society as 'multicultural'. Unable to come up with an alternative description, Howard was continually taunted by journalists trying to get him to use the dreaded 'm' word. Eventually, he finally conceded what he called the 'multiculturality' of Australia. He preferred to torture the language rather than admit defeat to his critics, although in 1998 he finally used the word 'multiculturalism'. Howard had failed to redefine Australian society so that it accorded with the cherished images of his childhood, although not for want of trying. Funding for multicultural programs was heavily slashed or abolished altogether and the Office of Multicultural Affairs was shut down.

For fifty years, there had been largely bi-partisan political support for Australia's mass immigration program that had brought millions of newcomers from Europe and, after the scrapping of the White Australia policy, from across the world. The program had not been free of troubles. There had been riots in the 1950s by European migrants disgruntled at the rudimentary conditions in their up-country migrant camps. And there had been resentment from some Anglo-Australians fearful of being swamped by 'wogs'. But overall it had been an outstanding success, providing a cheap labour force and an expanding population for a society that would not be able to procreate in sufficient numbers to populate the continent. Even the rise in unemployment during the late 1970s and 1980s did not dent markedly the immigration intake, although it was reduced during the prolonged recession of the early 1990s.

Howard had made a reduced immigration intake one of his election promises in 1996. With Asian immigrants making up a substantial proportion of the intake in 1995, and expected to constitute 15 per cent of the Australian population by 2030, promising a reduced intake was a coded message to One Nation supporters that the numbers of Asian immigrants would be reduced. There had been fears that the handover of Hong Kong to Chinese control could see an influx of educated and wealthy Chinese from that city into Australia, which consequently made it clear that they would not be welcome. As a result, Canada, the United States and Britain were the main beneficiaries of the limited exodus that resulted. The Labor government in the 1980s had also extended the family reunion component of the immigration program which allowed recent immigrants to bring out members of their extended families. Although strongly supported by Australians of European origin, it was also exploited by Asian-Australians in ways that alarmed One Nation supporters. So it too was targeted for cutbacks by Howard in 1996, and again during the 1998 election.

Apart from the officially sanctioned immigration program, there were also thousands of immigrants who entered Australia illegally or overstayed their visas. Most of the 'overstayers' were British or European and were dealt with leniently. Not so with the so-called 'illegals', many of who came by boat in desperate circumstances, fleeing from political or religious persecution or simply seeking a better economic life for themselves and their children. Vietnamese refugees had come following the Communist victory of 1975 and had been accepted into Australia in large numbers. Similarly, thousands of Chinese students were allowed to remain in Australia following the Tienanmen Square massacre. The Hawke government had been less sympathetic to several hundred Cambodian refugees fleeing for their lives from the strife that beset that country from 1989. Although a relatively small number of refugees, their arrival by boat along the isolated northern coastline revived memories of an Asian invasion and prompted the government to detain the refugees in isolated detention camps before returning most of them to Cambodia. Similarly, when refugees arrived from southern China by boat in the 1990s, they received a chilly reception, facing detention at isolated Port Hedland and, often, a quick return to China. Some, including young children, were detained illegally for years. In one case, a pregnant woman was returned to China to face a forced abortion for breaching that country's one child policy. Under new legislation by the Howard government, and supported by the Labor Party, those permitted to remain would be deprived of access to social welfare for two years after their arrival and be denied the opportunity to have their families join them in Australia.

The government's move was prompted by the arrival in the late 1990s of refugees from the Middle East, many of them from Iraq and Afghanistan. After making their way to Indonesia, they would engage Indonesian fishermen or crowd onto decrepit inter-island ferries to land them on Australian soil. Although most were later found to be genuine refugees fleeing the most terrible political or religious persecution, they faced confinement in a new detention centre constructed at Woomera, in the isolated desert country of South Australia. Howard and his immigration minister, Phillip Ruddock, took the sternest of approaches to these mostly Muslim refugees and helped to incite public hatred and fear towards them by suggesting that Australia was about to be swamped by an invasion of 10 000 of these so-called 'boat people'. The much-mooted invasion never eventuated and most of the detainees in the barbed wire camps were eventually assessed as being genuine refugees and allowed entry, albeit on conditions that denied them the normal rights of citizenship. Refugees from the conflict in the Yugoslav province of Kosovo were also denied a haven in Australia until public outrage forced the government to soften its stance. Kosovo refugees were then allowed temporary residence in Australia, many of them housed in former army camps, on the condition that they return to Kosovo as soon as it became safe to do so. Although the United States and other countries allowed such refugees the option of remaining permanently, Ruddock enforced this condition strictly, forcibly sending off to detention camps in early 2000 those refugees who were not prepared to return willingly to war-ravaged Kosovo. Once back in Kosovo, they would have the chance of applying for re-admission to Australia under the refugee quota. By October 2000, only one family, with the support of the Tasmanian government, had successfully negotiated the immigration formalities and returned to Australia.

The harsh measures enacted against refugees and 'boat people' recalled the time when Asian refugees had been forcibly deported in the late 1940s under the White Australia policy. It was a recrudescence of fears that many thought had been laid to rest during the 1970s and 1980s. But those liberal and left-wing activists who might have raised their voices in defence of the refugees were largely silenced by a growing view of Australia as a fragile ecological lifeboat that could capsize if too many people clambered aboard. Ironically, this view found common cause with Pauline Hanson and her ilk. They opposed not only illegal refugees, but also more immigrants of any description. NSW Premier Bob Carr was not alone in worrying about the effects of immigrants on his increasingly bloated capital of Sydney, to which many new arrivals were attracted. The labour movement worried about finding jobs for new arrivals when unemployment remained close to 10 per cent. Environmentalists worried about the damage already done to the continent's ecology and feared that further population would add to the stresses. As just one example, the increasing salinity of the Murray-Darling basin was expected to make Adelaide water unfit to drink by 2020. Although this was a result of inappropriate irrigation rather than of immigration, an alliance of convenience had grown between these environmentalists, supporters of 'white Australia', opponents of multiculturalism, and parts of the labour movement. Each, for their own very different reasons, agreed that the mass immigration that had characterised postwar Australia should now be scaled back. Some environmentalists even expressed equanimity about a decline of the existing population that would come with the ending of immigration altogether. At the same time, the birth rate had declined to such an extent by 1998 that it was lower than during the Great Depression. The average number of births per woman was just 1.76 in 1998, compared with 2.1 in 1976 and more than 3.5 in the early 1960s. It was predicted that deaths would begin to outnumber births by about 2030.

With Australia's claim on the continent seemingly secure, such developments could be regarded with relative equanimity. However, by the beginning of the twenty-first century, that claim had been cast in some doubt by the increasing belligerence of Indonesia and the conflicts that raged across its archipelago. To meet the challenge of these developments, the government planned to boost defence spending from its historically low levels. At the same time, old concerns surfaced about the adequacy or otherwise of the Australian population. There were renewed calls for boosting the immigration intake, which had been halved from the levels prevailing in the 1980s, as businesses found difficulty in recruiting skilled workers and the housing and other industries suffered from the slower population growth. Jeff Kennett, presiding over perhaps the most multicultural of states, was the loudest advocate for increased immigration. Constrained by the lingering electoral pull of One Nation, Labor leader Kim Beazley refused to back a large increase in immigration but did argue for a population policy that would set aims for population growth. With the increasing crisis in Indonesia, the idea of a static or even declining population seemed no longer to be such a desirable option.

After his election in 1996, Howard had declared that he would recapture Australian history for the Liberal Party. He quickly set about doing so. While acknowledging that there was much in Australia's past that was shameful, he argued that, on balance, it was a story of triumph of which Australians could justly be proud. Howard gave wide currency to the term 'black armband history', that had been originally coined by the conservative historian Geoffrey Blainey, and which was designed to denigrate the work of those revisionist historians who dared to take a critical attitude towards Australian history. That related especially to race relations and the decades-long conflict that flared across the Australian frontier as Aborigines attempted to resist their dispossession. Supporters of Howard's triumphant view of Australian history were appointed to the council of the new Australian Museum built on the shores of Canberra's Lake Burley Griffin and timed to open during the centenary of Federation celebrations in 2001. Others, including the former federal director of the Liberal Party, were involved in organising those celebrations. The year 2001 also coincided with the centenary of the White Australia policy, which had provided much of the impetus for the Federation movement, but there was no mention of that in the publicity. Instead, Howard, in launching the program in November 2000, declared that 2001 would be 'a year for great national pride'. It would begin with a ceremony at Uluru, even though the people of that region were still subject to random massacres and punitive expeditions at the time of Federation. There would be no replaying of those dark events. Instead, it would be a time of national backslapping or, as Howard put it, a time to glory in 'the sheer joy of being an Australian', rather than a time for serious reflection on the nation's sometimes appalling past.

Following his re-election in 1998, Howard claimed that reconciliation between indigenous and non-indigenous Australians would be a top priority of his government and promised to complete the process of reconciliation by 2001. It soon became clear that such a timetable would be impossible to achieve given the poor state of relations between the government and most Aboriginal groups. It was also not clear what Howard meant by reconciliation. It appeared to some observers that he was more concerned in reconciling Aborigines to their dispossession rather than working out ways in which the two groups could learn to share the country. He concentrated on what he called 'practical reconciliation' — improving the health of indigenous people and providing better facilities in their outlying settlements. Laudable as these aims were, Howard's intentions were essentially assimilationist. He wanted Aborigines brought into Australian society on his terms and opposed any move that would have the effect of acknowledging their distinct position as Australia's first people. He restricted the rights over Crown land that had been accorded them by the Keating government following the Mabo judgment, and limited their rights over leasehold land that had been accorded them by the High Court in the Wik judgment of December 1996. He denied the legitimacy of Aboriginal laws and he opposed a treaty with Aborigines that would have had the effect of acknowledging national status and recognising their pre-existing sovereignty over separate parts of the continent.

The process of reconciliation necessarily included recognition of Australia's lamentable record of race relations, including the drawn-out war on the Australian frontier and the forced removal of children from Aboriginal families and their assimilation into white society. Howard and many other non-indigenous Australians refused to make such an acknowledgment. They proclaimed the triumphs of white settlement while denying the damage that had been deliberately visited upon indigenous people. Although an inquiry in 1997 by the Human Rights and Equal Opportunity Commission into the so-called 'stolen generations' established the federal government's responsibility for removing tens of thousands of Aboriginal children from their parents, Howard downplayed the implications of this attempted 'genocide' of the Aboriginal people. It was done legally, argued Howard, and was benign in intent. He refused to pay compensation to Aborigines who had suffered harm through these policies, or even to make the formal apology to the victims that the Commission had recommended. He also vigorously contested at great expense any legal actions that sought to obtain compensation. His Aboriginal Affairs minister, John Herron, went even further, denying the existence of 'stolen generations' because, so he argued, only individuals, not entire generations, had been taken from their parents. In the face of the Howard government's refusal to push forward with the reconciliation process, and to say sorry for the wrongs that had been visited upon indigenous people, ordinary Australians went ahead and did so themselves. So-called 'sorry books' collected hundreds of thousands of signatures from people across the country. State governments and local councils, medical and legal bodies, schools and churches all made their own expressions of sorrow for past wrongs. Recognising the original Aboriginal owners of the country became a common part of public ceremonies and celebrations. Similarly, suburbs and towns acknowledged with signs the names of the original owners.

On 27 May 2000, at a public ceremony in the Sydney Opera House, the Council for Aboriginal Reconciliation submitted its final report to the government in which it recommended that Aborigines and Torres Strait Islanders be recognised officially as Australia's first peoples, that the state of Aboriginal health and education be regularly measured, and that an official apology be made to indigenous people. Howard put forward an alternative document that omitted mention of an official apology, concentrating instead on his familiar theme of practical reconciliation by addressing Aboriginal disadvantage. As political commentator Paul Kelly observed, it was Australia's loss to be led by a man who was incapable of bridging the gap between indigenous and non-indigenous Australians. 'Howard cannot heal or bind the past divisions', wrote Kelly, 'nor can he negotiate future advancement.' Frustrated by Howard's intransigence, many in the audience at the Opera House stood and turned their back on the prime minister as he spoke, while the following day around 250000 people marched across the Sydney Harbour Bridge in a massive show of support for reconciliation. Far above the crowd, an aircraft spelt out the word 'Sorry'. Howard refused to join the march and also prevented his deputy, Peter Costello, from attending. Instead of leading the way with the reconciliation process, Howard and his government had become part of the problem.

Over the following weeks and months, further marches were held in towns and capital cities across Australia. As in Sydney, they attracted huge crowds. Buoyed by the success of the marches, Aboriginal leaders demanded that the question of a treaty, which had languished on the political agenda for more than a decade, now be resuscitated. While Kim Beazley suggested that a treaty would be considered by a future Labor government, it was rejected out of hand by Howard and other conservative politicians as being divisive. It was not possible, said Howard, to have a nation within a nation. It was an argument that would have found favour with Pauline Hanson's One Nation supporters yet it expressed Howard's deeply felt convictions. Of course, it also ignored the fact that Aboriginal nations had co-existed with European society ever since the British landing in 1788. And it ignored the experience in countries such as Canada, the United States and New Zealand where indigenous people were recognised and their sovereignty was acknowledged by the victorious invaders. Ironically, while denying the existence of Aboriginal sovereignty, Howard's government conceded the sovereignty of

Torres Strait Islanders, who in 2000 were allowed to establish a governing body to control their affairs. While Howard might dismiss the notion of Aboriginal sovereignty, the argument will not go away. The force of legal logic, combined with political pressure from Aborigines and their supporters, will ensure that some form of sovereignty is recognised eventually, either by parliament or through the courts. It will come as non-indigenous Australians realise that such an acknowledgment will make their claim on the continent more, rather than less, secure. Indeed, an *Age* poll in November 2000 suggested that there was already considerable support for such a treaty, with a majority of respondents supporting the idea.

It seemed for a time that Aboriginal issues would dominate the Olympic Games in Sydney in October 2000, with predictions by the late Aboriginal activist, Charles Perkins, that his people's anger over the federal government's intransigence could see Sydney burning and Games venues blockaded by rioting demonstrators. In the event, Aboriginal protests during the Games were low-key, restricted mainly to a 'tent embassy' in an inner city park. Despite this, Aboriginal issues dominated much of the Games coverage in the media, with Cathy Freeman being chosen to light the Olympic cauldron and hundreds of Aboriginal dancers from around Australia being incorporated into the opening ceremony. A few days later, Freeman ran the race of her life to win the 400 metres and confirm her place in the affection of Australians. There were no demurring voices when she jogged a victory lap displaying both the Australian and Aboriginal flags. The sporting arena had allowed Australians to unite behind the idea of reconciliation as personified by Freeman, although Howard, who seemed to attend every event where Australians had the chance of a medal, was pointedly absent from the Olympic Stadium during Freeman's race and later played down the significance of her win for indigenous Australia. At the closing ceremony, Aboriginal issues were also to the fore when popular Aboriginal band Yothu Yindi performed their politically loaded song, 'Treaty', and rock group Midnight Oil displayed the word 'Sorry' on their clothes, much to the discomfort of the watching prime minister. In contrast, NSW premier Bob Carr thought that the Olympics had finally presented Aboriginal Australia 'as an integral part of Australia'.

Howard tried to put a favourable political spin on the events by arguing that the Olympics had shown that Australia was 'a lot more reconciled than many of the critics had allowed for'. Not that he was reconciled to Cathy Freeman's view of the past and her demand that he should apologise to the 'stolen generations' and their descendants. As the international spotlight shifted from Sydney, and the warm feelings about the Games gradually receded, Howard made clear that the events of those two weeks had not changed his outlook. When Phillip Ruddock was criticised for explaining the present state of Aboriginal disadvantage by pointing to them not having made use of the wheel before Europeans arrived, Howard backed Ruddock 'one hundred percent'. Anthropologists pointed out in vain that there was little point in Aborigines using wheels when there were no animals capable of domestication in Australia. Despite Midnight Oil's flaunting of the 'Sorry' word before the world's television audience, Howard still refused to make an official apology for past wrongs. 'We're all sorry for the mistakes that were made in the past,' he said, 'but we've got to get on with it and move into the future.' Describing government policies that caused the 'stolen generations', and which had as their ultimate aim the genocide of the Aboriginal people, as 'mistakes' revealed how far Howard had to go before he could be reconciled with Aboriginal Australians. In fact, he remained both emotionally unable and politically unwilling even to begin the journey.

The Sydney Olympics had brought Australians together for two weeks in an enthusiastic display of unity that had rarely been seen before. It not only celebrated the success of the athletes but also the ability of the nation to organise what the International Olympic Committee president, Juan Antonio Samaranch, called the 'best Games ever'. This coming together was akin to the Australian public's reaction to Gallipoli when Australians were described by outsiders as 'a nation of athletes'. The national self-doubt of the time was swept away. Now, in 2000, they could take renewed comfort as their athletes won more medals than ever before, coming fourth in the overall medal tally with fifty-eight medals, sixteen of them gold. It was testimony not only to the dedication of the athletes and their coaches and the 'hometown' effect, but also to the millions of dollars that had been set aside by a succession of governments to the development of sporting excellence ever since the failure of Australian athletes to win any gold medals at the Montreal Olympics in 1976. The new, high level of expenditure on training facilities, foreign coaches and stipends for athletes was all seen as worthwhile. As an Australian television commentator proclaimed upon their conclusion: 'These Games have shown the world Australia can do anything'. It was left to social commentator Hugh Mackay to remind Australians that it was just the Olympic Games: 'Now we must get on with our lives, our marriages, our parenting, our shopping, our exams, our politics, our reconciliations ... even, perhaps, our republic.'

Australia could organise the 'best Games ever' but it had been unable to organise the transition to a republic and the cutting of the last constitutional links to Britain and its distant monarch. The issue of the republic had been put on the political agenda by Prime Minister Paul Keating at the 1993 election and it was widely expected that the transition to a republic would be completed by January 2001, so that it could be celebrated with the centenary of Australian federation. Keating had used the republic as a way of dividing the conservatives and portraying them as politicians of yesteryear. It thereby became a party-political issue, with conservatives accusing Keating of wanting to be the republic's first president. This meant that it would be almost impossible to achieve, since any republican referendum would require bi-partisan support to succeed. Keating had put the republic squarely on the political agenda but had done so in a way that would ensure it could not succeed. Which is precisely how events transpired after John Howard neutralised the issue during the 1996 election campaign by promising, if elected, to hold a constitutional convention to decide on whether Australia should move towards a republic and what sort of a republic it should be. To ensure the desired outcome, Howard established a convention that was part-elected by the people and part-appointed by himself, with the appointed delegates being weighted in favour of those with Howard's values. As a result, when the delegates gathered for their deliberations in Canberra's old parliament house, they failed to reflect accurately the opinions of an Australian public that was largely republican. As well, by requiring the convention to decide on the form of the republic, Howard ensured that the groundwork would be laid for an unprincipled alliance between radical republicans and the minority monarchists. This, together with Howard's careful wording of the referendum question, produced the result he wanted. By a clear majority, Australians voted in 1999 against a republic in which the president would be appointed by parliament. Monarchists proclaimed it a great victory for their cause. Which it was, since they had connived to defeat the republic, something desired by most Australians, and to shift the issue back into the political shadows. Had the vote for the republic been taken after the successful staging of the Sydney Olympics, and the boost to national self-confidence that the Games had generated, it may well have turned out differently. Now the nation would have to wait for perhaps another ten years before having the chance to cut its final constitutional links to the old British Empire.

With the republic issue adroitly nullified, albeit temporarily, Howard celebrated those historic links to empire in July 2000 when he took hundreds of State and Federal politicians, bureaucrats and service personnel to London to commemorate the centenary of the visit by colonial premiers seeking Britain's approval for the proposed Australian constitution. Rather than celebrating at home the belated maturity of the Australian colonists in wishing to federate, Howard celebrated the supposed beneficence of Britain in allowing a federation that London had long been urging upon the Australian colonies. Such was the symbolism of a visit that saw Howard leave his calling card at all the old bastions of British power and influence. A visit by Howard earlier that year to Gallipoli and the battlefields of the Western Front in northern France had also done much to emphasise Australia's historic obligations to the British Empire. They were flashbacks to a distant era at a time when most Australians had moved on to new concerns and when Britain had been, for the most part, removed from its former place in the national psyche as the 'mother country'. There was another empire, much closer to home, that loomed larger in the minds of most Australians.

For more than half a century, Australia had supported the territorial integrity of the Javanese empire, or Indonesia, only baulking for a time at its incorporation of Dutch-controlled West New Guinea in 1969. Chastened by that experience, Australia gave its implicit blessing to the Indonesian invasion of Portuguese East Timor in 1975 and its subsequent annexation. Despite an ongoing resistance movement in East Timor, and substantial support for that resistance from concerned Australians, a succession of Australian governments, both Liberal and Labor, continued to recognise Indonesian sovereignty over East Timor. Only when the dictatorial and corrupt military leadership in Jakarta under Suharto was overthrown by popular protests in 1998, and the possibility of East Timorese independence was raised by the new Indonesian president, B. J. Habibie, did Australia support the East Timorese in deciding their own future.

Australia had backed the Javanese empire for half a century as a way of economising on its own defence by creating a bulwark against a future Asian invasion, whether from China or India or Vietnam. Australia's support for the incorporation of East Timor into Indonesia had been based on a conviction that it would remove a possible source of instability on Australia's northern doorstep. Instead, the ongoing war in East Timor from 1975–99 had destabilised Indonesia, encouraging other independence movements across the archipelago and creating a continuing source of tension between Canberra and Jakarta. Habibie's suggestion of an independence vote went further than Australia desired. But Howard grasped it anyway, helping to set in train a process that saw East Timor descend into anarchy and bloodshed as local militias, armed and directed by the Indonesian army, attempted to thwart the UN-supervised vote on independence.

As the East Timorese capital of Dili was laid waste by the rampaging mobs, and supporters of independence were targeted by the Indonesian army, Australia joined American calls for UN intervention to restore order and implement the decision of the East Timorese to separate from Indonesia. Eventually, after thousands of East Timorese had been killed and hundreds of thousands had fled from the terror, Australian troops led an international force into Dili to stop the violence and establish an interim UN administration. Despite US forces providing logistical support, it was a situation fraught with danger for the Australian troops, both from the undisciplined militia and from the Indonesian forces resentful at the Australian intrusion. Under the command of General Peter Cosgrove, the peacemaking operation was a political and public relations triumph, not least because of the relationships that had developed between Indonesian and Australian officers during the years of engagement that had been fostered under Bob Hawke and Paul Keating and which now annulled possible sources of friction. After several tense days, the Indonesians handed over control and finally withdrew from a territory they had been unable to subdue during twenty-five years of fighting.

The relatively peaceful takeover, after weeks of bloodletting, was greeted with relief in Australia. Riding high in the polls, it all went to Howard's head. As his defence minister John Moore talked wildly of Australian troops chasing the marauding militia over the border into Indonesian West Timor, Howard laid out a new strategic doctrine under which Australia would play the part of regional policeman, a deputy sheriff to the United States. It was a vision that recalled a past in which white colonial powers enforced their will upon Asian societies and, later, when Australia followed the United States into Vietnam. Not surprisingly, Howard's pronouncement was greeted with a mixture of ridicule and resentment both in Australia and internationally. In January 2000, the Philippines took over control from Australia of the ongoing UN peacekeeping mission in East Timor while, in May 2000, Australia watched from the sidelines as Fiji's and the Solomon Islands' elected governments were toppled by coups and held hostage. Although it quickly disappeared from the Australian foreign policy agenda, Howard's idea of Australia playing the regional policeman left an abiding impression of a government that had not come to terms with the new political realities of the region and which, under Howard's leadership, still thought in Menzian terms of Australia's place in the world as a British outpost 'bearing the white man's burden'. As foreign affairs commentator Greg Sheridan observed in December 1999, Howard was 'manifestly uncomfortable with Asia'. While scheduling his third visit to London, he had still not visited South Korea, Australia's third most important trading partner. Indonesia's new leader, the democratically elected President Abdurrahman Wahid, described Howard as 'childish' and continually postponed plans to visit Canberra while pointedly visiting every other continent in the world.

As Jakarta policy-makers had feared, the granting of independence to East Timor gave heart to other separatist movements. The increasingly sophisticated and militant independence movement in Irian Jaya, or West Papua, posed the greatest threat to Australia. It raised the prospect of another East Timor, supported by a growing band of sympathisers for the independence movement within Australia who are able to mount a strong political and moral case for the territory being taken back from Jakarta's control. Although Australia continued to recognise Indonesian sovereignty over the territory, as it did with East Timor, Jakarta became increasingly convinced that Australia was intent on breaking up Indonesia's far-flung island empire. The growing tension between the two countries was reminiscent of the last years under Sukarno during the 1960s, when Australian and Indonesian troops were engaged in hostilities in Borneo. Ironically, in questioning Jakarta's proprietorship over West Papua, non-indigenous Australians bring the proprietorship of their own continent under question and also possibly place that proprietorship under threat from the belligerent Indonesian military forces.

Ever since the First Fleet dropped anchor in Sydney Cove, white Australians have grappled with the issue of proprietorship — how they have the right to live on land that is claimed by descendants of the pre-existing Aboriginal society. The Australian predicament is not unique. It is part of a wider human story that continues to be played out across the world, and not just in the so-called settler societies. At some stage in their existence, most if not all societies have acted as supplanting societies, taking over the land of others, making it their own and defending it from further challenges. The Aboriginal communities of Australia would have experienced this prior to the British arrival, as the decline or demise of particular communities allowed nearby Aborigines to move onto their land. They would then have confronted a similar predicament to that faced by white Australians over the last two centuries — how could they justify and secure their occupation of that land? Such questions continue to be confronted by societies around the world. In the Middle East, Israelis on the West Bank resist the handover of control to Palestinians, claiming that they had a superior claim to the land based upon God's supposed gift of it to Abraham. In Bosnia, Bosnian Muslims defend their right to the proprietorship of their land by pointing to their 1000 years of occupation, something the Serbs, under Slobodan Milosevic, contested. In Ireland, too, the Catholic majority, who trace their roots to their Celtic ancestors from mainland Europe, often deny any right to share in the proprietorship of that tortured island to the descendants of Protestant people who arrived there more than 400 years ago. How then can European-Australians, after just over 200 years of occupation of the continent, hope to establish a claim of proprietorship that can compete with the claim of the Aborigines established over perhaps 120 000 years?

For much of the twentieth century, with indigenous Australians no longer posing a threat, white Australians were more concerned about securing their claim to the continent in the eyes of their Asian neighbours. To do so, it was believed that the continent had to be peopled, developed and defended. Much of the nation's modern history has been directed towards those ends. Only recently, with the emergence of the Aboriginal land rights movement and widespread acknowledgment that Aboriginal Australians are not a dying race, have non-indigenous Australians faced anew the problem of securing their claim. This time, though, many of them are seeking to construct their claim on the solid base provided by the pre-existing Aboriginal claim, rather than attempting to deny or destroy the Aboriginal claim. In his book, *Sharing the Country*, Jesuit priest Frank Brennan called for greater reconciliation between white and black Australians so that 'those of us who are not Aboriginal might belong for the first time without shame'. The subsequent Mabo and Wik judgments have the potential for achieving this objective, of conceding ownership of large parts of the continent to the Aborigines as a means by which non-Aboriginal Australians might more securely establish their claim over the continent as a whole. Such a strategy of effectively entwining the two claims together could strengthen the claim of Australians, both Aboriginal and non-Aboriginal, to the continent that they have come to share as against possible challenges from future supplanting societies.

John Howard's political success in 1996, and his subsequent rolling back of initiatives on land rights, the republic, multiculturalism and engagement with Asia, showed that many Australians remained unconvinced that their claim on the continent required making any such concessions for it to be secured. Many of these Australians lived in rural areas and felt themselves to have permanent and secure claims to their land. Like Howard, they were attempting to hold on to a version of the past that was no longer tenable but which they were unwilling to relinquish. They remained attached to the monarchy, they were suspicious of urban-based ethnic groups espousing multiculturalism, and their sense of identity was unsettled by Asian immigrants and the conceding of land rights to Aborigines. Many of them would argue that Governor Phillip had secured a claim of moral proprietorship, as well as legal and effective proprietorship, over the continent in 1788 when he proffered the gift of European civilisation to the 'barbaric' Aborigines and began the prolonged process of occupying their lands. They would argue that nothing further remains to be done by present-day Australians. The hundreds of thousands of indigenous and non-indigenous Australians who walked across Sydney Harbour Bridge in May 2000 and through the streets of Melbourne in December 2000 in support of reconciliation would disagree. Whether this people's movement can achieve meaningful reconciliation in the face of government opposition and thereby, as Cameron Forbes put it, 'give Australia moral legitimacy', will remain a pressing question in the twenty-first century. In the final analysis, though, no society can ever establish a completely secure claim of proprietorship over the territory that it occupies, although the drive to achieve it will remain an inescapable part of the human condition.

Recommended Reading

C. Bean, S. Bennett, M. Simms and J. Warhurst (eds), 1997, *The Politics of Retribution: The 1996 Australian Federal Election*, Allen and Unwin, Sydney.

Doug Cocks, 1996, *People Policy: Australia's Population Choices*, UNSW Press, Sydney.

Miriam Dixson, 2000, *The Imaginary Australian: Anglo-Celts and Identity, 1788 to the Present*, UNSW Press, Sydney.

Michelle Grattan (ed), 2000, *Australian Prime Ministers*, New Holland, Sydney.

Michelle Grattan (ed), 2000, *Reconciliation: Essays on Australian Reconciliation*, Bookman, Melbourne.

Geoffrey Gray and Christine Walker (eds), 1997, *The Resurgence of Racism: Howard, Hanson and the Race Debate*, Monash Publications in History, Melbourne.

Anna Haebich, 2000, *Broken Circles: Fragmenting Indigenous Families 1800–2000*, Fremantle Arts Centre Press, Perth.

Michael Leach, Geoffrey Stokes and Ian Ward (eds), 2000, *The Rise and Fall of One Nation*, University of Queensland Press, Brisbane.

Andrew Markus, 2001, *Race: John Howard and the Remaking of Australia*, Allen & Unwin, Sydney.

S. Prasser and G. Starr (eds), 1997, *Policy and Change: The Howard Mandate*, Hale and Iremonger, Sydney.

Marian Simms and John Warhurst (eds), 2000, *Howard's Agenda: The 1998 Australian Election*, University of Queensland Press, Brisbane.

G. Singleton (ed), 2000, *The Howard Government*, University of NSW Press, Sydney.

INDEX